Venezuela

LATIN AMERICAN HISTORIES

JAMES R. SCOBIE, EDITOR

James R. Scobie: *Argentina: A City and a Nation*, SECOND EDITION

Charles C. Cumberland: *Mexico: The Struggle for Modernity*

Rollie E. Poppino: *Brazil: The Land and People*, SECOND EDITION

Ralph Lee Woodward, Jr.: *Central America: A Nation Divided*

Henry F. Dobyns and Paul L. Doughty: *Peru: A Cultural History*

Franklin W. Knight: *The Caribbean: The Genesis of a Fragmented Nationalism*

Brian Loveman: *Chile: The Legacy of Hispanic Capitalism*

Herbert S. Klein: *Bolivia: The Evolution of a Multi-Ethnic Society*

John V. Lombardi: *Venezuela: The Search for Order, the Dream of Progress*

Venezuela

THE SEARCH FOR ORDER,
THE DREAM OF PROGRESS

JOHN V. LOMBARDI

New York • Oxford
OXFORD UNIVERSITY PRESS
1982

Copyright © 1982 by Oxford University Press, Inc.

Library of Congress Cataloging in Publication Data
Lombardi, John V.
Venezuela: the search for order, the dream of
progress.
(Latin American histories)
Bibliography: p.   Includes index.
1. Venezuela—History. I. Title. II. Series.
F2321.L58   987   81-9630
ISBN 0-19-503013-3   AACR2   ISBN 0-19-503014-1 (pbk.)

Printing (last digit): 9 8 7 6 5 4 3 2 1

Printed in the United States of America

For John Lee
and Mary Ann

Preface

This history of Venezuela owes its existence to Jim Scobie's initiative many years ago. His belief that this story needed to be told and that I was the one to tell it held firm throughout the years required to get ready to prepare the book. His advice and suggestions at various stages proved crucial, and his comments on the final draft most valuable. His sudden death kept him from seeing the results of his patience and encouragement in print, deprived the profession of one of its best historians, and left me bereft of a very fine friend.

My editors at Oxford University Press have also shown remarkable patience in waiting for the manuscript and unusual skill and sensitivity in preparing it for publication once they got it. Sheldon Meyer demonstrated admirable tact in inquiring about the book and great knowledge of the field in his comments on the final draft. Elaine Koss made many good suggestions for improving the text, and Vicky Bijur skillfully handled the final preparations for the press.

During the fifteen years I have had the pleasure of studying Venezuela, many Venezuelan scholars have given generously of their time and talents to help me understand the complexities and nuances of their country's history. There have been too many to mention them all here, but most appear in the bibliographical essay with their scholarly works. Venezuelans have also been most generous with their institutional resources as well, whether Carlos Felice Cardot or Ramón J. Velásquez at the Academia Nacional de la Historia, Mario Briceño Perozo at the Archivo General de la Nación, Manuel Pérez Vila at the Fundación John Boulton, or Fray Cesáreo de Armellada at the Archivo Arquidiocesano de Caracas. The guardians of these institutions and others always seemed to find a reason to open doors, indicate important materials, and encourage research. My debt to them is great and continuing.

In the course of preparing this book I had occasion to try out my ideas on a number of more or less willing audiences, and I imposed on the friendship and sense of duty of a number of colleagues to read and comment on the manuscript. They all made important, indeed often essential, criticisms. In most cases I took their advice, and this book is better because of it. Susan Berglund, David Bushnell, Judith Ewell, Robert Ferry, Mary Floyd, Herbert Klein, and Kathy Waldron read and commented on a draft. I hope they caught all my errors, and I thank them for trying.

The willing support of the International Programs Office at Indiana University made many of the difficult chores of preparing the manuscript easy. Darcy Lang typed a draft, Mary Hurt checked bibliographical citations, and Grace Bareikis kept the operation functioning. Indiana University's Latin American Studies Program and its Office of Research and Graduate Development provided research and logistical support at various times in the course of this project.

In Caracas, Don Pedro Grases, bibliophile, bibliographer, historian, and literary scholar, has advised me on things Venezuelan and historical ever since my first visit to that city. His friendship, generosity, and wisdom have provided me with an unusually rich vision of the Hispanic past and a much better understanding of its present than I could ever have achieved alone. In the library at Villafranca I have always found the necessary book and the generous sharing of experiences that occurs far less often than it should.

In 1972 the Midwest Universities Consortium for International Activities and the Centro de Estudios del Desarrollo of the Universidad Central de Venezuela sponsored a project to study the formation of the central city of Caracas. During the two years of the project I learned much about Venezuela's urban structure, and it is from that experience that much of the orientation of this book derives. Germán Carrera Damas, co-director and intellectual strategist for the project, provided his usual brilliant, incisive contributions. His critical perspective on the history and historians of Latin America has often helped correct or clarify my views of Venezuela's past, and his generous hospitality, enthusiastic collaboration on a variety of projects, and warm friendship have enriched my Venezuelan experiences. Thanks to his cooperation I have been able to see a Venezuela that would have otherwise been inaccessible.

The maps and figures throughout this book are the work of Cathryn L. Lombardi, whose support, patience, and bemused tolerance of my work are legendary. Our shared enthusiasm for things Venezuelan has made these explorations into Venezuela's past especially enjoyable. She has also managed to find many of my mistakes.

This book, then, while my responsibility, is nevertheless the result of the cooperation and support of friends and colleagues. They all have my thanks.

Bloomington, Indiana   J. V. L.
September 1981

Contents

Introduction 3

1 • The Materials of Venezuelan History 7

THE LAND, 7   THE RESOURCES, 30   THE PEOPLE, 40

2 • The Colonial Outpost, 1500-1650 59

CONQUEST AND EXPLORATION, 59   SETTLEMENTS AND MISSIONS, 71

3 • The Mature Colonial Society, 1650-1830 93

CONSOLIDATION, 93   THE COLLAPSE OF THE COLONIAL ORDER, 115
THE EMERGENCE OF THE INDEPENDENCE ELITE, 133

4 • The Commercial-Bureaucratic Outpost, 1830-1935 157

COMMERCE, CREDIT, AND CONTROL, 157
THE FIGHT FOR CARACAS, 187
THE INTRODUCTION OF THE TECHNICAL ELITE, 205

5 • The Technocratic Regimes, 1935-1980 213

AUTHORITY AND COMPETENCY, 213
THE DEMOCRATIC SOLUTION, 229

6 · The Narrative Tradition and the National Myth   252
   THE NARRATIVE TRADITION, 253   THE NATIONAL MYTH, 263

   Conclusion   265
   Chronology (by Mary B. Floyd)   269
   Bibliographic Essay   288
   Statistical Supplement   315
   Tables   319
   Index   335

Maps

The Physical Features of Venezuela   9
The Major Regions of Venezuela   11
The Coast   13
The Segovia Highlands and the Andes   19
The Coastal Ranges   22
The Llanos   25
Guayana   28
Venezuela   41
The Eighteenth-Century Provinces of Venezuela   111

Figures

1. Percent of Total Population in Urban Areas of 20,000 or More, and Percent of Total Population in Most Populated City, 1950-1975   38

2. Population of Principal Cities, 1976   39

3. Population Estimates, 1780-2000   44

4. Distribution of Major Immigrant Groups by Nationality, 1948-1961   52

5. Gain or Loss from Immigration, 1936-1975   53

6. Foreign Population, 1971   54

7. Population Growth Rate, 1900-1990, Annual Percentage Growth Rate Estimates   55

8. Gross Domestic Product, 1979, in US$ at 1978 Prices   215

9. Petroleum Production, 1920-1980   216

10. Per Capita Gross Domestic Product, 1960-1979, in US$ at 1978 Prices   231

11. Energy Consumption Per Capita, 1929-1976   232

12. Electric Lighting, Percent of Population Supplied, 1960-1973   233

13. Principal Export Commodities as a Percent of Total Exports, 1979   244

14. Share of Gross Domestic Product by Economic Activity, 1936-1979   246

15. Gross Domestic Product Per Capita Growth Rates, 1960-1979, in 1978 US$ 247

16. Imports as a Percent of Gross Domestic Product, 1960-1979   250

17. Exports as a Percent of Gross Domestic Product, 1960-1979   251

Tables

PART I   GEOGRAPHY

1. Geographic Location   320
2. Surface Area of Venezuelan Regions   321
3. Surface Area of the Coast   321
4. Surface Area of the Segovia Highlands   322
5. Surface Area of the Andes, 322
6. Surface Area of the Coastal Mountains   322

7. Surface Area of the Llanos   323
8. Surface Area of Guayana   323

PART II   POPULATION

1. Surface Area and Population Density by States 1941-1971   324
2. Population Estimates 1780-2000   325
3. Population Growth Rate 1900-1990   325
4. Population of Principal Cities 1976   326
5. Percent of Total Population in Urban Areas of 20,000 or More and Percent of Total Population in Most Populated City 1950-1975   326
6. Percent of Urban Population in Urban Areas of 100,000 or More and Most Populated City as a Percent of Urban Population in Areas over 100,000 1975   327
7. Gain or Loss from Immigration 1936-1975   327
8. Distribution of Major Immigrant Groups by Nationality 1948-1961   327
9. Foreign Population in 1971   328

PART III   ECONOMICS

1. Gross Domestic Product 1960-1979   328
2. Gross Domestic Product Growth Rates 1960-1979   328
3. Gross Domestic Product Per Capita 1960-1979   329
4. Gross Domestic Product Per Capita Growth Rates 1960-1979   329
5. Gross Domestic Product by Economic Activity 1936-1979   329
6. Imports and Exports as a Percent of Gross Domestic Product 1960-1979   330
7. Exports to and Imports from Four Countries 1912-1979   330
8. Principal Export Commodities as a Percent of Total Exports 1979   331
9. Petroleum Production 1920-1980   331
10. External Public Debt Service Payments as a Percent of Exports 1961-1980   332
11. Wholesale Price Index 1975-1979   332
12. Energy Consumption Per Capita 1929-1976   332
13. Electrical Lighting, Percent of Population Supplied 1960-1973   333

Venezuela

Introduction

Venezuela, as part of the Hispanic world, shares culture and history with the other countries of Latin America. Its language, values, and style combine to place it within this regional group along with Mexico, Argentina, Chile, and Colombia. This community, united by its common cultural and historical heritage, exists in an uncomfortable relationship with the North Atlantic world. As part of this world, Spanish America subscribes to the same general beliefs about progress, prosperity, and the content of a good life. But as a region whose historical experience has placed it on the economic periphery, Spanish America has been able to command only part of the complex set of attributes that define the dominant North Atlantic style.

In recent years, Venezuela's remarkable rebirth as a prosperous, dynamic, and democratic nation has attracted the interest of students of economic and political development who often explain this country's renaissance in terms of dramatic change, revolutionary breaks with the past, and similar metaphors that evoke images of new beginnings and abrupt discontinuities. A corollary of this general theorem is that, because the Venezuela of petroleum is such a transformed place, the country's Hispanic history since the sixteenth century is largely an irrelevant matter for those interested in current affairs. This view is seriously in error, for, if there are insights to be gained from the study of Venezuela's modern economic and political prosperity, they are only credible and useful when understood within the context of the country's past.

By focusing only on the twentieth-century history of Venezuela, modern analysts often see surface discontinuities as radical disruptions of historical trends. The Venezuela of the 1980s is in place, and functions as it does, as a result of the long-term development of forms and patterns of action. For students of change, modernization, and economic development—the cultural foci of our time—the evaluation of Venezuela's experience since petroleum became important requires a clear understanding of Venezuela's historical formation to permit an assessment of the degree of continuity and change in the country's current affairs.

This book provides a holistic view of Venezuela. Its basically chronological structure reflects the evolutionary and cumulative nature of the processes it describes. Its emphases illustrate the important surface transformations and underlying continuities that give this place called Venezuela its historical identity.

The contents of this discussion of Venezuela's search for order and dream of progress are arranged to reflect the design of the country's past. The first chapter identifies the material world, the resources of man and land. Here, the arrangement of space, the accessibility of resources, and the composition of population are emphasized in some detail not only because of their obvious relevance to the country's history, but also because these elements figure so prominently in the definition of Venezuela's national identity. This identity, which is an artificial, man-made construct, required an adaptation to the land and resources and also a redefinition of the geographic space so that, for example, the port of La Guaira and the city of Caracas could be seen as the premier city-port combination for Venezuela, a result not at all obvious from geography alone. Because so much energy went into the invention of a mechanism to connect and bind the disparate geographic regions into a functioning national entity, the chapter on the materials of Venezuelan history identifies these regions in some detail.

The subsequent four chapters describe the principal configurations of the country's organization. Because organizations always have a purpose, these chapters stress that purpose and demonstrate how the organization came into being.

Venezuela has operated in three organizational modes, the last two modifying the basic structure created to manage the first. This first mode, based on a carefully articulated urban system, was invented, imposed, and developed during the years from 1500 to 1650. Imperial bureaucrats consolidated the institutions and reinforced the structure during the late seventeenth and the eighteenth century to confirm the existence of a mature colonial society. This primary mode barely achieved its definitive form at the collapse of the colonial order and the emergence of the independence elite from 1810 to 1830. Because the principal structural elements of the mature colonial society persist throughout the subsequent surface reorganizations, the discussion of this remarkable artifact—the urban system focused on the central city of Caracas—provides the center of gravity for the book.

The second organizational mode, constructed to allow Venezuela to participate in the North Atlantic commercial prosperity of the nineteenth and the early twentieth century, made the country, through a long and often wasteful process, into an ideal commercial-bureaucratic outpost by 1935. Identified by the names of the leaders who best managed this organization, the years of José Antonio Páez, Antonio Guzmán Blanco, and Juan Vicente Gómez defined the essential elements of the commercial-bureaucratic order within the Venezuelan context.

But the perfection of this organizational style under Juan Vicente Gómez occurred precisely when petroleum and the expanding industrial economy of the North Atlantic world required a new organizational mode. Venezuela's response was to reorder the mature colonial society once again through the elevation of a technological elite and the creation of a sequence of technocratic regimes between 1935 and 1980. Although the main features of this organization appear solidly in place, it is, of course, too soon to know how long it will last or how successful it will be.

The conclusion provides a reprise of the themes in this book and serves as a counterpoint to the introduction. The three following sections—chronology, bibliographical essay, and statistical supplement—complete the cycle of this discussion.

The chronology, of course, is the device that anchors history to the specifics of time, place, and person. Because this is not a text or reference work, the chronology provides the necessary comprehensive and symmetrical listing of events.

The bibliographical essay, in addition to the utilitarian function of providing a guide to more information on Venezuela, indicates in a microcosmic way the emphases and preoccupations of Venezuelans and Venezuelanists who have studied the country's past. This literature, since it serves the same purposes as Venezuela's organization, fits the structure described in the text and illustrates the design traced there.

In our time the numerology of statistics enchants us all. But the statistical supplement in this book exists less because of a faith in the efficacy and validity of the data than because the tables give a sense of Venezuela's size, the orders of magnitude of the phenomena discussed in the text. This is important because Venezuela's history is a powerful model for analyzing developments in the rest of Spanish America, even though the relative magnitude of Venezuelan phenomena within the Latin American context requires constant emphasis.

This history, then, presents a grand design for Venezuela's past. It emphasizes the constant interplay between the surface discontinuities of regimes, reforms, and revolts and the structural continuity of an urban organization, focused on the central city of Caracas, that has provided the country with its identity and form since colonial times.

Chapter 1 • The Materials
of Venezuelan History

THE LAND

With its mountains, valleys, plains, deserts, jungles, rivers, and coastline, Venezuela shares most of the geographic characteristics of its Latin American companions in the hemisphere. Since the Spaniards first began their conquest of America, the country has been dominated by its mountains and its Caribbean coastline. The patterns of land use and settlement, and the organization of communication and transportation networks, responded to the requirements of Iberian conquest, settlement, and commerce. No history of Venezuela can afford to begin without an understanding of these arrangements.

This geography is as much a function of the observer's perspective as it is a consequence of the location of mountains, rivers, and the like. The values contemporaries placed on the facts of their physical universe greatly affected their perceptions of geography. The early colonial adventurers searching for gold saw Venezuelan geography much differently from the seventeenth-century cattlemen, whose perceptions of valuable natural resources coincided not at all with those of a twentieth-century petroleum executive.

This emphasis on the changing value of geography over time can, of course, be exaggerated. Venezuela in the last decades of the twentieth century has an urban arrangement that, while considerably different in size and density from its colonial prototype, follows the outlines imposed on the country's geography during the Spanish imperial centuries. For this reason the following description and analysis of Venezuela's landscape takes as its focus the development of the colonial model and then examines the changes brought during the republican and especially the petroleum periods of the country's history.

Physical geographers see Venezuela encompassing six major regions. The boundaries are defined by rivers, mountains, coastline, and the like, yet they also coincide with a similar set of boundaries that could be defined using historical criteria such as settlement, agriculture, transportation, or material culture. This convergence of boundaries illustrates the close connection between man and land in the Venezuelan context, a connection only recently weakened by the dissolving power of technology and wealth.

A glance at a relief map of Venezuela immediately reveals the country's major geographic features. Sweeping into the southwestern corner of Venezuela, a spur of South America's mightiest mountain chain, the Andes, curves northward dividing east and west to form the basin of Lake Maracaibo, losing height until it broadens out into the Segovia Highlands on the east and the Goagira Peninsula on the west, and then falling off gradually into the Caribbean. Directly east of the Segovia Highlands, a lesser range of mountains parallels the coast, effectively blocking off the interior of Venezuela from easy access via the Caribbean. These mountains run uninterrupted as far as Cape Codera, where they are broken by the Unare Basin, only to re-emerge again in the northeastern corner of the country. The remaining coast of Venezuela, lying south of Trinidad, is taken up by the magnificent Orinoco Delta. East and south of the Andes and the Coastal Range stretches a vast plain, descending very slowly from the foothills toward the Apure and Meta rivers on the south and the Orinoco River on the east. Below the Meta, these plains or llanos continue into Colombia

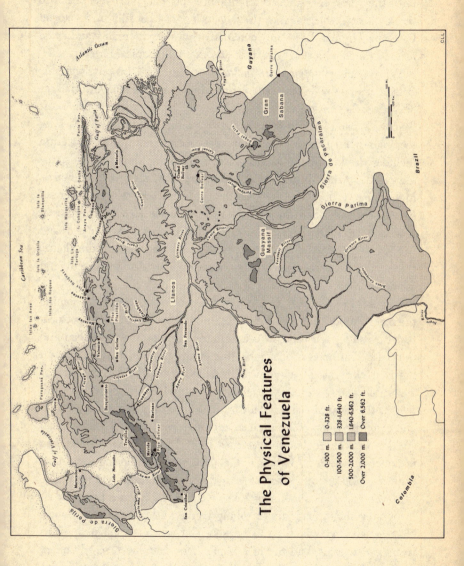

The Physical Features
of Venezuela

0-100 m. 0-328 ft.

100-500 m. 328-1,640 ft.

500-2,000 m. 1,640-6,562 ft.

Over 2,000 m. Over 6,562 ft.

Atlantic Ocean

Guyana

Gran
Sabana

Cerro Roraima

Sierra de Pacaraima

Sierra Parima

Brazil

Guayana
Massif

Orinoco River

Negro River

Colombia

Caribbean Sea

Gulf of Paria

Isla Margarita

Isla la
Blanquilla

Isla la
Tortuga

Isla Los Roques

Islas las Aves

Paria Pen.

Araya Pen.

Maturín

Paraguaná Pen.

Llanos

San Fernando

Lake Maracaibo

Gulf of Venezuela

Sierra de Perijá

San Cristóbal

Mérida

Pico Bolívar

Trujillo

Barinas

Barquisimeto

Valencia

San Carlos

Caracas

Maracay

Ciudad
Bolívar

Cerro Bolívar

Orinoco River

Apure River

Caroní River

Caura River

Paragua River

CLL

until they meet the Andean foothills. In the east, the llanos reach to the Orinoco, which marks the beginning of the still undeveloped Guayana Highlands, a land dominated by low mountains and large mesas covered with rich grasslands and extensive tropical forests.

Within this panorama, six major regions defined by physiographic criteria can be divided into subregions, divisions helpful in the analysis of Venezuela's historical development. First among these is the Coast Region, a band of low-altitude beach, plain, and rock which, after looping around Lake Maracaibo, borders the entire east-west coast and includes the fan of the Orinoco Delta. The Segovia Highlands, the second major region, displays a broken topography of low mountains, high plains, valleys, and semidesert, and forms a transitional area between the Andes and the Coastal Range. Surrounded by the coastal landscape around Coro, the Andean environment of Trujillo and Mérida, the Coastal Range of Caracas and Valencia, and the llanos, this region early became a major transfer point for settlement and administration.

The third region, the Andes, stretches south-southwest until joining the main trunk of that mountain chain in Colombia with its spectacular peaks and green valleys. As a highway between the Caribbean and the prosperous areas of Colombia, the Andes have served as a difficult but frequently used communication route, and in the earliest years as a possible path to the mythical kingdom of El Dorado. The fourth region, the Coastal Range, stands just behind the coast in the central and eastern portion of Venezuela. Although representing only a small fraction of Venezuela's surface area, the Coastal Range, in its rich intermontane valleys, has held the principal economic and political centers of the country since at least the mid-eighteenth century. The fifth, the vast plains or Llanos Region, forms the interior heartland of Venezuela and is made up of rolling land covered with grass, clumps of trees, and occasional palm forests. The area is dominated by its rivers and streams, and the inhabitants, who have lived mostly off of cattle and horses since the beginning of European settlement, have regulated their lives by the rains that swell the rivers and flood parts of the plains. Beyond the Orinoco lies Guayana, the sixth region, an

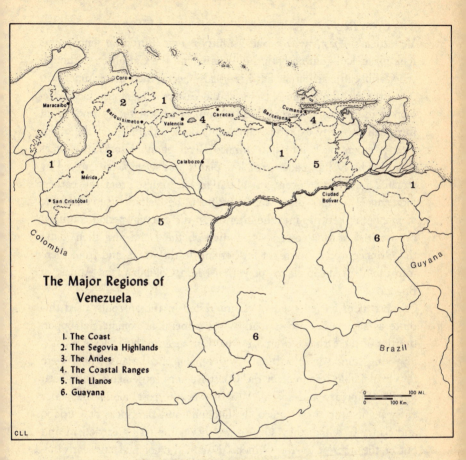

The Major Regions of
Venezuela

1. The Coast
2. The Segovia Highlands
3. The Andes
4. The Coastal Ranges
5. The Llanos
6. Guayana

area that has received effective settlement only in recent decades.
Today, as in colonial times, settlement hugs the edges of Guayana,
and notions of the region's fabulous riches remain for the most part
untested.

Each of these regions has had an important role in identifying and
defining the character of Venezuela's past. Over the centuries the
geographical focus has shifted from one region to another in response
to internal rearrangements and external demands. Before exploring
these changes in Venezuela's mental maps a closer examination of the
physical geography of the regions is necessary.

The Coast Region

Venezuela's coast, where the country's first European encounters took place, looks out on both the Atlantic and the Caribbean, although the Caribbean orientation has historically been much more important. Nevertheless, the Orinoco Delta at the eastern end of the Coast Region is an impressive geographical phenomenon, a natural wonder that intrigued the early explorers. Spanning about 250 miles on the ocean side, it tapers back into the Orinoco River channel some 125 miles inland. The Delta, made up of low plains and swamp, crisscrossed by streams and rivers, covers just about 23,000 miles. From the earliest moments of Spanish interest in Venezuela, the Delta has served as one of five natural entries into the interior. In the colonial period countless missionaries and explorers passed through the Delta and then along the Orinoco to the Apure, or farther still to the Meta, and from there into the Venezuelan llanos or perhaps into Colombia, the Andes, or Bogotá.

Subsequent entrepreneurs, less interested in Indian souls, used this route as a potential access road to the mineral or commercial opportunities of the Orinoco drainage area. But because the Delta itself is a low-lying humid land with a rainy climate, and because there were few exploitable resources in the Coast Region, settlements have been mostly temporary and sparse. Where they do exist, along the major entry points into the Orinoco, as Tucupita and Barrancas or Curiapo and Santa Catalina, they survive mostly on the traffic carried in and out of the interior on the Orinoco. But in the colonial and early national periods, this swampy, rainy, and hot subregion served primarily to announce the Orinoco and to lure the unwary into heroic efforts to open all of South America to direct trade with Europe via this great river and its tributaries.

Moving from this Atlantic subregion onto the Caribbean coast to the west, one must cut across the Gulf of Paria, swing around the tip of the Paria Peninsula, and go due west to the tip of Point Araya. This peninsular formation, with its narrow coastal beach and dry forests, stretches some 160 miles from tip to tip. The eastern peninsula is mostly arid desert; indeed, a major salt deposit, the Salinas de Araya,

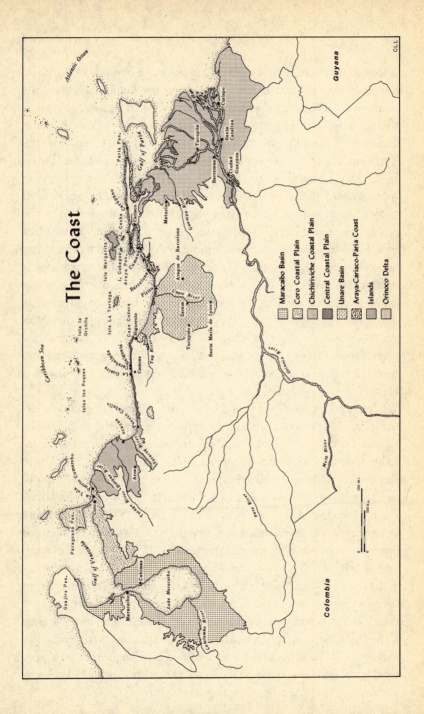

The Coast

Caribbean Sea

Atlantic Ocean

Guyana

Colombia

Marracaibo Basin
Coro Coastal Plain
Chichiriviche Coastal Plain
Central Coastal Plain
Unare Basin
Araya-Cariaco-Paria Coast
Islands
Orinoco Delta

Guajira Pen.

Gulf of Venezuela

Paraguaná Pen.

Lake Maracaibo

Maracaibo

Cabimas

Catatumbo River

Motatán River

Tocuyo River

Yaracuy River

La Vela

Coro

Islas los Roques

Isla la Orchila

Isla La Tortuga

Cabo Codera

Curiepe-Tacarigua

Higuerote

Tuy River

Caracas

La Guaira

Puerto Cabello

Morón

Aroa

Barcelona

Píritu

Aragua de Barcelona

Unare River

Zaraza

Tucupido

Santa María de Ipire

Isla Margarita

I. Coche

Cumaná

Araya Pen.

I. Cubagua

Paria Pen.

Gulf of Paria

Cariaco

Coro Coastal

Maturín

Guarapiche River

Barrancas

Ciudad Guayana

Santa Catalina

Curiapo

Tucupita

Orinoco River

Guarico River

Portuguesa River

Meta River

Apure River

100 MI.

100 KM.

CLL

is located there and has been exploited since pre-Columbian times. By
following the southern edge of Araya into the Gulf of Cariaco, the
coast changes into a beautiful subregion of narrow beaches, green
islands of semidry vegetation, and crystal blue waters from Araya to
Cumaná. This same type of coastline extends from Cumaná south-
westward about 60 miles past Barcelona to Píritu and the Unare
River. Two major rivers break this coast before the Unare: the Manzanares near Cumaná and the Neverí near Barcelona. From the Gulf
of Paria to beyond Barcelona, the section of the Cariaco-Araya-Paria
coast, there are no easy entries into the interior, since the coastline
from Paria to Barcelona is backed up by the virtually unbroken mountains of the Coastal Range. But if the coast appears forbidding, it
nevertheless provided the site for some of the earliest Spanish settlements on the mainland, places such as Cumaná, Barcelona, or Cariaco,
which drew sustenance from the pearl fisheries of Cubagua and Margarita islands some five to ten miles off Point Araya. This coastline
from Paria to Píritu which forms the Cariaco-Araya-Paria subregion
contains just over 1,600 square miles of surface area and stretches
almost 450 miles in length.

West of Barcelona, the terrain behind the beaches gradually de-
clines, until near the mouth of the Unare a substantial break in the
wall of hills appears, a coastal plain that seems to reach into the interior beyond the southern horizon. This subregion of the Unare
Basin is formed mostly by a flat, low-lying plain cut by the series of
small streams and rivers feeding the Unare. In the interior, the Unare
Basin is defined on the east by the Eastern Llanos, an area of flat land
broken by a system of mesas and drained by rivers and streams that
flow into the Gulf of Paria and the Orinoco Delta, and on the south
and west by the Calabozo Llanos, an area of savanna drained by rivers
and streams of the Ápure, Portuguesa, Guárico, and Orinoco systems.
Along the coast lies a band of low ground, beaches, and narrow plains
built up by currents that sweep from east to west depositing sand all
along the coast from Píritu to Higuerote. In all, the Unare Basin contains some 10,000 square miles of area and has long served as a principal entry into the cattle regions and petroleum fields of the Vene-

zuelan llanos. Before the petroleum boom created a major urban complex near the southeastern edge of this area at El Tigre, the subregion supported a scattering of villages and towns whose existence depended mostly on cattle raising and whose founders in the colonial period frequently had been missionaries in search of native souls to save in places such as Píritu, Tucupido, Zaraza, Santa María de Ipire, or Aragua de Barcelona.

West of Higuerote and along Cape Codera lies a strip of inhospitable beach and rocky mountainside which runs for over 125 miles to just east of Puerto Cabello. The lack of major attractions along this coast and the absence of outstanding harbors delayed the settlement of this subregion until the settlers recognized that the richness of the valleys in the Coastal Range made the effort worthwhile. In the hot oppressive climate, only a few hamlets and villages emerged in the colonial period: Naiguatá, Caraballeda, and La Guaira. Here and there along the coast a small stream or river can be seen making a patch of green and providing the space and soil for the cultivation of cacao and bananas, or, by the mid-twentieth century, a site for recreational complexes. By the late eighteenth century, this narrow subregion, covering only about 480 square miles, housed the major port for Venezuela. The emergence of La Guaira as the premier harbor stemmed not from its exceptional qualities, in which it is exceeded by such locations as Puerto Cabello, Tucacas, or La Vela, but from its proximity to the rich agricultural regions of the country in the Caracas and other valleys of the Central Coastal Range.

The coastal plain begins to widen near Puerto Cabello, and from that port city to just east of Puerto Cumarebo this wide Chichiriviche plain extends inland in a slow-rising formation along the rivers flowing out of the Segovia Highlands. The first of these is the Yaracuy River which separates the Coastal Range on the east from the Segovia Highlands on the west. This river provides one of the entryways into the interior plains, and because of its location and accessibility, it served as an excellent highway for the smugglers of the eighteenth century to transport contraband goods and products. North of the Yaracuy is Tucacas, an excellent port with no important hinterland.

North and west along the coast is the Tocuyo River, leading back
inland some 90 miles to a hot dry plain that attracted few settlers in
the colonial period. The last river plain of this subregion surrounds
the course of the Hueque River, an equally dry and unattractive area.
In all, the Chichiriviche Coastal Plain extends some 90 miles along
the coast and covers about 6,100 square miles.

Westward from the Chichiriviche Coastal Plain lies the Coro
Coastal Plain, a band of sand and low hills, interrupted by the Para-
guaná Peninsula, reaching almost to the mouth of Lake Maracaibo.
Although this desert and scrub brush terrain presents no obvious attractions, the area just east and directly south of the Paraguaná Peninsula became the site of one of Venezuela's earliest settlements.
Through the port of La Vela and its town of Coro some miles inland,
European adventurers entered the country to follow the southward-
rising mountains in search of El Dorado, or to roam the Segovia
Highlands, founding towns and establishing outposts that would serve
as bases for the exploration and settlement of the valleys of the Central Coastal Range and the prairies of the llanos. Coro survived as a
major center, serving as a gateway into the mountains and highlands
and as an early colonial administrative center. The coastal plain of
Coro, however, has never been able to support more than the Port of
La Vela and a minor fishing center at Puerto Cumarebo. West of the
Paraguaná Peninsula the coast becomes hotter and dryer and the
coastal plain widens out as it approaches the opening of the Maracaibo
Basin. It is an inhospitable coast that urges a traveler on toward Maracaibo. The Coro Coastal Plain and Paraguaná Peninsula cover an
east-west distance of about 160 miles and a surface area of just over
4,400 square miles.

Lake Maracaibo has fascinated travelers since the early colonial period. The great lake inspired dreams of commerce and prosperity
among Spanish colonists, who saw it as a mighty passage into the
heart of the Andes. The existence of several navigable rivers around
the lake, such as the Catatumbo and the Chama, encouraged these
dreams. Unfortunately, pirates, the impassibility of the Maracaibo Bar,
the hot humid climate, and the indifference of colonial officials pre-

vented the realization of this vision before independence. Indeed, not until the petroleum boom of the twentieth century did this lake come to have the importance it had had in the imagination of the conquerors. The eastern shore shows a band of low land, bordered on the east and south by the Segovia Highlands and the eastern spur of the Andes, and on the west by Colombia and the western spur of the Andes. The lake is some 125 miles from Maracaibo to the southern end and about 60 miles at the widest point. The Maracaibo Basin covers about 12,700 square miles, excluding the lake itself, which is about 5,000 square miles in area.

The remaining part of this Coast Region is composed of Venezuela's off-shore islands. Excluding Trinidad, once part of the Spanish empire, these Venezuelan islands add up to 700 square miles. The principal islands in this group lie off the eastern coast, just north of the Peninsula of Araya. Margarita is the largest with a surface area of about 500 square miles, followed by Coche and Cubagua. Vitally important during the early years of settlement because of the pearl trade, these islands rapidly declined in importance with the exhaustion of the pearl fisheries and the growth of mainland settlements. In recent years they have become recreation and commercial centers.

This, then, is the Coast Region, an area stretching the width of Venezuela, some 930 miles east and west, and covering some 59,000 square miles of surface. This is the subregion Europeans first encountered, and here they established their first settlements. From sites on the coastal plain came the expeditions that opened up Venezuela to European discovery, settlement, and exploitation.

The Segovia Highlands

After the Coast Region, Spanish exploration moved inland through the Segovia Highlands, a region of high plains and low broken hills lying mostly between 1,600 and 2,600 feet in altitude. In all, the Segovia Highlands cover some 9,300 square miles. The countryside south of Coro is hot, dry, scrub brush terrain. This Segovia Highland, however, is made up of four mountainous formations which loosely surround two principal savannas or plains. Along the northern edge of the Highlands rise the low Northern Mountains, broken almost in the middle to give access to the interior Plains of Falcón. To the west, defining the border of the Segovia Highlands with the Maracaibo Basin, lies another mountainous formation, the Barbacoas Mountains. Extending east from the northern end of the Barbacoas are the Baragua Mountains, a series of hills and mountains broken by valleys and small plains that separate the northern Plains of Falcón from the southern Lara Depression. The fourth mountainous formation just south of the Baraguas and almost parallel to the Barbacoas Mountains separates the Lara Plains around Barquisimeto from the Urama and Tocuyo river valleys.

Although cooler than the lower elevations of the coast, most of the Segovia Highlands Region is hot and dry. The towns established here in the colonial period could be found scattered along transportation routes, as is Pedregal; nestled against the hills, as is San Luis; located on important rivers or streams, as is Carora; or attached to a grassland, as are El Tocuyo and Barquisimeto.

The Segovia Highlands, formed by the Andes as they decline and spread before plunging into the sea, provided the locale for the second stage of Spain's expansion into western Venezuela. From Coro, the point of the first stage, Spanish captains moved to El Tocuyo and Barquisimeto, there to lay the base for the subsequent push into the Central Coastal Range. As a region with Indian labor and with the terrain to raise cattle and some food crops, the Segovia Highlands, and especially El Tocuyo, had the resources to support explorations.

The Andes

The Segovia Highlands gained considerable prominence in the early years of conquest and settlement as a transfer point for travelers and commerce from Coro on the coast to the llanos through Barquisimeto, or east and north to the mountains and valleys of the Central Coastal Range, or southwest into the Andes themselves. The inhabitants and geography of this region have always played an important role in Venezuelan history, whether as the road to El Dorado, the source of revenue from coffee cultivation, or the source of political power.

This Venezuelan branch of the South American Andes is composed

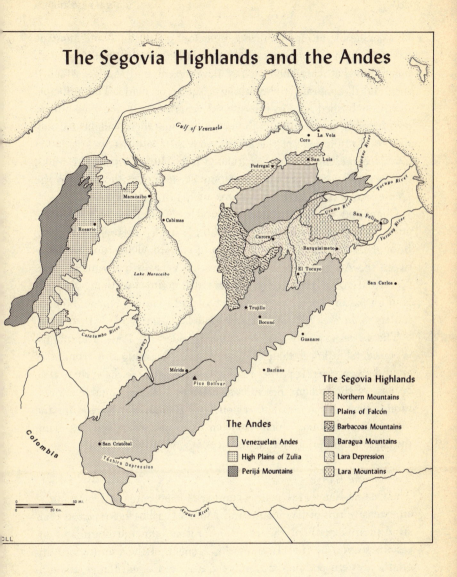

The Segovia Highlands and the Andes

Gulf of Venezuela

La Vela
Coro •
Pedregal ☗ • San Luis
Maracaibo •
• Cabimas
Rosario •
San Felipe •
Carora •
Lake Maracaibo
Barquisimeto •
El Tocuyo •
San Carlos •
Catatumbo River
Trujillo •
Boconó •
Chama River
Guanare •
Mérida • ▲
Pico Bolívar ▲
• Barinas
Colombia
San Cristóbal •
Táchira Depression

Huecue River
Tocuyo River
Urama River
Yaracuy River

The Segovia Highlands

- Northern Mountains
- Plains of Falcón
- Barbacoas Mountains
- Baragua Mountains
- Lara Depression
- Lara Mountains

The Andes

- Venezuelan Andes
- High Plains of Zulia
- Perijá Mountains

0   50 Mi.
0   50 Km.

Arauca River

of a double file of mountain ranges enclosing a series of intermontane valleys. This is a complex and spectacularly beautiful landscape with mountains that reach their highest elevations around Mérida, which is surrounded by peaks right at the 16,400-foot mark. The principal towns established here in the colonial years nestle in the high valleys and depressions which break the mountains into their complicated sub-regions. Trujillo, one of the lowest Andean towns, lies in a valley at 2,600 feet; nearby Boconó lies at 4,000 feet; Mérida, among the peaks, lies in a valley of 5,380 feet; and San Cristóbal, at 2,700 feet in the Depression of Táchira, is almost level with Trujillo.

Connected by winding mountain roads, these valleys still show the attractiveness that led settlers to establish stable, self-sufficient towns throughout the region. The difficulty of communication and trade between the Andean valleys and the rest of Venezuela is equally clear. Nevertheless, the presence of substantial Indian populations, of fertile land for pasture and crops, and of a cool and healthful climate brought settlers to the area long after the El Dorado dream had faded.

The western spur of the Venezuelan Andes, the Perijá Mountains, is considerably lower than the eastern spur, reaching a maximum of around 12,230 feet. It proved relatively unattractive to the early settlers because of the Indians' fierce resistance and a lack of suitable agricultural valleys. Some small towns such as Rosario did emerge on the high Plains of Zulia, which rise from 1,640 to about 2,600 feet along the edge of the Perijá Mountains.

The Coastal Range
The Coastal Range, the political and economic center of Venezuela, is an extensive run of low mountains. More a Caribbean formation than an Andean extension, the range is broken into a western and an eastern section by the Unare Basin. From the mid-sixteenth century on, the western portion, known as the Central Coastal Range, came to hold Venezuela's principal towns and cities, and by the late eighteenth century the main city, Caracas, controlled the region's political, judicial, commercial, and ecclesiastical institutions.

On crossing the Yaracuy Valley, the western section of this region

begins in the Nirgua-Tinaquillo Hills which border a plain that winds
its way north and east for forty or fifty miles. Another series of low
hills separates this plain from the Yaracuy River and the coast. The
route from the town of Nirgua to Montalbán passes through these
hills into the Valencia Basin.

This subregion, a lake surrounded by a fertile plain, forms a drainage area with no outlet to the sea. The town of Valencia itself lies at
the western edge of the subregion at an altitude of about 1640 feet.
Although rather hot, this valley constituted one of the major agricultural areas even before the eighteenth century. Extending some forty
miles east and west, the basin is bordered on the north by the Central
Littoral Mountains and on the south by the Central Interior Mountains.

From the Valencia Basin eastward appears a series of irregularly
shaped valleys and plains that interconnect and broaden out toward
the east until they reach the coastal lowlands. This subregion of interior valleys can best be seen as a system of three major divisions. The
first is the San Sebastián Valley, a small formation of some 90 square
miles drained by the upper reaches of the Guárico River. Continuing
eastward over a dividing series of low hills, comes the Aragua-Tuy
valleys, almost 770 square miles of fine agricultural land along the
Aragua and Tuy rivers. A major crop-producing region since the seventeenth century, this area is dominated by a series of farming towns
such as Cúa, Ocumare del Tuy, and Santa Lucía. This valley opens
into the Caracas valleys at the northeast corner through the Tuy River
channel.

The Caracas valleys take the shape of an irregular, narrow, isos-
celes triangle laid on its side, with the apex to the west and the base
running north and south in the east. Covering an area of about 580
square miles, the triangle's base lies at an altitude of about 160 feet
where it meets the coast and rises at the apex deep in the central coast
range to just about 3,300 feet. At the high point of the valley lies Caracas, the central city of Venezuela since the second half of the eighteenth century. These Caracas valleys of prosperous agricultural land
contain numerous towns, now mostly included within the Caracas
metropolitan area. From the southeast corner of the valleys, such places

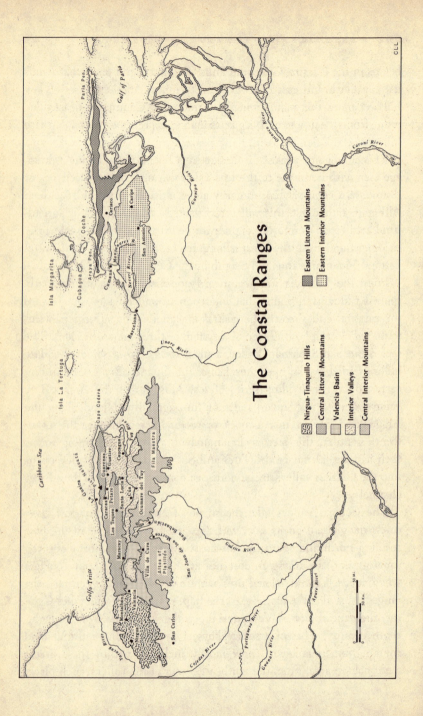

The Coastal Ranges

Legend:
- Nirgua-Tinaquillo Hills
- Central Littoral Mountains
- Valencia Basin
- Interior Valleys
- Central Interior Mountains
- Eastern Littoral Mountains
- Eastern Interior Mountains

CLL

Caribbean Sea

Isla La Tortuga

Isla Margarita

I. Cubagua I. Coche

Paria Pen.

Gulf of Paria

Araya Pen.

Cumaná

Cariaco

Manzanares River

Cariaco

Neverí River

Cariaco

San Antonio

Barcelona

Unare River

Guanipa River

Orinoco River

Caroní River

Gulfo Triste

La Guaira

Maiquetía

Pico Naiguatá

Cape Codera

Guarenas

Guatire

Petare

Caracas

Santa Lucía

Las Teques

Tuy River

Ocumare del Tuy

Cúa

Fila Maestra

Maracay

Montalbán

Valencia

Nirgua

San Carlos

San Sebastián

Villa de Cura

Altos of Pilatillo

San Juan de los Morros

Guárico River

Aroa River

Cojedes River

Portuguesa River

Cojedes River

Guanare River

Apure River

50 Mi.

50 Km.

as Caucagua, Guatire, Guarenas, and Petare mark the road to the head of the valley at Caracas.

The Central Littoral Mountains surrounding Caracas on three sides are a striking complex of green mountains that rise to a maximum elevation of almost 9,840 feet at the peak of Naiguatá north of Petare, and then fall precipitously to the rocky Central Coast of La Guaira and Caraballeda. In the colonial period the western-most section of the mountains was populated primarily along the southern foothills, as at Maracay, or in the scattered narrow valleys along the northern face. This held for almost the entire seaward side of the chain. Due south and then west of Caracas in the Los Altos Hills are a number of towns nestled in the small valleys or clinging to the hillsides, such as Los Teques. In all, the Central Littoral Mountain subregion occupies just under 1,900 square miles.

Parallel to and almost the same length as the Central Littoral Mountains are the Central Interior Mountains which run east and west separating the interior valleys from the llanos. These mountains, broken by numerous small valleys and openings to the plains, have two major formations of almost equal area. On the east are the Altos of Platillón and the Calza Hills, and on the west is the Fila Maestra. The major corridor to the llanos lies through these two, which helps explain the existence of the towns of San Juan de los Morros and Villa de Cura in the eastern foothills and Altos of Platillón and the town of San Sebastián in the interior valley of the same name that lies just north of the corridor.

To the east of the Fila Maestra, the Central Coastal Range gives way to the Unare Depression and rises again east of Barcelona. This segment has an interior range, the Eastern Interior Mountains, separating the coast of Cumaná from the Eastern Llanos, and a coastal range, the Eastern Littoral Mountains, running along the interior of the Araya and Paria peninsulas. Of these two formations, only the interior mountains attracted population in the colonial period to such places as Caripe and San Antonio. In all, these two mountain groups account for 2,700 square miles.

The Llanos Region

Southward from the Eastern Interior Mountains of the Coastal Range lies Aragua de Maturín and Caicara on the Llanos of Maturín. Bordered on the east by the Orinoco Delta, on the south by the Orinoco River, and on the west by the Unare Basin, this subregion has an eastern half of relatively flat grassland, populated during the colonial period mostly in its northern portion in such towns as Aragua de Maturín, Maturín, Caicara, and Aguasay. Most of the western half of the subregion is dominated by a series of extensive mesas which break the horizon around such towns as El Tigre and El Pao de Barcelona. From the early years of settlement through the nineteenth century and even to the present day, this subregion has served as one of the major cattle-raising areas of Venezuela, although the twentieth-century petroleum boom has dramatically expanded the town of El Tigre.

South of El Tigre and west around the Unare Basin begin the Llanos of Calabozo. This subregion is defined on the south and west by the Orinoco, Apure, Portuguesa, and Cojedes Rivers, and on the north by the Central Coastal Range. A large plain with rolling countryside, meandering streams, and flooded lowlands to the south, the region supported a scattering of towns based on large cattle-raising enterprises during the colonial period. More closely spaced near the foothills of the Coastal Range are towns such as Lezama, Ortiz, El Pao, Tinaco, and San Carlos, while to the south the population is sparser with more isolated centers such as Calabozo. Other than the major rivers, the Guárico, the Tiznados, and the Orituco, the only notable geographic feature to break the monotony of these rolling plains with their grass and scrub brush, clumps of trees, and palm forests, are the hills and mesas just east of El Baúl and the Baúl Massif.

West of the Cojedes River at El Baúl begin the Llanos of Barinas-Portuguesa. This triangular subregion has its base along the Andean foothills, its southern side following the Apure, and its northern side along the Cojedes-Portuguesa rivers. In the upper llanos along the Andean foothills lie most of its towns, such as Barinas, Guanare, and Acarigua-Araure.

The Llanos of Apure, stretching south of the river of the same name,

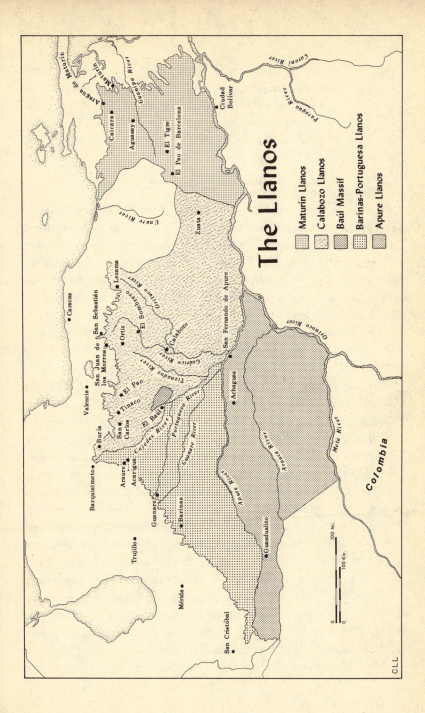

The Llanos

Maturín Llanos

Calabozo Llanos

Baúl Massif

Barinas-Portuguesa Llanos

Apure Llanos

Maturín • Aragua de Maturín • Guanipa River • Guarico River • Caroní River • Paragua River

Caicara • Aguasay • El Tigre • El Pao de Barcelona • Ciudad Bolívar

Caracas • Unare River • Zuata

San Sebastián • Lezama • Orituco River • El Sombrero • Ortiz • Calabozo • San Fernando de Apure • Orinoco River

San Juan de los Morros • Valencia • El Pao • Tinaco • El Baúl • Tiznados River • Guárico River • Achaguas

Burla • San Carlos • Cojedes River • Portuguesa River • Orinoco River

Barquisimeto • Araure • Acarigua • Guanare • Barinas • Guanare River • Apure River • Arauca River • Meta River

Trujillo • San Cristóbal • Guasdualito

Mérida

Colombia

100 Mi.

100 Km.

CLL

form a subregion of flat grassland, subject to frequent flooding by the overflow from the complex system of rivers running east into the Orinoco. The few towns in the subregion, for example Guasdualito, Achaguas, and San Fernando de Apure, are located mostly in a narrow band above the Arauca River. This area, like the rest of the Llanos Region, is supported by stock raising.

Guayana

Since the earliest days of Spanish exploration of the Orinoco River, the regions south and east have held a special fascination for adventurers, missionaries, entrepreneurs, and mystics. Venezuela's Guayana is one of the country's principal frontiers, not only because it has been the location of a long and often acrimonious boundary dispute but also because the plains and mountains seem to hold such a remarkable promise of mineral riches.

The thorough aerial mapping of this extensive geographic region in the twentieth century has dispelled most of the mystery surrounding its exact size and configuration. To be sure, numerous missionaries and prospectors in the colonial and republican periods traveled the Orinoco River and explored its major tributaries into Guayana—the Caroní, the Caura, and the Ventuari, for example. As the explorers followed the river channels out of the plains into the steeply rising mesas and mountain ranges, the dense tropical and subtropical vegetation and the resistance of the Indian residents conspired to prevent effective exploration. By clinging to the edges of the major rivers and streams, the eighteenth-century missionaries managed to maintain a string of religious establishments, churches, missions, doctrinas, and the like, which served to substantiate much of Venezuela's territorial claims in the area. But the stresses of the independence wars and the anti-clerical tone of republican governments destroyed this fragile web of Hispanic civilization in Guayana. By the 1830s there were far fewer outposts in Guayana than there had been in the 1780s, a situation which contributed to Venezuela's difficulties in maintaining its claims to the region as far east as the Essequibo River.

Although the map of Guayana shows seven subregions within this area, two types of physiography define the region. The plains, at an altitude of 160 to 1,640 feet, sweep in a wide band along the western edge of Guayana following the courses of the Orinoco and Casiquiare rivers. These are essentially sandy-soiled plains with relatively fragile grassland and scattered palm groves. Unlike the plains of the Apure, whose sturdy grassland can support cattle in the dry season, the Guayanese plains dry up when the rainy season ends to such an extent that large-scale cattle raising has never been possible. This difficulty, combined with the transportation problems presented by distance and geography, had an inhibiting effect on the development of stable Hispanic settlements in the region. While stock raising has always been an important local enterprise, its commercial possibilities could not be realized until modern roads reached into the region, roads built not to revitalize the cattle business but to support mining, manufacturing, and hydroelectric power installations in the second half of the twentieth century.

The rest of Guayana, a little less than half the surface area, is composed of a broken topography of mountains and mountain ranges which with their sharp rises, steep sides, and flat tops give the region its distinctive geographic character. The water flowing out of these mountains, most of which are in the 1640- to 2600-foot category with some portions rising about 2600 to 4900 feet, descends rapidly through the rugged terrain producing spectacular waterfalls, natural attractions that have provided picturesque scenery for the tourist industry for many years.

But more important for Venezuela's development, these mountains contain an impressive variety and quantity of minerals. Although the exact amount and quality of this resource endowment remain somewhat speculative, commercial amounts of iron ore have already been developed into a dynamic and prospering industry centered at Puerto Ordaz and exploiting the famous iron mountains of Cerro Bolívar. This resource, known to explorers and entrepreneurs since the late nineteenth century, has contributed a major industrial potential to the Venezuelan economy of the twentieth century.

These high mesas and mountains also contain commercial amounts

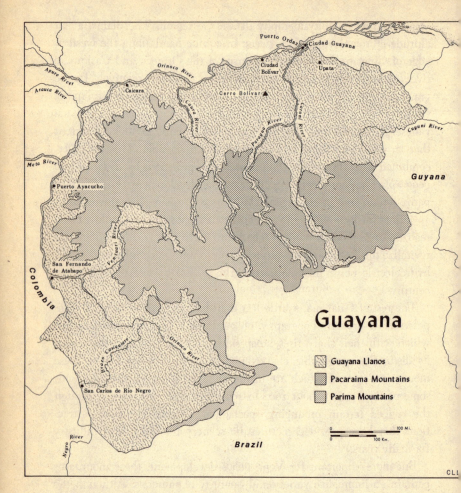

of manganese, diamonds, and gold, although the inaccessibility and limited quantity of the last two prevent a major rush for these rare materials. Whatever the value of the resources of this remarkable region turns out to be, it is sure to have a major impact on the country's economic future. This fact, so evident to Venezuelan and foreign observers since at least the late colonial period, has provided the logic for Venezuela's continuing boundary dispute. The country claims an ob-

long piece of territory about 100 miles wide and 450 miles long running north and south along the Essequibo River which Venezuela
regards as its proper eastern boundary.

The dispute, like all such matters in Latin American history, has
its origins in imprecise colonial boundaries, inaccurate geographic and
cartographic descriptions, and ordinary territorial acquisitiveness. In
this case, the villains, in the Venezuelan view, came from England,
whose agents in then British Guiana illegally pushed the western
boundary of that colony into Venezuelan territory some 90 to 100
miles during the decade of the 1840s. The Venezuelan protests of this
violation of their *uti poseditis juris* of 1810 began to get serious in the
1840s and continued with frequent pauses until the late 1880s, when
an international commission was sent to Venezuela and Guayana to
help establish the boundary. The results of this controversy, not settled
until 1899, did not please Venezuela at all. Even though the boundary
awarded by an arbitration tribunal gave Venezuela complete control
of the Orinoco Delta, the primary territory in dispute went to Great
Britain. Venezuela, naturally enough, saw the tribunal, composed of
Russian, United States, and British representatives, as rigged against
them, and they have never accepted the 1899 decision as binding.
When British Guiana became independent in 1966 as Guyana, Venezuela's recognition of the new nation carried a caveat about the common boundary between the two countries reasserting the claim of
sovereignty over the territory to the Essequibo River. Although the
claim is currently in a state of limbo, any major mineral discovery in
the disputed area could bring serious international consequences.

The boundary question and the mineral wealth provide the incentive for most of the development that has occurred in Guayana in
modern times. With the exception of the cities located on the Orinoco
itself, urban centers with origins in the colonial period, the principal
places in Guayana respond to mineral extraction or territorial claims.
But even with the populations established in places such as Upata,
Puerto Ayacucho, and San Fernando de Atabapo, this region is very
sparsely settled and immensely underdeveloped.

THE RESOURCES

The resources that make a region interesting or profitable depend on time and technology, and in Venezuela this truism is especially pertinent. Natural resources, like styles, have their periods of fashion and popularity. What excites the enterprise and greed of a sixteenth-century conqueror may be of only passing interest to the twentieth-century industrialist. So any discussion of Venezuela's resource endowment must always keep present the context within which a particular natural resource is valuable. For Venezuela, then, there are two major contexts for a discussion of resources. The colonial period and the nineteenth century shared a similar technological base, a concentration on agriculture, and a most primitive manufacturing capacity. Although there were some initiatives near the end of the period that made iron and petroleum more interesting, the capabilities of the Venezuelan economy in the 1890s were not very far advanced from those of the 1790s. The second period is, of course, the twentieth century, when Venezuela's petroleum revolution reordered the country's resources and redefined its wealth.

In the eyes of the early explorers of Venezuela's territory, the pre-eminent natural resources were precious metals and Indians. The first generation sought out the gold and searched in vain for the silver that might have made their fortune. Indeed, only in a few places near the valleys of Caracas in the mines of Buría did any Venezuelan conqueror find the gold of his dreams. Even here, the mines, while profitable, could only support modest levels of exploitation during the colony's early years. No great colonial fortunes came from these diggings, so Venezuela's settlers soon turned to other natural resources for their sustenance.

Because Spain's American adventure required many laborers, the Indian population of each region became as important a natural resource as any mine or cache of precious stones. So important was this resource that the basic political, social, and economic structure of the Spanish empire rested on the system invented to organize, control, and allocate this resource among colonists, clergy, and crown. Of course, the great debates over the Indian question had as their referents the Indian societies of the Caribbean and later Mexico, not Venezuela. But the preoccupation of Spanish authorities and colonists with Indian labor was a universal constant of the American empire and defined these native Americans as the hemisphere's strategic resource. Without Indian labor all the silver of Mexico or Peru, all the wheat, cattle, or cacao of Venezuela would have remained unexploited, uncultivated, or unharvested.

While most attention went to the organization and administration of the highly developed civilizations of Mexico and Peru, Venezuela's Indians attracted considerable interest also. Slave raids along the Venezuelan coast for Indians to replace the declining native population of the Caribbean islands set the tone of Spanish-Indian relations in Venezuela. The original size of this native population is beyond estimation. But in the valleys of Caracas alone in the late sixteenth century, at least 80,000 Indians were supposed to have combined forces to resist the Spaniards. Furthermore, substantial settlements of Indians in the fertile valleys of the Andes engaged in sedentary agriculture in relatively high density. Along the east coast as well, there were reasonably reliable reports of Indian populations. Information on the native inhabitants of the interior regions of Guayana and along the llanos of the Apure or Meta rivers is at best sketchy. That there were many Indians, we know, but how many is a question best left to others. Certainly these areas supported a sufficient native population to inhibit and resist the exploration of the region. Missionary accounts of life along Venezuela's major waterways indicate the constant presence of scattered bands of natives whose enthusiasm for Christianity was often undetectable. In any case, as natural resources, only the Indians of the coast, the major agricultural valleys, and the Andes served Venezuela's settlers during this colonial and early republican period.

As mentioned earlier, Venezuela's complement of exotic or precious substances proved relatively poor, but a few items caught the interest of the early explorers. Perhaps the most spectacular were the pearl fisheries in the waters around Margarita and Cubagua islands. The wealth contained on the ocean floor was substantial although quickly exhausted. The occupation of pearl diver claimed the lives of many an Indian before the bonanza played itself out by the mid-sixteenth century. Still, this brief moment of glory attracted Spanish settlement to the eastern coast of Venezuela and focused attention on a region relatively poor in other natural resources.

This eastern region also held another deposit, less romantic than pearls but more essential. The salt pans of the Araya Peninsula provided the attraction for numerous Dutch expeditions and the incentive for the construction of a major Spanish fort on the Peninsula. Although a valuable commodity, salt was not rare enough to justify elaborate exploitation and in any case remained a crown monopoly with a limited profit potential. Even today, the Araya salt works are a government enterprise.

The precious metal, gold, existed in very small deposits, principally in the mines of Buría and its environs, although some gold also appeared in isolated places in the Venezuelan Andes. The Buría gold, of limited economic importance, did serve to focus attention on the Caracas valleys and provided the initial impetus for the conquest and settlement of this rich agricultural region.

The only other mining activity of any consequence involved the copper extracted from modest deposits at Aroa in the Segovia Highlands. More important as a generator of settlement in Barquisimeto, the mines of Aroa remained active throughout the colonial period and into the nineteenth century. As part of the Bolívar family patrimony, the mines gained considerable notoriety in the extensive literature on the life and times of the Liberator.

The real wealth of colonial Venezuela, however, came from agriculture and stock raising. Because the colonial economy had two sectors, one for export and another for domestic consumption, the agricultural economy developed two structures. Cacao, of course, was the preeminent colonial export and thrived on the mountainsides and in the valleys of the Central Coastal Range. These trees, carefully tended by black slaves and mulatto, or *pardo,* workers, constituted Venezuela's principal capital stock and its most commercially valuable natural resource. Selling to a Mexican market reserved by Spanish commercial policy for Venezuelan cacao and to a growing European market, the cacao establishment of Venezuela came to represent the pinnacle of social and economic status. So lucrative was the trade in this fruit that the Basque monopoly, the Caracas Company, paid dearly and labored diligently to control the Venezuelan production and the European trade in this commodity.

With the changing fashions in European beverages and the destruction of the independence wars came a shift from cacao to coffee, a cash crop equally export oriented and using similar terrain and technology. By the middle of the nineteenth century coffee cultivation had spread out of the original cacao regions and moved up along the Andes into the valleys of Trujillo, Mérida, and Táchira. The social and economic pre-eminence that had once attached to cacao rapidly shifted to coffee production in response to the demands of Venezuela's external markets.

While cacao and coffee growers occupied an almost exclusively export-oriented place in Venezuela's economy, the cattlemen operated in both the export and the domestic economies. From the original areas of stock raising close to settlements, Venezuela's cattle expanded into the vast area of the llanos. Here they roamed mostly wild with only rudimentary care and supervision. Because the llanos south of the Central Coastal Range flooded on a seasonal cycle, the *llaneros'* primary responsibility was to get the animals rounded up and moved to higher ground before the rains that sent the rivers over their banks came. The meat from these herds supplied the needs of local consumption, and the hides went into local handicrafts and the export trade. While not as profitable as cacao or coffee, the cattle industry of the llanos and its counterpart industry in the Andean agricultural valleys provided the source of wealth and power for many a Venezuelan political leader. Scientific cattle breeding never caught on in Venezuela until the mid-twentieth century, primarily because Venezuela never became a significant participant in the international market for chilled beef.

For all of the emphasis on the export crops of cacao and coffee, the pre-twentieth-century Venezuelan economy ran a rather prosperous domestic agricultural industry. In the fertile regions composed of the intermontane valleys of the Central Coastal Range and the Andes, a diverse agricultural economy thrived cultivating the staple crops that fed the country's expanding population. Although a small portion of this production entered intercolonial trade, primarily to Mexico, most of the country's agricultural production went to feed the colony. Sugar cane, for example, grew in significant quantities in some of the low-lying coastal valleys, but never in sufficient amounts to compete in the sugar export market. Venezuela's sugar supplied local requirements, and the elite imported refined sugar for their fancy confections. The only significant exception was wheat, a crop in great demand to supply the Spanish fleets for the return voyage to Spain. The proceeds from wheat exported from the Caracas valleys to Mexico and Portobelo helped build the foundations of Caracas elite society in the early colonial years.

This pre-twentieth-cenutry period of Venezuelan history saw the absence of a well-developed transportation system as one of the impediments to continued and expanded prosperity. Although good roads and bridges hardly qualify as natural resources, they frequently determine the accessibility and utility of a natural resource. Because Venezuela's best agricultural crop land suitable for coffee and cacao lay in the valleys of the major mountains, the roads and trails that linked the urban network together concentrated there. Venezuela's geography and the country's dependence on cacao and coffee for so many centuries made most of the natural highways, the rivers and streams, the Maracaibo Basin and the Unare Basin, impractical as major transportation routes. Compounding this situation, Spanish colonial policy, continued almost unabated by the nineteenth-century governments, focused all national activity through Caracas. This made the country's least attractive natural port, La Guaira, the terminus of most of the country's export trade. Good only for mule caravans, most of Venezuela's roads became impassible during the rainy season for all but the most determined and foolhardy. Successive governments from the Caracas Company in the 1700s through Guzmán Blanco in the late 1870s promoted road-building and -improvement schemes, although with only modest success.

These activities resulted in the construction of some needed bridges, the improvement of the route from Caracas to La Guaira, and much urban street construction in Caracas, but the basic transportation network in 1900 looked remarkably like the road system described in eighteenth-century accounts. To be sure, the railroad came to Venezuela in the late nineteenth century, but it only improved the Caracas-La Guaira route and a few major short runs into the agricultural valleys outside Caracas. Steamship entrepreneurs negotiated ambitious contracts for the navigation of the Orinoco and Lake Maracaibo, but they failed to make any lasting impact on the country's transportation system.

In Venezuela, the roads permitted the extraction of the country's principal export products and allowed for an adequate intracountry trade. Any significant expansion of this transportation system would have cost far more than the government or anyone else could hope to recover from the increased commerce and production. Venezuela did not have large expanses of prime agricultural land beyond the reach of the road system. Although contemporaries complained often about the backward condition of their roads, it seems clear that until the petroleum boom changed the scale of the country's economy, the transportation network served Venezuela adequately if not elegantly.

If the pre-twentieth-century Venezuelan saw his country as an agricultural-export environment where good crop land constituted the principal source of wealth, his modern twentieth-century counterpart had a much revised view of the country's natural resources. Once the magic of the petroleum industry came to Venezuela, the country's economy was transformed in a few years. After the first years of adjustment to the new tokens of wealth and value, the Venezuelans of the 1930s and later saw their landscape in a new light. Certainly the agricultural and stock-raising land that had long been the staple resource of the Venezuelan elite remained valuable, but the relative value of this resource in relation to petroleum had suffered a precipitous decline. Because petroleum wealth came to Venezuelans at practically no visible immediate cost, its power to revise the country's notions of value proved extreme. Within a generation Venezuela, the most prosperous agricultural colony of the Spanish empire, could no longer feed its population and turned to the import of basic foodstuffs.

With the transformation of the country from an agricultural-pastoral economy to an extractive-mining economy came a parallel transformation in national ambitions. The incredible wealth that came to private citizens and public agencies made the modest economic goals of a Guzmán Blanco or even a Juan Vicente Gómez laughable. Now Venezuela could aspire to the command of a modern, world-class industrial economy. With this goal in mind, resources such as arable land lost their value and were replaced by iron ore, hydroelectric power, aluminum and manganese deposits, and of course petroleum reserves. These resources, in turn, because of their actual and expected locations at the edges of Venezuela's economically active territory, made the creation of a national transportation network, capable of high-speed, heavily loaded traffic, essential. Since the Venezuelan specialty was petroleum and the quintessential petroleum-based transportation system ran on paved roads with gasoline-driven vehicles, the country embarked on an orgy of road building and improvement that for the first time in history gave Venezuela rapid and mostly all-weather access to the settled parts of its territory.

These roads, while they permitted the development of newly valuable natural resources, such as power plants and steel mills on the Orinoco and petroleum fields in Maracaibo or the eastern llanos, also permitted an extraordinary resurgence of urban concentration. Venezuela's major urban centers remained the same places as in the colonial period and the nineteenth century, with a few petroleum additions, but their size and complexity increased almost geometrically. Because the petroleum wealth arrived so quickly and in such large amounts, Venezuelans thought little about the careful management of the petroleum bonanza. In the early decades of the industry only a few saw the foreign exchange earned by oil as just another natural resource expressed in the currency of exchange. Instead, the money seemed to be regarded as an inexhaustible gift to be spent as quickly as possible on improving the conditions of life in the capital and by imitation in the other major cities of the Republic. Without equivalent investment in the countryside, large numbers of rural Venezuelans migrated to the cities in search of the good life. Although this short-sighted pattern of petroleum expenditure has been modified by Venezuela's post-1958 governments, the flow to the cities has been very difficult to stop because the value Venezuelans place on urban life styles and opportunities makes the city one of the country's most sought-after resources.

Although Caracas alone received over a third of the population growth in cities larger than 20,000 between 1936 and 1971, its growth rate during those years had declined slightly from about 7 percent per year during 1936-50 to over 5 percent per year during 1950-71. Caracas continued its colonial role as the central city for Venezuela into the 1970s with over a third of all the urban population, over 40 percent of all manufacturing employment, and 60 percent of those employed in banking, insurance, and finance. Moreover, while other cities in Venezuela have also grown impressively during these years of petroleum, the size of Caracas relative to its closest competitor, Maracaibo, has grown from over twice as large in 1936 to over three times as large in 1971.

The massive government and private investment programs in petroleum, mining, industry, and agricultural development brought with them the transformation of a number of cities. In the decades 1950-71, five cities grew by more than 10 percent per year in response to the opportunities created by these investments. The most dramatic growth involved the emergence of Ciudad Guayana, a planned city that grew almost 20 percent per year during the period 1950-71. An indicator of the impact of this growth is that, while Caracas increased about eight times in the period 1936-71, Ciudad Guayana grew by almost 160 times; virtually all of this growth came from internal migration as Ciudad Guayana's strategic location for hydroelectric power and the iron and steel industries made it the focus of a major government development program that provided jobs and opportunity.

The expansion of Venezuela's cities has come mainly from massive migrations within Venezuela from rural to urban environments. In the petroleum period from 1936 to 1971 there has been an almost complete reversal of the rural-urban distribution of the country's popula-

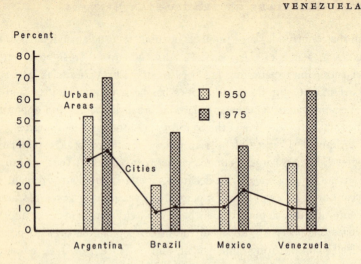

FIGURE 1: Percent of Total Population in Urban Areas of 20,000 or More, and Percent of Total Population in Most Populated City, 1950-1975 (Table II-5)

tion. In the 1930s over a quarter of the population lived in urban areas; by the 1970s just over a quarter lived in rural areas.

With the post-1958 emphasis on planned development, Venezuela has attempted to operate the national economy in accord with a rational development of the country's natural resources other than petroleum. This vision has led to the designation of regional development areas, geographic entities designed to focus attention and money on parts of the country little touched by the petroleum boom. Similarly, the post-1958 governments have recognized the need to make better use of the country's agricultural resources and have sponsored irrigation, technical assistance, and financial aid programs to improve the conditions and the yields of Venezuelan farms. Although some success has attended these efforts, including some progress in land reform, the country still imports basic foodstuffs, a reflection of the relative value of industrial- and petroleum-related investment to agricultural investment. The country's immense petroleum wealth is not sufficient to finance high standards of living, massive industrialization, and agricul-

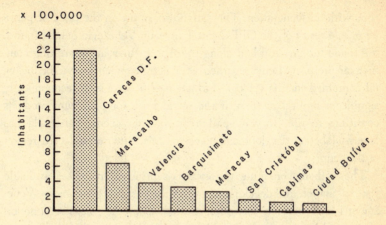

FIGURE 2: Population of Principal Cities, 1976 (Table II-4)

tural development. Because the country values the industrial and standard-of-living goals more highly than the agricultural goals, the modernization and expansion of farming and stock-raising sectors of the economy must move more slowly than some observers believe to be optimal.

The petroleum industry that provides the power for Venezuela's extraordinary program of economic improvement has come a considerable distance since the enclave days of the 1930s and 1940s. Because of Venezuela's aggressive pioneering of government participation in the control of and profits from petroleum extraction, the country has developed remarkably able technicians and managers. These people have managed the nationalized industry with enviable expertise since it was taken over by the government in 1975-76. But because the transition from private to public ownership occurred gradually and with considerable notice, the industry inherited by Venezuela had lost much of its dynamism and vitality by the time of nationalization. While the country has managed the existing industry skillfully, its record of exploration and expansion has not been as impressive. This is, of course, a critical problem, for without new techniques and new discoveries Venezuela's petroleum reserves will come to an end some-

time within a generation. The extraordinary rise in the price of petroleum as a result of the OPEC cartel, a group Venezuela helped found,
has made the tar-sand belt along the Apure River an interesting commercial prospect. Long regarded as a petroleum curiosity, the heavy
oil contained in this geologic formation will become an economically
significant natural resource if the world price for petroleum products
continues to rise. In anticipation of such an event, Venezuela has
begun elaborate development plans for this hitherto neglected region
of the country.

These, then, constitute the country's principal resources available
for exploitation and development. Over the past two generations, Venezuelans have become very sophisticated about the role and function
of natural resource identification, development, and management.
Whether this increased sophistication is adequate to maintain the
country's ambitious economic programs depends as much on events
outside Venezuela as it does on the internal management of resources,
although this skill will permit Venezuela to make the most of whatever opportunities appear.

THE PEOPLE

American Indians, Spaniards, and Africans provided the principal
components of the Venezuelan population. This human capital came
to the territory in a variety of ways. The Indians had been there since
prehistoric times; the Spaniards came at first as slave raiders, then as
explorers, and finally as settlers. Moreover, these Iberians came in a
steady stream of varying size until immigration was curtailed by the
democratic governments that came into power in 1958, providing
about four centuries of immigrants to Venezuela. Blacks came from
Africa, coerced through the slave trade. Although substantial numbers
of black slaves came to Venezuela throughout the colonial period, it
seems clear that the peak of this forced migration came in the second
half of the eighteenth century. The trade itself declined to almost
nothing in the first decade of the nineteenth century, and the first
independent Venezuelan government eliminated it in 1810.

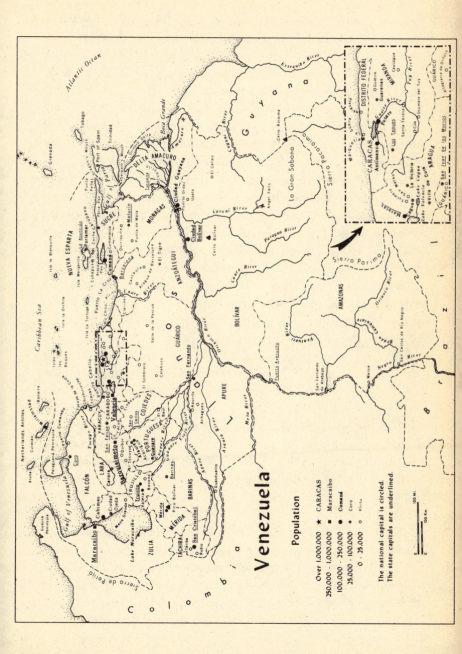

Venezuela

Population

Over 1,000,000	★ CARACAS
250,000 - 1,000,000	■ Maracaibo
100,000 - 250,000	● Cumaná
25,000 - 100,000	● Coro
0 - 25,000	○ Píritu

The national capital is circled.
The state capitals are underlined.

100 Km.
100 Mi.

Even though this basic composition of the Venezuelan population is relatively easy to describe on a general level, detailed analysis proves much more elusive. To be sure, ethnologists have provided a comprehensive inventory of preconquest Indian groups and modern indigenous survivors. Similarly, there is considerable information becoming available on the immigration patterns of Europeans—principally Spaniards, Italians, and Portuguese—into Venezuela in the second half of the twentieth century. We can also estimate with some confidence the numbers and composition of Venezuela's late colonial population, thanks to the diligence of the clerical bureaucracy. Our knowledge of Venezuela's modern, late-twentieth-century population is quite sophisticated. Although these sources permit partial glimpses at selected points in time of the area's population development, a continuous evaluation of the changes over time of each segment and geographic location within Venezuela still eludes scholarly inquiry.

With these limitations in mind, we can venture an assessment of this most valuable of Venezuelan resources, the country's people. Because the Indians were there first, they belong at the beginning of this discussion. Following the practice of the early Spanish explorers and conquerors, we rather inaccurately label all the native inhabitants of Venezuela as Indians. This, of course, obscures the wide diversity of ethnic groups and cultural styles represented among these people. In the eyes of the explorer and conqueror, several features of Indian civilization seemed especially important and determined Spanish behavior toward the native Americans. The Spaniards looked first for replicas of the civilizations found previously in Mexico and in Peru. By the late 1540s it had become obvious that Venezuela's hinterland held no mythical kingdom, no golden land equivalent to a Mexico or Peru.

But they did discover that Venezuela contained a large number of distinct linguistic groups, that the cultural levels of the various independent tribes ranged from stable sedentary farmers in the Central Coastal Range and the Venezuelan Andes through nomadic and slash-and-burn agricultural people in various parts of the llanos and other lowland areas, to hunters and gatherers in the coastal areas and along some of the major rivers. The Indians of the coast and immediate mountain valleys inland proved quite hostile to Spanish exploration, thanks in part to the sixteenth-century Spanish slave raids in search of replacements for the declining Caribbean native populations. In many parts of the Venezuelan coast the Indian population was much reduced by warfare and disease during the early years of exploration and conquest. Enough remained in the desirable areas of the Segovia Highlands, the valleys of Caracas, the valley of Aragua, and the Andean intermontane valleys to warrant the development of a substantial and durable variation on the Spanish *encomienda* system. The beneficiaries of the arrangement of assigning Indian tribute or labor to individuals were, of course, Spanish conquerors and settlers of influence; but the size and profitability of these arrangements never approached the magnitude of the similar operations in Mexico or Peru or Colombia. Still, the Venezuelan *encomienda* proved to be a most successful institution, outliving its counterparts in more prosperous Spanish American sites by at least a century. The abolition of this system was delayed in Venezuela until the middle of the eighteenth century.

By the close of the colonial period the process of adjustment between Spanish and Indian civilizations had virtually been completed. In the Andes there still survived substantial identifiably Indian populations, although the bulk of these people participated in Spanish society and the economy. In the Central Coastal Range the great increase in white and black populations and the inability of the native people to adapt to the demands of Spanish agriculture and stock raising resulted in the virtual elimination of Indians as an identifiable ethnic group. Many had died without the children who would carry on their traditions. Others fled into the llanos, where with other renegades they joined the nomadic *llanero* cowboys whose livelihood came from the cattle, horses, and mules ranging semiwild on the plains. Here, too, the notion of "Indian" dissolved as the *llanero* culture became a peculiar amalgamation of indigenous survivals, Spanish custom, and African cultural traditions brought by runaway slaves.

Outside the areas of intensive Spanish control, along the lower reaches of the Orinoco, the Meta, and the Apure rivers, for example,

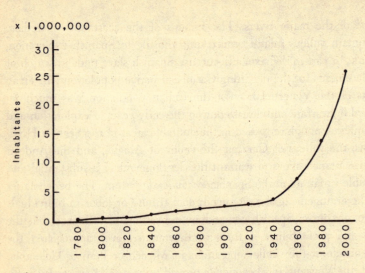

FIGURE 3: Population Estimates, 1780-2000 (Table II-2)

or in relatively unsettled areas such as Guayana or the Perijá Mountains west of Lake Maracaibo, the native American societies survived relatively intact thanks to the lack of Spanish contact. Many of these people remained unremittingly hostile to the missionaries and traders who tried to bring Spanish society to them, and others, protected by the vastness of the wilderness, lived virtually undisturbed until the twentieth century.

Because the Indian heritage in the principal settled areas of the country provided little lasting identifiable contribution to the dominant Spanish-American culture, Venezuelans have spent little time or energy on the reconstruction or preservation of the indigenous past. After independence, Venezuela's Indians ceased to be of much interest to anyone but ethnographers, folklorists, and missionaries.

If the Indian heritage merged with or was eliminated by the dominant Spanish culture, the African contribution to Venezuela's population base has been more difficult to absorb. These Africans came to Venezuela involuntarily, of course, as victims of the slave trade. Tierra Firme, as the Spaniards called the Venezuelan mainland, began its integration into the Spanish-American system as a source of Indian slaves and quickly became a market for black slaves. These Africans came to Venezuela through a variety of routes. Some arrived direct from Africa, others were traded from Colombia, but the majority appear to have come via the Caribbean islands.

Whatever the origin of these people, and there is a considerable, although somewhat inconclusive, literature on the African ethnic origin of Venezuela's slave population, the colony gradually acquired a substantial population of African ancestry, accounting for perhaps 60 percent by the last decades of the eighteenth century.

The slaves, those blacks attached through legal servitude, lived primarily in the coastal valleys and in the agricultural regions of the Central Coastal Range, although small numbers of slaves could be found in practically every part of Spanish-occupied Venezuela. They were predominantly field hands, but significant numbers of slaves lived in urban environments as household servants, coachmen, stevadores, artisans, and other service people. Within the Venezuelan social milieu, black slaves were either a capital good held because they produced wealth or a luxury commodity owned and displayed to indicate the master's ability to support such a significant expense on unproductive people. This use of slaves to show social and economic position involved picturesque but serious social rituals. Upper-class women of the Caracas elite, for example, would parade to and from Mass on Sundays accompanied by all their slave entourage, the well-dressed servants carrying pillow, missal, and such other accoutrements as their mistresses' morning excursion to church required. Status, of course, could be determined by the number and dress of the black slaves accompanying the women on display.

This custom, much commented on by visitors to the region, indicates the relative poverty of Venezuela's material culture when compared with the major centers in Mexico City or Lima. The Caracas elite, while possessed of considerable wealth and capable of some extravagancies in their life styles, could not imitate the metropolitan style where richly ornamented objects, extravagant carriages, and similar exuberant displays of wealth were much in evidence. The Venezuelan elite might manage a substantial one-story town house with some exterior decoration over the main door, some stylistic touches to the windows, and some decoration on the few pieces of interior furniture. But the colony's scale of consumption and style of life did not rest on an economic base sufficient for the support of more elaborate artifacts. Iron items such as locks and hinges usually had to be imported and therefore were rare and expensive. The gold and silver so much in evidence elsewhere in the Americas existed mostly in coin, always in short supply in Venezuela. Not having enough silver to conduct trade and commerce, Venezuelans could hardly afford to turn their small stock of precious metal into dinner plates. Of course, this is not to suggest that no silver plates, no gold ornaments existed in the province. Clearly the wills and inventories indicate that such treasures existed, but on a rather small scale.

This lack of accessible luxury goods available for display as status symbols accentuated the importance of the urban slave as a visible token of prestige and economic well-being. In fact, considerable evidence seems to indicate that the economic importance of slaves as field laborers, once a major consideration, had begun to decline by the end of the colonial period. Not only had the slave trade declined to insignificance, indicating the Venezuelan unwillingness to pay the world price for this human commodity, but the principal slave-owning class could never get exercised enough about the servile institution to mount an effective defense against abolitionist legislation of the early nineteenth century. It is not that they wanted to lose their slaves, but that they had no compelling economic argument to bring to the debate.

The remaining primary racial group in Venezuela's colonial population came from Spain. Although the records call these people whites and for the most part lump all Iberians into one ethnic category, the Venezuelans made somewhat finer distinctions. The principal Spanish stock in Venezuela mirrored that characteristic of the rest of Spanish America, but two subregions of Spain sent sufficient numbers to create relatively cohesive ethnic subgroups within the white category. The Canary Islands provided Venezuelan agriculture and commerce with a population group stereotyped as especially frugal, hardworking, and stable. The size, composition, and distribution of this group have not been clearly and definitively established, but the existence of a strong agricultural community in the Valencia region and a major concentration in the Candelaria parish of Caracas are obvious indications of their presence and their awareness of a special ethnic identity.

Basques, always present in colonial Venezuela, became a major component of the elite population by virtue of the Compañía Guipuzcoana or Caracas Company's monopoly of Venezuelan trade and commerce from the 1720s into the 1780s. These able and energetic entrepreneurs used their company and their unique economic positions to claim large parts of the local economy as their own. Basques came to Venezuela with the Company and rapidly integrated themselves into retail and wholesale commerce. With their accumulating wealth many bought land and urban properties and became, through marriage and wealth, members of the governing elite. Numerous studies have established the pervasive Basque influence in Venezuela's late colonial society and economy and, of course, many of the distinctive Basque surnames survive to the present day.

If the whites distinguished themselves in terms of provincial Spanish origin, they also worked hard to invent local methods of differentiation sufficient for the maintenance of a well-ordered and disciplined dominant class. The white elite of Caracas, whose wealth and connections were traceable in many cases to the early settlers of the valleys, occupied the pre-eminent position in local society. These *mantuanos*, so named for the elaborate lace *mantas* or *mantillas* worn to Mass by the women, used the Caracas town council as one of their primary instruments of social definition. But this visible manifestation of *caraqueño* elite status symbolized a much more interesting mechanism of social control and definition. By a complex interlocking network of clients, patrons, and middlemen, plus a sophisticated pattern of family alliances through cousin marriage, this colonial elite created a cohesive and mutually dependent structure capable of maintaining white supremacy within the multiracial Venezuelan society.

Without research into the organization and operation of urban elites outside Caracas it is difficult to project the context and style of white elite behavior. But the existing evidence seems to indicate an equivalent structure, albeit less sophisticated and complex. In any case, the Caracas elite set the tone and scale of white-group behavior, and the rest of the colony for the most part measured themselves against this standard.

The simple classification of white, Indian, and black does not accommodate the consequence of the rapid racial mixing that occurred in Venezuela. In some parts of the Americas elaborate classification systems became popular as reflections of the general interest in ethnic origin, but most places settled on some variation of a four- or five-category system. Venezuelans found it practical to recognize whites, Indians, blacks, plus a category called *pardo* and another called slave. The first three, of course, were the primary population elements, but by the end of the eighteenth century the category of black seemed to be falling out of favor, except possibly in reference to newly freed slaves. The *pardos* formed by far the largest ethnic group. Their distinguishing and identifying characteristics were mostly negative: being neither white nor Indian, neither black nor slave, they were called and called themselves *pardos*.

The slaves formed a group identifiable by their legal status as chattel, rather than their racial status which could only be black or *pardo*. Thus, while there is some coherence to the social reality symbolized by *pardo*, the label of slave tells very little about the life style, color, possibilities, or prospects of individuals carrying this name. City slaves working as artisans or domestics lived much better lives than the free agricultural peon. Because of the special character of this label of slave and the broad range of occupations covered by the label of *pardo*, analyses using these categories must proceed with caution.

From the white perspective, however, and after all whites invented the labels that articulated the ethnic arrangement, one characteristic made this system eminently practical. The labels permitted the white elite to control and manage the large numbers of subordinate people produced by the fusion of races that came after conquest and settlement. By enforcing the labeling and by providing for a whole range of special restrictions, organizations, privileges, and responsibilities applicable only to individuals within each group, Spanish policy created these ethnic groups and gave them identity and social focus. Whether in the form of religious brotherhoods reserved for *pardos*, militia units restricted to *pardos*, or dress codes, these devices displayed for all to see the separateness of white and non-white ethnic groups. In a society with no popular press, very limited literacy, and few other means of mass communication, the message of social structure, social limits, and social place had to be delivered through other media. So at each major milestone in life—baptism, marriage, burial—the ethnic category of individuals was emphasized in the recording of these events in the parish registers.

Similarly, the processions that formed such a prominent part of colonial Spanish-American life provided, in their order of march and in the grouping and dress of the participants, a visual paradigm of the proper organization of society. For this reason participants often contested bitterly their location in the parade, recognizing the importance of this for establishing their social place in the public view. This complex but imaginative system evolved and was consolidated during the centuries of colonial rule until by the eighteenth century the Spanish-American hierarchy had assumed a rather stable form, one that with a few modifications would survive until the dissolving power of twentieth-century mass-participation politics would begin to weaken its foundations.

Of course the system, designed to keep large numbers of people working under the direction and primarily for the benefit of a small number, had to contend with constant challenges. What is remarkable about these revolts, renegade black communities, challenges to racial classification, and random outbreaks of violence is not that they occurred but that they had so little lasting effect. The most spectacular challenge to the system came in the 1810-30 wars for independence, when the white elite's political and economic goals needed *pardo* and slave support. For a time during that turbulent generation, the possibility for a social revolution may have existed, but in the end the whites continued their system, having only to begin the dissolution of the no longer practical slave system and to eliminate the official ethnic labeling. Venezuelan society in 1830 or 1850 or 1880 or 1920 looked remarkably similar, and although a time traveler from the 1830s might have found some social customs strange in 1920, he would have had no difficulty picking up his ethnic cues.

Like most members of the Latin American white elite, the Venezuelan arbiters of social and economic policy worried about the ethnic composition of their population. Especially in the eighteenth century and after, when European fashions in racial ideology came into vogue everywhere in America, Venezuela's whites began to consider how they might improve their country's prospects by improving its racial stock. Although the elite was taken with this racist notion, there was little that could be done with it until after the independence wars. From 1830 on Venezuelans constantly sought ways of encouraging white colonization in their country, but very few of the colonization schemes attempted by the various governments from 1830 to 1950 had much success.

This failure to attract white settlers is not particularly difficult to explain, for Venezuela had little to offer the enterprising European immigrant. The good land that could be easily and profitably cultivated already belonged to the white elite, who had no inclination to offer it to immigrants. The road system did not encourage expansion into the less desirable land on the periphery of settled areas. Venezuelan trade did not flow in directions that encouraged a return current of migrants. Most importantly, however, the Venezuelan government never had the money nor the will to sponsor practical programs to encourage immigration, and the Venezuelan elite apparently saw immigrants as useful only for whitening the population and producing more and better laborers for the fields. This prospect, naturally enough, attracted few immigrants when options in Argentina, Brazil, and the United States seemed much more interesting. A few colonization efforts were made, such as the marginally successful small colony founded in 1842 by German Catholics. This Colonia Tovar outside Caracas in the interior Central Coastal Range proved to be a special case without any significant impact on Venezuela's population base or ethnic character.

The stability of this social system and ethnic hierarchy, reflecting the conservative agricultural economic base of the country, began to change only under the tremendous pressure of the petroleum-inspired and -funded industrial-consumer society of the 1940s and 1950s. Venezuela received two types of immigrants during these years. A small group numerically, but with influence and impact on Venezuelan life all out of proportion to their numbers, were the exiles from the Spanish Civil War. In the late 1930s and the 1940s several thousand intellectuals, politicians, and scholars left Spain to settle in Venezuela. In their adopted country they quickly found places of influence in government, universities, politics, and other activities. Although their impact is difficult to quantify, any casual survey of the best in Venezuelan literature, history, or arts will turn up Spanish Civil War exiles, and any census of doctors, lawyers, or political leaders will also provide more than a scattering of these energetic people. Their conversion of talent to the service of Venezuela has become so complete that their children for the most part are so Venezuelan as to be indistinguishable from the rest of the elite.

The second twentieth-century immigrant group provided a more complex addition to Venezuelan society. Composed primarily of Spaniards, Portuguese, and Italians, these post–World War II immigrants entered the country in large numbers in the mid-1950s in response to the economic opportunity and active encouragement evident in the regime of General Marcos Pérez Jiménez (1952-58). That military government saw these immigrants as enthusiastic and reliable participants in the plan to modernize Venezuela. Because the military plan was ill-conceived and called for extraordinary amounts to be spent on monumental construction projects in Caracas, the immigrants ended up primarily in the capital, where their industry and entrepreneurial spirit led them to capture portions of the construction trades, a variety of retail business categories, and a large part of the privately owned public transportation system.

When the military regime collapsed in 1958, the new popular government stopped the growth of these immigrant groups by shutting off the flow from abroad. The large concentrations of Spaniards, Portu-

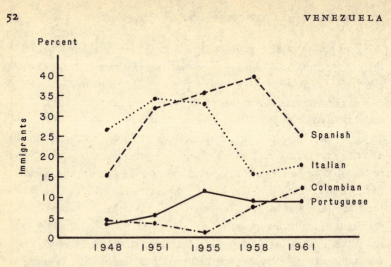

FIGURE 4: Distribution of Major Immigrant Groups by Nationality, 1948-1961 (Table II-8)

guese, and Italians in Caracas became one more political issue in the populist politics of the 1960s and 1970s. Because their period of greatest opportunity had come during the right-wing Pérez Jiménez regime, they tended to support right-of-center political movements, many of which threatened the stability of the post-1958 governments, further exacerbating ethnic-political tensions, although the immigrants did not constitute a significant voting bloc. Nevertheless, this will probably prove to have been a transitory phenomenon and may disappear as the second generation of the immigrant group grows up Venezuelan.

More complicated than the almost stylized conflict between Venezuelans and the 1950s immigrants is the current problem posed by the large number of Colombians who enter Venezuela illegally along the border in the Andes. Attracted to Venezuela by high salaries and jobs generated by the dynamic petroleum boom, Colombians, who had previously trickled across the border, became a flood in the 1970s. The illegality of these crossings makes the number of Colombians entering Venezuela difficult to determine. Current estimates are in the range of 100,000 a year during the mid-1970s, although not all of these people stayed in the country.

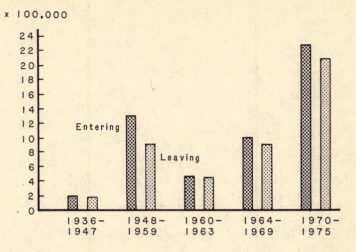

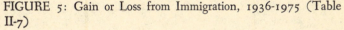

FIGURE 5: Gain or Loss from Immigration, 1936-1975 (Table II-7)

The Colombians take a wide variety of low-skill jobs in Venezuelan cities, and some work in rural employment in cattle raising or as seasonal workers on large agricultural establishments. In urban and especially industrial employment they will work for less than Venezuelans, and, as is the case in similar situations in other parts of the world, they are much less likely to cause labor problems that would bring them to the attention of immigration authorities. In 1980 Venezuela carried out a registration program designed to legalize the status of Colombians in the country, but, even though many registered with the government, significant numbers retain an irregular status.

The presence of these new immigrants has caused some political problems for the various elected governments. Some Venezuelans see these Colombians as taking low-skill jobs that ought to be filled by Venezuelans. The people displaced by the Colombians, it is argued, have no skills to compete elsewhere in the economy, and, being underbid by Colombians for the low-skill jobs, they become vagabonds, swelling the already disturbingly large unemployed sector in the cities.

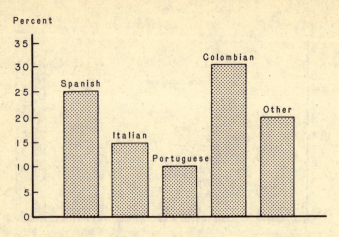

FIGURE 6: Foreign Population, 1971 (Table II-9)

With the growing integration of Venezuela and Colombia within the framework of the Andean Common Market, any corrective measures by Venezuela to stop the immigrant flow are likely to be increasingly difficult to implement.

These, then, are the principal population groups composing contemporary Venezuela. But there is one other significant set of individuals living in Venezuela whose historical influence is out of proportion to its size. The resident foreign community composed of business representatives, merchants, diplomats, and technicians has had a profound influence on the details if not the grand design of Venezuelan history. Most of the foreign community live in Caracas. Since the petroleum expansion began in the 1930s, however, substantial foreign communities have emerged in places such as Maracaibo or El Tigre, where large petroleum establishments have to be maintained.

The foreigners in Venezuela have played a role that has been fiercely denounced and praised throughout the country's history. Because these people came to Venezuela to manage the North Atlantic interests in the country, and because Venezuela had as its first priority full participation in the North Atlantic society, the demands and behavior of

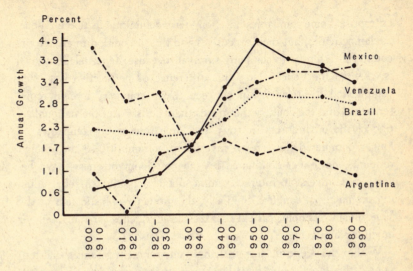

FIGURE 7: Population Growth Rate, 1900-1990, Annual Percentage Growth Rate Estimates (Table II-3)

these representatives were frequently accorded more importance than might otherwise have been appropriate.

Moreover, these foreigners, especially the merchants, businessmen, and technicians, brought with them the precious technological skills that Venezuelans required to transform their country into the modern industrial power of their dreams. So while the foreigners were sometimes regarded with suspicion and their motives frequently questioned, their participation in Venezuelan affairs remained large. In the prepetroleum decades, of course, this group was composed primarily of import-export experts, diplomats, and a few speculators and flamboyant entrepreneurs interested in contracts of one kind or another. In the postpetroleum years the technician, manager, marketing expert, and business executive have been the prototypical members of the resident foreign community. What distinguishes these people from the other foreigners who come to Venezuela, whether an exile from the Spanish Civil War, a Portuguese cab driver, or a Colombian migrant, is their temporary stay and their peripheral commitment to the Venezuelan

enterprise. Some companies have long-term commitments to their Venezuelan activities, but their executives and the corporation rarely see the
country as essential to company survival. Because Venezuela's survival
is essential for Venezuelans, this difference of perspective has often
complicated the relationship between these temporary foreign representatives and the country that needs their skills. After the nationalization of the oil industry in 1975, the large foreign oil companies no
longer dominated the foreign investment community, so the foreign
residents, no longer dominated by the petroleum business, have become more diverse in interests and economic activities, thereby reducing the potential conflicts. Similarly, the growing sophistication of the
Venezuelan technological elite makes the uniqueness of the foreigner
much less apparent.

Within this Venezuelan multiethnic environment serious social tensions certainly exist and have been present since the days of the conquest. During the colonial and republican periods this conflict had a
variety of dimensions. Within the white elite, Basques, Canarians, and
Venezuelans identified themselves or were identified as ethnic subsets
whose access to resources ought to be restricted, expanded, or controlled. Such conflicts, while very important to the participants, held
none of the danger of the much more serious tension between white
and non-white. In Venezuela the non-whites most susceptible to violent
resistance to white control were *pardos,* blacks, and slaves. Venezuela's
Indians, fixed in stable social arrangements in the Andes or isolated
in the wilderness, never posed a serious threat to Venezuela's social
order.

It is tempting, of course, to see the white-black conflict as an ex-
plicitly racial problem; but although race was a major component of
the phenomenon it did not define the conflict. The Spanish notion of
ethnic categories combined a variety of characteristics, qualities, and
goals into a system of ethnic hierarchy whose structure provided great
strength and rigidity and whose operation provided the necessary
mobility and flexibility. In Venezuela the ethnic system, and the economic class arrangements that formed part of it, passed through a

number of acute crises that severely tested the strength and efficiency of the system.

In the late eighteenth century, ethnic conflicts involved the courts, runaway slave communities, and the behavior of individuals who appeared to be exceeding their place. These led to the development of a curious legal avenue of ethnic transformation. Called the *Gracias al Sacar,* this procedure permitted certain worthy *pardos* to acquire the legal status of whites and gain thereby all the rights and privileges of the most favored ethnic group. Needless to say, the whites in Caracas protested against this weakening of their ethnic divisions, but with no success. As a practical measure of upward social mobility, this peculiar legal whitening had rather little effect, but its invention and implementation served as a symbol of Spain's recognition that the Venezuelan social and racial structure was too rigid for the times.

This eighteenth-century uncertainty about race and class manifested itself in other ways as well. Slave revolts, always a threat in Venezuela, became more common, and runaway slave communities, the *cumbes* and *quilombos,* also grew larger and their inhabitants more aggressive. While none of this seriously threatened the Spanish social system, it showed a high level of discontent that in the early nineteenth century would contribute powerfully to the independence wars. Indeed, only by a very narrow margin did Bolívar's generation of white leaders prevent independence from becoming a social revolution.

After independence, the elaborate racial and ethnic terminology maintained by the Spanish legal system disappeared, although slavery managed to survive in Venezuela until 1854. The postindependence generations contended with a serious ethnic problem with the *pardos.* The violence and banditry as well as the political revolts that filled the lives of the first two generations of independent Venezuelans had in almost every case an ethnic-racial content. Whether simply expressed by the mob as "death to the whites!" or by the recruitment of slaves to fight in uprisings or more elaborately in the periodical articles analyzing the causes of civil disorder in Venezuela, the racial and ethnic content of these activities was explicit and pervasive.

By the last quarter of the nineteenth century the racial theme had become considerably muted. With the emergence of a modern petroleum-based economy in the twentieth century, the conflicts gradually became related more to class than to color or ethnicity. Moreover, the Spanish, Portuguese, Italian, and Colombian additions to the Venezuelan population blurred the simple white-*pardo*-Indian distinctions and created in their place a more complex set of ethnic identities that sometimes conflicted with economic status distinctions.

Not until the 1960s, however, through the vehicle of mass-action political parties, did any significant number of *pardos* gain access to power and prominence in national life, and this increased *pardo* visibility is often lamented by members of the old Caracas elite. As the modernizing and industrializing of Venezuela continues, the country's ethnic patterns will become more and more like those in the countries of the North Atlantic: multiracial and multiethnic, with a strong tendency toward a social system based on economic achievement. But for the present, the economic and ethnic distinctions of the Spanish colonial empire still survive, attenuated and modified to be sure, helping to organize the complex social reality of twentieth-century Venezuela.

Chapter 2 • The Colonial Outpost, 1500-1650

CONQUEST AND EXPLORATION

Venezuela's colonial history flows from a rather modest beginning. There were no mighty Amerindian empires, no storehouses of golden objects, and no fabulous cities. Instead, the explorers and conquerors of Tierra Firme found a variety of hunting and gathering tribes, some Indians engaged in low-intensity sedentary agriculture, and many hostile tribes unwilling to cede control over their territories to the invading Spaniard. Within this environment, the expeditions of Venezuela's first fifty years had a certain grim desperation. Successive parties of Spaniards sallied forth from precarious outposts along the coast; they roamed the interior of Venezuela encountering generally unfriendly Indians; they often lost half or more of their troops to disease or accident or starvation or Indian attack; and they returned with little or nothing to show for their pains. If these tough, gritty conquerors failed to find El Dorado, that mythical golden king, it was not for lack of effort. In the search, the Spaniards gradually covered the major regions of Venezuela, so that by the 1550s the shape and extent of the land had become known. As the hope of finding El Dorado faded, the conquerors turned to the exploitation and development of the resources available in Venezuela, resources that permitted subsistence and some commercial agriculture with Indian labor, small-scale mining, stock raising, and, of course, commerce with the Caribbean Islands, Mexico, New Granada or Colombia, and Spain.

If the activities of these early years provide a remarkable contrast to the conquests of Mexico and Peru, they nevertheless share some characteristics with those more spectacular Spanish adventures. Except for a brief, if destructive, prelude during the German-controlled explorations in northwest Venezuela from Coro, discovery and conquest proceeded according to the same norms and in response to the same royal policies as the Mexican and Peruvian epics. The basic document, a species of contract or agreement, obligated the Spanish conqueror to follow a series of rules in his expeditions. These rules, designed to limit and direct the efforts of audacious, headstrong men, usually set geographical boundaries to the enterprise, imposed a time limit on the initiation of the expedition, stipulated the activities permitted, and specified the preparations required.

As we might expect, the Spanish monarchs of this early period had only the vaguest notions about the size and interior geography of the Americas and as a result often gave competing conquerors overlapping patents authorizing the exploration and settlement of the same territory. These *capitulaciones,* as the exploration contracts were called, provided a norm toward which the activities of the conquests generally tended. To be sure, conquerors often exceeded their instructions, trespassed on the territory of their rivals, intrigued against their competition, exceeded their authority to exploit the Indians, and in general played fast and loose with the letter of the agreement. These deviations from the terms of the contract, for all their frequency and the temporary local conflict they caused, failed to change significantly the major result anticipated by the crown: a network of urbanized Spanish settlements in America.

In many ways the Venezuelan experience provides an illuminating case history of Spanish-American imperial colonization. From the third voyage of Columbus, Spaniards were in intermittent contact with the Venezuelan mainland, or Tierra Firme. Spanish colonizers worked in the territory from the experimental days of the early 1500s through the stabilized conquest patterns of the late fifteenth and the early sixteenth century and on into the missionary explorations and missions of the seventeenth and eighteenth centuries. Practically every mode of conquest, settlement, and exploration observable in Spanish America took place in Venezuela, with of course the notable exception of the heroic assaults on the Aztec and Inca empires.

Although the detailed chronicle of conquest and colonization is complex and confusing, several distinct types or periods of expansion can be seen. Unlike the Mexican and Peruvian epics, where Spanish conquistadors struck directly at the major urban centers and where Spanish urban locations frequently followed the Indian plan, Venezuela proved to be an area settled from the coastal periphery inward toward the central valleys of Caracas, where the region's natural capital gradually emerged. It was from Coro on the western coast and the island-mainland nexus of Cubagua-Margarita-Cumaná on the eastern coast that Spanish settlement began. These two currents of exploratory energy joined, reluctantly and tenuously, only late in the eighteenth century in Caracas to form the political and territorial unit of Venezuela.

Venezuela's early years proved quite inauspicious. Activity during the first decades of the sixteenth century seemed dominated by four interrelated concerns. Most of Venezuela's early explorers and conquerors came to Tierra Firme via the main Caribbean islands of Cuba and Hispaniola. Indeed, the region was partly subservient to the political authorities of the islands until well into the colonial period. But in the early days, Spanish planters and entrepreneurs saw Tierra Firme as a likely place to acquire Indian captives for use as laborers on the plantations of Cuba or Hispaniola, where the Indian population had declined to practically nothing thanks to disease, malnutrition, and exploitation. The slave raids carried out along the eastern coast of Venezuela, especially the coast of Paria, left a legacy of Indian fear and hostility that plagued the conquerors for at least a generation. Raids of this kind contributed little or nothing to the Spanish settlement and colonization of Venezuela. That effort proceeded from two centers, one at the eastern and one at the western edges of the Venezuelan north coast.

In the eastern nucleus of Cubagua, Margarita, and Cumaná, the initial attraction for the Spaniards was pearls. The pearl beds off Margarita and Cubagua provided such a substantial income to crown and colonists for a short period in the early sixteenth century that drawings of the pearl fisheries grace the histories of America illustrated by Theodore D'Bry, alongside his engravings of the fabulous riches of Mexico and Peru. Yet, because the resources of the islands of Cubagua and Margarita were so few and their population base so small, the Spaniards found themselves obligated to move to the mainland at Cumaná and then later westward to Barcelona.

From the early 1550s until well into the seventeenth century the Cubagua-Margarita-Cumaná focus of Spanish settlement demonstrated more potential for generating strife than for creating a prosperous Spanish settlement in the New World. Jurisdictional disputes between rival conquistadores, each with a royal authorization that could be interpreted to cover the same territory, kept the precarious Iberian towns in Cubagua and on the mainland coast in intermittent turmoil. But for all the civil unrest these conflicts caused, the Indians' resistance posed a more serious impediment to the spread of Iberian control.

Because the mainland of Venezuela's northeast coast offered an apparently abundant supply of Indian labor but at the same time seemed to have no other easily extractable resource, Spaniards based in the Caribbean islands thought it perfectly reasonable to mine Venezuela for its demographic resources. Slave raids, even when prohibited by royal decree, began early in the sixteenth century and continued until well into the first decade of the seventeenth. This constant exploitation of the mainland population may have given some Spaniards a sizable short-term gain in the form of cheap labor for the growing Caribbean colonies and a supply of divers for the pearl business of Cubagua, but it left a bitter and destructive long-term legacy of Spanish-Indian hostility that not only delayed settlement on the mainland but defeated efforts at peaceful coexistence between Iberian civilization and Amerindian culture.

In spite of these difficulties, the pearl fisheries provided sufficient incentive for Spanish settlement to proceed, if not as easily as it might have. By the 1520s and 1530s there may have been a population of some 20,000 on Cubagua-Margarita. Although Cubagua lacked water, it was so well situated for the pearl trade that Spanish settlement persevered, drawing on the fragile Spanish connection with the mainland for agricultural goods and water. Even though the strong current sweeping along the eastern Venezuelan coast made communications between islands and mainland difficult, the link was never allowed to be broken for long. Even when Indian raids wiped out the few Spanish establishments on the coast, and on one occasion reached the settlement on Cubagua, the settlers returned again and again, gradually gaining control of the coast and mountains around what is now the city of Cumaná. An alternative and less determinedly hostile base appeared in Margarita, an island with fertile interior valleys suitable for cultivation. There the cities of Asunción and Pampatar arose to serve the pearl outpost on Cubagua, to help in the pacification of the mainland, and to serve as an intermediary position between the developed Spanish centers of Hispaniola, Cuba, and Puerto Rico and the fledgling Venezuelan mainland settlements.

By the end of the first century of Spanish presence on the northeast coast of Venezuela, some progress toward the implantation of Hispanic culture and control had been made. With the slave raids terminated and the coastal and island settlements reasonably secure, Spanish entrepreneurs, settlers, and clerics began the slow process of expansion into the interior, laying the basis for the cattle export economy that developed on the eastern llanos in the seventeenth century. Separated from the more dynamic sections of Venezuela by the Unare Basin, the eastern settlement cluster failed to develop the population density or economic complexity characteristic of the Caracas or Andean regions, and because the political, ecclesiastical, and trade links ran between the Caribbean and Cumaná, rather than between Cumaná and Caracas, the east coast found it difficult to participate in the expansion of the Caracas and Andean regions.

If the lure of Cubagua's pearl fisheries provided the attraction for Spanish settlements along the Venezuelan northeast coast, it was the myth of El Dorado that motivated the European exploration of the western coast and Andean hinterland. Of course, Spanish settlers had been aware of the general shape and characteristics of the coastline since the earliest voyages of Columbus. Indeed the houses on stilts built out from the Maracaibo lakeshore inspired the name "little Venice" or Venezuela. But the attractions of the pearl fisheries, the opportunities in the major Caribbean islands, and the subsequent epic of the Mexican conquest all conspired to keep interest in the Venezuelan northwest coast at a relatively low level. Spanish slavers occasionally raided the Coro coast in search of Indian captives, but initiatives toward serious exploration and settlement would have to wait until the late 1520s, when Juan de Ampíes took an interest in the Coro region.

Even then, the motive for expansion into Tierra Firme had little to do with an urge to settle and develop the mainland, but rather stemmed from Ampíes's hope of establishing a more efficient slave-raiding post from the Venezuelan mainland, one capable of extracting Indians more expeditiously for employment on the haciendas of Santo Domingo and Cuba. Ampíes moved his operations from Santo Domingo first to the island of Curaçao in 1527 and then in 1528 to a base near the present site of Coro. In that year, while busy negotiating with the local Indian chieftain for a steady supply of native captives, this promising commercial venture came to an abrupt end, as Ambrosio Alfinger arrived in Coro with a royal cedula granting the conquest and colonization of most of the Venezuelan coast and hinterland to a consortium of German bankers, led by employees of the Welser group.

Although the German period in the early history Venezuela lasted only a short time and left only the faintest of traces on the rest of that Alfinger arrived in Coro with a royal cédula granting the conquest and colonization that it has always fascinated historians. Not only did the Welser concession, awarded in repayment of a royal debt, make an unlikely breach in the otherwise stringent policy of excluding non-Spanish adventurers from the American enterprise, but the activities of the conquerors operating under German direction deviated from accepted Spanish norms. Instead of employing the leapfrogging procedure of establishing towns and villages throughout a territory, the Welsers devoted all their energies and resources to a frantic search for El Dorado, the mythical king and his fabulous civilization. During the twenty years of their explorations, expeditions sponsored by the Germans ranged widely throughout the Andes, the Maracaibo Basin, the llanos of Barinas, the lower llanos of the Apure, and the upper reaches of the Venezuelan Andes into what is now Colombia.

Without the space to detail the peregrinations of these expeditions, it is difficult to convey the sense of desperation and failure encountered time and time again. Whether studying the progress of Federmann's expedition southward from Coro in search of the Pacific Ocean, Alfinger's fatal trek into the wilds of Zulia, or Hutten and Espira's journey into the lower llanos to the Apure and Meta rivers, the chronicles tell much the same story. Leading bands of Spaniards and Indians, these conquerors traveled immense distances under deplorable conditions. Everywhere, they searched for evidence of gold, silver, and precious stones. Always, they sought evidence of the kingdom of El Dorado. Although the history of Europe's American conquest is hardly one characterized by humanitarian behavior toward native peoples, the exploits of the German-sponsored expeditions appeared to exceed even contemporary standards for brutality and destruction. Not only were these explorers particularly ruthless with the Indians who resisted the advance, they also appear to have retaliated against real or imagined threats with uncommon ferocity.

By the 1540s the German experiment ended. It was concluded not only because it failed to discover El Dorado, but also because its aberrant form of exploration and conquest became a nuisance to the crown. Of the principal German leaders in Venezuela, most came to a bad end. Federmann escaped from a royal inquiry by traveling the Andean route to New Granada, where he continued the search for El Dorado. Jorge Espira died in Coro in mid-1540 after being investigated by

crown agents. Felipe Hutten lost his head to a group of Spanish conspirators while returning with an expedition that had failed in its
mission. Ambrosio Alfinger died of wounds suffered in battle against
the Indians. The net result of this interlude can be expressed rather
easily: towns were founded, Coro securely and Maracaibo precariously;
geographic knowledge greatly increased; and Indian hostility substantially intensified. In the subsequent government inquiries, the greatest
charge leveled at the German management was their failure to establish
towns and create stable forms of Indian control. They did not allocate
Indians in *encomienda* to Spaniards living in regular towns, and in
their frenetic search for El Dorado they failed to fulfill the minimum
requirements for a proper Hispanic conquest.

After the conclusion of the German experiment, settlement began to
expand in the traditional Spanish fashion from the original base in
Coro. Apparently the first major settlement established from Coro came
as a result of the Coro region's inability to sustain more than a small
population in its arid, semidesert terrain. With an increase in the number of Spaniards, attracted by the possibility of new discoveries and the
lack of opportunity elsewhere, the resource base of Coro proved inadequate, and in 1545 Juan de Carvajal led a substantial band of settlers
and their retainers away from the city into the Segovia Highlands.
Stopping for a rest and reorganization in the valley of El Tocuyo, the
party soon resolved to establish a town. In part because of the fertility
and general healthfulness of the site and in part owing to the availability of Indian labor, this Spanish settlement soon prospered and rapidly
became the major focus of Spanish activity in western Venezuela, sup-
planting the older but less well-endowed Coro.

Indeed, the establishment of El Tocuyo marks the beginning of active, aggressive efforts to complete the conquest and colonization of
Venezuela. No longer seduced by dreams of El Dorado's kingdom,
these Spaniards from El Tocuyo spread out in search of the real Venezuela, a country whose prosperity would come from agriculture and
stock raising, not the quick riches of gold or silver.

From the perspective of the crown, Venezuela needed to become integrated into the framework of the colonial economic system. By the

mid-sixteenth century it had become clear that the exhausted pearl economy of the northeast coast could no longer be Tierra Firme's principal economic connection to the imperial system. Instead, the crown hoped that the western regions of El Tocuyo and the Venezuelan Andes could become a prosperous supplier of cattle and agricultural products to the mining regions of New Granada. In pursuit of this objective, Francisco Ruiz came to El Tocuyo with a royal order authorizing him to lead an expedition into the Andes in search of a usable route for cattle drives to New Granada. So many of the new settlers in El Tocuyo joined this effort in 1547 that the mayor, Juan de Villegas, feared for the continuation of El Tocuyo as a Spanish urban center.

He need not have worried, for El Tocuyo continued to attract Spanish settlers from Spain and the Caribbean through Coro at a steady rate. But for all of the city's apparent good fortune and favorable location it lacked two requirements for a major colonial center: an easily accessible port and a strong, diversified economic base. Because the settlers of El Tocuyo had no difficulty recognizing these impediments to their continued prosperity and growth they focused their exploratory energies on the coast and eastward toward the agricultural valleys of Caracas and Aragua.

The chronology of the subsequent town foundations clearly substantiates these preoccupations. Borburata, an indifferent port but relatively accessible to El Tocuyo, emerged in 1547-49. This coastal settlement served for a number of years as the entrepot for black slaves for the marginally profitable gold mines near El Tocuyo, but its relatively exposed position on the coast and its meager potential for development kept it from growing, and as Spanish settlement moved eastward into the central valleys, other more suitable ports appeared and supplanted the initial settlement at Borburata.

Within a decade of the founding of El Tocuyo, Spaniards had expanded eastward into what would become the major agricultural region of the country, the valleys of Aragua. Valencia, founded in 1555 at the western end of Lake Tacarigua, proved to be the Spanish frontier outpost in the Aragua area for over a decade. For although no Spaniard doubted the potential prosperity of the region, the various Indian groups already there refused to permit the Spanish advance past Valencia. Relatively well organized and ably led, these Indians managed to delay Spanish settlement in the central valleys for well over a decade. This is not to say that no Spanish expedition ever entered the region, but the succession of temporary settlements established in the valley of Caracas failed to survive repeated Indian attacks until the definitive settlement in 1567.

In the period between the foundation of El Tocuyo and the final conquest of the valleys of Caracas, a variety of other Spanish efforts to control parts of western Venezuela occurred. Barquisimeto, a settlement created to serve the small-scale mining operation in Buría, tried three different sites during the ten years before settling in its present location in 1563. This phenomenon of the migrating city also affected Trujillo, an Andean settlement that moved about the area in search of a healthy, stable, and accessible location. Between 1557 and 1568 the settlement moved five times before finding a site that promised good communications with Lake Maracaibo. The difficulties encountered in identifying prosperous, safe, and healthful locations for Venezuelan towns turned up time and time again. Maracaibo, for example, struggled to become a permanent settlement for twelve years beginning in 1562, but hostile Indians prevented a permanent location until 1574.

For students of Latin American history whose vision of conquest and settlement is inspired by the Mexican and Peruvian epics, the chronicle of Venezuela's settlement often appears incongruous. Spanish expeditions that failed to conquer relatively poverty-stricken tribes, towns created that disappeared, urban settlements that changed location every so often—these characteristics of early Spanish activity in Tierra Firme seem discordant with the general patterns of conquest and settlement prevalent elsewhere in America. But at the risk of over-emphasis, it is essential to recognize the reduced scale of conquest and colonization in Venezuela. These expeditions into the interior were usually small, varying in size but rarely exceeding one hundred Spaniards, with Indian servants numbering perhaps as many as one hundred more at most. Venezuela's varied Indian population ranged from

the most primitive hunting and gathering tribes to practitioners of reasonably sophisticated sedentary agriculture. But in no part of Venezuela were there large concentrations of urbanized Indians living under
centralized political control. Nor did the Spaniards exploring mountains, plains, and valleys of Tierra Firme have the advantage of surprise in their encounters with the natives. Slave raids along the coast
and the slow pace of expansion and settlement into the interior gave
Venezuela's Indians ample time to adjust to the practical demands of
warfare against the Spanish. Their lack of centralized control permitted
them to survive defeat after defeat, for the collapse of one group had
practically no effect on the capacity of the next group to resist.

These conditions did not, of course, offer any hope that the Spaniard could have been kept at bay forever. But they did contribute to
the tentative and often erratic pace of Spanish conquest and settlement
in Venezuela. The most successfully defended region of the country,
the Caracas and Aragua valleys, provides an interesting illustration of
these general conditions, although the scale of operation there was
larger than that in the rest of the country.

From the early days of Spanish exploration the attractiveness of
these central valleys had been appreciated. Exploration parties passed
through the region in the search for El Dorado. Settlement of the central valleys had to wait because they were isolated behind the coastal
range and situated a considerable distance from the eastern and
western foci of Cumaná and Coro. After the foundation of El Tocuyo
brought a stable Spanish base closer to the valleys, interest in the
region grew. In the mid-1550s temporary settlements in the Caracas
valleys failed to survive in part because the Spanish spent more time
looking for gold in the mountains than in establishing a stable settlement and in part because the Indians proved persistent, capable, and
effective enemies. The following decade saw a number of other attempts to bring Spanish control to the valleys, but they too failed. Possibly the conquering fervor of Venezuela's first generation had subsided as the conquerors grew older, and their sons may have preferred
the stable life of El Tocuyo to the dangerous expeditions to the central
valleys, expeditions with little promise of gold or silver.

The crown, more worried about the security of its American coast-line than lured by the possibilities for quick profit in the central valleys, finally intervened and sponsored an expedition to secure the region. Headed by Diego Losada, a man of fifty-four years with thirty of them in Venezuelan expeditions, the Spaniards of El Tocuyo put together a band of about 150 vecinos and 800 Indian bearers and soldiers. With them went cattle and other stock, a sure sign that they anticipated success in their endeavor. In the scale of Venezuelan conquests, this represents an extraordinary investment of men and resources, testimony to the importance attached to the Caracas valleys in the royal plan for a chain of strong cities defending the Spanish-American domain from French, English, or Dutch interlopers.

This time the expedition succeeded, not only because it had more men and resources but also because this effort had settlement and agricultural development as its goals. Although the 1567 foundation of Caracas by Diego de Losada was to endure, the settlement led an uncertain existence for much of its early years. An Indian confederation kept the Spaniards in constant need of an aggressive defense for at least a decade. But the Spaniards did not retreat, and Caracas rapidly became a major base for expansion into the rest of Venezuela.

Expeditions based in Santiago de León de Caracas pushed outward in all directions. North over the Coastal Range, Caraballeda (1565) became the port for Caracas, a location difficult to defend from Indian or pirate attacks. Eastward lay the Unare Basin and the overland communication route to the outpost of Margarita-Cumaná. But if the Indian resistance around Caracas appeared fierce, that encountered in the Unare region proved deadly. The failure of the Caracas expeditions to establish effective control over the region resulted to a large degree from this implacable hostility plus the relative poverty of the Unare Basin. Likewise, to the south, it seemed difficult to dominate the Venezuelan llanos, especially to secure a safe route for cattle into this vast natural pasture. Westward lay the major communication routes to the older Spanish centers at El Tocuyo, Carora, Coro, Trujillo, and Maracaibo. Constant vigilance was required to keep these routes west safe and secure.

This period of initial settlement lasted over a decade until smallpox greatly reduced Indian resistance. Apparently the plague hit the central valleys in 1580 and swept through the native population. Because the Indians had concentrated their population to resist the Spaniards more effectively and because they already suffered from fatigue and hunger as a consequence of the protracted fight, they succumbed to the disease in large numbers. Contemporaries thought the population might have fallen by two-thirds, from perhaps 30,000 natives in the immediate Caracas valley to only 10,000 or 12,000. The death toll in the outlying areas may have exceeded this, but in any case, the epidemic ended the major phase of Indian resistance and marked the beginning of Caracas's long history as a stable, prosperous, and expanding urban center.

During the years from the late sixteenth to the early seventeenth century, the development of Venezuela appeared to occur within relatively isolated geographic subsystems, each with its own urban network, its particular economic base, and its separate political arrangements. Although the interest and authority that would eventually make of Venezuela a reasonably cohesive economic and political unit had been traced by the early seventeenth century, it would take at least another century to turn those tracings into strong lines binding the country together. To appreciate the remarkable accomplishment that was the creation of Caracas as a central city, it may help to look more closely at the regional development of these subsystems to see Venezuela and Caracas from the provincial perspective.

SETTLEMENTS AND MISSIONS

Although the period from the last decades of the sixteenth century to the first part of the eighteenth century appears to contain a complex series of seemingly unrelated events—missionary expansion, regional economic development, shifting political alignments, widespread foreign intervention, and the like—several broad trends visible through the haze of daily life and bureaucratic operations give direction and coherence to the activities of those years. If we step back from the details of individual action and view Venezuela as a complex organism placed under stress by conflicting attractions, threatened by hostile forces, and capable of adapting to meet these challenges, it becomes possible to gain a clearer understanding of the history of these middle years of the country's colonial past.

During the century and a half from 1580 to 1720, Venezuela made its choices and determined to a great degree the shape of its future. In 1580, what we loosely call Venezuela was nothing more than a collection of small urban centers attached to limited geographic regions with independent lines of communication leading to New Granada, the Caribbean, or Spain. The economies of these semi-isolated, settled nuclei survived on trade in a variety of agricultural products and a limited amount of gold. While some intraregional trade existed with nearby towns, much of the production of such commodities as wheat, tobacco, chocolate, and sugar left the province in exchange for Spanish and European manufactures. But as the century wore on, this heterogeneous organization of Venezuela began to coalesce in response to external pressures and internal attractions.

The external pressures came from Spain, the Caribbean, Mexico, and Europe. Spain, of course, saw Venezuela as a secure bulwark of Spanish power along the southern edge of the Caribbean guarding the track of the fleet to Portobelo. Spain also expected this northern edge of South America to contribute a reasonable amount of revenue. But the realities of Spain's American empire tended to defeat these expectations with distressing frequency. Not only did the inhospitable Venezuelan coast fail to attract enough Spanish colonists to present a strong defense against the French, Dutch, or English interlopers, but the rocky shoreline seemed to invite successful pirate attacks. Not even Caracas, sheltered behind the Coastal Range, escaped assault. In 1680 buccaneers crossed the mountains through a little-used pass while the Venezuelan defenders guarded the more frequented one, and, finding no opposition in town, the pirates sacked and burned the city. Throughout this middle period, no part of the Venezuelan coastline from Cumaná to Coro proved capable of withstanding these attacks.

Of course, the entire history of Venezuela's interaction with European interlopers is intimately tied to the course of diplomacy and war in Europe. Depending on the state of international relations among the major European powers, Venezuela might have to defend against Dutch, English, or French pirate fleets.

Imperial-predatory raids on Spanish settlements seemed designed primarily to damage the structure and resources of the Spanish empire in a rather haphazard and opportunistic fashion. Non-Spanish adventurers sailed about the Caribbean in search of poorly defended Spanish settlements; they would then attack the port, sack the city, and sail away in search of another prize. The greatest hope of these adventurers was to fall on the Spanish treasure fleet at some undefended spot in the Caribbean. But the bread and butter of the pirates, privateers, corsairs, and other interlopers were assaults on weak outpost communities such as those at Coro, Borburata, Puerto Cabello, Barcelona, or Cumaná. The frequency and intensity of such incursions depended to a large extent on the situation in Europe. When Spain's diplomatic relations with its friends and enemies were reasonably good, and when Spain could spare ships and men to defend the Caribbean, then the pirates had slim pickings and the quasi-legal privateers little opportunity. But when, as was more frequently the case, Spain found itself engaged in foreign wars, intrigues, and complex diplomatic relations, then the Caribbean came alive with pirates.

The commercial motive for European penetration in the Caribbean was, of course, a much more important one, and represented a more serious threat to the integrity of the Spanish empire in America. Especially in the seventeenth century, non-Spanish activities in the Caribbean became quite intense; in the eighteenth century, aided by Spain's decline, non-Spanish possessions in the region increased. Basically what these European merchants were after was an opportunity to participate directly in the American trade. But contrary to popular belief, it was not principally the gold and silver shipments that Europeans hoped to acquire, but rather a chance to exploit a variety of lucrative local products. For example, recent research has demonstrated that one of the primary motives for the intense Dutch activity in that arc of the Caribbean sweeping westward from the Araya-Paria peninsula to the island of Aruba was the Dutch need for a secure supply of high-quality salt, a commodity in plentiful supply on the Peninsula of Araya opposite Cumaná. Indeed, the constant successful Dutch salt expeditions to this region finally induced the Spanish government to begin work on a very expensive fortress at Araya, for the region was much too sparsely settled to defend the entire coastline. In response to the Spanish campaign to deny foreign access to Araya's salt pans, the Dutch turned to the islands of Bonaire, Curaçao, and Aruba, where in the long run their activities proved more sucessful.

But if salt was the principal reason for the initial decision to invest in expeditions to Tierra Firme, the opportunities for clandestine commerce with Venezuela's north coast soon involved the Dutch in extensive trade in products such as the exceptionally high-quality tobacco from Barinas and excellent cacao from the Andes and the central valleys of Caracas and Aragua. Venezuelans proved eager to sell to the Dutch, and of course the English and French too, the cacao and tobacco destined by law for the Spanish trade to Mexico or the peninsula, in exchange for manufactured goods or species. The success of this contraband effort—and it is important to recognize that contraband was a way of life in Venezuela from at least the beginning of the seventeenth century until the fall of the Spanish empire—owed much to Spain's inability to defend the coastline. During the seventeenth century Spain's involvement in Northern European wars seriously reduced its ability to provide the warships needed to clear the Caribbean. This inability was also reflected in the erratic sailings of the Spanish commercial fleet to the New World. Although a regular, predictable legal trade did not eliminate contraband, it surely reduced the volume. But European wars curtailed legal trade with Spain, and Venezuelans found the foreign interloper the best and oftimes the only source of necessary manufactured goods.

It is easy to exaggerate the importance of this contraband trade. For one thing, there are no reliable estimates of its size, and this leaves much room for exaggeration. For another, Spanish officials and even Venezuelan colonials reacted to every change in the contraband situation. Either loud complaints about the scarcity of European goods came from the colonials or worried accounts of contraband increases accompanied local officials' requests for more money and troops. The natural tendency of officials and colonials to ignore the normal trade regulations with Spain and Mexico, and instead to concentrate their complaints and concern on the illegal trade, may tend to obscure the fact that this contraband, for all its importance in helping to bring down the Spanish colonial system, was probably not the main source of economic well-being for the colony. Venezuela, whether from its extremities of Cumaná or Maracaibo, or from its center at La Guaira-Caracas, traded primarily with Spain and Mexico in accord with the rules and regulations of the Spanish commercial system. The need to conform to these rules and regulations provided the rationale for the gradual consolidation of Venezuela around the central focus of Caracas, a process maturing in the late eighteenth century, and one well under way by the seventeenth century.

In the seventeenth century Venezuela had developed a diversified agricultural economy, producing for local subsistence and for trade in those export commodities most in demand in Spain, the Caribbean, Mexico, New Granada, and Europe. Although Venezuela exported a wide variety of products, the bulk of its external trade was composed of cacao, wheat, tobacco, and hides, with smaller amounts of cotton, indigo, gold, and copper. This stream of exports flowed in two principal channels and a number of considerably smaller tributaries. The largest volume of trade, especially in the seventeenth century, went to Mexico and consisted primarily of cacao and wheat.

From the late sixteenth and the early seventeenth century Venezuela enjoyed a protected market in Mexico for its cacao, and Venezuelan producers jealously guarded their monopoly against attempts by exporters in Guayaquil to break into Mexico. Although a great deal of Ecuadorian cacao entered the Mexican market anyway, the difficulties of this illegal intercolonial trade restricted the amount and raised its price, thereby keeping the Mexican market reasonably well protected for Venezuela. In any event, Venezuelan chocolate had an outstanding reputation for quality, being preferred by knowledgeable consumers. Apparently the Venezuelan cacao could be made into chocolate with only the smallest addition of sugar, while the Ecuadorian variety, being considerably more bitter, required sizable amounts of sugar. The Venezuelan product commanded a good price in the Mexican market, and throughout the seventeenth century that price tended to rise, reaching its peak in the last quarter of the century. As a minor note, this excellent Venezuelan cacao, traded also in contraband, provided the basis for the Dutch reputation for exceptionally high-quality chocolate confections. The trade in Venezuelan wheat went primarily to provision the Spanish fleet for its return voyage to Spain.

In exchange for their wheat and cacao in Veracruz, the Venezuelan merchants brought back small cargoes of manufactured products, many of them from Mexican producers, and large amounts of bullion. Rather than exchange their cacao and wheat for manufactured goods brought to Mexico through the legal Spanish channels, the Venezuelan merchants evidently found it more profitable to return from Veracruz with empty boats, carrying primarily the money from the sale of those products. This bullion, always in short supply in Venezuela, then went to purchase manufactured goods directly from Spain or, in many cases, from contraband sources. Ship arrivals in Venezuelan ports from Mexico, the Spanish Caribbean, or Spain were frequent enough to provide Venezuela with many of its manufactured necessities. But in times of international conflict, when the Spanish windward fleet could not make its annual passage along the Venezuelan coast, the country suffered considerable scarcity of goods. Of course, it was then that contraband became even more attractive.

In addition to the manufactured goods that made up the bulk of Venezuela's imports came a constant stream of African and American black slaves. These people, purchased to work the chocolate plantations along the coast and in the central valleys of Caracas and Aragua, were always in demand. Some arrived in foreign ships licensed by the Spanish crown, others in contraband trade, and some in quasi-legal forced landings. Although Venezuelan landowners complained constantly about the shortage of labor and the need for more black slaves, they apparently did not enjoy enough prosperity to pay the high prices required to attract slavers to the Venezuelan coast. In part the Venezuelan market was too small to be worth the risk, and in part the scarcity of money in the Venezuelan economy made quick and efficient contraband trade with foreign slave traders complicated. Throughout the seventeenth century and well into the eighteenth century, the black slave trade continued to be a matter of controversy and concern to colonists and crown, a situation not resolved until the mid-eighteenth century.

Although Venezuelan trade in cacao, wheat, tobacco, and hides provided the principal means of acquiring wealth in the country, we should not emphasize foreign trade through the major ports of Maracaibo, La Guaira, and Cumaná at the expense of the sizable internal trade within the region. This geographic area, which in the late eighteenth century would become Venezuela, operated economically as three identifiable economic subsystems. Although partially interconnected, each of these regions had much stronger economic ties with its external markets than with each other. This situation characterized Venezuela until the early eighteenth century, when the Caracas Company began the economic consolidation of the region, a process not completed until the late 1770s and early 1780s. Until then, Venezuela consisted of a center, composed of the central valleys of Caracas and Aragua with their plains to the south; an eastern periphery, composed of towns at Cumaná and Barcelona and a cattle-raising hinterland in the plains to the south between the Orinoco Delta and the Unare Basin; and a western periphery, composed of the Venezuelan Andean spur down to Coro, with its strong links to the llanos of Barinas and Cojedes and its elaborate trade relations with the Maracaibo Basin to the northwest and Bogotá to the south.

Because the history of Venezuela eventually led to a consolidation of these three major regions into a Caracas-centered unit, it is easy to underestimate the strength and independence of the regional economies in the seventeenth and even the eighteenth century. What statistics we have indicate that the volume and value of trade through Maracaibo and Coro, for example, although not as large as that through Caracas-La Guaira, were nevertheless considerable. This is especially so in terms of cacao and tobacco. Somewhat less commercial activity occurred in the east through Cumaná or Barcelona in hides, cattle, and other products. Likewise, the internal trade within these regions in wheat, meat, cotton cloth, and other minor products was significant, even if these activities did not show up in the import-export statistics. These regions of Venezuela—not great centers of wealth and prosperity on the Mexican or Peruvian scale—provided enough revenue through taxes of various kinds to support the royal bureaucracy, local officials, and necessary expenses. In some years Venezuela even managed to send a surplus to Spain or Mexico. The only project that exceeded Venezuela's local resources was the construction of the Araya fortress, designed to prevent the Dutch from raiding the salt pans. The Venezuelans had no major economic interest in the salt pans of Araya, and this military base, built to secure the northeast coast for Spain, required a constant subsidy from the Mexican treasury for almost a generation during the mid-seventeenth century.

One of the most interesting characteristics of these three subsystems in what is now Venezuela was their relative independence from each other. Although there was certainly considerable communication and commercial traffic between east, center, and west, the economic orientation of the regions was so overwhelmingly outward through the ports of Maracaibo, La Guaira, and Cumaná that no useful integration would have come to the area without external help. On a map of Venezuela this tripartite division of the country seems so geographically logical that the eventual consolidation of the country around Caracas requires explanation. Because the seventeenth century showed the closest approximation to this geographic model, we need to examine for a moment the reasons for the triumph of politics over environment.

Although there are perhaps five principal gateways into Venezuela from the north coast, two of these seemed especially promising to all observers and travelers: the Maracaibo Basin and the Orinoco River. Throughout the seventeenth century and into the eighteenth century the opportunity to develop these two routes into the interior gradually disappeared. Maracaibo served as a dynamic and prosperous port for the Andean hinterland during the seventeenth century, but the development of the region as a major urban center with prosperous and dynamic leadership failed in a contest with the hostile Indians of the Maracaibo Basin and the aggressive activities of pirates and smugglers. Furthermore, the sand bar at Maracaibo effectively prevented the entry of large ships, whether pirate or Spanish, thereby putting a limit on the strength of Maracaibo commerce. To add to these disabilities, Maracaibo could never hope to boast of a climate as healthful and pleasant as that in Caracas, making it difficult to attract the government and ecclesiastical authorities necessary to make the city a major Spanish imperial center. The trade from Mérida, Trujillo, and Barinas, which under other circumstances might have flowed through Maracaibo, was split into a number of smaller currents: some went south to Bogotá, some northward to El Tocuyo or Barquisimeto, other trade ran out into the llanos perhaps as far as Valencia or even Caracas, and a large current flowed into Maracaibo itself. The combination of these disadvantages held Maracaibo's development down as the bulk of Spanish commerce slowly shifted toward the central coastal range and its valleys of Caracas and Aragua.

The Orinoco entryway had an even less auspicious early history. The river system is magnificent, draining almost all of Venezuela east and north of the Andes through an extensive system of tributaries. The volume of water emptied into the Atlantic turns the ocean into fresh water for miles. So impressed was Columbus by this phenomenon that he imagined the river leading inland to Eden, the biblical land of paradise. The reality was not, however, that romantic. For all its majesty, the Orinoco proved to be a poor commercial route in the colonial and the early national period. Because of its rough course, broken by numerous falls and rapids, Spanish ships could penetrate only a short distance inland. Furthermore, the river and its principal tributaries of the Apure and Meta flow in a wide arc far south of Venezuela's main colonial settlements. The Indian groups along the Orinoco resisted pacification, although in the eighteenth century Spanish missionaries had some success in the region. The river emptied into the Atlantic, making communication with the major centers of the Venezuelan north coast and the Spanish Caribbean difficult.

Even more discouraging than these obstacles was the apparent lack of an easily developed resource, either in the form of an agricultural export crop or mineral wealth. The best the sparse Spanish population in this region could do was raise cattle and export hides, but even that activity was done more easily through Barcelona or Cumaná. Added to all these impediments to development, the Spanish authorities never showed much enthusiasm for encouraging activity in the Orinoco for fear that the thinly populated region would be too difficult to defend. As a result, the Orinoco-Apure-Meta river system never became a major commercial thoroughfare, although a considerable amount of local trade and transportation followed the rivers along the edge of the cattle-raising llanos.

These considerations help explain the failure of Maracaibo or the Orinoco to become principal centers of Spanish activity in Tierra Firme. The forces drawing the regions together around Caracas were considerably more complex. Although much of the consolidation came in the mid-eighteenth century or later, the origins of the Caracas-centered system could be seen as early as the late seventeenth century.

Prosperity and protection were Caracas's advantages over competing regions in the initial, formative years of Venezuelan history. Ensconced behind the protection of the Coastal Range, Caracas suffered relatively few pirate attacks, and its successful campaigns against the Indians eliminated all significant resistance by the end of the sixteenth century. Caracas enjoyed a tranquility unknown to the coastal cities of Cumaná, Coro, or Maracaibo. Because Caracas managed to establish and sustain an acceptable port at La Guaira, the city and its region preserved its protected position without paying the price of isolation. Even more important perhaps, the Caracas valleys and the adjacent valleys of Aragua demonstrated clearly their extraordinary agricultural productivity. To add a further attraction of considerable symbolic importance in the early years, the hills south of Caracas even produced a small but significant amount of gold. Were these advantages not enough, the city of Caracas had a fine healthful location with good water and a pleasant, disease-free, and temperate climate.

While other cities and regions in Tierra Firme may have had some of these distinguishing characteristics, no other place had all of them. But, even more important, Caracas had the right characteristics at the right time. This element of timing was crucial for the process of consolidation. The special place of Caracas came as the cumulative result of a long series of short-range decisions taken to achieve rather limited goals, decisions that gradually closed out opportunities for other places and opened them for Caracas. The combination of Caracas's advantages plus the royal decisions that, beginning in the mid-eighteenth century, made the city a submetropolitan capital and denied its competitors equivalent privileges, created the momentum for the formation of a central city. In the seventeenth century Caracas still had several major rivals, and the future central city had few responsibilities outside its own region.

Historical hindsight permits us, nevertheless, to see in the organization of the city's elite the beginnings of a special kind of self-consciousness, an elite sensibility and capacity that eventually gave the city the ability to press its interests skillfully. Although there is evidence suggesting similar elites in other cities, such as Coro, these competing groups do not appear to have become as complex and effective as their *caraqueño* counterparts.

As was the case throughout Spanish America, the basic *caraqueño* urban institution was the *cabildo,* or town council. But in other Spanish-American urban centers this town council's functions gradually declined as more powerful imperial institutions took over regional administration soon after the conquest. Not so in Caracas. Throughout the seventeenth century this *cabildo* remained the principal deliberative group for the central region. Not only did it control the administration of the prosperous city of Caracas, but it also presumed to act as the political representative for the jurisdiction of the Gobernación de Venezuela, the central portion of Venezuela. This presumption was possible only because Venezuela appeared too poor and minor a place to justify the crown expense of a regular royal court. To the Spanish empire, Venezuela seemed important as a producer of chocolate and wheat and a key piece in the Spanish plan to hold the Caribbean. Thus, Spain focused most of its attention on Venezuela's defenses, leaving the administration of local affairs to the governor and, in his absence, to the *cabildo* of Caracas. This custom of permitting the *cabildo* of Caracas to manage the province in the absence of the governor, while rare in Spanish America, clearly symbolized the sophistication and competence of the local elite.

Not only in political matters was the *cabildo* effective. Time and time again this elite spoke strongly and effectively on behalf of the economic interests of the city and its province. Whether in defense of the special monopoly for Venezuelan cacao in Mexico or in favor of increasing the slave trade, whether lobbying for new commercial privileges or against the imposition of taxes, the *cabildo* of Caracas often behaved as if it represented at least the province of Caracas if not all of Venezuela.

Part of the success of this elite can be traced to its ability to design a system of interlocking relationships that connected the rich and powerful as well as the not so rich and powerful in a close-knit network of obligation, patronage, and kinship. On the surface these linkages between individuals and families, merchants and landowners, appear exceedingly complex, but recent research has shown a rather elegant and orderly structure. Although this account may oversimplify the case somewhat, it indicates the essential features of the system.

Seventeenth-century *caraqueño* society can be seen as composed of four groups: patrons, clients, middlemen, and non-participants. The non-participants were usually individuals recently arrived and not yet integrated into the system, transients, or those too poor or too far removed from the city's mainstream to participate. The patrons, of course, were the elite members whose position, family, wealth, and property gave them the ability to dispose of or manage some resources—whether jobs, privileges, protection, land, commerce, credit, or the like. These individuals were most easily identified through their membership in the *cabildo,* their ownership of a dozen black slaves or more, or their landed wealth. Many of these people were also descendants of the city's founders and had Indians assigned to them in *encomienda.* Moreover, this elite managed to maintain the economic base of its pre-eminence through strategic marriages between cousins and other carefully arranged matches designed to permit the transfer of property relatively intact from generation to generation.

Clients, individuals of lesser means, might have been tradesmen, minor merchants or clerics, artisans, small landowners, low-level municipal or royal officeholders, and such. For these people to succeed they often required protection, credit, privileges, connections, and influence, and, lacking the ability to gain these resources on their own, they looked to a patron for support.

In between these groups stood the middlemen, whose principal function in this system seemed to be the coordination and connection of patrons and clients. The distinguishing feature of the middlemen was that, while patrons had clients and clients had patrons, only middlemen had both patrons and clients. The beauty of this system was that it permitted the elite to have access and a measure of control over a very large segment of the population without the need to create dependent relationships with large numbers of people. The middlemen permitted the creation of a remarkably cohesive elite-dominated society in seventeenth-century Caracas. With the *cabildo* as its primary institutional base, this elite had the will and the resources to press its interests in Venezuela, Santo Domingo, Spain, or Mexico; and its success in the seventeenth and the early eighteenth century contributed significantly to the eventual emergence of Caracas as a primate city. Even though the *cabildo* and its elite declined in importance as Caracas took on the role of submetropolitan capital in the mid-eighteenth century, the extraordinary social architecture created in the seventeenth century had made Caracas the center of power, wealth, and government.

Although Venezuela's early colonial experience in the sixteenth and seventeenth centuries held few spectacular achievements, with the possible exception of the sixteenth-century pearl fisheries of Cubagua-Margarita, the colony had achieved a considerable measure of prosperity by the beginning of the eighteenth century. Several symbols of this success existed, from the gradual growth of the urban network to the development of a prosperous trade in cacao with Mexico and Spain. The emergence of Caracas in the late sixteenth century as an urban place with a dynamic entrepreneurial elite and blessed with inhabitants who liked to think of themselves as specially placed to manage the affairs of the central portion of Venezuela indicated the direction of the region's development in the eighteenth century. Yet for all the progress of the first two centuries of Spanish interest in Tierra Firme, Venezuela in 1700 was still a region in formation. Its subregions in the west and the Andes, as well as those in the eastern coast and llanos, had only informal links to the central region around Caracas and few connections with each other. Administrative jurisdictions were still poorly defined, with the western portion oriented part of the time toward Bogotá and part toward the Caribbean connection at Santo Domingo. The east looked to Puerto Rico, Santo Domingo, Spain, and sometimes to Bogotá; while the central, Caracas area uneasily acknowledged some subordination to Santo Domingo but behaved as if its only overlords were the king and council in Spain.

This insecurity of administration reflected the uneven economic development of the region. While the cacao planters of a few selected valleys and mountainsides prospered as part of a sophisticated international market system, the cattlemen of the interior plains mostly supplied local consumers with meat and the external trade with hides. A small number of towns such as Caracas, Coro, Cumaná, Valencia, El Tocuyo, or Barquisimeto supported reasonable copies of traditional Spanish urban life, with most of the amenities and formality characteristic of thoroughly settled parts of the Americas. But not far from the elegant *caraqueños*, for example, Venezuela became untamed frontier country. The conquest of Venezuela continued throughout the eighteenth century, no longer the arena of roaming bands of adventuresome Spaniards searching for El Dorado but instead the province of the religious orders in pursuit of Indian souls. In the course of the eighteenth century these clerics created the modern map of Venezuela outside the principal cities. They defined the limits of the country and virtually completed its conquest with the exception of portions of Guayana.

Venezuela's last colonial century, given these conditions, was dynamic, prosperous, controversial, and creative. The preindependence history of this region does not chronicle the decline of old institutions or tired elites but tells of the creation of a mature colonial society. The independence of Venezuela in 1810 can be seen as the culmination of eighteenth-century growth and expansion, as an affirmation of Venezuela's maturity, and as a symbol of the region's readiness to participate in the world economy on its own account.

Much of the prosperity achieved by this Spanish-American colony appears to have sprung into being after 1700. The complex network of newly established institutions, such as the *consulado,* the *audiencia,* the intendency, and the captaincy general, were creations of the mid- to late eighteenth century. Likewise, the rapid growth of Caracas in this period, with its assumption of the role of Venezuela's capital city, seems to have happened with remarkable rapidity. Of course, few major historical processes have their origins and resolutions in the span of one or two generations, and the emergence of Venezuela as a Caracas-centered territorial unit was no exception.

We have already explored the development of Venezuela during its formative years in the sixteenth and seventeenth cnturies, with emphasis on the growing importance of Caracas as the center of its region and the most dynamic and prosperous city in Venezuela. It is now necessary to look at the Venezuelan hinterland and explore the history of the missionary activity of the regular orders that brought this territory into the Spanish sphere of influence. These missionaries appear at the very beginning of the Spanish enterprise in Tierra Firme, and their participation in the development of the region became especially important in the seventeenth and eighteenth centuries. Because the activities of these clerics foreshadowed the shape of Venezuela's late colonial development as early as the first part of the seventeenth century, a short survey of the activities of Franciscans, Capuchins, Jesuits, and Augustinians is in order here.

As happened elsewhere in America, the Franciscans came to Venezuela very early in the conquest. From the Antilles and from Spain, these missionaries traveled first in the late sixteenth century to the eastern pearl coast, where their heroic efforts to establish missions failed in the face of Indian hostility and Spanish weakness in the region. The Franciscans had much greater success in the west and central regions of the country, establishing their Province of Santa Cruz de Caracas in the Convent of San Francisco about 1576. From this base in the newly established provincial capital, the Franciscans spread their mission outward until by the middle of the seventeenth century their convents could be found in Trujillo, El Tocuyo, Barquisimeto, Carora, Maracaibo, Coro, and Valencia. These principal centers of activity received the addition of a convent in Guanare in the mid-eighteenth century, thus completing the institutional network of the province. Although the Franciscans of this province focused most of their activity on the settled regions of the west and center, they also spent considerable effort on the east, although with less solid results. From a base in Margarita beginning in the early seventeenth century, these Franciscans moved to establish a convent at Cumaná, an endeavor that brought modest success. The expansion of Franciscan missions and convents from Trinidad into the Guayana region had less happy results, although small establishments survived English attack into the eighteenth century.

The Franciscans, like many of their brethren in other orders, served the colony as interim parochial priests for Indian parishes and for Spanish towns without resident secular clergy. They cooperated in the Christianization of the natives in the more settled areas of the colony, and they ran schools to train novitiates for the order. The major Franciscan establishments became centers of culture and learning with the most impressive libraries in Venezuela. At the peak of their activity and influence in the eighteenth century, the Franciscans had an energetic program of education which provided the order with a steady stream of local recruits through the major convents. But if the eighteenth century saw the period of greatest Franciscan ascendance in the Province of Santa Cruz de Caracas, it also marked the beginning of rapid decline. In part, the Franciscans suffered from too much success. Their excellent education programs produced missionaries with few opportunities to work. The central part of Venezuela, their principal missionary theater, was firmly in the hands of the secular clergy, and other missionary orders reserved the unsettled areas to the south and east. With few outlets for their missionary zeal, many Franciscans migrated elsewhere in America, and the turmoil of independence plus the republican enthusiasm of a newly liberated Venezuela virtually eliminated the order as an important entity in the nineteenth century.

The accomplishments of this order were nonetheless substantial. More than anything else, perhaps, the Franciscans provided Venezuela with education and access to Spanish high culture. Through their libraries, schools, and churches they brought a level of sophistication to the region that Venezuela could not have supported on its own. Earlier than most other institutions, the Franciscan Province of Santa Cruz identified Caracas as the center of political and economic influence in Tierra Firme, and the network of convents, *doctrinas,* and missions affiliated with the province linked east, west, and center through Caracas long before the eighteenth-century economic and political reforms followed a similar pattern of consolidation. The disproportionate prosperity of the Caracas school, with its large number of novitiates drawn from throughout Venezuela, foreshadowed the typical configuration of the country in the late eighteenth century and afterward, an arrangement characterized by the predominance of Caracas within the territorial unit of Venezuela.

If the Franciscans of the Province of Santa Cruz de Caracas kept to the settled areas near major Spanish towns, their brothers in charge of the missions of Píritu in eastern Venezuela found a wider scope for their apostolic fervor. Píritu, the place from which the missionary activity draws its name, was a hamlet located about fifty miles west of Barcelona along the Unare coastline. Although the name Píritu was applied to the whole effort of the Franciscans in this region, their activities spread way beyond the immediate vicinity of that small town. These Franciscans of Píritu had no formal organizational connection with those of the Province of Santa Cruz de Caracas, and, while most of the Franciscans of Caracas were Creoles, Venezuelan-born, the Píritu Franciscans came almost entirely from Spain. The missionary activities of these dedicated clerics spread slowly in the second half of the seventeenth century. Arriving in Píritu in 1656 after a protracted campaign in Spain to gain permission to take on this mission, the

Franciscans began the difficult business of bringing Christianity and Spanish civilization to the scattered Indian settlements of the Unare Basin. In the course of the century and a half that these Franciscans labored in eastern Venezuela, they managed to found something on the order of fifty towns. Most of these, of course, congregated Indians, but a few were also Spanish settlements in the Barcelona llanos and along the Orinoco. Even more impressive, the majority of these places survived past independence to become permanent urban nuclei, whose elegant eighteenth-century churches still stand as monuments to the missionary spirit. In their expansion into the interior of the eastern region, the Franciscans depended, at least in matters secular, on the governors of the Province of Cumaná. For the most part, the missionaries and the royal officials cooperated; the clerics needed the assistance of the government to protect them from the depredations of implacably hostile Indians and adventuresome pirates, and the government often needed the assistance of the mission Indians to repel such attacks.

In the general plan of Venezuela's colonial history, the missions of Píritu followed an outline of expansion and decline similar to the experience of other orders. From the modest base at Píritu, the mission spread rapidly southward in the early part of the eighteenth century until by the 1730s these Franciscans had reached the Orinoco, and their missionary activity began to encroach on areas reserved for Jesuit or Capuchin missions. To avoid conflicts, representatives of these three orders met in Santo Tomé de Guayana in 1734 and agreed to partition the rest of Venezuela's hinterland. This pact reserved a substantial portion of Guayana south of Angostura and east of the Orinoco for the Píritu mission. During the rest of the eighteenth century the Franciscans expanded their work into the farthest reaches of the Orinoco, arriving at their deepest penetration at San Carlos de Rio Negro.

When the Jesuits left the Spanish-American domains as a result of nationalist Spanish policy in the late eighteenth century, and the Capuchins withdrew to Cumaná, the Píritu missionaries found themselves in charge of a number of missions previously in the hands of those orders. By the first decade of the nineteenth century some thirty-six Franciscan missions existed in Guayana, and some fifty members of the order administered these plus the other Franciscan establishments in the llanos of Barcelona. All told, the peak of activity in the preindependence years saw some seventy clerics care for just over seventy places. This accomplishment could not, however, survive the independence. The increasingly secular, if not anti-clerical, tenor of the new republican governments made the missions something of an anachronism, and this order, composed entirely of Spaniards and governed from Spain, could not make the political transition required by the protracted independence wars. Their legacy to republican Venezuela, the extension of Spanish occupation and Venezuelan control into the llanos of Barcelona and the far reaches of the Orinoco, helped define the Republic's territorial boundaries. The network of towns established by these clerics remained substantially as they left it, although many of the smaller and more remote mission communities disappeared. The Franciscan mission of Píritu also contributed to the separate identity of Venezuela's eastern region, for they reported through Cumaná and Barcelona to Spain with only tenuous contacts with the emerging central place at Caracas.

In similar fashion, although on a larger scale, the Capuchin order, also drawn almost entirely from Spain, carried Spanish control and civilization into those parts of Venezuela neglected by the conquerors. The largest of their missionary territories, and the region where they founded the most towns, included the vast expanse of the llanos of Caracas south of the Coastal Range and limited by the Píritu missions on the east and the Andes on the west. The Capuchins founded a scattering of towns that extended as far as the Apure, with a few establishments along the Meta and in the valleys of the Apure. In all, between 1658 and the independence, some 107 towns owed their existence to the missionary enthusiasm of the Capuchins. Moreover, because of the growing prosperity of this region serving the towns of the Caracas-Valencia agricultural area, a number of these missions became important Spanish towns engaged in the commerce of cattle, mules, and horses. The settlement of the principal Venezuelan stock-raising heartland owed much to the labors of these missionaries who served as the advance guard, the peaceful conquerors of the llanos. Where the Spanish settler saw a hostile wasteland, the missionary saw untamed Indians to control, Christianize, and Hispanicize. Through the efforts of these people, the llanos region became, in the course of the eighteenth century, an integral part of the Caracas-centered system.

The indefatigable Capuchins also took on the eastern llanos of Cumaná to the Orinoco, including the Delta. This mission, dating from the middle of the seventeenth century, founded some forty-five towns, of which about thirty-five survived until independence. In this mission, as was the case with most of the other Venezuelan missions, the greatest period of success and expansion came in the eighteenth century. In this late, but nonetheless impressive, missionary revival in Venezuela, the Capuchins could also be found deep in the Orinoco region along the river and its Rio Negro tributary. They worked for a time in Trinidad but abandoned that mission in the early eighteenth century to focus their attention on Guayana, where they founded some thirty-four towns as far as the Caroní. Although most of this activity occurred in the llanos and Orinoco-Guayana regions, the Capuchins also managed a couple of dozen missions in the Maracaibo Basin and the Goajira Peninsula.

These two orders, the Franciscans and the Capuchins, carried the bulk of Venezuela's missionary activity, but Dominicans, Augustinians, and Jesuits also contributed to the completion of the country's urban network. The Dominicans, although first involved in Venezuela in the sixteenth-century Las Casian experiment in peaceful conquest near Cumaná, contributed a string of towns, perhaps twenty in all, in the region of Barinas and Apure. They, like the Augustinians and the Jesuits, drew their support and direction from New Granada, an orientation that tended to create ties between the newly settled areas and that viceroyalty rather than ties to the center at Caracas. The Augustinians established their missions in the intermontane valleys of the Venezuelan Andes in the areas of Mérida and Trujillo. The Jesuits, based in New Granada, extended their Colombian missions of the llanos of Casanare into the Venezuelan lowlands near the con-fluence of the Meta and Orinoco rivers. Between 1721 and their expulsion in 1767, the Jesuits founded perhaps twenty towns.

This brief account cannot begin to convey the spirit and accomplishment of the missionary effort in Venezuelan territory. Although each missionary order had its own style and its special set of opportunities, difficulties, and circumstances, they all shared many of the same experiences. For the most part, the Venezuelan missions were precarious affairs. Usually a single missionary had the responsibility of bringing Spanish-Christian order to the nomadic hunters and gatherers of Venezuela's wilder areas. They sometimes enjoyed support from Spanish military expeditions, but more often they labored alone. The hardship and difficulties of these missions remind us of the tales in the chronicles of the early conquistadors of Venezuela. But where the conquerors left a trail of destruction as they passed through the Venezuelan backlands, the missionaries left a network of towns and villages. Some of these places may well have been most primitive, but the number of them that survived the independence to become permanent places on republican Venezuela's map is impressive.

Although the traditional Spanish practice of secularizing frontier missions occurred in Venezuela, too, the scarcity of secular clerics to take over former missions and the relatively short span of Venezuela's missionary activity left most of these late-seventeenth- and eighteenth-century towns in missionary hands at independence. The wars of independence brought much of the missionary network to ruin and abandonment, but the surge of evangelical zeal in the eighteenth century had already defined the limits of Venezuelan territory and had established European control over the scattered urban nuclei in the interior regions of the country. The century and a half of intense missionary action in the interior completed the work of exploration, conquest, and settlement begun in the sixteenth and seventeenth centuries in the mountains and along the coasts. Although these missionaries looked to Spain or to New Granada as often as to Caracas for their direction and leadership, their missionary achievement provided the material for the bureaucratic and ecclesiastical consolidation of Venezuela during the second half of the eighteenth century. Without the missions of the llanos, Guayana, and Apure, Venezuela's vast interior would probably have been very difficult to bring into the Caracas system. Thanks to the missionaries, these llanos became by the end of the colonial period a source of wealth and resources for the mature colony of Venezuela.

Chapter 3 • The Mature Colonial Society, 1650-1830

CONSOLIDATION

Although we always use the modern name, Venezuela, to identify that geographic region in the colonial period, the designation is misleading. Until the late eighteenth century Venezuela contained a number of distinct provinces, each governed more or less independently from the others. Not only did the political geography tend to divide this region, but the channels of communication and commerce also flowed in at least three directions. By the mid-seventeen hundreds, Venezuela had six regular provinces, each with its governor. In addition, the central province of Caracas and the eastern outpost of Nueva Anadalucía or Cumaná were administered by captains general, symbolizing their importance in the Caribbean defense network. Caracas, both city and province, held a pre-eminent position within this political context of Tierra Firme that came more from commercial links and economic prosperity than from any formal delegation of political authority.

To be sure, the Bishopric of Caracas (moved from its original seat

in Coro in 1636) encompassed an area larger than the provincial jurisdiction, but it controlled neither the Andean nor the eastern regions.
Moreover, the extensive missionary territories in the central and eastern
llanos came under the supervision of the several religious orders in
Spain until the end of the eighteenth century. The *cabildo* in Caracas
often spoke as if it did represent the interests of all Venezuelans, but
this presumption, while sometimes accepted as a matter of expediency
by other prosperous towns, had only the most circumstantial foundation in law. It is easy to exaggerate the fragmented state of Venezuela
before the eighteenth-century reforms and innovations, for, by controlling the port at La Guaira, Caracas managed a substantial majority
of Venezuelan trade. Even so, Maracaibo and Cumaná had their regular customers, too, especially the former, whose trade with Veracruz
remained substantial throughout the colonial period.

In practice, colonial Venezuela had three competing orientations.
The Caribbean drew the most from Venezuelan trade in crops such as
cacao, wheat, or tobacco through the ports of Maracaibo and La Guaira
and provided the most government supervision from the Audiencia of
Santo Domingo. Also from the Caribbean came most Venezuelan imports, either from Spanish fleets and merchants or from the smugglers
of the non-Spanish islands. But if the Caribbean connection appeared
the strongest at the beginning of the eighteenth century, it competed
with the strong links to New Granada and Bogotá and through the
Atlantic coast direct to Spain. The southern reaches of the Venezuelan
Andes from perhaps Trujillo through Mérida and San Cristóbal traded
as much with New Granada as with Maracaibo. Likewise, the cattle
and tobacco of Barinas often found their way into New Granada
rather than through the long-distance route to Maracaibo or Caracas-La
Guaira. The eastern regions with the Atlantic connection as close and
easy as the Caribbean contacts shipped their principal products of
hides and other stock-raising items in both the Caribbean and Atlantic
trade, but in either case they rarely traded through Caracas-La Guaira.

In the discussion of the commercial connections between Venezuela's
regions and the outside, the volume of interregional trade within
Venezuela is often forgotten. Even though comprehensive studies of

this phenomenon have yet to be prepared, every indication points to a steady, active, and prosperous trade system providing the inhabitants of Venezuela with the bulk of their daily needs. If the Venezuelan economy had little of the complexity and volume of the Mexican or Peruvian trade, the need to feed, clothe, house, and employ some half a million people in the settled areas and uncounted others in the missions provided the market for an active commercial system. If no other evidence existed, the minutes of the *cabildo* in Caracas with their constant preoccupation with food supply, construction, prices, and the market would be enough to convince us of the substantial nature of Venezuela's internal commerce. Moreover, the fact that Venezuela's cacao merchants preferred to exchange their product in Veracruz for cash rather than goods indicates that Mexico produced few things worth the cost of shipment to Venezuela and that the proceeds from the cacao sales went to fuel the chronically cash-short Venezuelan economy and to purchase luxuries and European manufactures direct from Spanish or illegal foreign merchants. While the economic reforms of the eighteenth century certainly modified some trade patterns and created others, they did not invent the economy nor rescue Venezuela from some form of excessive economic decadence.

This emphasis on the conflicting orientations and linkages is not to imply that the region could ever have developed in response to a non-Caribbean or non-European focus. Given the international conditions of the subsequent centuries and Venezuela's resources, the region was destined to participate in the Atlantic world economy. But the form of that participation and the organization of Venezuela to participate were determined by the resolution of these conflicting orientations during the revitalized Spanish Bourbon regimes in the course of the eighteenth century.

Each in its own way, the innovations Spain introduced in Venezuela during this century testified to the economic value and political importance of the colony within the Spanish imperial system. Venezuela's cacao, a product providing its growers and merchants with constant income and prosperity, encouraged Spanish Basque entrepreneurs to propose a trading company that would within one commercial institution begin resolving a number of imperial problems. This institution, whose history proved as controversial as its activities, would take on the trade in Venezuela cacao from La Guaira to Spain and would also guarantee the steady supply of European goods required by the colony. In return for this exclusive trading territory, the Compañía Guipuzcoana or Caracas Company agreed to patrol the coasts from Araya to the Gulf of Venezuela, eliminate the contraband trade with the Antilles, provide a steady supply of black slaves to the Venezuelan market, and develop the regional economy. Although the Caracas Company was the first and the best-known venture of its kind in Spanish America, it represented only one of a number of such attempts, for the notion of monopoly-mercantile enterprise captivated many entrepreneurs and government officials in the eighteenth century. During the years of the Company's greatest activity, from the late 1720s to the mid-1750s, Venezuela made considerable economic progress, and the controversies over the Company's policies helped define the role of Caracas as a central city for Venezuela.

In the broadest terms, the Company attempted to gain control over the entire cacao crop and then, with a corner on the market, make enough profit to finance the Company's other obligations involving the suppression of contraband and defense of the coast. To achieve these ends the Company, by law, had the exclusive right to purchase cacao in Venezuela for the Spanish trade. No Venezuelan producer or merchant could trade independently in the Spanish market. Naturally, with the power to act as a monopoly purchaser, the Company's activities led to a rather dramatic decline in the price paid for cacao in Venezuela, while the price paid in Spain stayed the same or increased. Theoretically, the excess profits earned by the company would subsidize their quasi-governmental activities in defense and public administration in Venezuela. Also in theory, the activities of the Company should have produced substantial benefits for the colonists. With the Company responsible for Spanish trade, the erratic flow of goods into Venezuela should have smoothed out, leading to regular commerce and thus increased prosperity. Likewise, the planned import of a steady supply of black slaves should have helped revitalize the agricultural economy.

In practice, the Company had little of the anticipated effect. To be sure, the contraband trade with the Antilles declined for a time, the Company did indeed introduce improved methods into the agricultural economy, and the monopoly proved quite profitable for the Company's stockholders. But the managers of the institution never succeeded in stabilizing their monopoly into a smoothly operating system. They expanded its coverage to include all of the present coastline of the country, bringing Maracaibo into the monopoly. They gained control over the tobacco trade, and they tried to capture the Venezuela-Mexico cacao trade. In spite of the considerable profits earned in the early years of the monopoly, the Company could not supply the steady stream of European goods required and found it impossible to fulfill the requirements of its contract to import black slaves.

Many of the Company's troubles can be traced to poor management, overextension, and uncontrollable complications involving Spain's increasingly complex diplomatic relations. But the principal difficulty encountered in Venezuela came from the Venezuelans. From an imperial perspective, the notion of a monopoly company buying cheap, selling dear, and using the profits to solve an imperial problem must have seemed eminently reasonable. From the colonial perspective, this arrangement appeared to be little more than an elaborate scheme to tax cacao producers and merchants very heavily to support a host of government services most colonials could do without. Although the Company did become thoroughly entrenched in Venezuela and did have a significant impact on the organization of agriculture and commerce, its long-term prospects were poor from the start. One of the biggest misconceptions in the project was the implicit notion that Venezuelan cacao producers would be prepared to change long-standing patterns of commerce, trade, and profit with relatively little resistance. In fact, the length of time it took for the colonists to rebel is eloquent testimony of their loyalty to and stake in the imperial system.

To be sure, the Company started slowly. In its early years the benefits to the colony in terms of a regular market for cacao and a steady supply of European goods appeared reasonable. Moreover, the distance between Company cacao prices and free market prices had not grown to the size it would later on. But during the next two decades of the 1730s and 1740s the company's control over the Venezuelan economy became more and more pervasive. Venezuelan merchants found their operations severely restricted by Company monopoly privileges, while the great cacao producers saw their margin of profit dwindle as Company prices stayed low and showed a tendency to sink even lower. Every town of consequence came to have its Company agent whose activities frequently abridged what the locals regarded as their rights. The agents acted above the law, holding special powers and exemptions in their role as customs agents dedicated to the elimination of contraband. These people became an isolated bureaucracy with little interest in participating in the local system of influence and cooperation. When the Company made an effort to control the Mexican cacao trade, a proposal that would have closed the one remaining high-profit outlet for Venezuelan producers as well as ruining the Venezuelan-owned trading fleet, the local producers protested with such vigor that the crown declined to award the Company this concession.

In the years of resistance to the Caracas Company, the most spectacular uprising involved the rebellion of Juan Francisco de León in 1749. Although on the surface this demonstration appeared to be nothing more than a local protest against the imposition of an unwanted colonial administrator in the town of Panaquire, the resistance actually represented an outburst of pent-up hostility toward the Company and its agents. This even has come to be known as a rebellion, but as rebellions go it was a relatively mild affair, although nonetheless dangerous for the participants.

León, a minor official whose job had been given to a Basque associated with the Company, gathered a respectably sized contingent of locals, mostly from the middle levels of society, and marched to Caracas to present his case. The goal of the rebellion turned out to be the elimination of the Company's monopoly privileges and the abolition of its quasi-governmental functions. Apparently the revolt had some tacit support from influential, wealthy local planters, although few of these individuals were foolish enough to become too closely identified with the León uprising.

In any case, with León in Caracas, the authorities went through the motions of accepting his demands, gaining his agreement to return with his people to Panaquire. But as it became clear that the Company continued in full vigor, León returned to the fight, this time in a much more threatening posture. So Spain sent a new governor with 1,500 veteran troops to resolve the difficulty, and resolve it he did, although with considerable severity. León and his followers tried to resist but had neither the weapons nor training required and rapidly fell to the Spanish troops. In the aftermath many participants were imprisoned, executed, or exiled. León was captured and sent to Spain, where he died in prison. By 1751 or 1752 the revolt appeared over with no apparent gain for the Venezuelans.

The importance of this event comes not from the immediate results, for the Company had its rights confirmed, nor from its uniqueness, for the revolt was only the most visible of a series of disturbances dating from the beginning of the Company's activities, but instead comes from the obvious and widespread support for the revolt's goals among the Venezuelan elite. Unlike previous revolts led by blacks or *pardos,* which had only ill-defined goals and dangerous social overtones, the León uprising appeared clearly political and economic in intent. León, from the lower reaches of the Venezuelan white elite, articulated his demands clearly, manipulated the Spanish government bureaucracy in Caracas skillfully to gain an official forum for his complaint, and achieved a detailed statement of provincial grievances against the company for a *cabildo abierto* in Caracas. To be sure, the crown could hardly tolerate the challenge to its authority represented by the León uprising, but, while upholding royal authority through the repression of revolt and punishment of participants, the Spanish authorities also listened carefully to the complaints from the most prosperous non-mining colony of the Spanish empire.

In the wake of the uprising, the crown dictated a series of reforms which, while confirming the Company's monopoly position, reduced its powers to the level of the Company's early years. In addition, a committee of local producers, Company agents, and the governor gained the authority to establish cacao prices. As a result of these improved conditions, cacao exports to Spain rose, and the province appeared well on the way to great prosperity. This prosperity did not seem to help the Company much, and its increasing financial difficulties tended to reduce its power and influence until by 1789 the Company lost its remaining monopoly privileges in the extension of Spanish free trade policies to Venezuelan ports.

Within Venezuelan historiography the assessment of the Caracas Company's activities in Venezuela generates considerable controversy. Some see the Company as a positive influence, bringing centralized economic direction to the fragmented local economies of the country. Others emphasize the destructive pricing, exploitative behavior, and exaggeration of monoculture agriculture as the negative features of the Company's regime. Both views are correct but incomplete. While there is little doubt that the Company paid less for cacao than other potential free market purchasers, and less than was paid in the protected Veracruz market, much of the profit from such transactions went into Company activities in Venezuela. The monopoly spent substantial sums developing port facilities, improving internal communications, and administering the Company bureaucracy. In addition, some of the profits from low prices in America amounted to a tax on local planters to support the Spanish imperial defense, for the Company on more than one occasion supplied ships and materiel for Spanish military campaigns. Venezuelan producers also subsidized the organization and consolidation of their country into a relatively coordinated economic unit centered in Caracas. The continuing coalescence of interest, influence, and control around Caracas, while regarded as a positive development by most Venezuelan historians, did not happen without cost. If the Venezuela of the 1760s was a more cohesive territorial unit with a better integrated economic network than it had been in the 1730s, much of the credit belonged to the Caracas Company.

But if the Company accomplished this, it must be recognized that it exacted a substantial price.

Because the Company had profit on its mind, and profit for investors in the Spanish Basque country, there should be no amazement that the balanced development of Venezuela's economy and the increased wealth of Venezuelan landowners and merchants carried a low priority in Company business. Leaving aside for the moment the question of the Company's competence and ability, we must see the Caracas Company from the imperial, the Basque, and the Venezuelan points of view. For the crown, the notion of a monopoly company must have had much appeal. Venezuela's growing importance as a profit center within the Spanish imperial system demanded more systematic attention. But the reorganization of Venezuela's economy would have been an expensive and complex undertaking, especially given the restraints of Spanish imperial law and tradition and the international complications of Spain's diplomatic troubles. The monopoly company, a mercantile device much in vogue at the time, offered the crown what appeared to be a cheap, efficient, and controllable way to tap the agricultural riches of Venezuela without the burden of new government bureaucracies. Furthermore, the Company would be required to pay now, and would absorb the costs of administration. Not the least of royal concerns, the Company would guarantee the steady supply of high-quality Venezuelan chocolate to the Spanish market. That the Company would also guarantee the integrity of Venezuela's north coast against pirates and smugglers was an additional advantage.

Had the Company's goals been in closer consonance with the imperial aims of the crown or, for that matter, with the local concerns of the Venezuelan elite, the result of this experiment in mercantile-capitalist monopoly would no doubt have been happier. But where the crown looked to the Company to carry out imperial duties in bringing Venezuela's prosperous economy more closely in harmony with the Spanish system, the Company saw its quasi-governmental obligations as expensive auxiliary services grudgingly provided in order to gain a commercial advantage. Thus the Company worked hard to convert Venezuela into an efficient cacao producer for the Spanish and world market. This perspective tended to minimize or ignore local interests and maximize short- to medium-term profit-making strategies. Where the crown might see coastal defense and regular supplies of cacao to Spain as the highest priorities, the Company would see these as distinctly secondary to the pursuit of efficient and cheap production of cacao for sale. Better, for example, to have some risk of coastal invasion and the possibility of interrupted supply to Spain than the expense of efficient coastal defense and the low profits of a conservative purchase and sales policy.

Both imperial and Company perspectives appeared seriously distorted to Venezuelans. The controversy over these differing perspectives provides an instructive glimpse of the tensions and diverging economic interests of Spain and America in the eighteenth century. Venezuela's history as an agricultural outpost of the Spanish empire prevented the development of powerful institutional links with Spain such as could be found in the *consulados* of Mexico or Lima or in the viceregal bureaucracies of those kingdoms. The growing tensions in the eighteenth century came from the first attempt of the Bourbon dynasty to bring Venezuela into closer harmony with the imperial system, an effort that almost succeeded in turning the country into a sophisticated Company store. But the strong resistance of Venezuela's prosperous planters and enterprising merchants, plus the burden of providing a surrogate imperial government, defeated the Company and encouraged the imposition of a different imperial mechanism on Venezuela. For the local economy, the Company's activities brought an improvement in the organization of commerce and a geographic expansion of agriculture, especially into the valley of Aragua. But the price was too high. The Company, in effect, required the abdication of the local elite and the subordination of local interests. Creole merchants had to give way to Company factors, Creole planters had to sell their crops at low Company prices, and Creole consumers had to buy at expensive Company stores. In the pursuit of economic gain, the Company behaved as if Venezuela was little more than a private farm, a place whose population had few major privileges, rights, or aspirations. Resistance to Company behavior was immediate and continuous, but formal resistance rare. A series of lower-class uprisings involving slaves and free blacks occurred in a number of prosperous coastal areas, disturbances directed at Company agents and apparently sometimes with Creole elite connivance. The Juan Francisco de León rebellion proved notable because of its mid-level white leadership and because it became transformed into a legal, notarized, and documented protest against the Company.

Venezuela, thanks to the Caracas Company, found itself even more dependent on one-crop agriculture, increasingly concentrated in Caracas, and much more integrated into Atlantic commerce. But the conflicts over the Company's role also demonstrated the existence of a self-conscious agricultural and commercial elite capable and determined to defend its interests. Speaking frequently through the Caracas *cabildo,* these notables prevented the transformation of Venezuela into a company store for the benefit of Spanish Basque investors. The significance of this for the future development of Venezuela's economy is difficult to determine, but the best guess may be that the Creole victory against the Caracas Company prepared Venezuela to become a company store for the benefit of the local elite and North Atlantic merchants in the succeeding century.

For all its importance, the Caracas Company was only the first in a series of eighteenth-century institutions in Venezuela whose cumulative effect would draw the country into a fragile interlocking network dominated by Caracas. This coalescence of the disparate provinces of Venezuela marks the coming of age, the maturity of the colony. Ironically, Venezuela matured so late that it enjoyed the status of sub-metropolitan capital for only a generation. Until 1808, few Venezuelans believed the future held much more than a gradual modification of the Spanish colonial system. This rather obvious fact helps explain why many of the controversies of the late eighteenth and the early nineteenth century fail to survive independence. Problems and solutions provoking intense controversy in 1800 within the context of the Spanish empire lost their urgency and their relevance by 1830 as Venezuela joined the North Atlantic commercial economy. Even so,

without the institutional and political development Spain provided
Venezuela in the last half-century of colonial rule, the country would
have been much less able to adapt to the requirements of the world
market. Because these colonial transformations came so late, Venezuela
experienced considerable difficulty managing its internal affairs in the
face of the pressures of that emerging Atlantic market economy.

Of all the reforms of the late eighteenth century, four institutional
innovations appear especially influential. In terms of Venezuela's economic development the creation of a *consulado,* or merchant-agricul-
turalist chamber of commerce, and the establishment of the intendency,
or royal fiscal and economic development agency, had the greatest
impact. Paralleling this arrangement in economic matters, the crown
established an *audiencia* in Venezuela, a royal court whose jurisdiction encompassed the whole country, thereby refocusing legal attention
from Santo Domingo or Bogotá to Caracas. Culminating this flurry of
activity, Spain created the captaincy general in Venezuela, an administrative and political jurisdiction consolidating the provinces of Tierra
Firme into one unit centered in Caracas.

The impetus for these reforms ranged from the fear of pirates and
foreign interlopers, through the need for more efficient and productive
management of colonial revenues, to the desire to rationalize the old
colonial administration to take account of the development of the
Americas since the 1600s. For Venezuela, these reforms achieved their
intent, and the eighteenth-century consolidation created a nation.

Briefly, the intendency, created in 1776, placed the six provinces of
Venezuela under one fiscal administrator resident in Caracas. This
official's mandate superseded in many respects the authority of a variety
of previous royal officials such as the provincial governors. The intendent's purview, while theoretically restricted to fiscal matters, actually
affected just about all government activity because the intendent's
acquiescence became necessary for any project of significance that required expenditures of royal funds or involved the production of government revenues. The Intendency of Venezuela brought together for
the first time the disparate provinces under one fiscal jurisdiction, but

because it did not include the administration of other aspects of colonial life it left the consolidation of Venezuela incomplete.

Perhaps more important in the process of integration, the Captaincy General of Venezuela brought the political and military authority of Venezuela together in a central office in Caracas. Established in 1777, about nine months after the intendency, the captaincy general represented one more attempt to resolve the centuries-old problem of Venezuela's defense coordination. By consolidating the provinces into one military district, the crown hoped to gain an efficient, strong bulwark against the increasingly threatening activities of Spain's enemies in the Caribbean. Presumably, the captaincy general would have the resources and revenue to manage its own defense without any need for royal support. This institution, more than the others, strongly influenced the political consolidation of Venezuela, bringing the lines of communication and administration together in Caracas.

But even this level of consolidation could not make Venezuela a major political unit while judicial matters had to leave the country for resolution in Santo Domingo or Bogotá. Recognizing this anomaly, the crown created the Audiencia of Caracas in 1786, a judicial-administrative jurisdiction that completed the major institutional development of colonial Venezuela. By having the *audiencia* in Caracas, Venezuela had achieved centralized control over fiscal, administrative, political, and legal affairs.

In the generation or so that Venezuela operated as a mature colonial center, these institutions contributed substantially to an increased prosperity and expanded level of activity. Cacao exports increased, and trade and commerce within Venezuela grew apace. The basic institutional structure of intendency, *audiencia,* and captaincy general acquired considerable stability, and a series of lesser institutions emerged to help complete the consolidation process. A *consulado* appeared in the 1780s after a long and vigorous campaign by the intendents. Unlike its Mexican or Peruvian counterparts, the Caracas Consulado included within its ranks both agriculturalists and merchants. The *consulado* had little time to make a major impact on Venezuela's econ-

omy, but its significance was more important in providing an institu-
tionalized system linking merchants and large planters from all over
Venezuela. The *consulado* maintained representatives in Venezuela's
principal ports of Cumaná, Barcelona, La Guaira, Puerto Cabello, and
Maracaibo, but its most important activities involved the Caracas-La
Guaira merchants.

Symbolizing Venezuela's newly acquired status, the Seminary of
Caracas was upgraded to a university in 1725, the Real y Pontífica
Universidad de Caracas. The Colegio de Abogados appeared in the
1780s as did a school of engineering and military science. Likewise,
the Church responded to the royal campaign for consolidation by
creating the Archbishopric of Venezuela late in this period in 1804,
an ecclesiastical reorganization that brought the Bishoprics of Mérida
de Maracaibo and Guayana-Cumaná under the direction of an archbishop in Caracas. The Church continued its program of secularizing
the missions, a campaign that tended to tie the remoter parishes of
Venezuela into the secular religious system based in Caracas.

While from a systemic perspective all this activity would appear as
rational and reasonable responses to Spain's imperial difficulties as well
as deserved recognition of Venezuela's expanded economic and agricultural prosperity, the reorganization and institutional innovations did
not please everyone in the country. Provinces such as Maracaibo,
Mérida, or Cumaná, which had long enjoyed considerable autonomy,
resisted the all-encompassing embrace of the new royal bureaucracy in
Caracas. The *caraqueños* also viewed this expanded bureaucracy with
some misgivings. In the old days, Caracas's local elite, working through
the agency of the *cabildo,* exercised an unusually wide range of attributes, including the ability to act in the place of the absent governor.
Beginning with the establishment of the Caracas Company in 1728,
the *cabildo* saw its universe gradually shrink, until by the end of the
century it found itself primarily concerned with the details of municipal administration. That these functions constituted the legitimate
mission of the *cabildo* provided small comfort to an elite used to controlling their province from the town council. Still, if the new system
reduced the prerogatives of the council, it also greatly expanded the

importance of Caracas within Venezuela and the empire. By placing the *audiencia*, intendency, and captaincy general in Caracas, the crown made the city a mature submetropolitan capital, and that status provided the city with great opportunities. The Caracas elite quickly moved to take as much advantage of these opportunities as possible, although the influx of Spanish appointees to the intendency, captaincy general, and *audiencia* limited their ability to gain control of the royal bureaucracy in Caracas. The *consulado*, however, was almost by definition a Creole institution and the Creole elite found it a useful forum for articulating their interests.

During the generation of reform and imperial reorganization, Venezuela appeared to be well on the way toward becoming a solid, institutionally connected administrative and political unit directed from a capital in Caracas. Had the Spanish empire survived another generation into the nineteenth century, the consolidation of Venezuela would no doubt have been completed. But the Napoleonic invasion of Spain in 1808 brought a crisis the empire could not survive, and Venezuela's fragile institutional network suffered drastic shocks from the imperial disintegration of the first decades of the nineteenth century.

Of all the consequences of the eighteenth-century reform, perhaps the most significant involved the dramatic expansion of the city of Caracas. The transformation of this town from a prosperous provincial capital to a mature colonial city, a central city for all of Venezuela, came as a product of a wide range of long-term developments, many of which matured in the late eighteenth century with the encouragement of Spanish royal policy. Caracas, for example, claimed special privileges in the seventeenth century when its *cabildo* reserved the right to serve as the provincial government in the absence of the governor; Caracas cacao planters and merchants presumed to speak for the provinces of Venezuela in commercial questions related to that profitable commodity; and the bishops for the province of Venezuela preferred to live in Caracas rather than the original diocesan seat in Coro from the late sixteenth century on. But these intimations of centrality did not make Caracas the central city for Venezuela. Until the late 1700s this prosperous and often arrogant urban cluster could claim no more than the position of largest and richest city in Venezuela. Cumaná, Barcelona, Coro, Maracaibo, and Mérida all operated more or less independently of Caracas. To be sure, Caracas's greater population, more advanced commercial network, and special royal privileges clearly made it the first city in the country, but these attributes, unsupported by substantial institutional structures, did not constitute the material of urban primacy. The eighteenth century brought Venezuela this institional support, providing Caracas with the apparatus required to function as a central city for that region.

It may help illustrate this process to summarize the remarkable series of events that combined to concentrate control of this institutional arrangement in the city. If a beginning point in the changing role can be identified, it would almost certainly be the establishment of the Caracas Company in 1728. The Company's activities proved controversial, and Venezuelan protests against its policies and practices began immediately and plagued the Company until its demise some half a century later. But the Caracas Company succeeded in concentrating the decision-making process in Caracas, at least insofar as the external trade of Venezuela was concerned. Important Company establishments existed in Puerto Cabello and at other sites, but Company officials made important decisions in Caracas or, of course, in Spain. By expanding the Company's role to include the entire Venezuelan coast, the crown effectively increased the intervention of Caracas-based authorities in the semiautonomous provinces of Cumaná and Maracaibo. Likewise, by attempting to control the cacao shipments to Veracruz as well as those to Spain, the Company increased the importance of *caraqueño* decisions for the trade from the west through Maracaibo. By intervening in the tobacco monopoly, especially in Barinas, the Company drew the interest of merchants and planters of the Andean and llanos regions into the growing web of the *caraqueño* bureaucracy. The Company, in the end, failed to create for itself a viable Caracas-based Venezuelan monopoly, but even in defeat and decline the institution helped accelerate the growth of the city. The Juan Francisco de León revolt, aimed at authorities in Caracas, proved to be the one protest against the Company to have a major impact, and this influence came from the mass of documentation generated by Caracas institutions such as the *cabildo* demonstrating the Company's deleterious effects on the province. It was as a result of *caraqueño* negotiation, intervention, or machination that the Company lost its special privileges.

Equally important, the consolidation of coastal defense and the refurbishing of Venezuelan fortifications accelerated the emergence of Caracas. The crown came to recognize the need for a connected and coordinated defense along the Venezuelan north coast, and it fixed on Caracas-La Guaira as the central port in this military design. The decision came not from any enthusiasm for the indifferent port of La Guaira, but from the recognition of Caracas's protected location behind the coastal mountains and of the town's relatively sophisticated government bureaucracy.

This notion, that Caracas should be the centerpiece for the north coast defense, may well have been the critical decision that created the central city. Once Caracas became manager of defense, the other governmental functions came quickly. If the coast from Maracaibo to Paria were to be controlled from Caracas, then the administrative, judicial, and fiscal organization that permitted Cumaná, Barcelona, and Guayana to the east and Mérida and Maracaibo to the west to operate independently of Caracas appeared irrational. The ministers of Charles III clearly sought to remedy that anomaly by the expansion of the *caraqueño* bureaucracy to encompass these peripheral areas. First came the intendency, then the captaincy general, the *audiencia,* the *consulado,* and finally the archbishopric.

Thanks to this activity, Caracas became the primate city for Venezuela. With a society richer and more complex than any other city in the country, with a range of institutional resources matched by none, and with a more skillful and specialized bureaucracy, Caracas came of age. As a measure of this primacy, it matters not a bit what index you choose, Caracas exceeded its closest Venezuelan competitor by orders of magnitude, not small margins. Its educational establishment, merchant community, urban structure, population growth, complement of artisans, and sophistication all grew beyond the ability of other places to compete. Moreover, as Caracas gained these advantages, its attractiveness to newcomers, for new enterprises and for government functions, increased. This self-reinforcing characteristic of central city growth proved irresistible from at least the 1770s, although some would give a date a century earlier.

But even though Caracas expanded into a complex primate city of some 40,000, the institutional network of which the city formed the center had less substance than might have been readily apparent. It should come as no surprise that, with only half a century, at most, of consolidation and reinforcement, and with many of the principal institutional connections formed within less than a generation, the network barely survived the wars of independence. The tensions and conflicts generated by the rapid expansion of Caracas's role in the colonial decades provided much of the disaggregating force of the independence and immediate postindependence period. Whatever the fragility and instability of these new, late colonial institutions, the basic relationships and resource patterns that had made Caracas the inevitable choice for primacy would continue into the nineteenth century, would be accelerated by the civil disorder of the first half century of republican rule, and would culminate in a Caracas even more in command of Venezuela by the end of the nineteenth century than it had been at the end of the eighteenth.

This mature colonial city of Caracas had little leisure to enjoy its newly acquired status, for hardly had it achieved maturity than it became the center of the civil war for Venezuelan independence. That continual movement for political emancipation from Spain seemed to obey a standard set of rules everywhere in Spanish America, rules less a function of the similarity of local conditions than a product of the uniformity of Spanish colonial laws and institutions. Because the independence movement in Latin America was but an auxiliary readjustment in the organization of Atlantic trade, it expressed itself in the language and style of international politics. Spanish-Americans spoke often and eloquently about the tyranny of Spain, the republican goals of their revolt, and the rights of man for which they fought. These leaders spoke of themselves as the champions of national movements, even in places that had neither the self-consciousness nor the substance

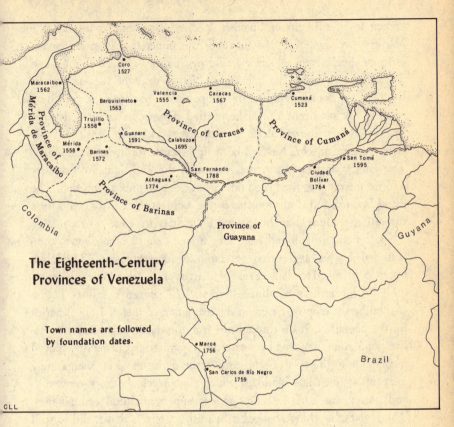

Coro
1527

Maracaibo
1562

Province of Mérida de Maracaibo

Barquisimeto
1563

Valencia
1555

Caracas
1567

Cumaná
1523

Trujillo
1558

Province of Caracas

Province of Cumaná

Guanare
1591

Mérida
1558

Calabozo
1695

Barinas
1572

San Fernando
1788

San Tomé
1595

Achaguas
1774

Ciudad Bolívar
1764

Colombia

Province of Barinas

Province of Guayana

Guyana

The Eighteenth-Century Provinces of Venezuela

Town names are followed by foundation dates.

Maroa
1756

San Carlos de Río Negro
1759

Brazil

CLL

of nationality. To say that Spanish America in 1810 had only the most rudimentary set of nation-states, territorial jurisdictions whose tenuous cohesion came more from Spain than America, is something of a commonplace. Our historiographic convention of referring to the colonial history of Venezuela when that entity barely existed in the late eighteenth century often leads us to project back on that colonial period, and onto the independence era as well, a conception of political identity invisible until much later in the nineteenth century. The Venezuelan experience illustrates the fragility of Spanish-American national identity as well as any other country on the continent.

In a formal sense, the chronology of this independence event is well known to all students of Spanish America. Beginning with the Napoleonic invasion of Spain in 1808, the imperial system suffered a series of shocks from which it would never recover. Even though it is difficult to exaggerate the importance of the events of 1808-10 for the future of the Spanish empire, the temptation to overlook the preceding years of Spain's decline must be resisted. From every perspective the Spanish system showed decay and disorder. The once sleek and efficient imperial mechanism had been in disrepair for at least a century. The energy and optimism that informed the mid-eighteenth-century reforms merely disguised for a time what was a terminal condition. The list of Spanish imperial problems in the eighteenth century could fill a substantial volume, but the general difficulties are easier to record.

Spain's empire suffered from an extreme case of obsolescence compounded by an aggravated condition of overextension. The obsolescence involved various levels of activity from the imperial design itself to the minutia of administration. The sixteenth-century notion of a bullionist empire, based on the extraction of metals from America for the benefit of Spain through the use of a docile and controlled native population managed by a carefully organized Spanish elite, proved inadequate to the task of adjusting to the demands of an increasingly mercantile, free-trade world in which the principal source of wealth and power was trade in manufactures and agricultural commodities. The remarkable thing about this Spanish empire is that it did so well for so long and that it adapted as much as it did before collapsing during independence.

The problems of empire began almost immediately after the conquest generations when the simplicity of sixteenth-century administrative structure gave way to the complexity of the seventeenth. Not only did the details of governance and control grow almost geometrically, but the simple economic system envisioned for America rapidly became much more complicated. America, it appeared, whether in viceregal Mexico or in outpost Venezuela, produced a wealth of its own in addition to metals and a few tropical export commodities. With the local production of wealth came the creation of substantial local interests with a perspective on the empire much different from the one seen from Madrid or Seville. Spain's sophisticated and capable bureau-cracy managed these conflicts and complications remarkably well, al-beit with declining vigor, until the end of the empire in 1810.

Because the bureaucracy proved to be Spain's greatest imperial con-tribution, it should be obvious that the failure of the empire came as much as anything from the gradual disintegration of that bureaucracy. To say this is not to deny the importance of Spain's international diffi-culties, the costly and exhausting wars that drained resources and at-tention away from the management of Spain's real source of wealth and power, and the debilitating peaces that gradually restricted and then reduced the scope and content of empire throughout the seven-teenth and eighteenth centuries. But even these international threats would have been tolerable had the imperial bureaucracy maintained some of its primitive energy and efficiency.

Unhappily for the empire, the elaborate civil service symbolized by its rule book, the *Recopilación de Leyes de Indias,* could not man-age the transition from a sixteenth- to an eighteenth-century world, even with substantial revisions and reforms. As in the case with every imperial organization, Spain's sought to fulfill the twin impera-tive of information and control. The design of the Spanish arrange-ment was ingenious, for it maximized information and control at the expense of efficiency. In the sixteenth century, when Spain's hu-man resources were limited and the details of empire relatively manage-able, the costs of this inefficiency could easily be borne. Without an expensive and complicated control mechanism, Spain could not have hoped to keep track of its representatives in America unless the mon-archs could establish a redundant information network. Because infor-mation collection was relatively cheap, the crown encouraged duplicate reporting from officials whose jurisdictions deliberately overlapped and conflicted. Although this system had guaranteed inefficiency built in, it also carried a self-correcting mechanism against gross abuses of power. Any significant deviation from royal policy would be reported by the official with the overlapping jurisdiction or by an aggrieved citizen. These reports, which were required and encouraged, would then lead to corrective measures; but if an official anticipated this sequence he would then be restrained from improper behavior in the first instance.

For such a system to work, every official, every individual, and every institution had to be in direct touch with the king, for if a hierarchy of communication existed, individuals would work to please the next echelon, not the king. Thus, in the Spanish system, the basic premise of preference within the empire specified that all patronage and preferment came from the king as a reward for service in his interest. Of course, much patronage in practice came from lower officials, but in most cases it came in the name of the king and required royal confirmation whenever the monarch changed. Within such a personalist arrangement, authority and legitimacy came from the royal connection, a symbolic juncture that tied the empire together.

This symbol of the crown's power to join carried over to the theoretical structure of Spanish and American regions as well. The empire, so the legal writ proclaimed, consisted of a conglomerate of kingdoms, including the American ones, united through the person of the Spanish monarch and possessing equivalent rights and status within the polity. Again in theory, the empire could be thought of as a cluster of lines of authority, loyalty, patronage, justice, and reward converging from every level of society on the king. Overlaying this primary pattern, a web of interlocking relationships connected the several parts, jurisdictions, and corporate entities, connections that, while they governed the daily interaction of individuals and made the king's business possible, never superseded the primary relationship represented by the lines of authority and responsibility from the monarch to each individual.

For its time, this was a remarkably flexible and sophisticated system of imperial management, one not equalled again until nineteenth- and twentieth-century British, French, and American civil services. But for all its flexibility and adaptability, the system had some serious flaws. As the empire grew larger and more complex, the ability of the primary, direct connection with the king to function became seriously compromised. The empire was too big and too diverse for most individuals or institutions to gain effective direct access to the king or even to know someone who had achieved direct access. As a result, a second network of interlocking jurisdictions came to be the principal arbiter of all things, but always in the name of the king. The system for gathering information about the empire worked so well that Spanish officials and the king's councilors could not even begin to assimilate or respond to all of it.

This situation worsened at the end of the seventeenth century, and the Bourbon monarchs came to Spain resolved to improve Spanish administration. Finding the existing system beyond their ability and resources to control or reform, they overlaid a third network of officials and relationships on the original Hapsburg arrangements. While imaginative and reasonably efficient, this new system simply covered up the weaknesses of the traditional system without replacing the traditional lines of authority and responsibility. These Bourbon reforms reduced the status and power of individuals and institutions from the traditional network without replacing them or altering their perception of their roles. Perhaps given another generation the Bourbon system might have supplanted the traditional network, but the Napoleonic invasion of Spain, the capture of the royal family (especially Charles IV and Ferdinand VII), and the installation of Joseph Bonaparte on the throne of Spain provided more of a shock than the system could absorb. In the ensuing guerrilla war in Spain against the French intruders, the American connection became frayed and then broken. Preoccupied by its campaign to rid the peninsula of the French and by its internal political turmoil over the rights and limitations of the monarchy, Spain never managed to bring the independence-minded Spanish-Americans back under control, and as a result, lost most of its American empire.

THE COLLAPSE OF THE COLONIAL ORDER

The epic struggle of Spanish-American independence has long fascinated historians. Not only do all of us enjoy a dramatic, decisive story filled with heroism, intrigue, intellectual excitement, and passion, but the striking surface similarity between Anglo-American and Spanish-

American independence invites continental comparisons and encourages hemispheric solidarity. Scholars from North and South America write enthusiastic comparisons of Simón Bolívar and George Washington; they note the structural similarities between formal constitutions and governments in the Americas; and they analyze the intellectual sources of both revolutions. Well might they do so, for Anglo- and Spanish-American independence did indeed form coordinate parts of the same complex international readjustment in the Western world, a reorganization of the Atlantic system that would recognize British, German, French, and later United States ascendancy in managing the affairs of the West.

Because of the temptation to include Spanish America's revolution in the same category as Anglo-America's, historians have often felt obliged to explain why the modern histories of these regions have diverged so dramatically, with the United States becoming the preeminent, technologically advanced power of our times and Spanish America acquiring the characteristics of underdevelopment. Of course, the explanation based on the notion of divergence since independence misses the point. For all the coincidental, superficial similarities of their independence movements, Spanish America and Anglo-America had been on divergent historical tracks since the seventeenth century at least. The differing developments of these regions should not come as any surprise, given their differing institutional traditions and economic structures.

The independence movement provides, in addition, such a convenient reference point for Spanish-American history that the majority of our texts and courses break the history of the region into two sections, colonial and modern, with the 1810-20 decade as the transition period. This organization is neat, practical, and seriously misleading, for it implies radical and fundamental changes in 1810, suggests a discontinuity in regional history, and focuses atttention on the apparent changes rather than on the enduring structures.

These remarks are not to suggest that Spanish America in 1830 had experienced little change nor to imply that the independence movement left those societies unscathed. Not at all. Independence does, of course, represent a major shift in Spanish-American history, but beneath the apparently cataclysmic events ran a series of social, intellectual, and economic continuities barely interrupted in the course of the independence generation. The important lesson of independence is not that Spanish America accomplished remarkable changes but that the region adjusted to changes in world political and economic alignments with so little need to change its own basic structure.

Venezuela is in many ways an ideal case study in exploring this notion of continuity through independence, and in analyzing the integration of Spanish America into the North Atlantic system. If great changes were to have come to Spanish America in the upheaval of independence they should have happened in the land of Bolívar, where institutions were recently formed and relatively weak, where the power and wealth of the local aristocracy appeared much less than in viceregal capitals, where the racial tensions of a *pardo* society appeared very high, and where the disorder and destruction of a decade of civil war provided an excellent opportunity for radical change. That republican Venezuela managed to preserve intact many colonial forms and most colonial structures is eloquent testimony to the strength of the Spanish-American social and economic system, one carefully created and adjusted to local requirements for three hundred years. What follows, then, is an exploration of the details of the independence decade in search of the elements that permitted such violence and destruction without allowing major social and economic changes.

The initiation of this Spanish-American independence movement, as happened with every other major Venezuelan historical event, came from the outside, in this instance from Spain and France. For all of the discontents, inefficiencies, and annoyances of the Spanish empire, few Venezuelans saw recourse to rebellion as a useful tactic to improve their lot. Such activity might be possible for a slave, but the elite and near elite preferred less drastic and less risky alternatives. Even the uprising of Juan Francisco de León, the only serious, elite-supported breach of peace, was actually less of a rebellion than an attention-getting device to impress on the king and his advisers the seriousness of Venezuelan complaints against the Caracas Company. Likewise, the

Venezuelan response to the conspiracy of Gual y España in the late eighteenth century, when the liberal propaganda of Picornell and his confederates started a minor uprising in Venezuela, demonstrated little enthusiasm for political innovations. Even that professional revolutionary, Francisco Miranda, could find no one interested in his liberating plans as late as 1806, when his expedition to the Venezuelan coast met with hostility and resistance rather than a general uprising.

Such reluctance to participate in these adventures is certainly understandable. Elite Venezuelans, those of the upper reaches of society or attached in some way to the elite, could hardly have wanted to plunge into rebellion and disorder on the thin pretext of a tract on the rights of man. Liberty is a relative thing. No one better understood that universal truth than Venezuelan landlords, slaveholders, and plantation managers. Disorder, the symptom of a malfunctioning society, implied slave and *pardo* uprisings, possibility of race war, destruction of crops, and the chance of another Haitian catastrophe with the elimination of the white ruling class. Only a rare oligarch would risk such consequences for the indeterminate benefits of a politically independent existence. Of course the Creole elite wanted freer trade, fewer peninsular officials, and better commercial ties with England. But no reasonable man would gamble for those gains against the possible loss of a social and economic system. The stakes were too high and the rules of the game much too vague to permit a clear calculation of the odds.

Between 1808 and 1810 events in Europe reduced the apparent odds and seemed to clarify the rules of the game to such an extent that the Creole elite could be persuaded to play. But even so, they probably had no idea that this independence would cost them so dear. Had they guessed, Bolívar would never have had the chance to create his continental dream in the Americas.

The sequence of events leading to Spanish-American declarations of independence is well known. Although the monarchy under the inept rule of Charles IV suffered from a lack of popular support, the misrule of the royal favorite Juan Manuel Godoy, the intrigues of the heir apparent Ferdinand, as well as a host of economic and diplomatic problems, it was not true, as Napoleon supposed, that Spain would welcome French rule, however competent. Charles, following the advice of Godoy, agreed in 1808 to permit French troops to cross Spanish soil en route to conquer Portugal. Napoleon took the invitation as an excuse to begin the invasion and occupation of Spain. Terrified, the royal family fled south, presumably with the notion of embarking for America. The family feud between Charles and his son, Ferdinand, became worse, and in Aranjuez, Ferdinand stirred up a popular mob, forcing his father to abdicate in his behalf. Charles promptly repented his action and tried to renounce the abdication. Ferdinand refused to agree, and Napoleon offered to help resolve the issue if the two principals would come visit him in Bayonne, France. Fearful of the advancing French troops and desperate to resolve the dynastic quarrel, the royal family left Spain for France and became Napoleon's captives. The Corsican's solution to the Spanish dynastic problem was, if unscrupulous, certainly innovative. He planted Joseph Napoleon on the Spanish throne and tried to keep him there with French troops.

This arrangement produced a civil uprising in Spain against the French invaders and the illegitimate king, and the Spanish patriots rallied to the banner of Ferdinand VII, the captive king. Without royal direction, and occupied by French troops, the country could hardly function normally, and, to supplant the captive bureaucracy, juntas or revolutionary committees appeared throughout Spain. These quasi-popular groups carried on the resistance to French occupation and, wherever possible, constituted the local, legitimate government. The Junta Central in Seville, which later moved to greater safety in Cádiz, attempted to rule Spain's empire in the absence of the king, and, when it became a regency, tried to assert its authority over the Americas and prepare for a general Spanish Cortes that would have American representation.

By 1810 the Spanish situation appeared bleak. Napoleon had control of most of the important places on the peninsula; the Junta Central, now converted into a regency, had only the immediate environs of Cádiz under its authority; and the remaining pockets of popular resistance must have appeared relatively minor to the French. The new king, José I, had begun sending his emissaries throughout America requesting vows of allegiance to the new ruler and the acceptance of francophile officials. But Napoleon greatly underestimated Spanish popular resistance to the French usurper, and the war of guerrillas on the peninsula prevented the consolidation of French rule and eventually forced the retreat of French troops required elsewhere on the Continent. The return of Ferdinand VII in 1814 was greeted with much popular rejoicing, but soon he demonstrated an absolutist temperament incompatible with the current movement for Spanish liberal reform. Ferdinand's constant clashes with his opponents, his attempt to abrogate the liberal Spanish Constitution of 1812, and the intrigues that accompanied this activity distracted the monarch from the need to bring America back into the empire. Troops that should have gone to America to suppress rebellions stayed in Spain to participate in domestic political action. By the time Spain had succeeded in sorting itself out in 1820, America had ceased to be part of the Spanish empire.

Throughout America the events in Spain had dramatic impact. The form of American response to these developments depended to a large extent on the strength of local imperial institutions. Where these colonial structures were old, the viceregal linkages strong, and institutional organization well developed, the imperial system survived the shocking news without major change. But where the structures of imperial control were new and weak, imperial linkages fragile, and where local interests had less substantial ties with their Spanish counterparts, the peninsular chaos produced immediate and often drastic action. Venezuela belonged to this latter category.

Although we like to speak of the events in Venezuela between 1808 and 1823 as the independence movement, the nomenclature implies a unity of purpose or a coherence of events that reflects historical hindsight more than contemporary experience. Venezuelans who participated in the early days of intellectual euphoria before the realities of civil war became apparent had little reason to suspect the magnitude of the adventure they had begun. Not the most experienced revolutionary, such as Francisco Miranda, or the most ambitious youthful firebrand, such as Simón Bolívar, anticipated the course of Venezuelan independence. Because the nature and costs of independence came as a surprise to the participants, it is possible to chart their changing perceptions of the Venezuelan experience through the rather clearly defined stages of the independence wars.

In broad terms, four styles of conflict characterized the independence era in Venezuela. Each had a chronological focus, a geographical trajectory, and an intellectual construct. Without some attention to these differing styles, the sequence of battles, invasions, counterrevolutions, reprisals, constitutions, and propaganda campaigns appears to be a chaotic manifestation of Creole bickering, an almost irrational struggle over the spoils of war. Although there was indeed a terrific struggle over these spoils, it was neither irrational nor particularly chaotic.

In general terms, the Venezuelan independence movement began with an elite rebellion, a species of elegant, intellectualized protest expected to produce modest changes in local conditions and to result in the substitution of *caraqueño* control for Spanish peninsular authority. After the failure of this style in the collapse of the First Republic in 1812, the notion of the heroic, lightning strike at Caracas became the organizing principle. Whether from the Caribbean or Colombia, the patriots' effort to implement this style proved succeesful only as long as the army stayed on the march. When Caracas fell to royalist forces for the second time in 1814, the style of combat changed again. This third, and decisive, style involved the thorough reconquest of Venezuela from a secure base on the Orinoco and the creation of a liberated resource base in Colombia. This style also called for the establishment of rudimentary institutions, the elaboration of networks of personalist alliances, and the conscious management of Venezuela's critical racial and social problems. Although this style succeeded in carrying the independence to its formal conclusion in 1823, it left the region unable to function effectively and forced a change to the fourth and last style of independence conflict, the caudillesque nationalism of the early republican era.

The continental vision that supported the reconquest style of 1814-23 failed to see the power of local elites who had little interest in paying further for the realization of any such chimera as a united

Spanish America. Instead, Venezuela, like other Spanish-American regions, spent some seven or eight years sorting out its caudillos, establishing the limits of its territory, and reaffirming the primacy of its traditional central city. The independence wars did not really end until Venezuela seceded from Colombia and claimed its political identity in 1830.

The first of these styles began, as happened throughout Spanish America, with the arrival of news about the events in Spain in 1808. The *mantuano,* or elite, rebellion in Caracas started innocently enough. In May 1808 the Caracas Cabildo recognized Ferdinand VII as the new Spanish monarch. But two months later, in July, the official news that Joseph I had taken the Spanish throne arrived. This announcement from an official French emissary came as no great surprise, for Caracas, like other Spanish-American capitals, had excellent communications with the peninsula. But the announcement, which the ruling captain general, Juan de Casas, tried to suppress, provided the Caracas Creole elite with an excuse to stir up a mob that forced the expulsion of the French emissary and made the captain general call the *cabildo* and *audiencia* into special session to consider the problem. Both of these institutions rejected Joseph I and swore allegiance to Ferdinand VII. None of these actions took place in an atmosphere of calm deliberation. Pro-independence, anti-French, pro-Ferdinand propaganda spread widely among the urban elite. Anyone with relatives or business associates in Spain or Europe must have received numerous letters about the Spanish situation; Francisco Miranda, for example, wrote often from Caracas to friends and acquaintances discussing the international situation.

Those within the *mantuano* group with visions of an independent Venezuela, a minority at this time no doubt, saw these weeks in early July as an excellent opportunity to further their cause, for the governor and captain general, Juan de Casas, had made no secret of his francophile sympathies. De Casas, whose political skills proved inadequate to manage this volatile environment, made the serious mistake of asking the *cabildo* members if he should create a Junta Conservadora de los Derechos de Fernando VII on the Spanish model. They, of course, quickly agreed. De Casas had second thoughts about the wisdom of this move and tried to retract his request. By November 1808 the *mantuanos,* emboldened by the quasi-legal agreement of the *cabildo* to the notion of a junta, called on the governor to establish it in a proclamation carrying forty-five signatures. The thoroughly elitist nature of these early *mantuano* maneuvers guaranteed that they would not succeed, and de Cassas, with the support of the *pardos,* artisans, and small tradesman, who had little reason to follow the elite who blocked their advencement in *caraqueño* society, put the signers under house arrest.

By mid-May 1809 Caracas received a new captain general, Vicente Emparán, more resolute and capable than his predecessor. Rumor, news, and speculative commentary kept the street corners, plazas, and social events of Caracas lively. Indication of hot-headed conspiracies or at least enthusiastic talk about conspiracies became frequent. But the Caracas elite would not reach any consensus leading to action until events in Spain forced a decision. In the first half of 1810, Spanish events encouraged these cautious rebels to act. Early that year, the Spanish Junta Central moved to Cádiz to escape the advancing armies of Napoleon, and in January it replaced itself with a regency, an institutional transformation designed to prepare for a national Cortes in which all Spanish provinces including those in America were to have representation. This move, principally an indication of Spanish liberal ascendance in Cádiz, brought considerable resistance in both Spain and America where liberal ideas had less enthusiastic followings. In Caracas, the governor continued to watch for conspiracies and, in fact, discovered another one at the beginning of April which forced him to send the guilty or suspect individuals out of Caracas.

All these activities, conspiracies, and discussions created an atmosphere of instability and irregularity, a sense of special times and special circumstances that made special actions possible. On April 19, 1810, the Cabildo of Caracas called itself into session as a *cabildo abierto.* Symbolically, this marked the beginning of Venezuela's independence movement, for a *cabildo abierto* could not, in theory, be called unless the governor did so, and Emparán had not done so. The *cabildo,* composed of the normally appointed members plus other representatives from the city, requested Emparán's attendance. He came, but a carefully prepared popular mob outside and inside the *cabildo* demonstrated for his ouster. Emparán, with no stomach for a fight, quit. This, of course, left the Spanish government of Venezuela leaderless and increased the *cabildo*'s claim to represent Spain's interests in Venezuela because of the long tradition of the *cabildo* governing the country in the absence of royal officials. To be sure, this tradition predated the establishment of the captaincy general, *audiencia*, and intendency, and there were several royal appointees in Caracas with excellent claims to represent the crown's interests. But of course the point of the exercise was to reclaim for the local elite their ascendance in Venezuelan affairs which had been so much reduced by the Bourbon administrative and fiscal reforms of the eighteenth century.

The *cabildo*, with the addition of seven self-appointed representatives of the clergy, the people, and the *pardos*, reconstituted itself as a Junta Conservadora de los Derechos de Fernando VII and, following the example of other Spanish juntas, refused to recognize the legitimacy of the Cádiz Regency and declared their loyalty only to the captive Ferdinand. As a political strategy, this maneuver, followed everywhere in America with minor variations, had striking advantages. It kept Venezuela's elite fully loyal to the king, it preserved the connection to the imperial system, it tampered not at all with any basic element of the country's social arrangements, and it guaranteed freedom of action until the monarch should return and be free to command the obedience of his loyal subjects. Although the evidence is incomplete, it also appears that the Caracas elite managed to gain the support or at least the indifference of the city's non-elite, for there was no lower-class movement in support of the governor, possibly because he quit so fast or because there were no available leaders to mobilize popular support for the established authorities, while there were several capable demagogues working on behalf of the *cabildo* and junta.

In any event, April 19, 1810, began Venezuela's existence as an independent political entity. Most of the participants would not have seen things in quite such clear-cut terms, but everything that happened after April 19 involved the effort of royalists to regain their control of Venezuela.

During the early days of junta government, the group worked to consolidate its position and hold off the radicals anxious for a complete break with Spain. In those first weeks the junta voted to compensate the military officers who had cooperated with the changes, and it appointed the Count of Tovar as Mariscal de Campo in charge of the local troops. The junta then turned to the organization of commerce, quickly eliminating a variety of sales taxes and reducing others while reforming the customs tariffs. Indian tribute was abolished and, rather late in this series of reforms, the junta declared the moribund slave trade to Venezuela over. The Patriotic Society for Agriculture and Commerce was created and rapidly collected the radical patriots to become a powerful lobby for political independence. Although technically the junta only existed to preserve the province for Ferdinand VII, these *caraqueños* rapidly claimed the jurisdiction and authority of a sovereign state. As they saw the situation, their principal and most urgent political task required the support of the other prominent cities of Venezuela and the recognition of their legitimacy by European powers, especially England. Representatives from the junta traveled to Curaçao, the United States, England, and New Granada with local messengers sent to the other Venezuelan provinces.

To the chagrin of the Caracas junta, neither foreigners nor locals seemed much impressed by the junta's claim to speak for Venezuela. In England, the messengers, who included Andrés Bello and Simón Bolívar, found the British government sympathetic, understanding, hospitable, but unwilling to recognize what could be regarded as an insurrectionary government, especially since Spain and England were, for once, united against the common Napoleonic enemy. Bolívar, twenty-three years old at the time, soon grew impatient and returned to Caracas in late 1810. He was soon followed by Francisco Miranda in December 1810.

The *caraqueños,* expecting their leadership in Venezuelan affairs to be recognized, found that many provincials failed to see anything special justifying that city's leadership. Of the nine principal Venezuelan cities, three refused to support the notion of juntas. Guayana, sparsely populated and with only the most tenuous connections with Caracas, chose to recognize the Spanish regency in Cádiz. Maracaibo, whose merchants had long competed for the Mexican chocolate trade and other commercial advantages with Caracas and whose leaders saw little reason to follow their *caraqueño* adversaries, firmly opposed the junta and remained staunchly loyal to Spain. Coro, the site of Venezuela's first Spanish government in the sixteenth century, proved especially hostile to Caracas's pretensions to leadership. If there was to be a coordinating junta for Venezuela, they responded, logic demanded that it be located in the oldest administrative city in the region, Coro. Refusing Caracas's offer of cooperation, Coro's leaders, like their counterparts in Maracaibo, promptly jailed the *caraqueño* envoy. Coro, in addition to the tradition of colonial pre-eminence, had a long history of social unrest and slave and *pardo* revolts, which in view of the Haitian experience made the Coro elite reluctant to become involved in anything disruptive of traditional order. Symbolically, these rejections of Caracas's authority serve as striking examples of Venezuela's fragile institutional network, the creation of only a couple of generations' work in the late eighteenth century.

Even without complete agreement, Caracas went to the next step in the process of separating from Spain: the junta called for a congress to discuss the situation and prepare for the future. As the delegates met in June 1811, radical, pro-independence propaganda orchestrated by the Patriotic Society increased. Miranda, in Caracas in time to get elected to the congress, provided a romantic and famous spokesman for independence, although the best of the *caraqueño* elite remembered him and his family as social upstarts of little consequence in elegant society. The congress debated at great length the wisdom of remaining loyal to Ferdinand VII and the practicality of declaring Venezuela's independence. With some help from a vociferous popular demonstration, the congress finally agreed to independence on July 5, 1811, a declaration lacking the signatures of representatives from Coro, Maracaibo, and Guayana. Nor did the remaining provinces represent a united front. Sentiment in Valencia, for example, ran strongly in favor of the king, and a serious uprising in July and August 1811 defeated the Marquis del Toro, whose troops required Miranda's seasoned military leadership to suppress the revolt. Yet with all these complications, the congress stuck to business and drafted a constitution that in form resembled closely the United States document. Unexceptional in design, the constitution preserved the privileges of the elite, their control of government and society, and proscribed only the already extinguished slave trade and the Spanish racial nomenclature and race laws while leaving slavery, the significant social institution, intact.

This December 21 constitution marked the official beginning of Venezuela's First Republic, or as Venezuelan historians have called it, La Patria Boba. The Republic would enjoy its newfound constitution in peace for only a few days before serious resistance to the patriot cause emerged in a wide range of places. The most serious threat came from Coro in early March, when the Spanish captain, Domingo Monteverde, and 230 seasoned royalist troops began the reconquest of Caracas for the king.

From practically any perspective the patriot effort in 1812 has to be considered a disaster. Not only did the patriots have to fight the loyal troops of the king supplemented by the majority of Venezuelans, but they also had to do so without the effective support of their own fledgling government. Nothing demonstrates as well the absolute inexperience of Venezuela's patriot politicians than the activities of the First Republic. While it is possible to understand why the *caraqueño* elite might have underestimated the complexity of civil government, especially in time of war, their complete misjudgment of their compatriots' political attitudes requires some explanation.

Statecraft, authority, legitimacy, and nationality are phenomena of considerable complexity, but, unless a national government and a people have at least a working consensus about these things, government becomes difficult if not impossible. The great error of the Venezuelan First Republic lay in its leaders' oversimplification of these attributes of the modern state. For example, the *caraqueño* patriots evidently believed that their authority to govern and the legitimacy of that government could be established by the stroke of a pen. What they failed to appreciate was that the authority of the officials and institutions housed in the city came not from any general Venezuelan acknowledgment of *caraqueño* superiority but from the recognition of

Spain's right to designate Caracas as chief city for the region. Caracas governed Venezuela by virtue of peninsular authority; its legitimacy came from Spain, and its authority derived from the Spanish monarch. If the independence movement and the troubles of the Spanish monarchy released Venezuelans from the bonds of imperial authority, this for many could include any obligation to recognize *caraqueño* supremacy. Freed from Spanish control, each locality of consequence in Venezuela believed itself fully capable of chosing its own destiny, and few local elites thought themselves less qualified than the haughty *caraqueños*.

Given this situation, the failure of the Caracas-based First Republic to gain the support of the rest of Venezuela's major cities is easier to understand. The need to send troops to subdue Valencia, Coro, Maracaibo, and Guayana should have made the leaders of the infant republic, La Patria Boba of Venezuelan historiography, realize the flaws in their national design, but because of their inexperience in statecraft these leaders found themselves helpless to salvage anything out of the first republican effort.

Apparently Venezuela's first republican statesmen believed statecraft to be a relatively simply extension of administration. Few *caraqueño* leaders thought themselves incapable of managing national affairs, believing that these could be seen as Caracas's business writ large. With a limited understanding of the interrelationship of legitimacy, authority, and statecraft, they blithely proceeded to create a completely impractical and unworkable institutional structure. In a region controlled for three centuries by the authority of an imperial monarch, these patriot visionaries tried to govern with a weak deliberative assembly. In a country where power and authority had most often been exercised by strong individuals—governors, captains general, intendents—the First Republic proposed a plural executive with rotating authority and restricted powers. In a country with a long tradition of tax evasion and smuggling, the First Republic expected civic virtue and voluntary compliance with the laws. The difficulties of this government stemmed from the inability to see the difference between the management of personal or municipal affairs and the management of national affairs. The state invented for the first Republic was an institutional structure without foundations in Venezuela's past or its reality. This government showed no skill in reconciling conflicting interests, and the leaders paid practically no attention to the problem of popular support.

In this sense the First Republic represents a peculiarly *caraqueño* creation, one that assumed the existence of nationalism. Evidently, these naïve republicans thought that a declaration of nationality was equivalent to the existence of national sentiment, and they further assumed that what Caracas saw as the basis of national consolidation would be acceptable to all Venezuelans. While this notion rapidly disappeared in the royalist counterrevolution in 1812, it revealed much about the perspectives of these *caraqueño* republicans. Because their experience of Venezuela came primarily from their role as submetropolitan intermediaries between the metropolis and the Venezuelan hinterland, the *caraqueños* saw their country in terms of its interactions with the Iberian empire through Caracas. This flow of information, products, legal activity, and people focused always by the Spanish imperial structure led the *caraqueños* to believe that Venezuela naturally focused through the lens of Caracas. It came as quite a shock to discover that, once the imperial orientation ceased, Venezuela scattered its light in all directions through Coro, Bogotá, Maracaibo, Cumaná, and Angostura. Nationality in the provinces of Venezuela, if it existed at all, was not Venezuelan but Spanish. The symbols of authority and legitimacy of this nation were king, royal officials, and the Church, not the *cabildo* or the notables of Caracas.

Although the short tenure of the First Republic hardly appears to warrant much notice, its importance is greater than its duration, for practically every problem encountered by the First Republic had to be resolved before Venezuela emerged triumphant in 1830. Not until the new leaders of the independence movement gained experience and perspective could they construct the nation envisioned in 1811 as the Republic of Venezuela.

The 1812 structure, however, had a very short life span. Domingo Monteverde's march to Caracas was a triumphal procession from Coro to the capital city. The First Republic vacillated, quarreled, and finally, too late, awarded Francisco Miranda the dictatorship. But that aging, elegant, intellectual revolutionary had none of the qualities necessary to save the day. As one long absent from Venezuela before independence, his hauteur and vast European experience made him unsuitable for the irregular warfare required to defend the Republic. Miranda tried. He declared martial law; he attempted to enlist the slaves; he hoped to defend Valencia, and thereby the capital, successfully. But the principal port of Puerto Cabello, in the hands of Simón Bolívar, fell to the royalists, and on July 25, 1812, Miranda surrendered his army to Monteverde. Miranda prepared to escape from Venezuela; however, the patriots captured him and turned him over to Monteverde. Bolívar, thanks to the intervention of a family friend, gained a passport out of the country. The rest of the patriots dispersed, were caught, or fled to the Caribbean. And that ended the First Republic.

In the years after 1812 the movement for independence began to change character. If the first phase of independence had been characterized by *caraqueño* elitism and Europeanized parliamentarianism, the second stage emphasized rapid military campaigns from secure bases at the periphery of Venezuela, campaigns aimed at the capture of Caracas. Furthermore, this second stage began the theme of regionalist caudillo leadership with the emergence of a strong and capable cadre of patriot chieftains on the eastern coast and plains of Venezuela. Through the battles of this period Simón Bolívar achieved a considerable measure of control over the independence process, but his leadership had by no means become pre-eminent. Finally, the campaigns of 1812-14 brought a wide range of social problems into the independence movement as a process of popularization of the war occurred.

While the details of the many military actions of those years are complex and confusing, the geographic dimension of the conflict became established in a pattern that would prevail for the rest of the war. All the participants in the independence movement recognized that Venezuela would never be free of Spanish control until the city of Caracas came under patriot command. This basic geopolitical notion dominated the strategic and tactical thought of the principal contenders throughout the conflict and underscored the primacy of that city in the Spanish imperial design for Venezuela. Even the partisans of regionalist interest, whether in the east in Cumaná or Barcelona or in the west in Coro or Barquisimeto, saw the necessity of a patriot-controlled Caracas. But if the capital city provided the goal for patriots and royalists alike, the decisive battles of the war occurred elsewhere. Perhaps the most significant development of the period following the First Republic came with the emergence of the popular forces of the plains, the *llaneros,* whose mobile cavalry and rough enthusiasm for a fight made them the crucial military element in the wars. Their decisive participation in the royalist campaigns of 1813 and 1814, especially under the command of José Tomás Boves, transformed the elitist *coup d'état* of April 19, 1810, into a wide-ranging civil war.

Because these people left few records of their thoughts about this independence conflict, their state of mind can only be approached through their behavior. If a leader like Bolívar or José Antonio Páez or Santiago Mariño fought in the wars to preserve or enhance their control of Venezuela's destiny and did so with a sophisticated command of European and American politics, the *llanero* fought for much more concrete and immediate goals. Clearly the abstractions of political independence can have had little influence on these people whose horizons were limited to the Venezuelan plains and whose contacts with the larger world came in villages and hamlets of two thousand souls or less. Instead, this nomadic community tended to follow the leadership of that individual with the greatest personal authority. Once the formal authority and traditional patterns of obedience and control came apart in the debacle of the First Republic, the *llanero* turned to the best among his peers or his superiors for guidance. Those local individuals, whose racial, social, intellectual, and especially physical gifts exceeded the norm, became the leaders of informal personal armies. This is not to suggest some democratization of the llanos, for the leaders in most cases were individuals with connections to the Venezuelan white elite. While in Caracas such people might not qualify for polite society, in the less sophisticated llanos their white color, their above-average education, and their greater understanding of the larger events within which *llanero* campaigns took place gave them the possibility of leadership. What made that possibility actuality were physical ability and opportunity, and the *llaneros* seemed equally content to follow their leaders in defense of the king or on behalf of independence.

Within a community proud of its horsemanship, endurance, plains-craft, and personal bravery, no city sophisticate, however clever, could hope to command. The leaders had to be as rough, brave, ruthless, and capable as the followers. Race, class, education, and intelligence might earn a chance at leadership, but the experience and ability to best the *llanero* at his games and compete on his terms proved crucial. For that reason the two pre-eminent *llanero* leaders, José Tomás Boves and José Antonio Páez, were transition figures. Both exiled from the mainline urban society for illegal activities, these members of the marginal white class had the education and intelligence for leadership, and their experience as outcasts in the llanos before the war had made them capable participants in the *llanero* community's life style. Having the skills and perspectives of both the small world of the nomadic *llanero* and the larger world of Venezuela and the Spanish empire, these popular caudillos mobilized their *llaneros* for the fight.

Understanding the origins of *llanero* leadership helps explain the behavior of the *llanero* armies of independence. Individual plainsmen probably followed their caudillos more for the immediate satisfaction of warfare than for any abstract political goals. The *llaneros* rode into battle because they expected to gain from the spoils of war, because the caudillo led them there, and because the alternatives were less attractive. Many contemporary observers and subsequent historians have remarked on the destructive character of the *llanero* campaigns, the propensity to sack and pillage, and the relative indifference to death and destruction. Although the *llanero* armies were nowhere near the bloodthirsty menace envisioned by the panicky urban white elite, they certainly did spread more than their share of death and destruction across the face of Venezuela.

To understand this behavior, we must see the *llanero* in terms of practical alternatives. The question is not what the plainsmen should have done but what they could have done. For example, a *llanero* cowboy faced with the disruption of authority caused by the independence and the First Republic could hardly have moved into a city and taken up a peaceful life. With no urban skills, what was such a man to do but continue in the llanos? Royalists and patriots alike called on these horsemen to come to the aid of their cause, and the *llanero* leaders mobilized their men to comply, but there was no paymaster, quartermaster, or supply train. The armies lived off the land and received their pay from the property confiscated in the course of battle. With no alternatives, the informal and frequently ruthless exploitation of urban centers became the wartime tax system. If royalist and republican causes required *llanero* armies, and if pay and subsistence could not be provided, then how else were these soldiers to survive if not through plunder? Further, in a community where physical prowess and violent combat determined status, few *llanero* commanders could afford to appear soft or to sacrifice the welfare of their followers for the convenience and safety of townspeople.

With the involvement of the *llaneros* and the similar involvement of slaves and *pardos* from the coastal and central mountain regions in the war, Venezuelan independence ceased to be a mere political realignment and became transformed into a decade-long civil war. The weakness of both patriots and royalists prevented a quick decision; the longer the war ran on, the more popular participation spread. The need for popular support preoccupied royalists and patriots throughout the 1812-14 period and, indeed, until the end of the war in Venezuela in 1823.

THE EMERGENCE OF THE INDEPENDENCE ELITE

The activities of 1812-14 focused on three fronts. In the eastern region the patriots managed a constant series of guerrilla actions. From a base in New Granada, a second group of patriots prepared and launched an assault down the Andes to Caracas. From Caracas the royalists directed a pacification campaign designed to return the colony to a normal state of quiescence.

With the successful conclusion of the royalist campaign of 1812, the patriot cause appeared almost beyond redemption. The leaders of the Patria Boba had been captured, exiled, imprisoned, or killed, and what passed for a patriot army had been dispersed. Domingo Monteverde, a reasonably effective military man but a poor peacemaker, had firm control of Caracas for the empire. Small bands of patriots remained in the countryside, but with the exception of a group that escaped westward into New Granada and sporadic activity in the eastern llanos, little remained of the independence movement.

In spite of this failure, the movement survived into 1813, drawing strength from the patriot successes in neighboring New Granada. It survived thanks to the growing successes of the guerrilla bands in the east under Santiago Mariño and Manuel Carlos Piar and in Margarita under the Arismendis, and the patriots revived when Bolívar's successful military ventures in New Granada gained him the troops and support to contemplate a reconquest of Venezuela.

Of considerable assistance to these patriot heroes, the incompetence and disagreements in the royalist camp kept the imperial authorities from carrying out a successful pacification program. Monteverde seemed unwilling to follow a conciliatory policy in Venezuela and in any case fell from favor in Spain. His replacement, Mariscal de Campo Juan Manuel Cajigal, appeared more tractable, but even so he could not command the support of his royalist field commanders, especially José Tomás Boves and Francisco Morales, who controlled the bulk of the *llanero* lancers.

Although it is tempting to concentrate on the heroic efforts of the patriot leaders and their royalist adversaries, such an approach to independence tends to obscure some of the important material, social, and political conditions that to a large degree determined the course of the independence wars. For example, in 1813 the royal presence in Venezuela appeared overwhelming. Not only had the First Republic disintegrated, but the people of Venezuela from all classes and all regions had shown themselves indifferent or hostile to the fledgling government of 1811-12. In spite of this apparently strong position, the royalist counterrevolution lasted only about a year.

On paper the royalist position may have looked strong, but in reality it proved impossible to sustain. For pacification to take place the royalists would have had to find a way to return the country to some version of the *status quo ante*. But because large segments of the *caraqueño* elite had been directly involved in the independence action and a greater number implicated indirectly, the royalists, whether Monteverde or Cajigal, had to choose between two equally undesirable options. One alternative would have been amnesty for the participants and a program designed to reintegrate the dissidents into the Spanish system. This might have reduced the incentive to continue to revolt, but it ran counter to all imperial policy in that it would appear to permit treason and rebellion without appropriate punishment. Furthermore, such a policy could only alienate those Venezuelans who had remained loyal to the crown. A second possibility would have been a policy of rigorous punishments and confiscations designed to eliminate or frighten troublemakers and rebels. This, of course, would have required such a massive campaign against the Caracas elite that at the least it would have left a legacy of hostility and resentment and at the most would have rekindled the rebellion.

Faced with two unattractive possibilities, the Spanish authorities vacillated. One moment the reprisals would be swift, severe, and arbitrary. At other times, generosity and forgiveness characterized official Spanish behavior. Confusion, insecurity, and a lack of confidence in royal authority resulted. Those punished severely, and their families and friends, harbored a resentment made all the more bitter by the inconsistency of royal policy. Those forgiven or sent into exile felt little but contempt for the weakness of the Spanish government, and the exiles plotted and acted energetically to continue the war and reclaim their rights and privileges in their homeland.

In assessing the royalist position in Venezuela it is important to remember that, while most Venezuelans outside Caracas appeared unwilling to follow the *caraqueño* elite into independence, neither did they welcome the re-establishment of strict royalist control. Furthermore, and even more significant, royalist success in crushing the patriot army and government did not lead to the restoration of civil order or much of the rest of that fragile *status quo ante*. Every interest, and friends, harbored a resentment made all the more bitter by the events of 1808-12. The *llaneros* rode in the name of the king, but the king's representative proved incapable of controlling the *llanero* chieftains. The urban elites, unwilling to follow Caracas's example of independence, likewise failed to show much enthusiasm for the inept and often arbitrary rule of the royalist conqueror Monteverde. The rural masses, especially black slaves and the lower order of *pardos*, sought a variety of escapes from the normal difficulties of their lives. Slaves who had fought for the king found precious little freedom as their reward. *Pardos* who had supported the restoration of royal rule found that their efforts had simply helped preserve the arrangements limiting their advancement in society.

As is always the case, it turned out to be much harder for the royalist government installed in Caracas in 1812 to reconstitute social, political, and economic order than it had been for the patriots to destroy it in the euphoria of independence. Perhaps a united Spain with an enlightened colonial government in Venezuela and a reasonably healthy treasury could have retained this rich agricultural province in Tierra Firme, but in 1812 Spain had few of these characteristics. Although Domingo Monteverde, little beloved in Venezuela, was replaced by Juan Manuel Cajigal, a much more able and pleasant individual, the royalist cause began to fall apart in early 1813.

Two geographic theaters of war that would provide the bases for activities of the second stage of Venezuela's independence wars developed in 1813: New Granada and the Venezuelan east. Although the twin pressures from the armies of the Bolivarian troops from New Granada and the eastern caudillos would recapture Caracas in 1813, the character and basis of these two efforts were much different.

In the east the independence spirit remained strong, partly because the eastern section of Venezuela had long been relatively free from energetic royal supervision and in part because this region had an extensive history of independent action against pirates or on behalf of smugglers. In any case, under the leadership of such caudillos as Santiago Mariño, Manuel Carlos Piar, and Juan Bautista Arismendi, the eastern region, including Margarita island, once again came into patriot hands in mid-1813. This movement, characterized by the participation of local leaders, drew its support from the immediate countryside. It was a home-grown revolt made successful by local soldiers and local chieftains, with a more reliable base than that enjoyed by Bolívar in his campaign from New Granada.

It is, of course, in the campaign from New Granada, or Colombia, that Simón Bolívar emerged as a military leader of consequence. In the days of the First Republic he had been little more than an ambitious, eloquent, and hot-headed participant in the patriot enthusiasm. His military experience was limited, his diplomatic credentials slim, and his administrative capacity untested. But between 1812 and 1819 he became the principal leader in Venezuela, then in Colombia, and from that base his power and authority extended as far as Peru and Bolivia for a short time in the 1820s. By every account, the man possessed extraordinary gifts, and before discussing the first successful military command of his career, some assessment of his abilities may help put the subsequent account of the independence wars into better perspective.

From any point of view, Simón Bolívar differed from those around him. This difference has been glorified, exaggerated, and condemned by contemporaries and historians for reasons of party, jealousy, and profit. But to make any sense out of the independence of Spanish America we must come to an evaluation of Bolívar. It will not suffice, for example, to view him as a slightly more successful general than all the rest, nor will it help much to speak of some sort of mystical genius guiding the fortunes of Spanish-American liberation. Instead, we need to determine the peculiarities of his time and place that permitted his extraordinary qualities to achieve full development.

Among the heroes of independence, Bolívar stood out in several dimensions. First, he survived all of the setbacks, defeats, and catastrophes of those turbulent years. Although this may appear obvious, it is also significant because so many of Bolívar's generation, of his background, and with his education did not survive long enough to make much of an impact. A Bolívar dead in 1818 would have warranted only a few lines in a book such as this. Second, the disasters of 1812 and 1814 in Caracas, with the failures of the First and Second Republics, reduced dramatically the number of Venezuelans whose talent and training could have competed with Bolívar's. In other words, the steady attrition among the leaders of the *caraqueño* elite left Bolívar with fewer and fewer competitors as the war continued.

Bolívar also had a range of personal qualities that made him especially well-adapted to the circumstances of 1810-30. Something of a dandy, vain and proud, Bolívar had great ambition. But unlike so many vain and ambitious men, Bolívar was intelligent, well educated, and capable of big ideas. He also had something of the fanatic—the visionary—in him. In more tranquil times, these traits would have made him a dynamic local figure, perhaps a troublemaker, or even a minor-league rebel. But the independence wars provided a unique set of circumstances, conditions that combined to accentuate each of Bolívar's special qualities and make him for a very short moment in history the embodiment of Spanish-American independence. Other men were wiser, better educated, more intrepid, vainer, stronger, more ambitious, and wealthier. But none combined so well the characteristics that fit so perfectly the conditions of those disorderly years of independence.

Bolívar's prominence in Venezuelan and hemispheric historiography of independence often leads to an assumption that he controlled the movement from beginning to end, but that notion seriously misleads. Bolívar's moment as supreme leader in the independence was short, for his unique position depended on an equally unique and unstable combination of circumstances. Bolívar emerged as the chief leader in Venezuela by 1817, and his authority declined rapidly after 1824. To be sure, those seven years of glory have yet to be equalled in the hemisphere, but because history is by nature conservative, tending to a relatively low level of innovation and change, the Bolivarian interlude could only have been short.

In the end, what distinguished Bolívar from all of his contemporaries was his continental vision of America which transcended local concerns, and his willingness to sacrifice anyone's interests, including his own, to realize that vision. Bolívar's failure was to misjudge the force of circumstances, to expect that his special qualities would be sufficient to rechannel the currents of three hundred years of historical experience. This error, of course, is common among those who choose greatness and glory in turbulent times.

However great he became in subsequent years, the Bolívar who led the lightning strike on Caracas in 1813 was only one of many patriot leaders. Young, energetic, messianic, and capable, he succeeded in Colombia against royalist troops, and by that success he gained the opportunity to re-enter Venezuela from the Andean city of Cúcuta. In a swift campaign through the Andes, down onto the llanos of Caracas, and then through the valleys of Aragua to the capital itself, this army carried Bolívar on his first major victorious campaign, known in Venezuelan history as the Campaña Admirable. Once in Caracas, he assumed supreme command of the government, determined to do better than the leaders of the First Republic.

Several features of the independence movement became clearer in the course of this rapid march to the capital. For one, the lack of national consciousness and the remoteness of independence ideology became explicit on June 15, 1813, when Bolívar and his generals promulgated the decree of "War to the Death." This remarkable document reflects in the formalistic and bombastic language of independence pronouncements the difficulty patriots had identifying their cause with their countrymen. In essence, this decree attempted to separate Spaniard from Venezuelan, to create two classes of individuals within the country—a native-born group whose rights and immunities exceeded those of the Spanish-born group. Those individuals considered native sons, moreover, would automatically be regarded as loyal to the patriot cause unless they actively joined and supported the royalists. Those considered Spanish-born would be regarded as declared enemies of the patriot cause unless they enthusiastically joined and supported the independence effort.

This decree received its name from the penalties outlined for the Spanish-born who would not actively support the patriots. It proclaimed a war to the death against such individuals, guaranteeing the destruction or confiscation of their property and goods on behalf of loyal patriots.

Much has been made of this decree, as if by the stroke of a pen Bolívar had initiated a new and more ruthless form of civil warfare in Venezuela. In fact, the notion of a total civil war did not emerge in the famous decree. Instead, the decree tried to legitimate the style of civil war developing in Venezuela. For example, it made the property of the Spanish-born easily forfeit in the cause of independence, and Bolívar as well as the other Venezuelan generals recognized the necessity of large-scale confiscations to support their armies. Likewise, the note of ferocity in the decree, the recognition of a license to hunt and kill Spaniards for the simple crime of having been born in Spain, represented less the initiation of a new and more brutal phase of the war than the recognition of the growing harshness of the conflict and an effort to channel the ruthless enthusiasm into directions supportive of the patriot cause.

Finally, this decree is of a piece with the consistent effort of Bolívar to involve the European powers directly in the independence movement. Although none of the principal European nations had any interest in a direct commitment to the Spanish-American revolt, many, Bolívar thought, might be persuaded to provide some assistance if the conflict could be presented as an international struggle between Venezuelans and Spaniards. To achieve this end, he lost no opportunity to underline the difference between Americans and Spaniards. In this sense, the decree of War to the Death became one more item in his elaborate diplomacy.

The Campaña Admirable of 1813 also illustrates the centrality of Caracas to the Venezuelan independence movement. Bolívar's rapid advance down the Andes, across the llanos, and into the capital indicates the importance of the city to the success of independence. Unless and until the Caracas connection lay in patriot hands, there could be no freedom from Spain. Still clinging to the notion of a rapid solution to the military problem of independence and with a belief that from Caracas the country could be controlled, Bolívar made no effort in his campaign to organize or pacify the regions between Colombia and Caracas. It was quite enough for him to receive the acclamation of the townspeople in each city and village along the way because the war, in his mind, would be won in Caracas.

This erroneous notion had been, of course, one of the reasons for the failure of the First Republic, but because that regime also suffered from incompetence, irresolution, and foolishness, the major strategic flaw in its military arrangement was not immediately evident. Bolívar's solution to the problems of the First Republic required efficient, autocratic administration of public affairs and the suppression of revolt wherever it might occur. But he failed to understand that without control of the Venezuelan hinterland, especially the llanos, political independence proclaimed in Caracas would be almost impossible to maintain. That hinterland, as he was to discover, while totally incapable of controlling the country or managing a government, had the capacity to destroy or disrupt any Caracas-based government. In short, Caracas could not govern without the hinterland's support or at least sufferance, and no one could govern without Caracas's bureaucratic expertise.

In the fall and winter of 1813-14 all of this became painfully clear as the *llaneros* rose in revolt against the patriot government in Caracas, following the leadership of one of the war's outstandingly successful caudillos, José Tomás Boves. The government created by Bolívar in Caracas in late 1813 and early 1814 had all the proper attributes—efficiency, dictatorial power, progressive management—but these virtues were as nothing against the well-directed assault from the llanos. Boves, a master of cavalry tactics and a charismatic leader of the plains cowboys, fought enthusiastically, winning battle after battle, until the patriots, defeated on every front, fled from Caracas in disorder toward the eastern city of Barcelona. Fortunately for the patriots, one of Boves's most decisive victories at the battle of Urica on December 5, 1814, also brought him a mortal wound, leaving the much less capable royalist leader Francisco Morales in charge of the *llanero* horsemen.

Throughout the historiography of Venezuelan independence, José Tomás Boves has acquired the status of the archetypical royalist villain, a caudillo whose low morals and ruthless slaughter of innocents and opponents alike set him apart from the rest of Venezuela's combatants. Certainly Boves proved a ruthless competitor, willing to confiscate and sack anything of value that came his way. But his bloodthirsty reputation appears much exaggerated. Patriots used his methods with equal enthusiasm as they, in their turn, worked to reconquer Caracas. Everyone involved in this destructive civil war found it necessary to loot, pillage, and burn in order to survive to fight another day. Perhaps Boves's singular contribution was that he brought the horrors of the hinterland warfare right up to the gates of Caracas in a campaign that so terrified the patriots that many of them fled en masse—women, children, the aged, and the infirm—with the remnants of the patriot army toward Barcelona. Perhaps several thousand individuals in all deserted the city in 1814; many never made it to Barcelona, falling prey to the hazards of the rough terrain and hostile environment.

The collapse of the Second Republic had its lessons for the patriots and for Bolívar. In addition to the clear demonstration that Venezuela could not be governed from Caracas without some degree of control in the hinterland, the short lifespan of the Second Republic illustrated some interesting features of political legitimacy. Bolívar evidently believed that a proclamation, a contrived popular assembly in Caracas, and an energetic and efficient administration would provide him with the legitimacy and authority required to govern. But in the eyes of his compatriots, Bolívar represented just one more successful general, although he, at least, had excellent social credentials. For the competing patriot caudillos, especially Santiago Mariño from the eastern region, Bolívar must have appeared in 1813 as a much less legitimate ruler of independent Venezuela than Mariño himself. After all, Bolívar's triumph came thanks to Colombian support while Mariño's success came from campaigns within Venezuela. By what measure, then, should the caudillos be judged?

In this early period of independence, there appear to have been a number of shifting criteria applied to the conferral of legitimacy, and an interesting perception of the permanence of authority. Although this is not the place for a general exploration of Spanish America's complex history of authority and legitimacy in government, some discussion of the Venezuelan version of the general problem is necessary. This is especially so when exploring the course of independence, for this movement between 1810 and 1830 has as one of its principal themes the creation of an authority system remarkably different in form and operation from the Spanish imperial model. In these early years of the independence wars the participants began experimenting with the criteria by which their leaders were to be chosen and supported.

The Second Republic demonstrated in two ways the principle that no caudillo would legitimately control Venezuela unless he also controlled the city of Caracas. Bolívar's Campaña Admirable, with its target of Caracas, illustrated his understanding of this principle, but of course as a *caraqueño* born and bred he would have been expected to see things this way. More interesting was the behavior of Santiago Mariño, whose patriot forces from the east also marched to gain Caracas. When he did not get there first, Mariño apparently accepted the Bolivarian *fait accompli,* reluctantly recognizing Bolívar's position as prime ruler of Venezuela, at least for the moment.

Unfortunately for the peace and public order of Venezuela, the authority conferred by possession of Caracas had little basis in any enduring social or political agreement. Although direct evidence is hard to find, the actions of everyone involved indicates their understanding that the legitimacy earned by conquering Caracas would last only as long as the incumbent, in this case Bolívar, kept his military forces strong, and as long as his enemies refrained or were unable to depose him. The inhabitants of Caracas had, to be sure, named Bolívar "Liberator," settled dictatorial powers on him, and sung his praises to the heavens. But these protestations of enthusiasm neither represented the sentiments of the other cities of Venezuela nor implied total *caraqueño* dedication to the cause of their titular leader.

Caracas, by 1813, was in its third year of the revolt, had already seen two governments changed in the city, and suffered the reprisals of one conquering army. Prudence alone dictated a public welcome for the next conqueror. Those who had no use for patriots or independence could expect that the unstable conditions of the recent past would continue to contribute to the weakness and insubstantiality of any new regime. The rapid demise of the Second Republic, the flight of prominent patriots to the east, and the collapse of Bolívar's flimsy government all demonstrated the lack of a secure touchstone for authority and the impermanence of the government created in Caracas.

The difficulties the patriots had in uniting behind a leader came, of course, from the difficulty in identifying that leader. By what alchemy was a Bolívar substantially different from a Mariño? By whose agreement did a Mariño subordinate his ambition to Bolívar's? These critical questions demanded clear, simple answers. A wrong answer could well bring death as a traitor, or at least the unenviable position of having backed a loser.

As often happens in times of civil disorder and social instability, the touchstone of authority and legitimacy in Venezuela became the quantum of force commanded personally by a pretender to the position of supreme authority. As a basis of civil order there is nothing in theory wrong with force, but in the conditions of the independence movement it proved to be a poor instrument of government. Because the force available to each claimant derived from that individual's personal prowess and charismatic leadership, its potency varied from day to day, depending on the energy and success of that leader, and its range of variation fluctuated widely and rapidly. One moment Bolívar appeared to be in personal command of large numbers of armed men and firmly in control of the government, the next he found himself exiled to the Caribbean with a handful of followers and an accusation against him for having betrayed the patriot cause.

Under such conditions, what society in its right mind would make enduring commitments and willingly suffer sustained sacrifices to support any individual caudillo? The strategy developed by Venezuelans and other Spanish-Americans in similar circumstances required short-term, tentative commitments to apparent winners, careful cultivation of apparent losers, constant alertness to changes in the quantum of force available to each contender, and consistent efforts to minimize personal sacrifice. While there were many individual exceptions to these rules of behavior, which produced the heroes and martyrs of Venezuelan history, the bulk of the population followed this strategy, some more successfully than others of course.

Peasants, blacks, *llaneros*, slaves, clergymen, merchants, landowners, and bureaucrats: all operated in this mode, although their tactics differed in accord with their class, wealth, race, and opportunities. In the case of the lower classes of society, this opportunistic behavior responded to a rather grim set of alternatives. The wars for independence and the accompanying dissolution of the old order often translated into more personal freedom, less immediate personal supervision, and greater geographic mobility. But the conditions in the countryside also meant increased danger, high risk of property confiscation or destruction, irregular or no work opportunities, and a constant threat of forced enlistment. These unpleasant conditions of life varied in intensity from region to region and from time to time throughout the war. In the course of the two-decade struggle practically every part of the country experienced the scourge of civil conflict, the central and eastern regions suffering repeated campaigns. Obviously, this picture of disruption and turmoil must not be exaggerated. People went on living; they married, raised families, cultivated the land, paid their debts, and went to market. Daily life continued in between the sporadic outbursts of major violence associated with the independence wars.

The general instability described above contributed to a high level of background violence in the years after 1810. Without even reasonably stable, consistent, and continuous civil government, people learned to depend on the local or regional chieftain for protection or for the resolution of civil complaints. Furthermore, as long as the collection and maintenance of personal and occasional armies remained the *sine qua non* of political power within Venezuela, the ambitious young man could hardly find better employment than in the troops of a successful caudillo. Evidently life in the countryside proved so unstable and so precarious that the campaigning armies often collected substantial baggage trains of non-combatant civilians who moved with the successful armies from the smaller towns to the larger cities where opportunities for work and security were better than in the countryside.

To be sure, this general description of life among the lower classes must be mostly speculative, for these people rarely wrote about their experiences. But as a group they did behave in visible ways that indicated these pressures and conditions. We can track with some accuracy their movement from place to place within Venezuela, and although colonial society before the war was also characterized by considerable population mobility, the magnitude and composition of these movements take on a different character by 1814. In any event, the necessity for patriots and royalists to recruit substantial numbers of troops from the population at large, and the long duration of the instability and warfare almost institutionalized this opportunistic behavior. By 1830, when Venezuela finally determined its political boundaries and began regular, relatively stable government, an entire generation of young adults in Venezuela had grown up knowing nothing of the complex and stable civil government of the Spanish regime, individuals whose principal experience in solving civil disputes involved violence and force at varying levels of intensity.

Although the impact of these conditions on the elite had somewhat different manifestations, their survival strategy proved no less opportunistic than that of their lower-class neighbors. Bureaucrats, merchants, and landowners cooperated, by and large, with every conquering hero, whatever the political persuasion or personal qualities involved. The elite or near elite constantly tried to limit their material contributions to the causes of king or republic, while at the same time they sought the protection of the conqueror and competed for the privilege of selling or buying under special protection from the reigning caudillo. If this scramble for security and profits failed to provide the material for heroic tales, it nevertheless demonstrated a keen understanding of the risks and opportunities in troubled times. Profiteering, quick sales at exorbitant prices, gross bureaucratic corruption—all were the tactics of an elite whose grasp on the future seemed tenuous. Only a few of the elegant *caraqueños* who engineered the declaration of independence survived the twenty-year war to enjoy the rewards of the Republic, and while many upper-class families did survive the wars, it was at the cost of exile, or as a result of the participation of their fathers, sons, and brothers in the leadership of the patriot armies. Clearly, under the constraints of the times, the elite looked for quick returns wherever they could be found. Who, for example, would plant cacao trees that would not mature for eight years at best knowing that within those years the labor to cultivate the trees would be drafted, the plantation animals would be confiscated, and the plantation looted? Better to preserve what was already produced, hoard real assets for the future, and sell what was salable before some caudillo confiscated it.

Given the disruption of normal trade and commerce, the irregularity of harvests, and the general instability, energetic entrepreneurs found ample opportunity to gain from the war. Often royalist and patriot commanders would pay handsomely for supplies, exorbitantly for arms. Risky though this business was, especially with limited recourse to civil law, the profits were correspondingly high. Similarly, as the war progressed after the fall of the Second Republic in 1814, both sides worked diligently to create the forms and institutions of normal civil existence. Royalists appointed officials, supported the courts, settled disputes, and collected taxes. Patriots issued decrees, promulgated constitutions, set up civil jurisdictions, and collected taxes. Patriots, always short on funds, issued large numbers of promises to pay, claims on confiscated royalist property or state-owned land, and similar fiat values. Because these pieces of paper had a worth determined by the fortunes of war and politics, they were heavily discounted by speculators who bought them up in exchange for food, clothing, supplies, arms, and similar necessities. Among these speculators, of course, were the patriot commanders who exchanged supplies and loot for these slips of paper. After the war, these claims would constitute the economic base of the new republican elite.

All these consequences and states of mind had as their cause the wars for independence, which in 1814-15 passed through an especially critical stage for the Venezuelan patriots. Although the formidable Boves had died in the battle of Urica, thereby removing the most capable popular royalist hero, the patriots had fled in disarray to the east. Not only had their central government in Caracas collapsed, but the principal caudillos had little use for each other, each one believing his version of the patriot cause deserved the support of all the others. Bolívar traveled in disgrace once again to the Caribbean, then to Colombia, where his military experience gave him some success, but his political enemies cast him out. By 1815 he had returned to the Caribbean, to Haiti, where President Alexandre Petión became his protector and patron.

In Spain, Ferdinand VII returned triumphant to the Spanish throne at the end of 1814, promptly rejected the liberal constitutional reforms established in his absence, and initiated a campaign to re-create the Spanish empire of old by reconquering America. Early in 1815 General Pablo Morillo arrived in Venezuela with several thousand seasoned Spanish troops to begin the pacification of Venezuela and the reconquest of New Granada for Spain. Morillo proved capable, honorable, and successful in his efforts, and had he been able to count on strong support at home, he might have kept northern South America for Spain.

While the Spanish cause appeared successful in much of northern South America, the small bands of patriot guerrillas maintained their activities at a high level of intensity, especially in the east. Their small victories there gradually cumulated throughout 1816 until much of the east had returned to patriot control. Bolívar, after considerable success in Colombia, found himself once again in exile in the Antilles, and in September 1815 he issued his famous Jamaica Letter, a document outlining his vision of American independence. Although written principally for a foreign audience, especially a British one, the letter is a striking example of Bolívar's continental perspective on American independence. In the following years, Bolívar's notions about the details of an independent continent would go through a variety of forms depending on his audience and the circumstances, but the one constant, the monomania of his greatness, remained the dream of a united, powerful, independent America. More than any other characteristic, this continental perspective separated Bolívar from his contemporaries and in turn constituted the fatal flaw in his strategic design.

In early 1816 Simón Bolívar was still little more than a brilliant, ambitious South American general whose short military and political career had been characterized by an erratic record of brilliant successes and dramatic failures. But the advantages of education, culture, and wealth permitted him to overcome adversities that might have destroyed less able men. The President of Haiti, Alexandre Petión, was one of those to fall under the charismatic spell of Bolívar, and with the help of Haiti, the Liberator organized a new assault on the Venezuelan coast.

The plan this time, as in earlier attempts, envisioned a rapid assault on the capital and the surrounding valleys in hopes of executing a surprise strike that would deliver Venezuela back into patriot hands. The expedition sailed from Haiti in May 1816 and successfully landed its troops along the central coast at Ocumare. Not only did the local inhabitants fail to rally around the patriots, but the main column under General Carlos Soublette crossed the coastal mountains only to be defeated by the royalists. The remnants of that column marched eastward until they reached comparative safety in Barcelona. Bolívar himself, stranded on the beach at Ocumare with the supplies but no troops, found it necessary to return to Haiti. His fellow patriot generals took this opportunity to blame Bolívar for the defeat and accuse him of a long list of crimes and errors.

By the beginning of 1817, then, the patriot cause remained successful only in the eastern regions of the llanos and in parts of Guayana plus the central plains, especially in the territory of the lower llanos where José Antonio Páez continued his campaigns to control that territory. New Granada, in the meantime, had been mostly returned to royal control, thanks to the skill of Pablo Morillo and his Spanish expeditionary force. Bolívar, still without an army of his own, had finally come to recognize the necessity of pursuing the liberation of Venezuela from a secure base in the east, but his many rivals, some with armies of their own, conspired to keep control of the movement. Pablo Morillo, clearly aware of the threat posed by Páez's successful *llanero* campaigns and the continued rebelliousness of the Venezuelan east, returned from Colombia to lead the royalist pacification efforts.

For a time he had some success. Barcelona fell to the royalists. But even though the participants were surely unaware of it, the contest had begun to turn in favor of the patriots.

For one thing, the continued success of Páez in his element of the plains posed a constant threat to royalist control. For another, the fractious republican leadership began to consolidate during 1817. Bolívar, without an army but endowed with charisma and powerful allies among the patriot commanders, spent much of 1817 and 1818 working to create the structure of a successful patriot government. His tireless travels to meet with Páez in the llanos and his other comrades and rivals in the eastern regions of Guayana and along the Orinoco kept the potentially destructive patriot fractionalism within bounds. Perhaps as important as the charisma and leadership of Bolívar in establishing his ascendancy in this violent milieu was his ruthless disposition of his least discrete rival, General Manuel Piar.

This able eastern caudillo committed a series of political blunders that permitted Bolívar to isolate him from his supporters and unite the other caudillos against him. Piar made the mistake of failing to recognize the limits of personal power. He chose, instead, to disavow any obligation to cooperate with the emerging patriot coalition of caudillos unless his pre-eminence was recognized. Such ambition did not make Piar unique, but when combined with his lack of prudence and his military weakness it brought about his demise. Piar, because of his presumed mulatto ancestry, could never have been regarded as the social equal of such as Mariño or Bolívar or Bermúdez, all members of the white elite. These patricians could ignore Piar's ancestry as long as the man remained a successful general and appeared to support the proper social order. But when Piar appeared to encourage the blacks and *pardos* to assert their claims for social change, the quarrelsome patriot leadership joined together under Bolívar's direction to capture, judge, and execute Piar for his treason against the cause.

This demonstration showed Bolívar's rivals that drastic measures could and would be part of the Bolivarian plan. Clearly, the cost of an unsuccessful challenge to patriot unity would be high, so the other patriot caudillos tended to move against Bolívar only with great caution.

In pursuit of a more stable base of patriot unity, Bolívar, with the support of General Páez and a number of other patriot leaders, organized the famous Congress of Angostura and established the influential patriot newspaper, the *Correo del Orinoco*. The congress convened in 1819, named Bolívar president of Venezuela, and established the Third Venezuelan Republic. With this institutional backing, Bolívar began the series of military campaigns that would liberate northern South America from Spanish rule. The first of these set the tone of his successful military career. With a sizable, if inadequately equipped army, Bolívar marched from Angostura across the Andes to a battlefield at Boyacá. There the surprised royalists collapsed, leaving the road to Bogotá open. Bolívar entered the city triumphantly with his army some days later. But, as would continue to occur throughout the next decade, no sooner had Bolívar left his home base than his enemies and rivals conspired against him. The patriots in Angostura rejected Bolívar's leadership and set up a substitute government. Bolívar, covered with the glory of a successful conquest returned to his base, in this case Angostura, to re-establish his authority. In person, and with the authority of military success, Bolívar seemed irresistible, but, although his presence and army constituted the essence of patriot authority and legitimacy, the local factionalism could only be suppressed, not eliminated.

In late 1819 Bolívar's triumph in Boyacá and Bogotá gave him the authority to ask the Congress of Angostura to legitimate the Bolivarian strategic design of a united greater Colombia composed of Venezuela, New Granada, and Ecuador. The congress, of course, agreed, and Bolívar, with the title of provisional president of Colombia, began his conquest of northern South America for the patriot cause.

Although the independence of Spanish America dragged on for a number of years, the end had been announced in 1820, when the Spanish liberals in Spain required Ferdinand VII to accept a variety of liberal reforms. Preoccupied with internal political turmoil, the Spanish government lost the will to recover America. The conservative American royalists who had defended the king to preserve the old order now found the old order abandoned even in Madrid. In Colombia, the patriots moved from success to success. They began a successful siege of Cartagena, the principal remaining royalist stronghold in Colombia. Bolívar, marching down the Andes toward the central valleys of Venezuela, agreed to an armistice with Morillo in Trujillo. Early in 1821 the patriots seized the port of Maracaibo, breaking the truce. Morillo, without support at home, was recalled and replaced by a considerably less able substitute. In June 1821 Bolívar's forces from Colombia via the Andes and the troops of Páez from the llanos of Venezuela combined to defeat the main royalist force in Venezuela in the battle of Carabobo outside Valencia. Although a royalist unit held out in the castle at Puerto Cabello until 1823, the battle of Carabobo in June 1821 and the fall of Cartagena in the same year signaled the definitive liberation of New Granada and Venezuela. From this secure base, Bolívar then organized a strong government at Cúcuta on the border of Venezuela and New Granada complete with constitution, laws, and a bureaucracy. With this structure to support him. Bolívar began the southern campaigns that eventually would liberate Peru and Bolivia.

For Venezuela, the creation of the government at Cúcuta in 1821 marks the end of the independence period and the beginning of national reconstruction. After the 1821 Cúcuta constitution, Bolívar's activities in Peru and Bolivia ceased to be of primary concern to Venezuela except insofar as they required material assistance or disturbed the bureaucracy of Colombia. But for the most part, Venezuela spent the next decade gaining self-confidence and establishing the limits of its territory and sovereignty.

Although included within the structure of Colombia, Venezuela felt uncomfortable with the consolidation of former colonial *audiencias*. As early as 1822 the town council of Caracas objected to the constitution promulgated in Cúcuta. The intendent of Venezuela, Carlos Soublette, found it almost impossible to administer the country according to the directions from the central government at Bogotá, especially when these contradicted the wishes of either the Caracas elite or the plans of General José Antonio Páez. In spite of these difficulties, the administration of Colombia in Venezuela gradually took hold. Taxes, materiel, and men were collected and sent to support the Bolivarian campaigns in Peru and Bolivia. State and municipal government settled down into a reasonably normal rhythm, and for at least a few years the energies of Venezuela's independence heroes, especially Páez, remained focused on the elimination of pockets of royalist resistance at Maracaibo, Coro, and Puerto Cabello. But by the end of 1823, Venezuelan territory stood completely free of Spanish imperial control, and as a result, the military heroes of the independence epic turned their attention to the management of the country they had fought so hard to liberate.

From the Venezuelan perspective, the experience with Colombia in these early years promised little reward for faithful cooperation. Santander and the Colombian congress, even with its Venezuelan members, rarely appeared to have Venezuelan interests in mind. Venezuelans thought that they should be allowed to rebuild their economy in peace, without heavy taxation and administrative meddling from far-off Bogotá. From every perspective except the Bolivarian, the Colombian consolidation was a colossal mistake, an error of perception made into a temporary reality by the military prestige and personal power of Simón Bolívar. The idea of a combination of independent American states had wonderful theoretical possibilities, none of which escaped Bolívar's brilliant imagination. But the conditions, history, and geography of America combined to render this notion nothing but a chimera.

In Venezuela's case, the previous half-century before independence had been dominated by the drive to create an autonomous administrative and economic unit centered on Caracas. The great accomplishment of the late colonial administration had been the concentration of country-wide institutions in the Caracas submetropolitan center. Not even the sophisticated managers of the Spanish empire could arrange an institutional network that would link Venezuela and New Granada, though they tried any number of times throughout the eighteenth century. Part of the difficulty came from the complex geography of northern South America. Caracas, Cumaná, Coro, and Maracaibo communicated more easily through the Caribbean and with Europe than overland via the Andes with Bogotá. Maracaibo and the cities of Trujillo,

Mérida, and San Cristóbal had strong connections with New Granada in the extensive Andean trade through the port of Maracaibo. Cumaná and Barcelona, at the other extreme, hardly felt favorable toward Caracas, but felt even less so toward far-off Bogotá.

Further complicating the realization of Bolívar's united America, the logic of the independence movement itself guaranteed the failure of Colombia. If there is one identifiable characteristic common to all of Spanish-American independence, it is the centrifugal force evident throughout the continent, splintering the monolith of the Spanish empire into autonomous fragments. The size of those fragments depended on a variety of circumstances, but the basic fault lines of the Spanish empire appeared to run along the colonial *audiencia* boundaries. This centrifugal force that split the empire continued in attenuated form within each fragment, attempting to split the remnants of the empire into even smaller pieces. The fragmentation ended, of course, when the pieces reached a size controllable with the resources and administrative expertise of a central city. Bogotá, in our case, did not control sufficient resources or expertise to keep the Venezuelan fragment attached to Colombia, and with the end of the threat of reconquest, Bolívar's fragile creation split into its *audiencia*-based parts.

Before the Colombian confederation fell apart, however, it had the glory of participating in the grand conquests of Peru and Bolivia. Bolívar, president of Colombia and supreme leader of the liberating armies of independence, led his troops southwards, where he and his generals completed the liberation of America at the battles of Junín and Ayacucho in 1824. But the triumph and honors conferred on the Liberator by the enthusiastic crowds of Lima did little to help the cause of civilian government in Bogotá and Caracas where, in his absence, every effort was being made to dilute his influence. In the year of exhaltation in Peru during 1825, the situation in the north grew more and more difficult until by 1826 Bolívar had no choice but to return to Bogotá and Caracas or give up his dream of a united America. In Bogotá, his enemies worked to separate him and his supporters from all involvement in Colombian affairs, and in Caracas, General José Antonio Páez had become the center of a separatist protest against the authority of the Bogotá government.

The Venezuelan incident involved a minor altercation between Páez and the Colombian intendent for Venezuela, a Venezuelan himself. Páez, in recruiting soldiers, had used what the intendent regarded as excessive force. The intendent protested the action to Bogotá, and the congress called for Páez to come to the Colombian capital to explain his behavior. The good citizens of Valencia, a Páez stronghold, expressed great outrage at this insult to their hero and organized an assembly that proposed the separation of Venezuela from the Colombian confederation and nominated Páez to lead Venezuela. Thus by the end of 1826 Bolívar found Venezuela on the verge of separation from Colombia. His presence in Caracas in 1827 calmed the passions of the moment, but only at the price of confirming Páez's supremacy in Venezuela. When Bolívar rushed back to Bogotá from Caracas to defeat an anti-Bolivarian conspiracy there, he left a Venezuela nominally still part of Columbia. In the subsequent two years Bolívar's elaborate struggles with his political opponents and his declining health presented a tragic spectacle. Unable to anticipate the end of his era, he continued his efforts through an ill-conceived dictatorship in 1828 and then witnessed the collapse of the Colombian structure in 1829 with the separation of Venezuela under Páez. Defeated and broken in health, Bolívar withdrew from American politics too late to save either his health or his fortune. The Liberator of northern South America died in a little Colombian coastal town along his road to exile in December 1830.

This unhappy conclusion of a heroic epic in Spanish-American history symbolized the transition from the chaotic phase of Spanish America's independence to the institutional or proto-institutional phase. The Bolivarian style, with its emphasis on continental solidarity, local sacrifice, and authoritarian rule, turned out to have only a short life span, one permitted more by the lack of a substitute style than by any lasting enthusiasm for the Bolivarian mode itself. The reorganization of the Spanish-American polity and economy along the norms of northern European merchant capitalism could not have been managed in a continent-wide procedure simply because the relevant economic units that had to adjust managed more easily and profitably without central direction on a continental or even regional scale. But the independence experience had a profound effect on the possibilities, opportunities, and style of the readjustment process in Venezuela.

Chapter 4 • The Commercial-Bureaucratic
Outpost, 1830-1935

COMMERCE, CREDIT, AND CONTROL

After almost twenty years of insecurity, disorder, warfare, and destruction, the Venezuela of 1830 found itself free to organize without the overwhelming influence of Bolívar or the complications of the Colombian confederation. The process proved harder and more lengthy than any of the leaders of the Republic imagined in 1830, and the difficulties stemmed in considerable measure from the legacies of the war.

The most obvious difficulties involved the resolution of the authority and legitimacy problem of government along with the re-establishment of Venezuela's economy. The dissolution of the Spanish imperial government left Venezuela, as well as the rest of Spanish America, without the traditions and institutions of civil order and political control. Because the spirit of the Spanish authority system derived from the general acceptance of the king's and his council's right to rule, because none doubted the legitimacy of the king and council, and because the majesty of Spanish government existed in remote Spain, the transfer of the habit of obedience to a local leader, the recognition of authority, and the acceptance of legitimacy proved very difficult to manage. Not that there was any lack of pretenders to the position of Venezuelan supreme authority. The problem was to choose an authority and then, once chosen, to agree to limit individual gain for the common good.

Without the assistance of royalty to help identify leaders and separate them from the rest of society, Venezuela had to discover a new method of distinguishing its chiefs. That method, of course, became the organization and employment of personal armies. This sounds rather crude as a system of political selection, but as done in Venezuela and as developed from the experience of the independence wars, the system gained considerable flexibility and subtlety, if not elegance.

Supreme authority in Venezuela required two key ingredients. First, the successful leader needed to control or to have the ability to control at short notice a large number of armed men willing to march and die for their leader and the spoils of combat that he provided. Second, anyone who hoped to command Venezuela had to control the bureaucrats of Caracas and the elite of the capital city. These basic requirements of leadership had completely different origins. The role of violence as the selection mechanism for leadership came to Venezuela as a direct result of the wars for independence, for one of the consequences of those decades was a change from a civilian and legalist base to a violent and coercive base. Where before the war the expected response of an aggrieved individual or group would have been a complex and lengthy law suit, after the war the expected response was an uprising of armed men marching on the capital. This change reflected not only the lack of acceptance of the reigning power's authority to resolve contentious issues but also the greatly shortened time sense of society at large. Before the war, a litigant had little expectation of a speedy resolution of his claim; often sons carried on the legal battles of their fathers. This willingness to wait responded to a general acceptance of the legal mechanisms of conflict resolution, the lack of acceptable alternatives to judicial and administrative processes, a secure belief that the process would have the time to reach completion, and the knowledge that when completed the judgment would be enforced.

After the experience of almost two decades of violence and disorder during independence, individuals and groups could no longer afford to wait out judicial resolution. Not only was there every chance the judge was bought, but even if he were honest, he might be deposed by the next armed barbarian to march on Caracas. The citizen with a judgment against a caudillo had few legal means of seeing that judgment enforced. Under these conditions most people sought more direct and expedient modes of resolving their conflicts, especially when the stakes in the dispute were very high. In this way the problems of reorganizing civilian society and government after the wars were often resolved arbitrarily, and that arbitrary behavior made the reinstitution of legalistic, civil authority difficult. With the short time frame of expectation in postwar Venezuela, few major leaders could afford the patience and forbearance required for the construction of stable, impersonal institutions.

In the enthusiasm to identify and comprehend the insecure, dramatic manifestations of violent and coercive personal authority, it is easy to overlook the very powerful bureaucratic structure Venezuela inherited from three centuries of Spanish rule, a structure that with numerous changes in appearance and titles maintained its basic functions throughout the wars and emerged in the early years of the 1830s substantially intact. To be sure, the formal institutional organization of the Spanish empire did not survive the fall of Puerto Cabello. Rather, the uncodified networks of administration, trade, family, and geographic relationship sustained Venezuela during the uncertain independence and provided the substance of the republican governments. Each of these networks, linked one to the other at various points in the system, contributed to the fragile cohesiveness that kept the country from splintering into eastern, central, and Andean mini-states. Because these networks were in many cases of recent formation and therefore weak, the threat of disintegration was real enough. In the east especially, the independence leaders Santiago Mariño and the Monagas brothers, José Tadeo and José Gregorio, went so far as to proclaim an independent republic in 1831, and only the prompt intervention of José Antonio Páez prevented the secession movement from degenerating into another civil war.

Fortunately for the territorial integrity of Venezuela, the organization of these regions around the central city of Caracas, consolidated in the late eighteenth century, remained intact. From that base the new Republic, freed from Spanish and Colombian control, began to reconstruct its economy and reorient its society to gain maximum advantage from world trade. Indeed, the participation of Venezuela in Atlantic commerce provided, in the republican as well as in the colonial period, the primary reference for the management of the country's internal affairs. In the early colonial period, perhaps as early as the last half of the seventeenth century, Venezuela participated in the Spanish mercantilist system in which local American products, in Venezuela's case principally cacao, were exchanged with the North Atlantic world through Spain, and manufactured goods came to Venezuela via Spanish exporters. Of course, during the colonial period this neat arrangement gradually became more and more complex as Venezuela's Mexican trade and its lively contraband commerce made the economy more closely attuned to American and North Atlantic needs than to Iberian requirements.

Independence, to a great extent, allowed Venezuela to refocus its economy, society, and government completely toward the satisfaction of European needs without the restraints previously imposed by the Spanish colonial system. Yet if the accomplishment of independence presented extraordinary opportunities for wealth and profit in international trade, these gains required the existence of a reasonably sophisticated interface between the primitive social and political environment of most of Venezuela and the sophisticated European world of merchant capitalism. Only Caracas, it appeared, could fill the need for this connection, and this quasi-monopoly on the skills and services required to trade with European merchants and capitalists strengthened the city's control over the rest of Venezuela.

Throughout the rest of the nineteenth century, Venezuelan history can be seen as a complex argument among the country's elites over the precise terms of Venezuela's adjustment to the requirements of North Atlantic trade. In addition, it can be viewed as a dispute over which individuals representing which interests and regions would manage the adjustment. From this perspective it becomes clear that the turmoil, violence, and disorder intermittently characteristic of the country throughout the nineteenth century came less from the struggles of an independent nation in search of its identity than from a competition over the right to organize and manage the country for the benefit of the local elite, and through them, European and North American commerce. Although when presented this way, the bare skeleton of this arrangement appears excessively stark and mechanistic, it nevertheless provides a powerful analytical device for explaining and understanding the kaleidoscopic rotation of individuals, factions, interests, and conflicts that constituted Venezuela's nineteenth-century history.

Because the Venezuelan elites had as their principal goal greater participation in the life and commerce of European and North American societies, they found themselves obligated to operate in two environments simultaneously. When looking outward, the elites had to be sophisticated, educated, refined, and technically competent in the finer notions of trade and finance. When looking inward, they had to be ruthless, crude, exploitative, and violent to manage their potentially prosperous but underdeveloped economy and society. In the countryside, the niceties and fine distinctions of Paris, London, or New York had no meaning. In New York, London, or Paris, the rough, crude arrangements governing the Venezuelan interior provided picturesque material for the readers of high-class monthly magazines but caused neither concern nor excited more interest than bemused curiosity. These two worlds came together in Caracas, where the Venezuelan elites and especially the Venezuelan bureaucracy provided the skills and apparatus that helped Europeans profit from Venezuela's agricultural wealth and Venezuelans profit from European trade.

By the terms of this arrangement, European merchants, bankers, and their governments established a set of minimum requirements for the participation of Venezuela in the Atlantic trade. Unless Venezuela was to remain in virtual isolation from the modern world, it had to find ways of meeting these minimum requirements. The country, then, found it necessary to guarantee the security of property, and even more, the sanctity of contracts. The elites accepted terms of trade and finance suggested by Europeans and encouraged the government to maintain a bureaucracy capable of handling the details of commerce and of guaranteeing the enforcement of these minimum conditions. The range of deviation permitted from the suggested norm depended on the European demand for Venezuelan products, but the existence of the norm was beyond question.

Within this environment, the constant political instability of the nineteenth century reflected an internecine conflict among Venezuela's elites over control of the connection with Europe and the major benefits to be acquired from the management of the country to European specifications. Because the North Atlantic community concerned itself primarily with the product of the Venezuelan system and not with the process that created the product, the Venezuelan elites felt free to operate their internal affairs much as they pleased. If this system wasted lives and resources, they were, after all, Venezuelan lives and resources and therefore of relatively little concern to European financiers, manufacturers, and merchants. In times of maximum turmoil within Venezuela, Europeans withdrew their investments, short-term obligations in any case, and continued to trade at the fringes of the conflict. When a victor emerged capable of keeping Venezuela's external behavior closer to the norm and its internal conditions reasonably stable, the traders and capitalists returned to carry on their business. Not controlling any vital resources or managing any agricultural monopoly, Venezuela lacked the leverage to modify the terms of its connection with the North Atlantic nations, and so, until the early twentieth century, the country worked to establish the ideal commercial-bureaucratic regime in Caracas, a process that had a most promising beginning under the regimes of General José Antonio Páez.

Páez, born in 1790 in the rural region near Acarigua, grew up with only the most rudimentary education. From the age of sixteen, Páez became independent, first as a peon on a llanos cattle ranch and then as an aide to the ranch owner. During the early years of the independence, Páez fought intermittently, primarily with the patriots. By 1816 he had become a significant plains leader and by 1819 the major cavalry leader of the lower llanos. His willingness to work with Bolívar and his success in the concluding years of the independence warfare made him a major figure in the postindependence era. As Venezuela's pre-eminent military hero, Páez engineered the country's separation from Colombia and emerged as the arbiter of the country's first republican decades until 1848. A man of modest intellectual attainments, Páez proved to be a skillful manager of men. He captured the bureaucratic apparatus of Caracas to manage the country on his behalf, but the fall of coffee prices and the consequent economic difficulties of the 1840s could not be resolved by charismatic manipulation, and in any event Páez had lost touch with his *llanero* supporters by 1848. Exiled to the United States in 1850, Páez returned again in 1858 to serve as the Conservative party president-dictator of Venezuela. This futile attempt to recapture the glory days of the 1830s failed, and in 1863 Páez left Venezuela for the last time to spend the rest of his years in exile in the United States and Argentina. He died in New York in 1873.

For many historians the years 1830-48 mark the beginning of Venezuela's modern period, the first years of regular government after the centuries of Spanish colonial rule and the turmoil of the independence decades. From another perspective, the Páez years belong to that critical transitional century in Venezuelan history running from the mid-eighteenth century to the mid-nineteenth. In the framework of Venezuela's gradual integration into the Atlantic commercial world and the geographic and administrative consolidation of the country's institutions accomplished under Bourbon rule, Páez's regime marks the end of the transition as much as it does the beginning of the commercial-bureaucratic regimes of the nineteenth and the early twentieth century. The principal controversies of this period carry the echo of the past and concern more the nature of Venezuela's readjustment to the world than the simple argument over which elite faction should manage the bureaucracy, although this was also involved. Likewise, Páez suppressed the last serious separatist revolt. After his period of supreme command ended in 1848, Venezuela no longer struggled with the separatist dilemma, although regionalist interests and localist perspectives limited the nation's ability to modernize well into the nineteenth and the early twentieth century.

With Venezuela free from the confining relationship with Colombia,

Páez and his countrymen began to design the society and polity that they believed would keep the country modern and attractive for foreign investment. Although politics, economics, and social order represent interdependent phenomena, actions in one area influencing the events in another, the analysis of this regime should consider these things separately.

Politics, of course, is the art of compromise, and even when armed force provides the basic mechanism of authority and legitimacy, compromise limits the costs and risks of political combat. Thanks to the military supremacy of Páez during this period, Venezuela escaped continuous civil war for almost two decades. Although the great *llanero* chieftain was poorly educated when he began his rise to power in the guerrilla campaigns of the llanos, he proved in the years of republican rule to have a keen appreciation for the basic balance of forces within his Venezuelan world.

Without losing his sensitivity to the perspective of his *llanero* supporters, Páez came to understand the requirements of the new era. He, unlike many of his competitors, clearly saw that Venezuela required peace, civil order, institutional stability, a modernized set of national economic laws, and a healthy, prosperous bureaucracy in Caracas to manage the country according to the needs of European traders and the demands of the Venezuelan milieu. Although uncomfortable with the sophisticated urban folkways of Caracas, Páez rapidly learned that he and Venezuela needed the capital city if both were to prosper.

Under his protection, and of course with his approval, the representatives of Venezuela's provinces met at a congress in Valencia and issued a constitution in 1830 similar in content to the earlier constitution for Colombia. With some similarity to the United States model, much in vogue at the time, Venezuela created a government of three powers—legislative, judicial, and executive. Few, except visionaries and intellectuals, believed that these would be equal powers, for all recognized the significance of the executive position within the government. The constitution made Venezuela a democratic, representative republic with limited suffrage. Eleven provinces, corresponding closely to colonial subdivisions, acquired legal status with governors and provincial assemblies but without autonomous authority except in limited circumstances. Through the control of provincial government budgets, the federal bureaucracy guaranteed the centralized control of the country. This constitution, like its predecessors, continued none of the Spanish colonial laws regarding social and racial distinctions, but unless specifically changed, most of the rest of Spanish law served the Republic until more modern codes could be adopted. With the capital established in Caracas and Páez dutifully elected president for the first term, 1830 to 1834, Venezuela entered the ranks of the American republics.

In the detailed account of the regimes of José Antonio Páez, several symbolic events can stand for the principal contributions of his years in office. Coming from the chaotic period of the independence and Colombian conflicts, Venezuela required nothing more urgently than civil order and rural peace. The wars and general instability had loosed on the countryside two kinds of disruptive violence. The first, involving the poor, the dispossessed, and the angry manifested itself as endemic banditry. Small groups of lawless men plagued the highways of rural Venezuela with assaults, robberies, and extortion. During the wars, of course, such activity had its place as quasi-legitimate military action against the enemy; with peace and the establishment of the Venezuelan republic, such violence could no longer be tolerated. Not only did it give lie to the authority and responsibility of the national government, but it also impeded the successful economic revival of Venezuelan agriculture. In November 1813, with his customary energy and the skills of his *llanero* training, Páez met and tamed the most fearsome of the bandits, one Dionisio Cisneros, whose depredations had disturbed the Tuy valleys for some time. With Cisneros under control, the military forces of the Páez government had little trouble reducing rural violence to an acceptable level. All of this is not especially remarkable except that the bandit Cisneros did not submit to the authority of the state; he did not really acknowledge the supremacy of civil law, but instead subordinated himself to the greater personal power and charisma of Páez, the national caudillo. Thus the peace and civil order brought by this submission came as a direct result of the caudillo's personal authority and not through the government's claim on its citizens' loyalty. To be sure, Páez was president of the Republic, but the significant element in the maintenance of public order came not from this anointment by civilian government but from the enforcer's personal authority. Páez made the government legitimate, not the other way around.

The second challenge to public order involved a more serious institutional threat to the integrity of Venezuela in the form of a separatist revolt in the Venezuelan east. Led by Santiago Mariño, one of the eastern caudillos of independence fame, this movement had a disparate and contradictory set of goals. Claiming to represent the military heroes of the wars, Mariño called for a return to the Bolivarian ideal of a united Colombia or, if that were not possible, the separation of the Venezuelan east from Caracas's control. This disingenuous program could not have been taken at face value, even though the threat to Páez's Venezuela was real enough, and the supreme caudillo quickly marched to the east to negotiate a settlement based on superior military strength. The incident never became a major revolt, but it presaged decades of tension and conflict between the national government in Caracas and the eastern periphery. Although the ostensible basis of this conflict has been traced to rampant regionalism, such a notion provides an incomplete explanation of the phenomenon.

The eastern caudillos, Mariño especially, may well have had illusions of an independent eastern Venezuela, but that chimera had less attraction than an alternative vision—a united Venezuela controlled from Caracas by members of the eastern regional elite. It was this latter form of regionalism that characterized Venezuela's republican politics throughout the modern period. In this country, regionalism did not imply the relocation of authority, decision making, economic power, or cultural centers into one of the peripheral areas, but the accession of a regionally based elite to the Caracas-based and managed central government. In fact, even the separatist rhetoric, only half-hearted at its peak during and immediately after independence, disappeared by the end of the 1830s.

Venezuela's territorial integrity proved relatively easy to define and maintain for a complex set of reasons. Not only had the Spanish colonial regime carefully delimited the national boundaries, but the human and political geography of the place made it difficult to split the country into pieces. The only natural break would have been at the Unare River, and this gave some plausibility to the rhetorical flourishes of the eastern caudillos. Even that division had no real chance of success, for the east had no potential capital city. Both Barcelona and Cumaná would have claimed that status, but lacking institutions, traditions, and economic links with the European world, their claims would have been difficult to sustain long enough to create these missing elements. Perhaps even more significant, however, the European merchants of England, France, and Germany evidently saw little benefit in the separation of eastern Venezuela. Better to deal with one intermediary elite in Caracas than with two, with the addition of an eastern city such as Cumaná. The eastern separation received little foreign encouragement, and that by itself indicated the futility of the separatist spirit. In fact, the only serious, early complication about Venezuela's borders came in the extreme east, in the Guayana region, where very early in the republican period the British colony at Georgetown in British Guiana claimd territory that Venezuela considered its own. This dispute, which endures to the present day, had relatively little significant impact, however, on the consolidation of the country around the central city of Caracas.

In the course of resolving these challenges to his rule of Venezuela, Páez gradually set the tone of his administrative style. Never much interested in the details of finance and bureaucracy and evidently anxious to acquire the acceptance of Venezuela's elite, he surrounded himself with a talented group of individuals characterized most prominently by their wealth, commercial expertise, and lack of significant participation in the independence epic. With a few notable exceptions, such as José Rafael Revenga and Carlos Soublette, Páez relied on men who had little connection with the military heroes of independence. This predilection for cultured, capable civilians without revolutionary prominence indicated Páez's shrewd judgment of the Venezuelan political environment.

Most of the heroes of independence would have made exceedingly poor allies, for if not part of the pro-Bolívar faction, and therefore anti-Páez by definition, they were independent caudillos anxious to supplant Páez in the role of Venezuela's protector. The Páez strategy involved waiting out each caudillo, forcing them one by one to declare themselves, and then pacifying them individually with the force of his *llanero* armies, paid of course from the national treasury. Because he never broke completely with any of them and because he carefully kept his position separate from the civilian politics of the capital, his military rivals never could be sure how he would react. They often based their plans on the assumption that he could be induced to join them or at least remain neutral. Until 1848, when his political judgment failed him, Páez kept them all at bay and gave the Caracas bureaucracy time to establish the links with North Atlantic commerce that would make Venezuela and its elite wealthy participants in world trade.

This policy of relying on the civilians of Caracas for the management of his administration fooled the *caraqueños* into thinking that they had the authority and legitimacy to govern. By the end of Páez's first term, the country appeared relatively tranquil, and the rapid inflow of foreign capital had begun a revival of Venezuelan agriculture. In the election of 1835, two principal candidates appeared: General Carlos Soublette, the only major independence hero loyal to Páez, and Dr. José María Vargas, a lukewarm patriot who had sat out the wars in the safety of the Antilles. Vargas, the candidate of the *caraqueño* elite, had little of the ruthlessness required of a president of Venezuela, but his supporters saw him as a dedicated believer in the supremacy of civilian authority over armed rule. In Vargas, these *caraqueño* leaders believed they had someone who would manage Venezuela in their interests, an individual without an independent source of power who could be counted on to put them first on the national agenda.

Thanks to the enthusiasm for Vargas, the doctor was duly elected president, and Páez, his candidate defeated, retired to his rural properties. Evidently unwilling to be the cause of civil disorder or rebellion, Páez simply chose to wait, perhaps knowing Vargas would never last as president. Indeed, hardly had the civilian regime begun when it faced an uprising led by a number of independence-era generals dissatisfied with their rewards from the Republic and appalled at the indifference of the Vargas government to their claims. This Revolución de las Reformas, aimed against a government without an army or the capacity to raise one, quickly succeeded in deposing Vargas, who fled back to the Antilles. But as the revolutionaries knew, even if Vargas and the Caracas civilians did not, without the participation or at least neutrality of José Antonio Páez, no *coup d'état* in 1835 could be secure.

It is eloquent testimony to Páez's political craft that he waited until everyone of political consequence in the drama of this little revolution had declared himself before he chose sides. Then he came thundering out of the llanos with his lancers to destroy the revolution, restore civilian government, and escort José María Vargas back to the presidential chair. At one stroke, Páez identified his rivals and enemies among the remaining independence heroes, labeled them as rebellious dissidents, and greatly reduced their ability to challenge him. At the same time, he impressed on the civilian elite of Caracas, the managers of the profitable and essential connection with the Atlantic world, their absolute dependence on his personal prestige and authority for the civil peace and social order required for Venezuela to prosper.

Early in 1836 Vargas, evidently frightened by his experience with the revolution, proposed severe punishments for its leaders, but Páez and the wiser members of the Caracas elite refused to permit retaliation more severe than exile. Frustrated in his efforts to govern, Vargas resigned the presidency which, after passing through the hands of a couple of interim officeholders, fell to General Carlos Soublette, who finished out Vargas's term.

By 1836, then, the basis of a stable republican government, which would last more than a decade with the same individuals and a century in the same form, had been established. The elements of this arrangement have been mentioned before but deserve added emphasis. In essence, Venezuela would operate from 1836 until the death of Juan Vicente Gómez in 1935 under a system of political action that involved two principal poles of power. At one pole was concentrated the expertise needed to manage the complex connection between the world of rural Venezuela and the world of sophisticated North Atlantic finance, manufacturing, and trade. This expertise was concentrated in the central city of Caracas in the hands of a growing civilian bureaucracy and merchant elite whose prosperity depended on their ability to make the connection between Venezuela's agricultural production and North Atlantic markets. By the very fact of their urban, sophisticated, expert life style, however, these people rarely possessed the skills required to control Venezuela's unruly peasant population or the authority to command the allegiance of Venezuela's popular caudillos. They could not, in effect, keep the peace or secure public order.

At the other pole congregated a succession of popular caudillos, individuals or shifting coalitions of individuals with the charisma, experience, and resources to generate temporary personal armies. Although originating in a variety of geographical locations, these caudillos provided the authority and legitimacy that the civilians of Caracas could not provide. They exercised the force that kept social order, and they expected to get rich for performing these services.

Within this system, the individuals in this constellation of force and bureaucracy tended to change with unpleasant frequency, but the system itself remained stable for a century, centered in Caracas and dedicated to the organization of Venezuela's internal economy to serve best the needs of Atlantic trade. Because this system, for all its durability and longevity, had a weak institutional structure and a constant and recurring incentive for internal social disorder, Venezuela spent much of the nineteenth century in varying states of civil war.

The lack of internal stability, the absence of smooth transitions of power, the constantly high level of endemic social unrest—all came from Venezuela's peculiar situation and complex history. Having destroyed the basis of civilian government with the destruction of Spanish rule and the dismantling of the royal bureaucracy, Venezuela had neither the time nor the resources to create a substitute with similar durability, legitimacy, and authority. Socialized rather abruptly and in many cases brutally into a short-term, quick-return mentality by the decades of war between 1810 and 1830, Venezuelans could little afford to adopt a patient, civilian attitude toward matters of state or politics. Furthermore, the characteristics of Venezuela's postindependence agricultural and economic recovery, determined to a great extent by the terms of Atlantic trade and finance, accentuated the quick-return syndrome, making this mode of operation one of the strongest features of Venezuelan public and private existence.

Within this framework, the frequent outbursts of political violence observed throughout the nineteenth century represent a form of institutionalized, almost ritual, warfare. The caudillos who rode at the head of their informal personal armies sought no basic change in the structural relationship of Venezuela to the world; they wanted no reorganization of the economy and society, nor did they seriously propose a relocation of the central city of Caracas. Instead, they simply pursued national prominence and personal advancement within the bounds of behavior established during the independence years. These norms, of course, were wasteful and disruptive in the extreme. At intervals throughout the century, uprisings, rebellions, and successful revolts took workers from the fields and paralyzed agriculture, trade, and commerce in large sections of the country for months at a time. Government revenue that might have been spent on roads, piers, irrigation, and other national needs went instead to support the government's troops in the field. Although Venezuelan civic leaders, publicists, and generals recognized the cost of these disturbances of public order, they were unable to find alternatives to the short-term opportunities for personal advancement and profit. Lacking the institutional structure and the social and political consensus that makes waiting possible, the Venezuelan elite pursued their interests with skill and success, whatever the long-term costs to the nation.

Such a system, with its built-in disorder and instability, could only have been possible in a society managed by a small elite with a firm hand on the country's social organization. While Venezuelans saw nothing extraordinary in the disorder of the para-military uprisings that constituted their political selection mechanisms, they showed remarkable unanimity in maintaining the social order. Elite-led revolts with political goals upset the normal rhythms of daily life and were roundly denounced by the government. But revolts with social goals, led by renegades from the elite or members of the lower orders, posed a threat to the entire system and brought an elite reaction that in its ferocity and hysteria betrayed a fear of any fundamental challenge to Venezuela's political and social arrangement.

This system worked as well as it did and lasted as long as it did because the regime of José Antonio Páez enjoyed a period of unusual economic prosperity between 1830 and the late 1840s, a prosperity that permitted the country substantial wealth and, consequently, the possibility of peace. With the coffee boom, enough money flowed into the country to induce the elite to accept Páez's rule and to allow the political and social institutions a momentary respite after the wars. Although the prosperity lasted only a few decades, it did give the Caracas-based political system a chance to coalesce.

The Páez regime witnessed and aided a remarkable transformation of Venezuelan agriculture. From the cacao-oriented colonial economy, Venezuela became transformed within a decade or so into a coffee-producing international economy. The change received considerable help from the physical destruction of the independence wars. Those planters whose cacao estates had been damaged or destroyed by the warfare, or more often by neglect, during those turbulent years found it better to replant their acreage in coffee than to try to resurrect their cacao groves. Coffee, not only an export fruit of preference in North Atlantic markets, also had a relatively short maturation period of five years instead of the eight or ten required by cacao. Even more important, these planters found that they could get large loans for replanting in coffee from European merchant houses established in Caracas. To be sure, coffee trees had been widely scattered about Venezuela's landscape since the late eighteenth century, but the large-scale, almost monoculture, of this fruit came only in the 1830s.

This reorientation of the Venezuelan economy under the watchful protection of Páez and his governments carried a host of consequences for Venezuelan agriculture and the management of the national economy little suspected by most of the elite. Busy getting rich on the credit generously distributed by European merchants and their Venezuelan agents, most agriculturalists failed to see or at least to worry about the subtle changes in their economic arrangements, changes that in a global sense merely reflected the completion of the transfer of American dependency from an Iberian connection to a North Atlantic connection. The local manifestations of the new economic order were fairly clear, involving conditions of trade, credit terms, and legal arrangements within Venezuela.

Under the new regime, Venezuela rapidly completed the conversion of those parts of its economy that dealt directly with the export market to a liberal, free-trade model without substantially modifying the domestic economic arrangements of internal trade, labor relations, and landholding patterns. This meant practically no restrictions on trade and a tariff designed only to provide government revenue. In the years after independence, Venezuela cleaned away most of the remnants of the complex Spanish economic legislation designed to restrict and control trade. These reforms were made more easily in Venezuela than elsewhere in Spanish America because the country's colonial tradition of corporatism and corporate colonial economic institutions had been very weak. With a strong tradition of individual entrepreneurial commerce either through contraband or legitimate channels, Venezuela found the free-trade doctrines of the North Atlantic relatively easy to assimilate insofar as their dealings in international commerce were concerned.

In return for the improvements in Venezuela's economic regulations, the merchants and banks of England and other North Atlantic trading nations offered Venezuelans virtually unlimited credit for a while on the promise of coffee crops and the security of agricultural properties. Symbolizing this new approach to economic development, this rejection of the Spanish paternalistic commercial rules, the Venezuelan congress passed a credit law in 1834 that eliminated all Spanish controls on contracts. After April 10, 1834, any contract legally executed would be enforced by the state. No matter that the terms were injurious or the interest rates outrageous, the enthusiasm of the liberal Republic saw no reason to protect the weak and foolish. Of course, the

April 10 law represented the subordination of domestic interests to the
impersonal and indifferent vagaries of world trade. Venezuelans, little
experienced in these matters and in any case determined to squeeze
maximum advantage out of the coffee boom of the 1830s, seemed anxious to show European bankers and merchants their willingness to
organize Venezuela in the most favorable way for capital and trade.

The liberalizing of Venezuela occurred so rapidly and so completely
in the trade-oriented part of the economy that by the mid-1830s practically nothing of the old colonial system for world trade remained.
The completeness and rapidity of this transformation owed much to
the Páez hegemony, which allowed the peace and agricultural development on which prosperity depended, and the absence of strong institutional interests prevented the formation of an effective opposition to
this liberalization. The Church, never particularly strong or wealthy in
Venezuela, expressed little interest in these matters, being more concerned with the restoration of its preferred position with the state and
the reconciliation of prelate and government after the wartime conflicts. The merchant group in Venezuela had to some extent been destroyed by the wars, but in any case Venezuelan merchants had only
weak ties with the powerful and privileged commercial elite in Spain.
For most of these local entrepreneurs, Spanish colonial economic legislation had rarely been of economic benefit, and then primarily in favor
of the cacao trade. Those merchants who survived the wars seemed
glad to see the colonial apparatus dismantled.

Landowners, however, agreed to this liberalization of the trade economy for somewhat different reasons. Desperate for the credit that
would permit them to rebuild and expand their export production of
coffee, they would have welcomed European money on practically any
terms. With coffee prices high, they saw no reason to refuse credit
that could easily be repaid. For the most part, then, even the coffee
producers enthusiastically supported the April 10 law and other liberal
economic measures.

Having gained the credit and the markets of Europe, Venezuelan
planters engaged in an orgy of planting and expansion, all financed
with money borrowed from European-controlled export factors. Al-

though credit and high debt were nothing new to Venezuelan agriculture, the terms of the credit were indeed different. In colonial times Church agencies served as the principal bankers for agriculture, placing money in long-term loans at relatively low interest rates rarely exceeding 6 percent per year. This kind of credit, ideal for the agriculturalist, permitted the planters to spread their losses and gains over a long cycle without fear of precipitate foreclosures. Under the liberal regime, however, the credit available, while abundant, came on commercial terms at higher interest rates. Not only did planters have to pay 12 percent interest or more, they had to liquidate the principal or refinance the loan in periods ranging from nine months to a year. If coffee prices were high, as happened in the 1830s, then credit was easy, and planters had no difficulty rolling over their loans and even increasing their debt. Any decline in the world coffee price had an immediate impact on the Venezuelan credit market. Not only were no new loans available, but existing loans came due rapidly as the nine-month or year-long terms drew to a close. Under the guarantees of the April 10 law, it took only one creditor unwilling to refinance or renegotiate to force a planter into bankruptcy and foreclosure. These consequences of a decline in the world coffee price had such an impact in Venezuela partly because no local providers of capital existed. Venezuela had no banks of consequence, and the money available for loans came mostly from Europe and could be withdrawn as rapidly as it had been offered.

The new organization of Venezuela's export market intensified these precarious financial circumstances. Under Spanish colonial rule, Venezuela had long enjoyed a privileged position in both Spain and Mexico for its cacao exports. The price for that commodity, while variable, was set by the government with the participation of the Venezuelan producers. Violent swings in the price and rapid changes in the market occurred mostly as a result of Spain's international military problems, which closed the trade routes to the peninsula from time to time, and not as a result of market changes. To be sure, the Caracas cacao prices reflected changes in the market, but slowly and moderately. While this system of protected markets and buffered prices kept Venezuelans

from making windfall profits, it also kept them from suffering catastrophic losses. All of this apparatus disappeared during the independence in the switch from cacao to coffee and in the creation of the
liberal Republic.

The coffee boom of the 1830s, while it provided the prosperity that
helped Páez keep the peace, also had other effects on Venezuela's postwar development. In the rush to expand coffee production and to
bring new land into cultivation, Venezuela's elite discovered that there
was a labor shortage. In the heady days of the early independence,
Venezuela had eliminated the moribund slave trade from its shores.
From all indications, Venezuela's labor force in the decade or so before
independence proved adequate for the requirements of the cacao industry, and few planters much wanted to spend the money necessary
to purchase slaves. In addition, some evidence indicates a decline in
cacao production, which would also have reduced the demand for
labor. In the period of the independence wars, both patriot and royalist
commanders had found it expedient to free slaves who would fight
their battles, and victorious patriots under Bolívar had incurred an obligation to free the slaves in return for Petión's help in Haiti. Thus, the
Venezuelan congress at Angostura had passed a free-birth measure,
and the congress at Cúcuta established the free-birth legislation that
would be ratified by the independent Venezuelan congress in 1830.

By the 1830s, then, the slave trade had been irrevocably eliminated,
and the captive, controllable slave population had entered a period of
gradual decline as the children of slaves grew up free. To be sure, as
the demand for labor grew along with the coffee boom, planters did
everything possible to slow down the process of manumission and to
delay the entry of freeborn children of slaves into the uncontrolled
labor force. These devices could not, of course, do much about the
labor shortage suffered by Venezuelan agriculturalists after the mid-
1830s. This apparently reflected less an absolute shortage of hands
than a lack of willing laborers. When profits from the coffee boom
reached their peak in the early 1830s and planters paid well for labor,
few complained about the absence of workers. But as the price of coffee fell in the late 1830s and early 1840s, more and more complaints

about labor scarcity and irresponsibility surfaced. Clearly, the Venezuelan rural laborer had a choice between subsistence agriculture and paid work on coffee plantations. As long as wages remained high, rural workers could purchase a higher standard of living by working in the coffee fields for wages, but when those wages fell with the fall in export prices, the alternative of subsistence agriculture grew more attractive. Most workers probably opted for a combination of plantation work and subsistence farming, the proportions of each depending on the return for their labor in the coffee groves.

As planters spread coffee trees onto new land, they required labor to clear, plant, care for, and eventually harvest the coffee. But with production expanding much faster than the labor supply, shortages inevitably occurred. The planters responded with a series of police laws designed to fix the labor force in the employ of individual hacendados and restrict the mobility of peons from one coffee plantation to another. These devices failed because no police force existed to manage the laws and the planters could not restrain each other from the practice of offering bonuses to lure peons from neighboring haciendas.

This labor problem occupied the periodical press throughout the late 1830s and the 1840s and suggested an even greater complication. Venezuela, in the throes of the coffee boom, had more expansion than its institutions could manage. Everyone who could took maximum advantage of the easy credit, high prices, and boom-time psychology. Because the institutional structure that might have helped diversify Venezuela's prosperity did not exist, the country rapidly became devoted to coffee monoculture with a thoroughness never known in the colonial cacao economy.

While prices remained high, the country and especially the coffee regions prospered, although the prosperity was unevenly distributed. Coffee grew in all parts of the country, but most of the exports came from the central region, the valleys of Caracas and Aragua, and the slopes of the coastal mountains. This pattern reflected the agricultural economy of those areas before the wars, a development that made rapid transition to coffee from cacao relatively easy. It also reflected the ease of transportation and communication with the coast ports of Puerto

Cabello and La Guaira plus the proximity to Caracas, the center of credit and finance for the expansion.

This concentration around the capital greatly enhanced the centralizing power of the Caracas bureaucracy, for the prosperity of its hinterland flowed through the city and into the hands of the coffee merchants whose main Venezuelan offices carried out a lively import-export business from the city. The credit that sustained this prosperity almost invariably came from the agents of European merchants and banks resident in Caracas. José Antonio Páez guaranteed the peace, the government reorganized the financial and legal structure of Venezuela to accommodate foreign finance, and the coffee boom seemed to justify these efforts.

By the 1840s, then, Venezuela had achieved a degree of order and progress. The country had a reasonably competent government bureaucracy in Caracas; the forms of a constitutional republic had been established in law; the basis of a thriving economy had been laid; and the vital connection with the North Atlantic community had been made. The country appeared ready for full participation in world trade, and with the prosperity from that trade, Venezuela would progress until it became as modern and powerful as any North Atlantic power. Or so hoped the Caracas elite.

That future, the constant dream of Venezuelans, was not to be, at least not for a century. Instead, the economy, precariously based on the monoculture of coffee, overburdened with debt, and operating inefficiently, began to falter in the late 1830s and fell into disorder by the late 1840s. The clearest signs of trouble, as often happens with export monoculture economies, came with the decline in the world price for coffee. That, in turn, set off a chain of related calamities throughout the economy. As prices fell, the planters found their creditors unwilling to refinance their loans. Creditors demanded payment from Venezuelans, whose debt was too high already. Inevitably, some of the weaker operations failed, and in the late 1830s, and increasingly in the 1840s, bankruptcy auctions became a common activity in Caracas under the provisions of the April 10 law.

All of this did not happen overnight. The crisis had begun slowly in the late 1830s and became the central national political issue by the mid-1840s. As a result of growing concern over labor and credit problems, the Venezuelan elite began to divide into two main political groups which in the 1840s would become political parties. One faction, calling itself Conservative or called by its opponents *godo,* to associate it with the Spanish imperial past, coalesced around the figure of José Antonio Páez and brought together what the propagandists of the opposition saw as a coalition of merchants, money-lenders, and the agents of foreign commerce. The other group organized around the quixotic figure of Antonio Leocadio Guzmán, an individual whose marriage into the Bolívar-Blanco family gave him the independence-era credentials and the elite status required of a major political figure in Venezuela. This party, calling itself Liberal more for rhetorical effect than from any doctrinal conviction, claimed to represent the agricultural interests of the country—the planters, in other words.

Both parties included individuals engaged in agriculture and in commerce, although the Liberals did espouse a consistent policy line that favored debtors at the expense of creditors. As most agriculturalists were debtors, there was some logic in the Liberal claim of being the party of agriculture. But an issue-oriented political party could not have lasted long in nineteenth-century Venezuela, and the Liberals also drew strength from the familial, regional, and independence-era rivalries of the country's past. The eastern caudillos, opposed to Páez mostly because he had prevented their rise to prominence, appeared to view the Liberals with favor. The pro-Bolívar families and associates who had been excluded from Páez governments came to support the Liberals. The political exiles from the abortive coup against President José María Vargas in 1834 returned to the country under a general amnesty in March 1842, and many ended up working for the Liberals.

Out of this collection of debtors, Bolivarianists, disaffected military heroes, and political exiles, Antonio Leocadio Guzmán and his associates created a political party. The mechanism for the party's expansion was a newspaper, *El Venezolano,* founded in 1840 to propagate the party line and organize the party's program. Throughout the 1840s the newspapers of Liberals and Conservatives blasted their opposition's ideas, programs, and leaders with flashy prose, reasoned articles on the state of the economy and the remedies for its problems, personal invective and slander, and clippings from foreign newspapers. In the battle of words, the Liberals had an advantage, for they described a very real crisis, and the government's remedies showed little concern for the plight of the debt-ridden planters. While the Liberals raged against the iniquity of foreclosures, the forced sale of agricultural property well below true value, and the ruthlessness of creditors, the Conservative government suggested that the credit squeeze came primarily from the profligacy and mismanagement of the planter class.

Each group had its remedy for the crisis of the 1840s. Liberals called for a modification of the April 10 law because it enforced all contracts whatever the terms. Liberals wanted specific protectionist legislation enacted which would permit planters to delay their payments, get judicially approved waiting periods before foreclosure, and, under some conditions, eliminate their debts altogether. In addition, Liberals called for the creation of an agricultural land bank that would provide loans to planters at low rates over long periods of time. The Conservatives viewed most of this program with considerable alarm. As the party charged with managing Venezuela's connection to North Atlantic commerce, they had assimilated the European merchant's horror at the thought of disturbing the sanctity of contracts, and from their participation in that trade, they had come to understand the importance of good external credit for the continued prosperity of Venezuela's export economy. From the Conservative perspective the failure of a few imprudent planters seemed a small price to pay for the maintenance of Venezuela's reputation for fiscal and financial responsibility in the North Atlantic community.

Few political controversies proceed with clear issues and reasoned discussion, and this one was no exception. The Liberals, led by the impetuous oratory and polemical propaganda of Antonio Leocadio Guzmán, became deeply involved in the elections of 1842 and 1846, elections the Liberals believed to be fraudulent. In the wake of the 1846 affair, bands of Liberal-led ruffians sacked a few haciendas owned by prominent Conservatives and stirred up the specter of civil disorder and race war. Because the hard times and low coffee prices affected the wages and opportunities of rural workers, most of whom were *pardos* in the coffee regions, these people were easily recruited into bandit raids under the cover of Liberal party slogans. The slave population, although not very large, still constituted a reservoir of oppressed and discontented people that both Conservatives and Liberals believed ready to flood the country with the death and destruction of a race war.

Although the Liberals managed to stir up considerable social and political unrest, the government and Páez proved adequate to the challenge. President Carlos Soublette presided over these turbulent times with tranquility and faith in his mentor, Páez, if not with imagination or initiative. In any case, the government, finally goaded beyond endurance, arrested Antonio Leocadio Guzmán and sentenced him to death for his role in instigating the popular uprisings. While Antonio Leocadio had indeed written inflammatory propaganda, no evidence shows him actively involved in the instigation or direction of the bandit raids. The evidence indicates that the violence and racial overtones of the bandit fury frightened Guzmán as much as it did any *caraqueño* oligarch. But to terminate the Liberal excesses, the government sought to eliminate the local leadership, hence the sentence against Antonio Leocadio Guzmán.

In political terms this sentence caused more trouble for the government than it could possibly have prevented. Not only did the death penalty appear excessive, especially for the crime of injudicious propagandizing, but it went against the Venezuelan tradition of exiling elite troublemakers rather than executing them. Furthermore, to many the action appeared more a reprisal against the Liberal party than a sentence against a dangerous individual, and the Liberals had quite a significant following among the agricultural elite. Under these conditions, the election of the next president of Venezuela took on unusual importance, for that individual would not only have to cope with the worsening crisis of the coffee industry but also would have to carry out the sentence against Guzmán.

The outgoing president, Carlos Soublette, had little to say about his successor, that privilege falling to General José Antonio Páez, the supreme caudillo. As usual the popular press scurried about collecting rumors, but at the proper moment the national hero, Páez, proposed General José Tadeo Monagas, the eastern war hero with some Liberal sympathies. The choice surprised many because Monagas had never been in the center of Venezuelan politics and had participated in the eastern separatist activities of the 1830s. However, he had not taken a position on the party politics of the 1840s, and Páez may have seen the presidency as a way of bringing Monagas into the Conservative coalition and preventing any movement to attach him to the Liberal cause.

Páez's approval meant automatic election, and the Liberals appeared certain that the elections had been fraudulent. In any case, Monagas took office in 1848 and began an administration that very rapidly disturbed and surprised Páez and his Conservative supporters. In his appointments to the cabinet and other government positions, Monagas showed a decided preference for individuals with Liberal sympathies. Gradually he changed the complexion of the upper layer of the bureaucracy from monochromatic Conservative to predominantly Liberal. The crowning insult to the Conservatives was the commutation of Antonio Leocadio Guzmán's death penalty to one of exile. This represented a complete break with the Conservative group and signaled Monagas's independence from Páez.

Early in 1848 the government had traveled so far along the Liberal track that Páez believed intervention to be necessary, and the ageing caudillo once again raised his banner and called out his *llanero* horsemen. But in 1848 the conditions of the llanos did not permit a major response to the caudillo's call. The name of José Antonio Páez no longer represented a vital, dynamic leader to the young *llaneros* who had only the tales of their fathers to introduce them to the General. The elite leadership of much of the country saw little use in a Páez campaign against Monagas. The result came in a quick defeat of Páez and his exile to the Caribbean and the United States.

If the Liberals had expected a renaissance of Liberal reforms and a flowering of democratic principles, they were disappointed. Monagas permitted the congress to pass a series of debt relief laws, repeal the controversial April 10 law on contracts, and attempt to establish an agricultural land bank, all key elements in the Liberal program. But if he was willing to allow the Liberals their pet programs, he had no intention of letting them control his government. His regime, which lasted for a decade more or less, turned into a family affair, with José Tadeo alternating the presidency with his brother José Gregorio; then, in an ill-fated experiment, José Tadeo had his son-in-law elected to the vice-presidency in 1857, a prelude to the reform of the constitution in 1857 which extended his presidency for two more years.

Unfortunately, the Liberal measures of the Monagas government failed to bring the anticipated revival of the Venezuelan economy. Not only did coffee prices remain depressed, but the credit squeeze brought on originally by the decline in prices remained severe. In part, Venezuela's liberalized format must have appeared much less attractive to European and United States merchants and bankers. Moreover, the Liberal Monagas government found itself often preoccupied with the problems of civil order.

The constant alarms and disturbances in the countryside represented more a symptom than a cause of Venezuela's malaise, but it monopolized the government's resources and attention during the Monagas years. The bandit raids and general instability of the social order came from the poor economic conditions of the late 1840s and the 1850s plus the lack of a ruling consensus within the elite. Conservatives—Páez sympathizers—took every opportunity to stir up trouble. From the Antilles the exiles sent propaganda and some assistance. From the countryside came sporadic uprisings against this or that government official. All these activities drained off government resources that might better have gone into solving the agricultural crisis of Venezuela.

The Monagas dynasty's difficulties in this period form part of the larger pattern of Venezuela's past. The Liberal Oligarchy (as some historians have called the Monagas regimes), in much the same way as its predecessor governments under Páez, tried to make Venezuela a better participant in the North Atlantic trading community. But in this instance the pressures of high debts and low coffee prices combined to reduce the elite's enthusiasm for the North Atlantic model of a free-enterprise, agricultural-export economy. They attempted to construct a limited, modernized version of the Spanish colonial economic system that would have preserved the benefits of world trade and foreign capital but would also have protected the interests of local land-based elites from the most severe consequences of unrestricted enterprise. Here, as earlier in Venezuela's republican history, these elites pursued their short-term interests with single-minded intensity. Whereas in the 1830s the quick profit came from dismantling the Spanish colonial commercial system and contracting for an excess of credit, in the 1850s the rush was to protect the assets of the elite from the consequences of easy credit and volatile world export prices.

This behavior of Venezuela's controlling class, whatever the party, shows remarkable consistency throughout the country's modern history. The basic mechanism operated as follows: the local Venezuelan elite, always eager to cash in on whatever short-term benefits were offered in the North Atlantic market, stood ready to rearrange their economy and polity to take advantage of those opportunities, whatever the possible long-term cost to the country at large. Likewise, when those opportunities ceased or changed, the elite quickly used its government to protect its interests until the next cycle of opportunity arose. Because these activities took place against a background of a society with very impermanent political institutions and political parties without significant organization or doctrinal consistency, the transition from expansion to protection often became violent because the elites had no other way of distributing the costs of retrenchment and protection. Because the cycles came at times and under conditions determined by events completely beyond Venezuela's control, the transitions were frequently rapid. Further, these violent and rapid transitions prevented the consolidation and maturation of an institutional structure capable of buffering the shocks of the export cycle. The basic features of the export-monoculture economy accentuated all of these problems by eliminating the possibility of economic diversification, a tactic that might have eased the impact of rapid export price changes. But with no institutions to manage such a diversification, what elite member would sacrifice his profits in a high export market to help the country survive a low export market? Who, in short, would give up big short-term gains for the possibility of moderate long-term gains?

From this perspective the unstable governments and political-civil unrest that gradually grew worse from 1848 to 1858 becomes easier to explain. In an international context, Venezuela struggled during those decades to find a way of continuing its profitable participation in North Atlantic export markets without having to suffer the consequences of easy credit, high debt levels, and falling export prices. Such a utopian solution could not be found, and the declining economic conditions prevented Monagas—as it would have any alternative caudillo—from gaining either the resources to eliminate his rivals or the prosperity to satisfy them. Added to these complications, Monagas proved to be something less than astute. His ineptness and excessive nepotism made it relatively easy for his rivals to attack the administration.

On a national scale, the events of 1848-58 operated in accord with a different logic. The interaction between the North Atlantic trade and the Venezuelan response to that trade and Venezuela's domestic social, economic, and political traditions complicates the analysis of the country's nineteenth-century history. This curious phenomenon of a dual national existence came from the failure of the independence wars to effect a significant social revolution or to change the basic domestic mechanisms for distributing wealth. Under Spanish rule, Venezuelan social, political, and economic values operated more or less in consonance with Spanish America's economic participation in the world market because the Spanish economic system, with its controls restricting free enterprise, buffered that participation. The wars of independence and the subsequent republican governments eliminated those economic controls without much changing the underlying mechanisms of social control. Throughout the nineteenth and into the first decades of the twentieth century, a dual existence resulted that often brought substantial contradictions. While the elite struggled to integrate their trade, values, and life style with the modern rhythms of the North Atlantic nations, they also worked diligently to maintain their archaic social system and domestic political economy intact, free from the influences of modern practices and theories.

In good times, with the export market strong and the country prosperous, the contradictions of this dual-track development could be disguised or moderated by a sort of subsidy from the modern system to the archaic. In bad times, the elites fell to quarreling, and the suppressed contradictions within the archaic system expressed itself as social unrest and popular movements. Most of the elite had every interest in maintaining the archaic system that supported their status. But the discontent and unrest among the non-elite in the archaic system also presented a wonderful opportunity for out-of-power factions to gain troops and to harass the government. The trick was to exploit this advantage without bringing on a social revolution capable of destroying the archaic system that, after all, made the elite possible. Throughout the decade 1848-58 the Conservatives and Liberals carried out a contest according to these rules, but because neither party could gain complete control of the archaic system or neutralize the modern system, the conflict degenerated by 1858 into a full-scale civil war.

The social content of the conflicts of those years can easily be followed through the sporadic debate over the questions of slaves, slavery, manumission, and people of color. Although the slave trade had ended by 1810, the Venezuelan slave population survived Bolívar's freedom decrees and the good intentions of other independence-era laws. In the years from 1830 to 1854 the slave population slowly declined from the effects of free birth, manumission programs, and attrition by death. Venezuelans held no brief for slavery, and all members of the elite saw the end of the institution as inevitable. The existence of slavery posed too great a contradiction between the archaic and the modern systems, and Venezuela stood ready to eliminate it, slowly. But with the turmoil and unrest of the 1840s and 1850s, slavery became more trouble for the ruling elite than it was worth because the out-of-power Conservatives seemed willing to stir up slave revolts in agricultural Venezuela as a means of destroying the Monagas dynasty's hold on the government. To deny their opposition this weapon and to keep Conservatives from looking philanthropic in the North Atlantic world, President José Gregorio Monagas and the Venezuelan congress abolished the institution and promised compensation to slave owners in March 1854, thereby earning his administration a line in all our histories.

THE FIGHT FOR CARACAS

The various Monagas family regimes between 1848 and 1858 failed to revitalize the economy, in part because export prices remained low and in part because the debt-relief legislation increased the risk for foreign investment in the country, thereby helping to keep the inflow of capital low. The Monagas years demonstrated that any effort to restrict the free operation of North Atlantic enterprise would seriously impair the participation of Venezuela in the modern sector of world trade. It took Venezuela a long time to learn this lesson because of the strength of the country's archaic system and the weakness of the elites as the result of internecine quarrels. But the Federal Wars—as the civil conflicts of 1858-63 are called—helped convince a new generation of Venezuelan caudillos of the importance of maintaining the modern system at all costs.

These Federal Wars, with their prolonged campaigns and considerable loss of life and property destruction, resembled the independence years, and some scholars have seen this conflict as a second war of independence. But this time the heroes had no foreign power to defeat, no continent to liberate, and no Bolívar to carry the civil war to heroic dimensions. Although the detailed inner history of the conflict has yet to be written, apparently the Federal Wars represented primarily a conflict within and among Venezuela's elites over the control and exploitation of the federal government. Warfare provided the only available mechanism for the resolution of uncompromisable conflicts between the major caudillos and their civilian supporters. The weakness of the economy and the excesses of the corrupt Monagas regimes made the wars easier to start and harder to bring to a satisfactory conclusion.

Ostensibly, these wars had their rationale in a principled fight over the question of whether Venezuela should be federalist or centralist. That is, the rhetoric of states rights and regional autonomy dominated the propaganda. Clearly, regional and local dissatisfaction with the Monagas central government had much to do with the origins of the civil war. Mixed into the complex of regional and personal rivalries was a subsidiary and little-debated argument over the role of the state in encouraging national progress. Part of the Federalist rhetoric could be seen as continued resistance to Caracas's control over the North Atlantic connection, a theme rarely articulated in the propaganda of the period, at least not directly.

More interesting than these elements of the complex mix of the Federal Wars was the regional shift in Venezuelan politics that these wars represent. If the independence wars drew their strength from the eastern stronghold on the Orinoco and from the caudillos of Cumaná and Barcelona, the Federal Wars remained a peculiarly western phenomenon, drawing leadership and locating campaigns in the regions of Coro, Barquisimeto, San Carlos, and other parts of the Segovia Highlands. The principal leader and subsequent president of Venezuela, General Juan Crisóstomo Falcón, came from that region, and the eventual triumph of his troops signified a shift in regional power away from the easterners such as Monagas and toward the west, the Segovia Highlands, and into the lower Andes.

Much has been made of Venezuelan regionalism, and rightly so, for the history of Venezuela is replete with regional caudillos, political movements, and aspirations. Nevertheless, the constant discussions of regional demands, the Venezuelan preoccupation with the regional origins of its leaders, heroes, and villains tends to obscure the function of regional activities within the country's past.

After the mid-1830s at the latest regionalist behavior ceased to have separatist pretensions. The local caudillos of the rest of the century never appear to have seriously contemplated any fundamental reorganization of the country with their regional capitals as center. The regional movements and the regional caudillos worked to gain control of Caracas and, through the *caraqueño* apparatus, control of the country. Naturally, every successful regional caudillo saw to it that his friends, neighbors, and family prospered, a behavior that often required the diversion of resources from one region to another. The significant point of the exercise was not that regionalist conflicts represented a weakness in the Venezuelan national design, but rather that the conflicts appeared to strengthen at every change in regime or regional preference the importance of the Caracas bureaucracy and its connections to the outside world.

In a country without ideological or interest-group politics on a national scale, a regional affiliation provided a point of cohesion for caudillesque political movements. In fact, it may well be that the caudillo-based politics of nineteenth-century Venezuela required regionalist justification. The caudillo form of political action, of course, specified substantial short-term personal armies or irregular military forces, without which a bid for national power was inconceivable. Of necessity, the mechanics of collection, organization, and maintenance of these irregulars implied a local or at most a regional base of operations. Without communications systems, rapid transportation, or political organizations, the geographically defined regional bloc formed the natural subdivisions which individual caudillos effectively controlled. In the national arena, caudillos competed to capture Caracas and the resources it controlled, use those resources to support the regional army long enough to defeat challengers from other regions, and keep the resources of the central government working to maintain the capability of recruiting the regional army when needed. In hard times, when the export market failed to keep Venezuela rich or when the personal vigor and skill of the reigning caudillo waned, the resources from the export connection through Caracas would be inadequate to resist another regional challenge. The old caudillo would then be replaced by a new one, sometimes from the same region, sometimes from another region, but always in Caracas. If Venezuela was lucky, the conflict required to effect the change would be short, as when Monagas succeeded Páez; in others, such as the Federal Wars, the issue required a long, drawn-out civil war to resolve.

From this system, then, came the Federal Wars of 1858-63, in which a variety of caudillos competed for ascendancy. In addition, the Federal Wars also had social overtones, as often happened in prolonged Venezuelan conflicts. The popular hero in this affair was Ezequiel Zamora, a military leader of exceptional ability. Whether his short but brilliant career would have matured into something different from that of the traditional caudillo is impossible to determine, for he was killed by a sniper before he had a chance to show his long-range promise. The Federal Wars then ground on until 1863. General José Antonio Páez's forces lost to a caudillesque coalition headed by Juan C. Falcón, a general whose success can be partly attributed to his associate and adviser, General Antonio Guzmán Blanco, son of the famous Liberal, Antonio Leocadio Guzmán.

Although traditional historiography shows the Federal Wars ending in 1863 with the ascendancy of Juan C. Falcón to the presidency of the Republic, it is difficult to distinguish the pre-1863 years from the post-1863 years. Venezuela's long period of instability in the nineteenth century varied primarily in intensity. The Liberal-Federalist regimes of Falcón and his successor Guzmán Blanco, the interludes presided over by the likes of Andueza Palacio and Joaquín Crespo, plus the transitional years of Cipriano Castro all had in common high levels of civil disorder and constant outbreaks of more or less politically inspired caudillesque revolts. What differentiates these presidential regimes is the relative success of the series of national caudillos in suppressing these uprisings while at the same time bringing some measure of peace and progress to most of the country.

Within this sequence of national leaders from Falcón to Cipriano Castro, the most interesting individual is General Antonio Guzmán Blanco. A fascinating character bringing together a variety of archetypical Latin American traits, he exemplified the ideals and the drive behind the Latin American commercial-bureaucratic state. Páez, in an earlier generation, had understood only the realities of local Venezuelan affairs. His comprehension of the North Atlantic export market and the mechanisms of finance, credit, and trade was at best rudimentary and derivative. His success in the 1830s and 1840s came first from boom-time coffee prices and second from his willingness to leave the management of the export connection to those *caraqueños* who understood the requirements of the North Atlantic market while spending his energies on the task of keeping archaic Venezuela in order. Guzmán Blanco, son of the great Liberal demagogue and founder of the Liberal party, Antonio Leocadio Guzmán, became the first Venezuelan president, with the possible exception of Bolívar, to belong both to the archaic and the modern worlds. Not until the post-Gómez regimes of the 1950s did Venezuela have such a versatile leader.

Antonio Guzmán Blanco received his education in the principles and realities of archaic Venezuela in the course of growing up in the middle of the Liberal-Conservative controversies of the 1840s. During the Federal Wars, he received the obligatory baptism under fire and the title of General, and, what proved considerably more important, he gained a clear understanding of the dynamics and structure of Venezuelan caudillo politics. As a tactician and strategist of civil war, Guzmán Blanco had excellent credentials. His teachers, Juan C. Falcón and Ezequiel Zamora, provided him with the practical experience in the occasional warfare of Venezuelan politics that helped make his years as manager of Venezuela so successful. Skillful local warriors, however, were common enough in nineteenth-century Venezuela. What made Guzmán Blanco special was his integration into European society, his ability to live and succeed in both archaic and modern worlds, and his efforts to change Venezuela into a more successful peripheral North Atlantic state. To be sure, the man was exceedingly vain, had an enormous appetite for adulation, and eventually found the strain of living in both worlds impossible to support. Yet for almost thirty years his presence and influence brought about a remarkable revitalization of Venezuelan government and a rebirth of Caracas.

For Guzmán Blanco, the Venezuelan problem had three principal and closely related dimensions. The first, recognized by every thoughtful citizen, involved the establishment of public order. No progress or prosperity could be achieved with the country mired in intermittent civil war. The first part of the Guzmán Blanco strategy attempted to reduce the level of organized violence to a minimum. The second dimension, also widely understood within Venezuela, involved the revitalization of the economy and the stimulation of the export trade. The final dimension of the problem, less commonly discussed, required the expansion of the Caracas bureaucracy and the modernization of the city to increase its ability to serve as the connection between modern Europe and archaic Venezuela.

In the decades of the 1860s and 1870s the Illustrious American, as he liked to be called, created a commercial-bureaucratic system to solve these three problems. His innovations in detail and tactics were many, and the integration of his approaches to internal and external difficulties were original. His principal contribution to Venezuelan national government was the foreign contract and loan. Previous caudillos would, of course, have been delighted to take money available in European banks and commercial houses, and some did. Guzmán Blanco was the first Venezuelan leader to see the connection between foreign contracts and loans, national government resources, the suppression of local revolts, and personal wealth. Although Páez and Monagas had certainly grown wealthy through their public careers, their fortunes came at the expense of public lands and contemporary Venezuelan income. Guzmán Blanco, however, learned how to skim the cream off of foreign contracts as well as to acquire vast holdings of national property for his own estates. In effect, his exceptional business skills permitted him to loot Venezuela's wealth in the form of property and acquire a portion of Venezuela's future wealth by skimming contracts and loans that the nation would have to pay back in years to come. This innovative personal aggrandizement, much condemned by contemporaries and historians, did not differ in kind from the behavior of previous national leaders, although it did exceed in quantity the rustic depredations of a Páez or a Monagas. At least Guzmán Blanco gave the country something for the fortune he took out, a record not equalled by many of his successors.

Whatever the caudillo's personal probity, he had superb political skills. To a country weakened and tired from years of war, Guzmán Blanco offered a way of keeping the peace. His system involved the creation of a powerful national bureaucracy and the acquisition of significant resources to distribute through that bureaucracy. With his aggressive program of foreign loans, Guzmán Blanco greatly increased the ability of the central government to reward the cooperative and punish the rebellious. This money freed the central government, at least for a time, from dependence on the uncertain revenues from customs duties, revenues easily disrupted by fractious caudillos. In the federal system managed by Antonio Guzmán Blanco, local caudillos governed their localities in any way they saw fit so long as public order was not greatly disturbed and the local government supported the national government. In return for their support and the civil order they maintained, local leaders received money in the form of regional subventions and federal troops in case competitors' uprisings became too large to handle.

Unlike earlier arrangements between national and regional caudillos, for the most part based on balances of personal power and expectations of future gains, Guzmán Blanco's system required the participation of a technically competent and sophisticated bureaucracy. The Illustrious American, for all his understanding of archaic Venezuela, had little ability to create his own personal army. Skillful and able though he was, the charismatic politics of the popular caudillo exceeded his grasp. Instead, Guzmán Blanco used his skills to acquire the money needed to purchase the charismatic leaders his system required. His strenuous efforts to fix an efficient bureaucratic system on the country are a reflection of his distrust of the popular appeal that had served as one of the bases of archaic Venezuelan politics.

In practice, the centralized bureaucratic regimes needed better communications than Venezuela had and closer personal attention than Guzmán Blanco wanted to give. He hoped to build such an efficient system that he would gradually withdraw from day-to-day supervision and leave the operation of the government to the bureaucrats. This notion, surprisingly modern in outlook, supposed a much more rapid change in Venezuela's archaic system than could possibly have been achieved with the economic resources available or without major changes in the attitudes of Venezuela's popular leaders. While the regional caudillos could be convinced to support the central government in exchange for generous subventions and to moderate their ambitions in recognition of Guzmán's superior tactical and financial skills, they would not respond to the directives of faceless bureaucrats in Caracas or accord Guzmán Blanco's surrogate presidents similar respect. Thus, the organization of Venezuela in a modern, centralized, and bureaucratic mode simply systematized traditional political practices, but it changed the basic behavior of political aspirants very little, and it continued to require the strong hand of a supreme leader to keep the ambitious regional caudillos within the confines of the bureaucratic system.

Before Antonio Guzmán Blanco lost his enthusiasm for modernizing Venezuela, his regimes made a significant impact on the organization and capabilities of the central government. At the center of his design for Venezuela lay the city of Santiago León de Caracas. The colonial town, which continued with the same buildings, streets, and public places in 1865 as it had had in 1810, seemed poorly equipped to play the role of modern national capital. With large sums flowing into the national treasury from a revival of the coffee trade, based this time on Andean groves, and the much improved Venezuelan credit abroad, the Illustrious American rebuilt Caracas in the Parisian mode. Boulevards, arches, massive public buildings, new plazas, and commemorative statuary (much of it to the glory of Guzmán Blanco)—all these came to grace Caracas. The city got water, sewers, and electrical services; its public transportation, both within the city and connecting Caracas to its major port and in the other direction toward its principal agricultural suburbs, became much more efficient. A telegraph web linked the capital with the important provincial centers of the country. The national army gained a more professional organization and access to modern armaments, especially new rifles. Within this setting, the Caracas bureaucracy grew to new levels of complexity and technical ability. Experts in finance, international contracts, and import-export trade all concentrated their skills in the capital city.

The overhaul of the physical features of the capital city seemed designed to create an image of Caracas that could be projected outward to the North Atlantic trading community and inward to the provincial caudillos for different effects. The external image aimed at the bankers and merchants whose interest in Venezuela focused to a considerable extent on the stability and responsibility of the national government and by extension on that government's ability to guarantee the completion of contracts and pay the interest on the national external debt. By making Caracas look new and modern, by presenting

the chiefs of North Atlantic trade and finance with a familiar, Northern European environment, Guzmán Blanco increased his credibility
as head of a responsible government. In the commercial-bureaucratic
world, these North Atlantic entrepreneurs and financiers rarely concerned themselves with conditions beyond the port and the capital;
and as a result, Guzmán Blanco's strategy of concentrating everything
in Caracas proved successful for a time.

For his fellow Venezuelan caudillos, the Caracas facelift had a different message. Before Guzmán Blanco, the capital city had been the
biggest, most sophisticated, and wealthiest city in the nation; indeed,
since the seventeenth century, Caracas had exceeded competing cities
in size, prosperity, and power. Yet for all of its centrality and advantages, Caracas differed from its competitors mainly in degree, not in
kind. Bigger, to be sure, but its buildings, streets, public places, and
services had little to recommend them over similar facilities in Coro,
Mérida, Cumaná, Trujillo, Barquisimeto, Valencia, or other places.
After Guzmán Blanco's reforms, the capital not only held more skills
and resources than any other place in the Republic, but it looked
completely different. What provincial visitor to the capital could fail
to recognize the quantum jump between the physical character of his
own town, a colonial village grown large, and Caracas, a metropolitan
center with a style drawn not from the Iberian colonial past but from
the Northern European present? This increased visual distance between capital and provincial center helped Guzmán Blanco create the
national system that was his goal. Since the skills that Caracas monopolized and the abilities that made the city central to Venezuela were
those invisible skills of administration, credit, and finance, the physical
facelifting of Caracas served as a visible symbol of the city's greater
knowledge of the modern world.

Guzmán Blanco eventually found the dual role of archaic caudillo
and modern urban sophisticate too difficult to play continuously.
Marveously skillful at the manipulation of his less sophisticated associates, a master of the reward-and-punishment technique, he kept
Venezuela reasonably under control when he devoted himself to the
task. Nevertheless, the process of modernization and bureaucratization

of Venezuela could not progress fast enough, and gradually the Illustrious American began spending more and more time in Europe, returning only to repair the system that kept him rich and famous when it appeared on the verge of collapse. Finally, in 1888, he left for Europe for good, never again returning to Venezuela.

Although Guzmán Blanco's stable system of central government control failed to start the country on a new political and economic track, his long period of domination left a considerable mark on the country. The role, resources, and appearance of Caracas became greatly enhanced. In addition, the massive debt contracted abroad significantly reinforced Venezuela's attachment to the world economic system of trade and finance. By introducing the modern mechanisms of communication and armament, however, the Illustrious American had changed the terms of political conflict in ways not made clear until the regime of Juan V. Gómez at the beginning of the twentieth century. Telegraphy made it virtuatlly impossible for regional caudillos to plan and organize revolts within the grace period permitted by poor communications. With the telegraph, news of disaffection reached the capital instantly and could provoke rapid and efficient countermeasures. Of course, the central government had to be reasonably capable for the system to work, but the telegraph made provincial revolts more risky than before and the central government more secure.

Similarly, the introduction of modern repeating rifles and other sophisticated war goods increased the ability of the central government to suppress provincial uprisings. The increased technical requirements of domestic warfare placed a premium on subverting the national armed forces if any opposition revolt were to succeed. No longer could a provincial caudillo collect his peons, armed with lances and knives, and march them toward Caracas with any hope of success. Although the overwhelming advantage of superior firepower did not become part of the national arsenal until the very end of Guzmán Blanco's regime, the Illustrious American deserves full credit for bringing modern military hardware into Venezuela and for beginning the creation of a national standing army with professional aspirations.

Curiously, the introduction of telegraphy and especially modern arms into the Venezuelan political process reinforced the close involvement of foreign representatives in Venezuela's internal affairs. By raising the technical requirements for civil war, Venezuela became dependent on the suppliers of the necessary hardware. A regional chieftain could not expect to conquer Caracas and then begin dealing with foreign commercial agents. Instead, under Guzmán Blanco, insurgents had to equip themselves with borrowed hardware and provisions from foreign bases in the Caribbean for an assault on the government. An aspiring caudillo had to make deals, at least with arms traders and frequently with governments, before launching an attack on Caracas. This not only made these external revolts more difficult but led to onerous terms as the aspiring caudillo dealt with foreigners from a very weak position. From the supplier's point of view, these upstart rebels represented very risky business partners, and their low success rate justified exhorbitant terms.

Antonio Guzmán Blanco's regimes left a heritage of a technically competent and worldly-wise *caraqueño* bureaucracy, an apparatus capable of managing the details of import-export trade in a world commodity market and in administering large national revenues from foreign contracts and loans. This structure, which Guzmán Blanco created but did not have the energy to perfect, survived the erratic, picaresque regime of Cipriano Castro to be inherited by a man who knew how to use it, Juan Vincente Gómez, the creator of modern, petroleum Venezuela.

In the twenty years that run from the end of Guzmán Blanco's regime in 1888 to the beginning of Juan Vicente Gómez's administration in 1908, Venezuela's political and economic systems experienced some dramatic changes in content and in style. Each succeeding caudillo-president brought the country closer to modern, technical, bureaucratic, and professionally managed styles of government behavior. Although the regime of Cipriano Castro found itself more enmeshed in the affairs of the world, more sophisticated in armaments and communications, and less dependent on archaic structures of the

colonial past than was that of Guzmán Blanco, there was little fundamental change in the arbitrariness, the personalism, or the violence
that characterized government in Venezuela.

This distinction, between the modernization of the tools and techniques of government and warfare and the absence of change in presidential prerogatives and civic norms expected by society at large, is
important to emphasize, for it demonstrates the strength of archaic
notions about leadership and legitimacy. In the years from Guzmán
Blanco to Gómez, Venezuela struggled to outlive the legacies of the
Federal Wars and the regional caudillo coalitions that gave the country what little political stability it had enjoyed. These years present an
almost continuous panorama of civil violence, uprisings, and instability. Clearly, the caudillo regimes based on regional alliances would
not die an easy death, but there could be little doubt that they would
eventually go.

As the Federalist leaders of the 1858-63 wars grew older, the new
generations coming of age in the 1870s found the traditional career
patterns of the successful national caudillo closed to them. In earlier
years the regional revolt or participation in a major civil war had provided the training and visibility required for an ambitious man to
aspire to important regional and national office. The key quality in an
aspirant for national leadership had been success in these wars, and
the constant stream of intermittent civil rebellion had provided the
mechanism Venezuela used to train and select those individuals most
able to manage the fractious, violent Venezuelan polity. The notion
of civic virtue in the form of elections, honestly and peacefully conducted, held little attraction for Venezuelans of the nineteenth century. To be sure, constitutions and elections existed, and most national
caudillos made rather heroic efforts to cover their political behavior
with a blanket of constitutional legitimacy. Because their requirements
often fell outside contemporary constitutional norms, those legal arrangements changed to fit the needs of the successful caudillo. Sometimes this meant a new constitution, at other times it meant managed
elections with predetermined results.

Many European and American observers, with the myopia common to imperial nations, saw this behavior as contemptible examples of public hypocrisy. Missing the point of the system, seeing only the surface features of Venezuelan behavior, they read the constitutions, took them literally, and then imposed on Venezuela a judgment based on the notion, never current in that country, that constitutions should not be changed. With such ad hoc criteria, of course, Venezuela could easily be dismissed as a nation of anarchic local chieftains, a collection of constantly warring tribes without any other law than the lance. While such an interpretation was convenient for the vigorously expanding commercial imperialism of North Atlantic enterprise, it distorted the complexity and rules of Venezuela's nineteenth-century political system.

That country's political organization, based not so much on a legal structure as on a social structure, derived its organizational stability from territorial arrangements and bureaucratic functions. What organized Venezuela in the nineteenth century was the Caracas-based bureaucratic and territorial structure inherited from the Spanish empire. Within this system of great stability and permanence, individuals and groups competed to gain ever larger shares of national prosperity. The rules of competition derived not from the forms of constitution and legal code but from the material realities of land-based wealth. Individuals with land and with control over the people who lived on and worked that land had the basic requirements for an active political life. Success in a political career at the regional and national level depended on the ability to use those resources of land-based wealth and followers to gain sufficient force or threat of force to impose policy on the national or regional bureaucracies. Because more aspirants to regional and national command existed than opportunities, a mechanism for sorting out these competitors had to be developed. In Venezuela, civil war proved the most appropriate means of selecting national and regional leaders. Expensive, to be sure, but in a country without a political tradition and without political institutions, it is hard to imagine a more effective means of choosing national leaders.

In this system, then, the laws and constitution served several important functions. For example, the bureaucracy acted according to and by virtue of the laws, and its continuity from regime to regime owed much to the existence of constitutional and legal forms. Of course, the conquering caudillo often violated the laws, but more often he got his way by having inconvenient legal forms modified or reinterpreted to fit his needs. Rarely did Venezuelan strongmen manage regimes without the law and the constitution, although they certainly believed themselves to be above that law. Within this frame of reference, the legal system and the constitution established a set of norms to which governments and bureaucrats subscribed. No one with experience in the Venezuelan milieu expected the laws to be literally obeyed at all times. One could expect governments and bureaucrats to stay reasonably close to the law much of the time, and if that should prove impossible, the law was usually changed to fit the circumstances. In many ways, the legal system and the constitutional forms operated to restrain the enthusiasms of successful caudillos whose rise to power almost always came from violent episodes during which the rules were suspended. On accession to national power and responsibility, the bureaucrats and ministerial elite of Caracas generally proved quite able to contain much of the caudillo's official arbitrary behavior within a constitutional framework.

Because Venezuela's nineteenth-century history revolves around men whose wealth and prominence derived primarily from large land holdings, the stability of property ownership concerned all the competitors for power and wealth. Although the chronicle of constitutional changes in Venezuela gives the impression of rapid and dramatic modifications of the country's political arrangements, these new documents for the most part changed only minor items in Venezuela's political system. Most of the constitutional change involved reducing or enlarging the number of states making up the Venezuelan Republic or the number of years allotted a president. Some caudillos wanted fewer states in order to have few state governments to control, while others wanted more states in order to have more state offices to distribute to their faithful followers. Since the territorial reorganization of Venezuela required a constitutional change, the list of new constitutions grew quite long. Most conquering caudillos believed, at least at the beginning of their regime, that their government would last longer and be more successful than those before, and so to start everything off right, a new constitution would be promulgated to symbolize the beginning of a new era. The reach of these would-be heroes usually exceeded their grasp. When the government next changed hands, the incoming caudillo generally repeated the process. Beneath the ever-changing date on Venezuela's constitution lay essentially the same document.

If the basic respect for private property, especially land, remained enshrined in Venezuela's basic law because Venezuelans of the elite wanted it that way, the respect for property rights proved essential for the country's foreign relations as well. Few incidents better demonstrate this than the response of the major North Atlantic powers to Cipriano Castro's casual attitude toward foreign claims. Although the details of the incident are not very edifying, and neither Castro nor the large powers set high standards of diplomatic conduct, the incident clearly outlined the basic requirements for an export economy within the Atlantic system. Export economies must, it appeared, recognize the property rights of foreign nationals, must make every effort to protect those rights, and must be prepared to pay damages if those rights are abridged in any significant way. These property rights included such items as real estate, commercial establishments, and contracts within Venezuela as well as debts contracted between Venezuela and foreigners outside the country. Furthermore, as long as Venezuelan legal forms and processes operated and produced results within North Atlantic standards of equity and fairness, local laws would be respected by the big powers; if not, then some form of intervention would produce this equity. Until the regime of Cipriano Castro, most Venezuelan governments managed to keep foreigners reasonably content and pay enough on Venezuela's debts to keep foreign intervention to the level of ambassadorial remonstrance and threat. But the penury of Venezuela's treasury, the excesses of the dictator, and the cumulative effect of over a decade of almost constant regional uprisings exhausted the patience of the big powers and produced the 1902-3 blockade of the Venezuelan coast, the bombardment of Venezuelan ports, and a coerced settlement of the foreign claims.

While all of this damaged Venezuela's self-respect, the events nevertheless produced important benefits for the Venezuelan elite. The existence of the North Atlantic export and credit market enforced on the country a minimum level of financial responsibility. The caudillos of the civil war could kill, destroy, and confiscate, but in the end property had to be respected at some reasonable level, or Venezuela would be excluded from participation in the North Atlantic economy; and without participation in that economy the good life coveted by all and enjoyed by a few was unattainable. Likewise, Venezuela could hardly have accorded significantly better treatment to the property interests of foreigners than it did to members of the national elite, if only because foreign and national elite interests often coincided. Thus, the enforcement of minimum norms of economic behavior by the big powers redounded to the benefit of Venezuela's elite, however much they might deplore the insult to national honor implied by the diplomatic interventions and the exaggerated measures of blockade and bombardment.

These conditions should help clarify the confusing decades between the end of Guzmán Blanco's regime in 1888 and the beginning of Juan Vicente Gómez's rule in 1908. Of the succession of presidents to pass through Venezuela's government in those years, the most picturesque, and in many ways the most significant, was Cipriano Castro. Aside from the man's peculiar personality and extravagant personal style, his regime symbolized the transition from the traditional, caudillesque political system perfected by Antonio Guzmán Blanco to the modern, technology-supported, militaristic political system perfected by Castro's protégé, Juan Vicente Gómez.

Although to our technologically sated senses the Venezuela of Cipriano Castro may not appear especially advanced, within the context of the 1890s the expansion of the telegraph network to cover all of Venezuela's major cities, the construction of some miles of railroad in the central and central coastal region, and the growing sophistication of the national arsenal signaled a revolution in Venezuelan political styles. The regime of Cipriano Castro proved an almost unrelieved disaster from economic, political, and diplomatic prespectives, but his presidency prepared Venezuela for the disciplined and prosperous rule of Juan Vicente Gómez. For instance, the political selection process involving rebellious regional caudillos disappeared for good during Castro's regime. Under the able command of Gómez, the national army acquired technical equipment and training unattainable in some regional stronghold. This forced all aspirants to presidential power to work within the government and armed forces, or it drove them to work from a foreign base with foreign support and arms. In his campaigns across Venezuela, which eliminated the last vestiges of regional, caudillo opposition to Castro's government, Juan Vicente Gómez learned about the potential of a well-equipped professional army. This is not to suggest that Venezuela possessed a military machine on a par with European armies of the day. However, government soldiers provided with Winchester repeating rifles and a modest level of training proved far superior to the temporary forces of regional caudillos.

This dependence on modern weapons and a telegraph network brought with it a much closer participation of foreign interests in the internal affairs of Venezuela. The price of rifles was Venezuelan dependence on the foreign suppliers of those weapons, and the cost of rapid, efficient communication was foreign control over the telegraph and, although of lesser importance, the railroads. In reasonably good times, when government revenues covered the cost of debts, and when foreign and domestic capitalists saw Venezuela as a land of opportunity, the participation of suppliers of these strategic services and products seemed benign enough. When export income declined, government revenues were dissipated in the suppression of civil disorder, and debt payments fell behind; then foreign intervention in Venezuelan affairs became considerably less benign. Although the Winchesters could not be taken away from the government, the foreigners could slow up shipments of cartridges or they could supply revolutionary groups in New York or the Caribbean with equivalent armament for an invasion. The telegraph, in the hands of French operators and technicians, could become inefficient enough to impair the government's ability to coordinate its forces against domestic uprising or coastal invasions by exiled Venezuelans as was demonstrated during the blockade crisis.

As the opportunity and the ability to meddle in Venezuelan politics grew in the years between Guzmán Blanco and Gómez, so too did the incentive. While Venezuela's relationship with the North Atlantic world remained that of a supplier of commodities and a purchaser of manufactures, the composition and structure of trade changed gradually in the last decades of the nineteenth century. Instead of simple import-export connections through modest commercial establishments in ports and the capital, the trade began to involve long-term capital investment, first in basic services, such as the railroad, the telegraph, electricity, and the steamship lines, then in primary material extraction such as asphalt, and finally in the big industry in the 1920s, petroleum.

In the earlier years, the transactions with North Atlantic trading nations were relatively short-term, agricultural purchase agreements and financing. If times turned bad in Venezuela or in the world markets, the foreign trader had little in the way of fixed assets to lose or fixed costs to maintain. To be sure, importers and exporters liked stable, pro-trade governments. They frequently had their diplomats pressure the Venezuelan government for better conditions or for reparations for damages suffered in the civil wars. Their resources for direct intervention in Venezuelan affairs proved as limited as their direct long-term investment. Beginning with the modernizing regime of Guzmán Blanco, with his long-term contracts for the reconstruction of Caracas and the creation of the telegraph, railroads, and steamships, and accelerating during subsequent regimes until the beginning of petroleum investment on a massive scale in the 1920s, foreigners found themselves with much more to lose in the complicated and violent political process of Venezuela. Faced with high risks, and having the means of influencing the internal dynamics of Venezuela's political process, these foreigners and their governments began to take an active, participatory interest in domestic politics.

The big power blockade and bombardment of the Venezuelan coast showed the inexperience and lack of subtlety of these North Atlantic imperialists in the exercise of their new ability and in the protection of their Venezuelan interests. It also demonstrated to any unconvinced Venezuelans that the country must behave within rather wide margins of North Atlantic respectability or it could not participate in the benefits of modern industrial society. If Cipriano Castro thought he could defy the industrial powers with impunity, Gómez, his number-one henchman and the creator in subsequent years of petroleum Venezuela, quickly grasped the essential dimension of this lesson in international comportment.

As the century began, Don Cipriano Castro, in a sense a relic of Venezuela's caudillesque past, could not keep up with the changes in the times, styles, and skills. In poor health and reduced vitality, he survived primarily because Juan Vicente Gómez had subdued his enemies. In 1908, when Castro left the country for Europe to seek renewed good health, Juan Vicente eliminated him by having Castro charged with the murder of a revolutionary general.

With the accession of Juan Vicente Gómez to the presidency of Venezuela, the country entered the modern age. His regime, one of the longest and most stable in Venezuela's history, brought the country into the technologically advanced world of the twentieth century; but curiously enough, his system of government, for all its modern trappings, had the underpinnings designed by Antonio Guzmán Blanco a half-century earlier.

THE INTRODUCTION
OF THE TECHNICAL ELITE

For all of his unpleasant characteristics, and in spite of the brutal suppression of dissent, disagreement, and discussion, Juan Vicente Gómez brought Venezuela into the modern world. This achievement came not because Gómez had vision and statesmanship nor because the dictator wanted it so, but, instead, because the peace he brought to Venezuela permitted the development of the petroleum industry after the

First World War and because the petroleum boom unleashed on the country a range of modernizing forces barely contained by the efficient and ruthless apparatus of the dictatorship. At the beginning of the regime, Gómez inherited a Venezuela still very much in the nineteenth-century tradition but without the possibility of successful regional revolts. He had an army, carefully organized and equipped with the best modern weapons, that guaranteed civil order and efficiently suppressed any of the traditional forms of challenge to the reigning caudillo. Yet in spite of this formidable apparatus, the Gómez years saw their share of civil disorder and revolutionary outbursts. The principal difference between the challenges of these years and the revolts in previous regimes lay in the short-lived unsuccessful trajectories of the anti-Gómez movements. Never seriously challenged, Gómez ruled the country from 1908 until his death in 1935 with skill and ruthless competence.

This twenty-seven-year episode, remarkable not just for its tranquility and its prosperity, set the stage for Venezuela to emerge in the 1930s and 1940s with a new generation of leaders almost completely unconnected with Venezuela's political past. Divorced from a political tradition and free from any historic concerns, the generation of politicians who gained their experience and education primarily in exile would return to Venezuela after Gómez and begin public life anew, basing their programs and tactics on models drawn not from the Venezuelan past but from the international present. In a matter of a few years, Venezuela passed from the old-style authoritarian regime of Gómez to modern, mass-action, ideological party politics. It is this abrupt transition to contemporary styles of governance and political action that makes the history of the Gómez regime so compelling.

In the early years of his regime, most observers underestimated the colorless, conservative Andean general. Many contemporaries thought this man unable to maintain control for any length of time. Unschooled in and uncomfortable with the urbane maneuvers of the Caracas elite, Gómez made a poor impression on the capital's social and economic leaders. Confusing style with substance, they failed to appreciate the skill and vision of Juan Vicente Gómez. Worse yet, many misjudged his ruthless, vindictive spirit, a temperament that led to the persecution of his enemies, real or imagined.

Juan Vicente Gómez invented nothing new in the way of government, he showed no imagination in his organization and administration of Venezuela, and his years in office produced nothing of consequence in the realm of political theory. Instead, this taciturn Andean general, who began his career as an accountant and cattle rancher, applied the same principles of sound patriarchal management to the task of running Venezuela that he had applied to the job of raising cattle on his rural properties. His system for resolving political problems could not have been simpler or more effective: he eliminated them by removing the individuals responsible, either through admonition, imprisonment, torture, or exile. Some individuals were simply killed.

This system worked better for Juan Vicente than for any of his predecessors because he came to the job with an unusual set of personal qualities and enjoyed a unique set of resources, a combination that produced the twenty-seven-year interlude of order and progress in Venezuelan history. Unlike all his predecessors, Gómez cared not one whit for the opinion of the sophisticated *caraqueño* elite, nor did his reputation in the economic and cultural centers of Europe or America concern him. This indifference to the best opinion left him free to pursue the interests of Venezuela as if they were his own. In applying his sound management techniques, the army became a private guard, organized and administered by his trusted subordinates. The purpose of this guard was to keep the peace on his place, that is Venezuela, and expel or punish those who failed to observe the rules of his house. Within this system, notions of political or human rights had no currency, for in a domestic economy only the patriarch's word was law. As on any well-managed family estate, the patriarch tended to put his brothers and other relatives in charge of the important activities of the ranch, in part because these people could be trusted and in part because a patriarch had an obligation to his kin. Similarly, in delegating tasks, Gómez preferred his Andean neighbors to Venezuelans from other regions because he believed that these mountain folk understood his style better than the elegant *caraqueños*.

The immense power and wealth that became Gómez's as a result of the successful application of this patriarchal authoritarianism never seemed to tempt him with the excess and pretension that destroyed or weakened his predecessors. His distaste for the elegant and the decadent remained as strong in the 1930s as it had been in the early 1900s, when he had managed Cipriano Castro's army. By all accounts, the dictator, in a perverse way, was incorruptible, and this consistency of purpose gave his regime great strength.

To be sure, managing Venezuela proved to be a good deal more complicated than operating an Andean cattle ranch, and Gómez, like all of his predecessors, found it necessary to rely on the Caracas elite to manage the technical details of administration. Lest they forget the patriarch, his principal advisers were required to report often to him at his ranch in Maracay in the rich agricultural valleys outside Caracas. This device not only freed him from the distasteful tedium of diplomatic protocol, but served to symbolize the fact that Caracas worked for Gómez, not Gómez for Caracas.

This pleasant arrangement existed because of the excellence of the national army and Gómez's careful control of this instrument. During the previous regime of Cipriano Castro, Juan Vicente Gómez had organized, equipped, and led the army on what turned out to be the last of the caudillesque campaigns. By 1908, Gómez and his army had eliminated the regional caudillo as a force in Venezuelan history, and, as president, Gómez made sure the army remained the bulwark of his authority. In many ways the army proved a clumsy instrument of oppression. It could keep the peace, prevent mass demonstrations, patrol the borders, and discourage revolts, but it performed poorly in ferreting out the individual dissenter, the quiet intellectual or political conspirator, the reformist student, or simply the disaffected individual. Gómez turned to a private secret police dedicated to the task of finding and punishing any who failed to accord the patriarch proper respect. Gifted with the confidence of the dictator and free of any concern for individual rights, the police indulged in every conceivable excess in their zeal to eliminate undesirables and malcontents. Prison and torture became the commonplace fate of those suspected of anti-Gómez beliefs as well as those whose behavior irritated the regime in any other way.

This closed system, for all its brutality and primitive political behavior, nevertheless brought Venezuela its first extended period of order and progress since the days of José Antonio Páez, not because Gómez became a genius at economic development but because the North Atlantic world needed Venezuela's oil. Because the oil boom began after the Gómez system had become well-established, however, the system absorbed the terrific impact of a boom-time economy relatively easily. Indeed, the greatly increased scale of economic activity that occurred in Venezuela after the First World War provided the dictatorship with renewed resources and greater strength.

Even with the advantages of wealth and stability, however, the Gómez regime could not survive indefinitely. Venezuela, as a Gómez fief, could not be passed on to the dictator's heirs, for they proved incapable of maintaining the system while the dictator lived. The next generation of Venezuelans never became fully integrated into the ethos and austerity of the Gómez system. In effect, the elimination of politics within Venezuela during the first third of the twentieth century made the shift to modern, world politics very rapid and complete in the years following the dictator's death. Although the cattle-ranch model of management enabled Gómez to postpone or hide the inevitable transformation of Venezuelan society and economy caused by the oil boom, this system could not prevent it. After 1935 the country burst into the contemporary world with an explosive series of economic, political, and social changes made all the more dramatic by delay.

Even though the Gómez regime appears to have been a long peaceful interregnum, an anomalous break in the violent history of Venezuela, the surface calm projected by the regime obscured a number of fundamental transformations in the organization and structure of the country. For the most part these changes came as a consequence of petroleum exploitation, for even though the country's participation in the oil enterprises remained low throughout the Gómez period, the increase in government and private income was large. On the government side, the greatly increased revenue brought an expanded Caracas bureaucracy dedicated to spending the money on public works and, of course, the salaries of its members. Similarly, the military, seen in this context as an extension of the bureaucracy, also gained in status and equipment, validating the new role of the professional, technically proficient, and technologically sophisticated soldier. Petroleum exploration and the production of crude oil for shipment to refineries outside Venezuela required a basic infrastructure in the form of roads, housing, minimal public services, and port facilities. Since the oil bonanza provided the wherewithal to pay for these improvements, the regime found it easy to build what the petroleum companies required.

This increased level of economic activity provided the private Venezuelan enterprise with previously unheard-of opportunities for wealth. Friends of the regime made themselves rich by acting as middlemen in the transfer of petroleum rights from the state to one of the foreign oil companies. A host of entrepreneurs built fortunes providing services to the oil companies or building the roads, houses, ports, and other facilities required by the industry. What had been a minor-league class of small-time merchant middlemen in the prepetroleum years became a self-conscious, entrepreneurial middle class with capitalist ambitions and values. As their interests in enterprises within Venezuela grew, this group came to project a point of view and defend a set of interests distinct from those of the traditional agricultural import-export class or even the government bureaucracy. Of course, until the death of Gómez, any active development of such a special-interest group remained suppressed, but, once the old man died, these people, along with many others, began articulating their perspectives on national order and development.

While the magic influence of petroleum expansion captivated the Venezuelan elite, the country began a fundamental change in structure and organization that endures to the present. When Gómez sent Cipriano Castro off to Europe in 1908, Venezuela's was a quintessential agricultural, export economy. Basically, the country earned its foreign exchange by selling coffee, cacao, and cattle products abroad. The overwhelming majority of its citizens lived and worked in rural areas in agriculture. The Caracas of 1908, with the exception of a few new buildings and the Guzmán Blanco facelift, existed much as it had since the last days of the Spanish colonial empire a century earlier. Indeed, the principal cities, trade routes, and economic organization of the country had changed hardly at all, and a visitor to Venezuela from the independence era would have had little difficulty adapting to the first years of the twentieth century.

The oil expansion marked the beginning of a radical transformation of Venezuelan society, polity, and economy, a set of changes that in two generations would remake the nation. More rapid structural changes occurred in Venezuela between 1920 and 1960 than had occurred in the years between 1780 and 1920. The generations active between 1920 and 1960 experienced a compression of historical time and an acceleration of cause and effect that stuns the observer. From a primitive, rural, isolated, agricultural dependency on North Atlantic markets, Venezuela became a complex, sophisticated, urbanized, industrializing, extractive, mining society closely attached to the ebb and flow of North Atlantic politics and economics.

Venezuela's history shows such a peculiar discontinuity in its political and economic development that it is possible to tell the story of the country's last generation without much reference to the political behavior, party development, or economic activities of the late nineteenth and the early twentieth century. Part of the reason for this abrupt transition in the country's past can be found in the policies of the Gómez regime. By spending twenty-seven years suppressing political discussion, party development, and critical analysis of Venezuelan affairs, by eliminating every vestige of the country's traditional political parties, and by exiling or imprisoning the next generation's leaders, Juan Vicente Gómez left the country free to start its political system from scratch in 1936. To be sure, the armed forces continued, representing the only major inheritance from the Gómez political apparatus; but the army had neither the experience nor the expertise to create a government or direct a nation, and so the reorganization of Venezuela fell to the exiles. These were people whose understanding of politics and economics came from an international, North Atlantic perspective. They returned to Venezuela after 1935 with internationalist models of economic and political development, and their efforts to establish these norms met with practically no opposition from what could be termed authentic Venezuelan political traditions.

Juan Vicente Gómez did, inadvertently perhaps, begin the greater integration of Venezuela's internal affairs with the life, economies, and policies of the North Atlantic community when he encouraged the development of the country's oil resources. Petroleum exploration and extraction required a new dimension of foreign involvement in Venezuela. The import-export economy of coffee, cacao, and hides had made Venezuela's elite dependent on North Atlantic markets, and the North Atlantic powers had never hesitated to dictate Venezuela's external behavior. But the level of interference and the type of control exercised through the import-export mechanisms were usually characterized by relative indifference to the styles and behavior of Venezuelan government within the country. If Venezuelans wanted civil war, poor sanitation, rudimentary public services, and an archaic political system, the North Atlantic merchants only cared to the extent that damages resulting from this behavior be paid. Even the excesses of Cipriano Castro brought a demand only for control of the customs houses, not for any change in Venezuela's internal affairs.

By encouraging the petroleum extraction industry to expand within Venezuela, Gómez changed the terms of the country's relationships with the North Atlantic economy. Because the petroleum business is complicated and capital intensive, because the oil companies had to invest on a long-term basis in expensive machinery and facilities, and because significant numbers of foreign technicians, oil-field workers, and managers had to live inside Venezuela and outside the capital city, the oil companies and their governments began to take a close interest in Venezuela's internal affairs. Contributing to this greater interest was the strategic importance of petroleum, a matter of concern in the First World War, and increasingly a critical resource as the Second World War approached. The need to guarantee the supply of petroleum meant a need to have confidence in the Venezuelan government's ability to keep the country peaceful and deliver the oil.

With the death of Gómez in 1935, Venezuela became open to the full impact of all these influences, and the absence of any tradition made the transformation to the contemporary styles of politics and economics very rapid.

Chapter 5 • The Technocratic Regimes, 1935-1980

AUTHORITY AND COMPETENCY

The new Venezuela of 1935 to 1980 falls rather neatly into two parts, the post-Gómez military regimes from 1935 to 1958 and the demo-cratic-populist regimes since 1958. Although this division demarcates rather substantial differences in style and content, the direction of Venezuelan development has remained virtually the same from the death of Gómez to the present. That orientation, determined by the existence of petroleum wealth, involved a series of related themes. Beneath all the political turmoil of those years ran a strong consensus about the need for Venezuela to become a more complete participant in North Atlantic affairs. With the growing stream of petroleum riches, many observers believed that Venezuela might be able to purchase a place at the center of the dominant North Atlantic hegemony. This national obsession with modernity reached an ever-widening range of Venezuelans as the impact of the petro-boom spread and grew through-out these decades. Because one of the first consequences of the boom increased government revenues beyond any level imaginable in the nineteenth and the early twentieth century and because these governments tended to spend the money on public works and public services in the capital city of Caracas, that urban center began a period of rapid growth that continues to the present. Of course, the lure of an urban existence caused similar rural-urban migrations in other places in Latin America too, but in the Venezuelan case the abrupt shift from an agricultural to a petroleum-based industrial economy greatly accelerated this process. Moreover, the rapidity of growth produced a reinforcing pressure on the national government to provide more services, public works, and amenities for the residents of the capital.

Why this phenomenon should have happened is no mystery, for practically all of the money, benefits, decisions, and growth flowed through channels dredged out during the colonial years and maintained and strengthened during the civil wars of the nineteenth century. With no other mechanism available to handle the multiple problems and take advantage of the numerous opportunities than an administrative system of colonial origin based in Caracas, the windfall profits went to projects that benefited the residents and especially the elite of the capital. Furthermore, the fact that this petroleum wealth was unearned and unanticipated meant that the money exacted no immediate cost or obligation from the state.

The simplicity and miraculous nature of this wealth-generating machine called petroleum can hardly be exaggerated. Oil, it turned out, took less effort to produce than the gold and silver of the Spanish empire's halcyon days. Petroleum was discovered and extracted in commercial amounts by foreign firms with foreign capital and technology. These companies came to Venezuela equipped to do their job without any need for Venezuelan assistance except for a few cheap, low-skilled laborers, of which the country had an excess. To reap the riches of petroleum, it appeared, the government had only to provide scraps of official paper granting rights to drill on relatively worthless agricultural land, or even better, the empty bed of Lake Maracaibo. No other imaginable enterprise could have provided Venezuela with such a handsome return, so quickly, for such a tiny short-term cost. For Venezuela, petroleum was a good deal.

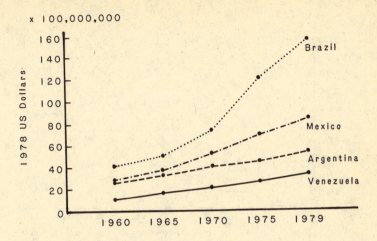

FIGURE 8: Gross Domestic Product, 1979, in US$ at 1978 Prices (Table III-1)

The very ease of the oil bonanza, the lack of any requirement for getting the wealth, made the country totally unprepared to extract the possible long-term benefits. Blessed with a short-term investment philosophy as a heritage from the unstable conditions of the nineteenth century and obsessed with the need to live as well as possible and to be as modern as possible, Venezuelans of all social strata rushed to improve the surface features of their lives. Who could possibly have expected any other behavior? While in retrospect the massive expenditure on public works and life style may appear short-sighted and frivolous, at the time few knew how long the boom would last or when they, personally, would have a better chance to get ahead. Thus, the rich built extravagantly, lived elegantly, and traveled extensively. The rural poor moved to the cities, especially to Caracas, where they found life more exciting, opportunities for subsistence more promising, and social and economic advancement for their children more likely.

As the years after Gómez wore on and the dimensions of the petroleum bonanza became clearer, the governments of Venezuela came to take a greater and greater interest in petroleum affairs and to become

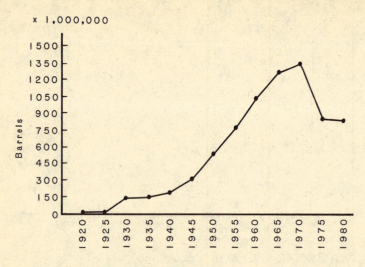

FIGURE 9: Petroleum Production, 1920-1980 (Table III-9)

increasingly concerned with patterns of government spending. Because the generation of Gómez exiles had studied and lived abroad in Europe, the United States, and Mexico, they had ample opportunity to observe the behavior of responsible, development-oriented governments, to absorb the basic folklore and science of industrialization. When they returned to help re-create Venezuela's future, they brought with them sophisticated notions about investment, production, industrialization, social welfare, and individual rights. These new people did not subscribe to the old-fashioned notions of Venezuela as rural hacienda, a theme popular in the days of Gómez. Seeing, instead, a country in the process of becoming a major international power, they returned home with ready-made models to apply, models derived from and influenced by the experience and values of the North Atlantic nations. Many of these new leaders, imbued with nationalistic pride and burning with the need to see Venezuela freed from a demeaning dependency, advocated the creation in Venezuela of a North Atlantic replica society that, because it was the same, need not be dependent on the United States or Western Europe.

This idea, although dressed in the newly popular rhetoric of Marxist or quasi-Marxist analysis or democratic-republican ideologies, was hardly new. Antonio Guzmán Blanco in the late nineteenth century had operated on much the same premise. What gave the post-Gómez leaders a different perspective was their ambition, an ambition born of the infinite possibility promised by petroleum. They dreamed of a North Atlantic replica for all Venezuelans, not just the elite, a society in which the nomadic cattle ranchers of the llanos would have the opportunities of a Texas rancher, where the Andean peasant could live like an Iowa farmer, and where the *caraqueño* artisan could have the benefits of a Detroit auto worker.

This design for Venezuela's future came not, of course, from a native Venezuelan notion, from the llanos or the Andes, not from the classrooms of the Central University of Venezuela, but from the ideologues, economists, missionaries, social democrats, Marxists, and reformers of the North Atlantic. Because Gómez had eliminated most of Venezuela's political traditions except the military, these new plans could be transferred to post-Gómez Venezuela virtually unchanged. The new leaders could create their own rural organizations, their own labor unions, their own mass action political parties with only the slightest attention to the Venezuelan political past. Similarly, they could bring back from exile a whole complex of ideological and economic controversies current in the North Atlantic core, controversies that had little to do with Venezuela's experience but which, for lack of native controversy, became the central issues of national debate.

Had there been no petroleum revenue, the death of Gómez would have certainly released a tempest anyway. The exiles would have returned with their new ideas, moving the country toward the modern age, but the poverty and limited resources of a non-petroleum Venezuela would have restricted the possibilities for reform and would have required a readjustment of North Atlantic models to the realities of a rural, agricultural country. As a result, the dominant institution of Venezuela today would probably be the military, not the technocratic elite of industrial development.

But petroleum revenues were there to support the grand design of the new apostles of economic development. Before they could implement this model, one continuing Venezuelan institution had to be tamed. The armed forces had to be convinced to relinquish their right to determine the destiny of the country. The process occupied Venezuela for almost twenty-five years in a complex interaction between the old-style military dictatorship patterned after Guzmán Blanco and Juan Vicente Gómez, the new-style technocratic military regime with aspirations of North Atlantic respectability, the imported tactics of mass-action politics, and the all-encompassing and uncontrollable influence of petroleum wealth. This last element, the oil money, subsidized the experimentation required to work out the contradictions of competing notions of national management. Without that money, the country could never have afforded the luxury of so many years of complex political action and debate, nor would the outcome have favored the non-military technicians of development.

In terms of Venezuela's political chronology this process of interaction and resolution involved three military presidents before the victory of the technocratic developmentalists in 1958 and five civilian presidents since that victory. The political events of the years 1935-80 reflect in an unusually clear way the underlying process described above.

While the inevitable reaction to the death of Gómez brought people into the streets to celebrate their release from the oppressive regime by sacking the residences of prominent *gomecistas*, the army that had been his personal instrument of control remained in charge of the country. Part of the reason for its continued success when many of the other elements of dictatorship ceased to function came from the absence of a viable alternative to the military. No political parties existed, no organizations or institutions approached the armed forces' national constituency or their organizational ability to take charge of national affairs. Furthermore, the death of Gómez had been a surprise to no one in the government and military elites. Daily and hourly rumors about his health had been the pre-eminent topic of conversation for years.

As a result of the extended period of failing health, members of Gómez's coterie had ample opportunity to think through their survival strategy. Because Gómez lasted too long and developed unusually suspicious attitudes toward his family and associates in his old age, they turned to palace intrigue. With the dictator growing even more capricious, senile, and physically infirm, and with the Gómez clan divided and fighting, third- and fourth-level Gómez enforcers came to wield extraordinary power in the last period of the dictatorship. These individuals, notable for their enthusiastically brutal methods, could sow terror only so long as the dictator lived and sanctioned this behavior. While the bulk of the army elite no doubt viewed these activities with distaste, any attack on the thugs would have been construed as an attack on Gómez. So, being personally above most of the unpleasantries perpetrated by the dictator's minions, the military leadership waited for a better time. When Gómez died and the popular fury came down on the most visible symbols of the regime—family, chief ministers, and especially the secret police—military officials failed to intervene, being too occupied with the problem of managing the transition to a new regime to protect the discredited leaders and enforcers of the old. When the initial outburst passed and the country had purged itself of the most visible members of the old regime, the military remained practically unchanged.

Given these circumstances, the emergence of General Eleazar López Contreras as the military's answer to the problem of national leadership seemed entirely natural. As an officer in the army he commanded the loyalty and recognition of the military; as an Andean native he appeared to pose no threat to the regional clique that had dominated Venezuelan affairs for the previous twenty-seven years; as a former Minister of Defense he could reassure the many other participants in the Gómez hegemony that there would be no wholesale reprisals for past behavior; and as a well-traveled, well-educated officer, López Contreras showed considerable sensitivity to the need for a less repressive political style. Indeed, thanks to a fortuitous combination of qualities and circumstances, López Contreras can be seen as the first twentieth-century Venezuelan president.

The relative freedom of action and expression permitted in the López years provided the opportunity for large-scale organization of political parties and mass participation in public affairs. The leaders of this new form of activity came primarily from among the group of former students who had experienced the repression and exile of the dictatorship as a result of their activities during the student movement of 1928. This earlier anti-Gómez manifestation, while completely futile as political action, had identified a generation of student activists who returned to Venezuela after 1935 with a sense of mission unique in the country's political history. During the decade of exile, these student radicals had studied, traveled, and conspired abroad. At the death of Gómez, their political apprenticeship in the North Atlantic world appeared complete, and they returned to Venezuela to put their knowledge and theories to the practical test of competition and power.

Still, the freedom of action sanctioned by López Contreras proved only relatively better when compared to Gómez's policies. It did not permit political freedom to everyone in the rapidly expanding political spectrum. Indeed, as the discussion of national problems and the style of discourse grew more and more exaggerated, the *lopecistas* became less and less tolerant of the political activities around them. This led to a rather selective suppression of individuals and groups, a strategy that could not succeed in the long run because, in a short time, Venezuela had adopted wide-open political discussion as a national enthusiasm.

If the years 1936-41 sparkled with political controversy, they also produced new institutions. From the government came an interest in national development expressed in the creation of an industrial development bank, a central bank, and an expanded agricultural and livestock bank. These entities, while not operating on any massive scale, signified Venezuela's re-entry into the contemporary world. Where Juan Vicente Gómez would have seen no need to develop such institutions to manage the affairs of the great hacienda Venezuela, López Contreras and his advisers shared the growing national preoccupation with modernity. Not only did they believe that their country ought to have a range of institutions similar to those in more progressive Latin American nations, but they also wanted their political landscape to resemble more closely the North Atlantic norm. For López and his military colleagues, the future of Venezuela lay not in the closed vision of

Juan Vicente Gómez, a vision that saw an agricultural-pastoral economy, but in the examples of Houston, Miami, New York, or Paris, a future that thanks to petroleum would be modern, technocratic, sophisticated, and urban. Banks are modern urban institutions, and the development of three of them symbolized the new dedication to close international cooperation. These banks helped facilitate closer links with the North Atlantic hegemony and facilitated the flow of knowledge and capital that would remake Venezuela in the modern image.

This rapid advancement of the country from the arrested development of the Gómez years included an opening-up of the political system. Long-suppressed political groups began to organize and campaign for influence, even if within considerable restrictions. Reasonably honest indirect elections with a limited suffrage occurred. The obvious military dominance of political action declined, as, for example, the number of officers controlling the twenty-three state governments fell from nineteen to four. The habits of decades do not disappear overnight, however, and the increased opportunity for political action produced more activity than López Contreras could tolerate. When the newly formed labor unions under the direction of the Partido Democrático Nacional (PDN) of Rómulo Betancourt staged a general strike early in López Contreras's regime, the General quickly suppressed both the union and the party. This behavior, the liberalization of politics and then the suppression of the political action that resulted, illustrates a pattern in post-Gómez Venezuelan politics. Some observers saw this behavior as indicating the insincerity of López's commitment to democratic or participatory political systems, but the phenomenon is more complicated.

As has occurred throughout Venezuela's independent history, the conflict between the archaic structures of the country's past and the desperate search for a respected place in the North Atlantic hegemony produce the oscillation between progressive liberal forms and repressive archaic behavior. The Venezuela of 1936-41 had none of the institutional infrastructure of the Western democracies. It had none of the political experience that teaches limits and turns restraint into traditional virtue. Thus, the sudden expansion of political opportunity brought exaggerated responses from the principal actors. The exiles of the generation of 1928, symbolized in Venezuelan history by the person of Rómulo Betancourt, returned home with a range of skills and political abilities learned in the school of North Atlantic politics. They had acquired tactical skill and organizational ability, but they still lacked the judgment of experience and tradition. Untested in Venezuelan political action, these leaders applied their talents and skills to an energetic campaign of politicization, a campaign so successful that the force created could not be wielded with any delicacy. The generation of 1928 shocked the government and its supporters with the power of ideology and mass organization used indiscriminately, and López Contreras proved unable to respond with flexibility or imagination. When seriously pressed in 1930, he simply outlawed the PDN and dissolved the party's labor unions.

Curiously, both *lopecista* and *betancurista* groups were after the same image, but with different content. Both government and opposition wanted Venezuela to look more like a North Atlantic nation. But while Betancourt and the generation of 1928 wanted to achieve this through radical reorganization of Venezuelan institutions to fit a North Atlantic pattern, López and his government wanted to preserve the essence of traditional Venezuelan politics while presenting a modernized façade to the watching Western World. Because neither group had any significant experience in the operation of popular political action, the result could only have been excesses on both sides. When the generation of 1928 found their organizational skills rewarded with strong mass-based movements, the government became frightened of the disruptive force represented by mass politics. The result was, of course, repression.

This pattern repeated itself in the 1940s after the election of General Isaías Medina Angarita, López Contreras's Minister of War, to the presidency by the Congress. Although Medina made the PDN legal again—now renamed as Acción Democrática—and in general seemed to pursue a more permissive policy toward the energetic reformers, he could not appease the generation of 1928. Even with the successful elevation of Venezuela's share of petroleum revenue to 30 percent and the creation of an income tax, social security legislation, and agrarian reform laws, the reformers remained dissatisfied. They doubted Medina's sincerity; they believed themselves to be the bearers of the true word; and while sure of their future, they expected that future to begin immediately. The rhetoric and examples of the Second World War also contributed to the reformers' belief that their time had come. Democracies and socialism appeared to be fighting one last crusade against totalitarian militarism, and Venezuela ought to shed the vestiges of its archaic military past and accept the leadership of the masses as expressed through Acción Democrática. For a time it appeared that Medina and AD might agree on a transitional president. But when the chosen neutral, Diógenes Escalante, became too ill to serve, AD tried to cut short the process of political maturation and helped sponsor a military coup.

In October 1945, Acción Democrática, in collaboration with a group of young military officers from the Unión Patriótica Militar, took over the government and set up a civil-military junta to transform Venezuela into a showcase of reformist democracy. Having found the traditional Venezuelan political system too strong and inflexible to permit the rapid changes they believed necessary, Acción Democrática and its military collaborators proposed to reorient that system in one short operation. Once revised, in theory, the system could then be left alone and everyone could resume activities in accord with new roles and under new rules. In a frantic flurry of activity, the AD-dominated junta proceeded to reorder Venezuela's political and economic life.

During these years of the junta, and through the brief period of the popularly elected Rómulo Gallegos regime, AD demonstrated a remarkable ability to organize popular support, as demonstrated by the overwhelming margins of the party's victories, not only in the presidential election in 1947 but also in the preceding election for members of a constituent congress. Bolstered by these signs of acceptance, Acción Democrática believed itself to be the chosen party whose doctrinal positions and political solutions ought to be implemented rapidly. While few doubted that AD had remarkably strong popular support, the party leaders' inexperience led them to overestimate their practical strength and underestimate the ability of other groups to resist the AD program.

As the party rushed to implement newly passed laws, improving the lot of the peasant through land reform, the workers through an organized labor movement, and the national economy through improved participation in petroleum profits, its support in other political parties, in the armed forces, and among the Venezuelan elite dwindled. The newly created Christian Democratic party, COPEI, formed by prominent Catholic intellectual leaders in 1946 to permit a more moderate student-intellectual presence in Venezuelan politics, rapidly became an important conservative force, with its primary base of support in the Andes. Similarly, the personal party of Jóvito Villalba, one of the original leaders of the generation of 1928, began to assert itself in opposition to the aggressive AD style. This group, the Unión Republican Democrática (URD), chose to represent the middle-class urban population whose principal interest was an orderly government, not the disruptive reformism of the AD ideologues. The leaders of the new AD government, whether in the junta or the early months of the Rómulo Gallegos presidency of 1947, had been absent so long from Venezuela that their perception of the country's realities appeared to have become stylized. They believed their own rhetorical excesses about the sovereignty of the peasants and the workers, and they failed to pay close enough attention to the traditional organization of the country. Because they were new, energetic political activists creating a new political consensus, they made the fatal mistake of seeing the other parts of the Venezuelan socio-political matrix as being essentially equal competitors. Since AD had the electoral support of the masses, the party leadership believed they had a free hand to remake Venezuela in the modern social-democratic image.

Like many reformers without practical experience, AD misjudged the strength of traditional ways; party leaders misread transitory popular support as a durable political consensus, and they believed their view to be so compelling that they need not cooperate with other, competing political groups. The years of the AD junta were so filled with controversial reforms precipitously enacted and arrogantly implemented that the popular enthusiasm for AD's aggressive, contentious style rapidly waned. Although the AD margins in the elections during this period stayed impressively high, the participation rate of the electorate declined by almost half. More serious than these defections was the military dissatisfaction with AD style and content. The officers who had initiated AD into the conspiracy of 1945 had not anticipated their own eclipse. They had expected to be closely involved in the decisions of the new government, not to be ignored and in some cases excluded from the mainstream of political action. Many officers also found AD's taste for revolutionary rhetoric and the party's energetic reformist program too radical.

These problems finally resulted in a military ultimatum to President Gallegos that called for the inclusion of COPEI in the government as a moderating influence and the exile of Rómulo Betancourt, the party leader and symbol of AD's revolutionary spirit. Gallegos, of course, refused. Consequently, on November 24, 1948, the military took over the government, ending for ten years the experiment in mass political action. In retrospect, the errors of the 1945-48 interlude seem all too apparent. Excessive zeal, lack of experience, overreliance on doctrine, failure to create a wide political base, and an aggressive combative political style all contributed to the inability of Venezuela's first mass action political party to build a solid, durable government.

The decade from 1948 to 1958 took a heavy toll on the party leadership and apparatus, but it also made the leaders who survived those years of persecution very sensitive to the realities of the Venezuelan political environment. Any illusions that the military, the local elite, or the foreign elite would be easily controlled were painfully dispelled by the harsh experience of this decade, especially under the persistent persecution during the regime of General Marcos Pérez Jiménez. The AD that survived the decade returned in 1958 much chastened, more experienced, more practical, and less ideological than it had been in the heady days of the junta and Gallegos governments.

In present-day Venezuelan political mythology, the military regimes initiated in 1948 represent an unfortunate interlude in the country's progress toward a modern, popularly based, representative government.

There is considerable merit in that notion. Yet the military governments of this unpleasant decade—especially that of Pérez Jiménez,
which really determined the tone and style of the period—represented
more a throwback to earlier forms. Pérez Jiménez bears a closer kinship to Juan Vicente Gómez and Antonio Guzmán Blanco than to any
modern military chieftain.

The style of Marcos Pérez Jiménez combined traditional personal
politics and brutal political repression with a nineteenth-century passion for public works of the monumental style. Thanks to increasing
petroleum revenues from the greater participation of the Venezuelan
government in oil profits, an accomplishment of the AD government,
Pérez Jiménez and his collaborators had the resources to initiate a massive construction plan in the city of Caracas. Highways, high-rise office
buildings, extravagant officer clubs, the famous Hotel Humboldt at the
crest of the mountains separating Caracas from the sea, and other projects of a similar nature became the trademark of the regime.

Brutal persecution of political opponents also became symbolic of the
Pérez Jiménez approach to government. Among Venezuela's ruthless
leaders, few have achieved the reputation earned by this mid-twentieth-
century dictator. Secret police, political assassinations, torture, and
similar behavior characterized the regime. Correctly identifying AD as
the most dangerous threat to his government's stability, the dictator
spared few resources in the effort to stamp out all vestiges of the party's
apparatus. Nevertheless, its leaders persevered. Exiled, assassinated, imprisoned, or tortured, AD's people paid a high price for the party's survival as a political force during those ten years. Especially hard hit was
the young generation of local party activists. The older, original party
leadership, forced into exile by persecution by the regime's secret police, also found it increasingly difficult to maintain control of their
party workers inside Venezuela.

Other political organizations did better under the Pérez Jiménez
regime. The communists collaborated reluctantly. The Catholic, Christian Democratic party COPEI, under the leadership of Rafael Caldera,
followed a line of uneasy participation, as did the middle-class URD,

the party of Jóvito Villalba. These groups, while reasonably happy to have AD out of the way, found their own sphere of action limited by the arbitrary behavior of the dictator. Nevertheless, they participated in the 1952 elections designed by Pérez Jiménez to demonstrate the legitimacy of his government. The election did not work out as planned. URD and Jóvito Villalba, with the tacit support of AD sympathizers, appeared to be winning the election when Pérez Jiménez stopped the vote count and revised the results to give the election to the government party. This intervention effectively eliminated all hope for a peaceful, legal defeat of the regime. Coupled with the dictator's increasingly arbitrary and incompetent management of national affairs, this helped create the dissatisfaction and resistance that eventually brought the regime down in a military-civilian coup in January 1958.

Although the Pérez Jiménez regime proved to be an expensive pause in Venezuelan history, it provides a fascinating opportunity to assess the strengths of the country's traditional structures and values. Within the grand sweep of Venezuelan history, this decade's peculiar character gives it an anachronistic cast. Of course such an interpretation depends on the perspective, for if we look at the Pérez Jiménez years from the perspective of 1930, it is the three-year AD regime of 1945-48 that appears out of place, a futuristic discontinuity in the traditional pattern of Venezuelan affairs. Be that as it may, the critical defect of the Pérez Jiménez years was the regime's inability to adapt itself to the requirements of petroleum prosperity. The regime failed to understand that participation in the material benefits of mainstream North Atlantic commerce, trade, and industry brought with it demands for the adoption of North Atlantic norms of political and social behavior.

This is not to suggest any simple-minded notion of external coercion by North Atlantic capitalists busy dictating behavior to Venezuelan dependents. Quite the contrary, it was the Venezuelans who, in acquiring the benefits of North Atlantic trade and capital investment, also acquired new values. As their expectations of physical and material comfort changed, so did their expectations of political participation. Like many other dictators of his time, Pérez Jiménez failed to recognize that the wholesale importation of the North Atlantic industrial complex included the introduction of North Atlantic political norms.

The failure of the Pérez Jiménez regime, then, stemmed not from its excessive brutality, not from its persecution of political opponents, nor from its denial of personal freedom, but instead from its nineteenth-century understanding of the political process and the role of the state. This system of values and beliefs represented a pretechnocratic society characterized by personal relationships, informal alliances, and restricted opportunity. But by the 1950s Venezuela had bought into the North Atlantic commercial-industrial world, paying the price of petroleum extraction, a price that included the rapid technical transformation and material modernization of a wide range of Venezuelan concerns. The petroleum industry's expenditure of large sums of public and private money on technologically complex goods and services created in much of Venezuela a growing, technologically sophisticated elite. Whether petroleum workers or lawyers working in international business, whether electronics repairmen or airplane mechanics or construction engineers, these people absorbed a set of behavioral norms with their technologically sophisticated training. The basic tenet of those norms was orderly, systematic, predictable, and rational behavior. The primary desideratum of the technological society is the elimination of chance, of fate. Capriciousness and irrationality defy the very premise of a precise, machine-oriented society.

In Venezuela, the irrationality and unpredictability of the Pérez Jiménez regime displeased the elites from labor, finance, Church, military, and politics. The lack of interest in technical competence turned the military against the regime. The failure of Pérez Jiménez to project any understanding of the needs of the new material culture eventually brought his government down. Symbolic of this basic problem, the triggering political event for his fall came from the simple-minded, technically incompetent, and naïve effort to stage a fraudulent plebiscite. In a new Venezuela, such a flagrant insult to the political intelligence of the elite could not be sustained, and Pérez Jiménez had to pack his bags of money and take a plane to Miami.

In ten years of dictatorship, Venezuela's political leadership in exile or underground had changed. For AD, especially, this period forced the party leadership to come to an understanding of Venezuela's practical possibilities as well as revise the party's ideological and theoretical doctrines. In the months preceding the 1958 coup, party leaders in exile from AD, COPEI, and URD met in New York and set out the ground rules for political competition and national government in a liberated Venezuela. This agreement symbolized AD's recognition that majority electoral support could not justify a one-party government, a basic principle that would go a long way toward resolving some of the difficulties experienced during the Gallegos government.

With the collapse of the Pérez Jiménez regime, Venezuela was once again put under the control of a temporary military junta, led by a naval officer, Wolfgang Larrazábal, who would become something of a popular urban hero. The junta's job, carried out with considerable dispatch, was to prepare for a national election that would re-establish mass-based political democracy. In this they succeeded, in spite of a number of right-wing military revolts. The political parties campaigned energetically, but AD's superior organizational skills and the national image of its candidate, Betancourt, proved too powerful for either COPEI or URD to match. In January 1959, Rómulo Betancourt took charge of the government and initiated the period of mass-based party politics and democratic government that is still with us today.

THE DEMOCRATIC SOLUTION

The two decades of presidential government since 1959 have helped complete the transformation of Venezuela begun under the military regime of López Contreras in 1936. The changes of government style, the development of political parties and mass-action movements, and the overblown rhetoric of politics and propaganda are signs of the inexorable current of modernization that, whatever the government, would have transformed the Venezuela of Juan Vicente Gómez. That current of change flowing into Venezuela came in exchange for petroleum and as a consequence of the national consensus in favor of participation in the North Atlantic world community. One of the more obvious manifestations of this change occurred in government, where the size of the federal budget grew exponentially between 1935 and 1980. Although many Latin American governments have had bigger budgets, the size of Venezuela's, in relation to its population or in relation to the size of the non-petroleum economy and the ever-accelerating growth in the budget, made this petroleum boom a unique phenomenon in Latin America. Not only did the government have inordinate amounts of money to spend, but the private entrepreneurs also experienced a similar bonanza. Petroleum profits paid construction companies to build for the industry itself or for the government, and these companies paid their workers relatively well, especially when compared to the real wage in agriculture. Because the various elites managing the petroleum money preferred to follow Venezuela's traditional pattern of urban public and private construction, the money had its greatest impact on the cities and especially on Caracas.

It is easy, in retrospect, to fault Venezuela's elites for their extravagant expansion of Caracas, for their neglect of agriculture and stock raising, and for what appears to be a slavish imitation of the surface features of the North Atlantic model. In the abstract, such criticisms are correct; in practical terms, Venezuela's experience is remarkable, not so much for the amounts squandered or misinvested but for the basic investments actually made.

In the early years of the petroleum boom, the prevailing norms for public expenditure and private investment were those of a primitive agricultural, export-oriented economy, and a poor one at that. The first proceeds from oil quite naturally went to improve the life style and environment of the elite. They saw no contradictions in wanting to imitate as fast as possible all the amenities and surface efficiencies of a North Atlantic metropolis. This notion, embedded in Venezuelan tradition since Guzmán Blanco and derived from Spanish colonial patterns, had led to the refurbishing of the capital in the last years of the Gómez regime and peaked in the extravagant construction program of Pérez Jiménez. As the boom continued, however, new generations of Venezuelans came to realize that oil could be made to do more than

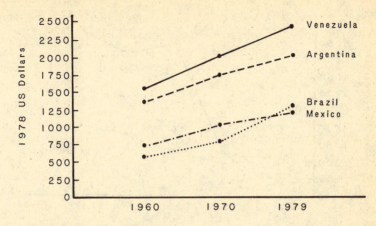

FIGURE 10: Per Capita Gross Domestic Product, 1960-1979, in US$ at 1978 Prices (Table III-3)

improve the life of *caraqueños,* that this bonanza could be made to sustain long-term investments in the infrastructure, that oil, in short, could buy Venezuela a place in the North Atlantic center—not just an imitation society on the periphery, but the real thing.

Such a program involved more change than most people envisioned and proved far more expensive than the technicians of social and economic transformation had anticipated. Yet Venezuela, unlike other Latin American countries, could afford the mistakes and misjudgments of the technicians and could withstand the temporary setbacks and occasional failures in an ambitious program of development. Even more importantly, Venezuela discovered that it might be possible to reorganize society and restructure the economy without having to deny any important Venezuelan interest group a share of national prosperity. To be sure, some groups received more or less than they and others believed proper, and this difference of opinion about the allocation of resources led to acrimonious, turbulent, and sometimes violent confrontations. Although contemporaries and participiants saw these disagreements as catastrophic conflicts whose resolution narrowly averted chaos, the long-term perspective indicates that few important interests in Venezuela were prepared to risk losing their share in petro-prosperity

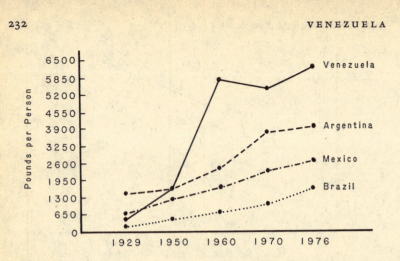

FIGURE 11: Energy Consumption Per Capita, 1929-1976 (Table III-12)

by breaking completely with the consensus managers of the national wealth.

Two experiences had taught most Venezuelans the cost of such disruptive behavior. During the Trienio, 1945-48, AD had tried to monopolize the petroleum benefits for a reduced segment of Venezuela's interest groups, excluding others from a share. The cost of this plan was high as it brought on the military coup that exiled AD's leadership for ten years. Likewise, the Pérez Jiménez interlude proved not only exclusionist but incompetent in the achievement of oil-derived prosperity. As a result of these experiences, the democratic government in 1959 returned with an informal agreement on a set of norms for the management of national resources.

First, no major interest group within Venezuela could be excluded from participation in the growing prosperity, although the relative degree of gain and the mechanics of participation could be changed. Second, the government in power must adhere to a minimum standard of technical competence in the management of Venezuela's affairs. If these two rules were kept, then Venezuela's various interest groups would support the electoral system and compete for shares of the wealth within the norms of democratic political action.

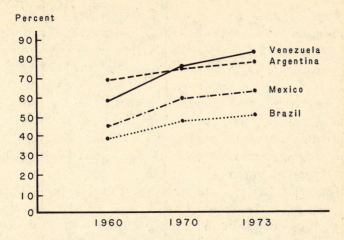

FIGURE 12: Electric Lighting, Percent of Population Supplied, 1960-1973 (Table III-13)

Although very neat and civilized in theory, the system proved hard to sustain during the first decade of democratic rule. Not only did the government require strong popular support but it also needed a host of technically competent and politically wise bureaucrats to implement the various facets of development envisioned by reformist leaders from the principal political parties. Such people simply did not exist in sufficient numbers within Venezuela. While a few problems could be solved by foreign technicians, these temporary assistants in Venezuela's development campaign did not represent a permanent solution. Venezuela would have to train its own. Until the technically proficient middle class grew large enough, poorly trained people would attempt complex jobs. The result was often inefficiency, fraud, and incompetence in the first decade of democratic revival.

Further complicating the basic consensus pattern of government established in 1959, significant minority segments of Venezuela's politically active population refused to acquiesce in the middle-class developmental program. Some of the dissidents came from the economic elite, whose notions of prosperity and development did not involve land reform, nationalized industries, government planning, or a controlled and regulated economy. Their dissatisfaction appeared in a variety of ways, from the funding of dissident political groups dedicated to the return of the dictator Pérez Jiménez, through the withdrawal of capital from the Venezuelan economy in times of economic difficulty, to the active encouragement of military conspiracies. Alone, and confronting a strong, confident government, such behavior would not have been a matter of great concern, but in the early years of the Betancourt presidency the government's hold on the details and machinery of political control was often tenuous.

Similar and much more dangerous opposition came from a dialectical drama played out between left-wing revolutionary activists operating in the spirit of and with some help from Fidel Castro and right-wing military officers tempted to restore order and civilized political behavior through returning control of the government to the armed services. In the left-wing scenario, terrorist activities, if not immediately successful as a popular revolution, would provoke the armed forces into a *coup d'état* and result in a repressive military regime. With democratic government discredited and the armed forces repressive, popular support would, the dogma ran, coalesce behind the revolutionary program of the left. In pursuit of this synthesis a significant, dangerous, and very destructive terrorist campaign operated in Venezuela beginning in the early part of Betancourt's presidency. It peaked in the early 1960s as an essentially rural movement led and staffed primarily by urban university students. The failure to attract many peasant supporters and the success of the armed forces in persecuting the rural cadres led to a shift of emphasis to urban terrorism, a tactical change with some short-term success. Nevertheless, by the end of the Leoni presidency in 1969, the guerrilla threat had subsided to a low level, dangerous to those caught in a crossfire or picked as victims, but powerless to disturb the stability of the government.

This leftist threat to the continuance of democratice government is especially interesting because it represents the only coherent doctrinal opposition to the ideology and practice of progressive, technically competent developmentalism. Precisely because this opposition was ideological and doctrinal in nature, it could not easily be bought off with greater participation in the system. What the left wing most wanted was the destruction of the system and its replacement with another based on a Cuban rather than a North Atlantic model. Yet for all the intellectual power of Venezuela's guerrillas and their supporters in the universities and in the Congress, they never made successful contact with the masses. This failure, which spelled the demise of the movement, came partly from the divisions and mistakes of the left and partly from the skillful political action of the government. While the guerrillas from the city spoke to the peasants about world revolution and the need for radical social change, the government, especially AD, spoke about housing, land reform, education, electricity, highways, and health care and in many cases delivered enough of these services to validate the promises. The land reform program is an excellent example.

Venezuela's democratic governments, especially Acción Democrática, have had a strong commitment to land reform. Dating from the 1930s, the principle of support for a redistribution of the country's agricultural property became an article of faith in party platforms and rhetoric to such an extent that the elected governments of the 1960s found it necessary to invest substantial resources in this program. Unlike other countries in the hemisphere, however, the Venezuelan land reform proceeded on the basis of compensated expropriations, distribution of publicly held land, and provisional titling of beneficiaries. Such policies responded to a variety of political necessities. By compensating the owners of expropriated land at market prices, the government avoided the worst consequences of an outraged landowning class and reinforced its moderate, responsible international reputation. By awarding provisional titles to peasants who lived on or had invaded agricultural properties, the governments of the 1960s managed to deliver land to a relatively large number of households without resolving the many difficulties involved in awarding final, legal title to the land. In the early and mid-1960s, when the governments headed by Acción Democrática confronted radical efforts to mobilize the peasantry for revolutionary action, this program to deliver provisional titles rapidly gave the government an excellent opportunity to demonstrate its commitment to the principles of land reform.

Under the provisions of the 1960 land reform law, moreover, landholdings may be of any size; hence large estates, if judged to serve a useful social purpose, could be left intact. Additionally, Venezuela had developed in the 1940s and 1950s a significant sector of commercial farmers operating on a large scale such as occurred in the dairy industry. These people organized effectively to press their interests in agriculture before the national government, interests often at variance with some of the goals of land reform programs. Venezuela's unusual wealth permitted a substantial sum to be spent on land reform during the decade of the 1960s, something on the order of 2 to 3 percent of the national government's direct expenditures. This may have provided land of some kind for perhaps 166,000 heads of household during those years.

While the work of the land reform program has had a significant impact on agriculture in Venezuela, its primary force seemed spent by the close of the decade. As Venezuela's population continued the migration to the cities, the competing claims of urban Venezuela for a share of the country's resources has grown. The growth in urban concentration has made the logic of AD's commitment to a rural-based electorate less and less compelling, while the failure of the rural revolution in the 1960s has also removed considerable incentive to continue the expensive land reform program. Emphasis seems to have shifted to an analysis of ways of improving agricultural productivity. Although Venezuela has indeed improved its productivity, it is still not sufficient to feed the country.

The success of government-sponsored social programs weakened the impact of revolutionary rhetoric. Furthermore, the Venezuelan left has never been able to agree on a basic program; in the years since 1959 the number of purges, splinters, defections, and doctrinal quarrels has been legion. When political groups such as these thrive on messianic devotion to principle, compromise contaminates the purity of doctrine and weakens the party's hold on its members. Thus the left found itself in an unresolvable dilemma. If party doctrine were kept pure, the left's strength would be fragmented; if compromise were attempted, the left's constituency would desert. In the two decades of democratic rule, the left both compromised and fragmented. By the 1978 presidential elections the parties of the left were dispersed and relatively powerless.

The armed forces response to technocratic, democratic reformism proved ambivalent. In general, most of the officers adhered to the basic premise of the political system agreed on in 1959. By and large they preferred civilian government, not necessarily from any profound belief in the moral superiority of non-military governance, but because they believed development expertise was more efficiently managed by civilian technocrats than by military men. Moreover, the Pérez Jiménez era and the experience of the AD-dominated Trienio of 1945-48 showed the officers what difficulties could come with military management of political affairs. Socialized to respect competence and expertise, the officers could be convinced that civilian politicians and technocrats provided the necessary expertise for governance and development, and, as such, should be allowed to do their job. Further, the North Atlantic model, to which officers as well as most of the civilian elite aspired, is essentially a civilian model with a strong predisposition toward military restraint and the maintenance of civilian control.

Even so, some officers found the inefficiencies of the early Betancourt years almost impossible to take. Conspiracies and rumors of conspiracies abounded with considerable frequency during the Betancourt years and into the Leoni regime as well. These sometimes resulted in action such as the mobilization of isolated garrisons, but in every case the attempts failed to draw enough popular support or military cooperation to succeed. The majority of the armed forces stayed with the government, not only because of their predisposition to civilian government but also because that government gave them a mission and the resources to carry it out. Thanks to the guerrilla threat from the left, the armed forces had a job of internal security to accomplish, and the government lost no opportunity to equip the soldiers well and honor their leaders extravagantly. Military conspirators found themselves retired or sent abroad as attachés to Venezuelan embassies. Through the presence of military men in the cabinet and the provision of excellent support to the armed forces, the government succeeded in keeping them loyal. A government with fewer resources than Venezuela's would probably not have done as well. Moreover, new generations of officers may not hold the value of democracy as highly as the previous generation.

Not every threat to Venezuela's consensus political system came from outside the political process. Internal political, generational, and personal conflicts also threatened the stability of these arrangements. Two sorts of divisions have characterized Venezuela's democratic politics in the decades since 1958. The tensions and contradictions inherent in a regime based on cooperation between competing political parties made successful coalition government almost impossible, especially when no single party had control of both houses of congress, a situation relatively common throughout these years. Moreover, most political leaders saw a threat to their own political identity in appearing to collaborate with the dominant governing party. There were benefits from collaboration, such as a significant share of patronage, control of major national bureaucracies, and a platform for statesmanlike behavior. Under Betancourt the coalition between the parties URD, AD, and COPEI held up until URD withdrew in late 1960. COPEI stayed with Betancourt's government throughout the five-year presidential term but refused to continue the collaboration into the Leoni administration, and this seriously weakened the government's ability to get its policies enacted in Congress.

The second division came from a series of threats to party solidarity from a variety of sources. Sometimes the party quarrels derived from a sense of frustration at successive electoral failures. URD is perhaps the best example of this. Trading on the popularity of Jóvito Villalba, a leader of the anti-Gómez generation of 1928, and mindful of its strong showing in the election aborted by Pérez Jiménez, this party tried to find an identity somewhere between the energetic reformism of AD and the Andean conservatism of COPEI. Its failure to capture significant electoral support led in successive presidential terms to defections and further reductions in political importance. Essentially, the URD was a one-man party, strong on rhetoric and fatally weak in organizational skills. The party could not survive the intense political competition, and its electoral support declined steadily until by 1978 it was only one of many minor parties. It stayed barely alive on the mystique of its caudillo and the fading tradition of its glory days in the 1940s and 1950s.

In striking contrast to URD, COPEI managed to survive the handicap of a one-man party. As the vehicle for Rafael Caldera's political program, this party succeeded in gaining strength under AD rule and successfully challenged the government party to win the presidency twice—once under the leadership of Caldera in 1969 and then again a decade later under a second generation of party leadership with Luis Herrera Campíns. COPEI, originally a very Catholic party, gradually broadened its appeal by shifting its political objectives to the left without abandoning its moderate image. This strategy captured a strong position in the left-reformist area while maintaining for the party its reputation for moderation and conservative tendencies. Although occasionally challenged by internal disagreements, COPEI showed skill at resolving these conflicts short of party divisions. Part of this success can be traced to the astute management of party affairs by Rafael Caldera, a leader with a superb political talent.

In comparison, URD failed because it never established a clear identity between the moderate conservatism of COPEI and the moderate reformism of AD. When COPEI gradually moved left, and AD gradually moved right during the 1960s and early 1970s, URD found itself a party without political space. This ambiguous position, combined with URD's notoriously poor organization, determined the decline of the party and left COPEI as the only major party able to challenge AD.

As the dominant Venezuelan popular organization since the Trienio of 1945-48, AD has demonstrated extraordinary vitality. Surviving the intense persecution of Pérez Jiménez in the 1950s, the party reemerged in 1958 with its senior leadership still active and its second generation hardened by the experience of clandestine political action in Venezuela. Under the firm control of Betancourt and his classmates of 1928, the party built its strength on a combination of political tactics. If there were to be a single motto for this party, it should be Organization. Every hamlet, town, village, or urban district was served by a unit of the party bureaucracy. This organizational mania also included unions, businessmen, and professionals in associations integrated into the party mechanisms. This elaborate bureaucratic structure permitted the party to translate Rómulo Betancourt's personal popularity into an institutionalized electoral base.

The Betancourt party bureaucracy provided the strength necessary to survive the series of defections that split the party in the 1960s. These internal conflicts occurred over two sorts of issues: ideological and personal. Although the ideological dispute within the party was rather complex, its essential dimension was the belief of younger party activists that the old guard had lost touch with the party's revolutionary mystique and that their failure to step aside for the new generation indicated an unwillingness to move to the left, where, these dissidents believed, the future lay. The split engendered by this disagreement severely reduced the party's youth group. It created to the left of AD a vocal and able collection of revolutionary parties unable to gain major electoral strength but capable of provoking intense political debate in the Congress and the press. These debates frequently challenged AD's legitimacy as a left-reformist party.

The personal dimension of conflict within the party occurred with the failure of the party bureaucracy to support the presidential candidacy of Raúl Ramos Jiménez in 1961. With the party in support of Raúl Leoni, Betancourt's choice, the Ramos Jiménez group split from the party into a leftish opposition, further reducing the party's younger contingent. The final split in AD occurred also over the presidential candidate, this time in 1967-68. When AD nominated Gonzalo Barrios, the supporters of Luis Beltrán Prieto Figueroa and Jesús Angel Paz Galárraga left the party. This last division apparently so weakened the party that AD lost the presidency to Rafael Caldera and COPEI, although AD still controlled Congress.

Throughout these conflicts AD survived primarily because of its great organizational strength and the personal stature of its grand old

leader, Rómulo Betancourt. Although the party lost important segments of its leadership group in these divisions its organizational base
remained intact. Most of the prominent dissidents have never returned
to AD, but many of the second-line supporters have come back to the
fold. Because of the ideological orientation of the groups left of AD,
these small parties have never agreed on a major coalition, and, worse
still, have not competed on an organizational level with the established
parties. As a result, the party of Betancourt continued its organizational work and in 1973 elected their man, Carlos Andrés Pérez, to
the presidency.

This chronology of political party behavior should indicate the basic
features of Venezuela's democratic landscape. The remarkable thing
about the parties and the democratic system within which they operate
is that the system survives at all. Venezuela, in the same way as other
Latin American countries, found itself with an incredible array of
obstacles to the successful management of a democratic regime. Yet
as country after country in Latin America turned to military or authoritarian solutions to national and international problems, Venezuela
remained an open, politically flexible, and democratically managed
society. What makes this survival especially interesting is the nation's
lack of a democratic tradition and the absence of long-standing democratic institutions. Most of Venezuela's democratic experience dates
from the death of Juan Vicente Gómez in 1935. The institutional basis
of democracy hardly existed until after 1958. The Venezuelan experience, because it appears to contradict cherished notions about the formation and maintenance of democratic regimes, deserves some consideration.

Venezuela's success as a democratic society demonstrates that no
extensive long-term development of institutions or tradition is necessary. Democratic government, it would appear, need not be preceded
by an articulate, literate electorate; it need not have traditional multi-
generation political parties; and it need not develop within an elaborate institutional framework. Indeed, given the right package of resources and the proper world conditions, a country can construct and
maintain a full democratic system, complete with institutions and

traditions, in a generation's time. The combination of circumstances that makes this possible is, of course, most unusual.

In Venezuela's case a combination of domestic and international conditions and opportunities permitted the emergence and survival of the country's current participatory system. Internally, the virtually complete absence of any traditional, historical political parties, organizations, or doctrines in Venezuela as of 1936 permitted an extremely rapid discussion and acceptance of the democratic canons of the new political leaders. With no serious opposition and no competing political apparatus, AD, URD, COPEI, and to a lesser extent the communist parties rapidly established themselves as the principal actors in the domestic political drama. This lack of opposition is unequalled anywhere else in Latin America and reflects the country's remarkable institutional weakness. The Church, politically ineffective since colonial days and crippled as a national institution by the anti-clerical reform of Antonio Guzmán Blanco in the late nineteenth century, had neither the resources nor the following to oppose the democratization of Venezuelan society. Because one of the major participants in this process, COPEI, represented the Church's interests in Christian Democracy, what little political energy this institution commanded went to the support of COPEI, and indirectly to the support of the democratic system.

Only the military had the institutional tradition, organization, and ability to block the development of a democratic process directly. As mentioned above, the officers, because of their participation in the North Atlantic technocratic society, much preferred to be honored defenders of competent civilian regimes than the managers of a dictatorial government. Not only did direct government not mesh well with the ideal type of North Atlantic society, but the military recognized its inability to mobilize adequate technical talent to manage the increasingly complex Venezuelan economy. To be sure, this reluctance to take power and the tolerance of democratic processes all depended on the civilians' efficiency and technical competence. Were that to fail, then military rule certainly would result.

The extraordinary success of Venezuela's political parties in creating an articulate, institutionalized democratic process in a generation's time can only partially be attributed to the ability of the generation of 1928, the astuteness and restraint of Betancourt, Villalba, Caldera, and their collaborators. These men indeed demonstrated unusual political and organizational skills, but they needed the benefit of a weak political tradition and nonexistent political institutions, and they required the North Atlantic connection to make their accomplishment possible. While it is the petroleum money that supports this democratic regime and resolves the inevitable conflicts, it is important to recognize the sources of the Venezuelan political design.

All of the generation of 1928's political doctrine, organizational strategy, and democratic norms come from abroad. Whether discussing the left reformism of AD, the Christian Democratic doctrines of COPEI, or the Marxist revolutionary philosophies of the left, the conclusion is the same. These parties operate in Venezuela not from a Latin American or Venezuelan context but from a North Atlantic context. The sources of political ideology and doctrine are not Bolívar or Sucre but Jefferson, the French Revolution, the Russian Revolution, Marx, Lenin, De Gaulle, and John F. Kennedy. The models of political behavior, organization, and discipline come from France, Italy, Germany, the United States, not from Venezuela or Latin America.

This generation of political leaders and military officers have a working political consensus derived from their North Atlantic context, and it is this consensus that permits them to agree to import and implant in Venezuela a fully developed, doctrinally consistent, and internationally respectable political system in the span of three decades. They did not have to create institutions or develop ideologies, only install slightly modified versions of North Atlantic political processes. The operation succeeded because there was very little in the way of old institutions to remove and the country had adequate petroleum money to purchase and install the imported institutions. Just as Venezuela imported hydroelectric power plants and steel mills, it imported its political arrangement.

Although petroleum wealth alone would not have achieved the democratization of Venezuelan society, neither would the process have

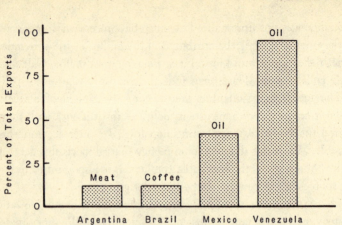

FIGURE 13: Principal Export Commodities as a Percent of Total Exports, 1979 (Table III-8)

occurred without petroleum. Moreover, oil provided more than money. As mentioned above, petroleum extraction placed a set of requirements on the Venezuelan government that had not existed in the agricultural export economy. Within this complex event, two broad, interrelated processes can be identified. The first was a rapid increase in the demand for sophisticated technical, social, and government services. The second was a rapid increase in the funds available to purchase these services. The petroleum industry in Venezuela demanded a level of social services in excess of those required for coffee. Some could be supplied on an enclave basis, such as adequate worker housing, paved streets, special schools, and the like. But adequate electrical service, regular supply of construction materials, good health conditions, efficient communications, and a transportation network, for example, proved difficult to create within the enclave. The demonstration effect of the clean, healthy, well-kept petroleum compounds also proved difficult to resist. The inefficiencies of an agricultural rural economy could not be allowed to complicate the oil business, where technological competence reigned as the supreme criterion for success. Although it was not within the oil companies' power to transform Venezuela overnight, the demands they made on the bureaucracy and the wealth they contributed in return did, in a relatively short time, refashion the face of Venezuela.

The agents of this change were not so much the oil executives from Dallas, Houston, and New York, but the Venezuelan elite, intermediaries between the technologically sophisticated foreign oil enterprise and the rural simplicity of the Venezuelan coffee economy. Because the initial phases of this transformation took place within the controlled environment of Gómez's Venezuela, many of the shocks of change were buffered by the repressive rigidity of that familial dictatorship. Ironically, the very strength of Gómez's cherished hacienda-based government, dedicated to rural cattle-raising values, made possible the rapid transformation of Venezuela's economy and society into an urban, technological, and quasi-industrialized copy of North Atlantic models.

The elite who managed this change came from the Gómez circle of families plus representatives of the traditional *caraqueño* and provincial urban elites. They processed the paper that granted the oil companies the privilege of operating in the country, and they demanded in return enough money to purchase the externals of North Atlantic metropolitan life styles. Moreover, because the oil business needed a variety of sophisticated services, it created a demand for construction and other skills that the Venezuelan elite was quick to fill. As wealth generated by the petroleum expansion increased, the prosperous elite found that the good life promised by the imitation of North Atlantic models required more than the simple ability to duplicate consumer styles. This realization led the government, beginning in the final years of the Gómez regime and continuing to the present day, to embark on ambitious development programs. All are very expensive, and all are based on assumptions and techniques imported from one North Atlantic country or another. The basic presumption of the early stages of this development exercise was that petroleum extraction required a certain level of material well-being and a certain

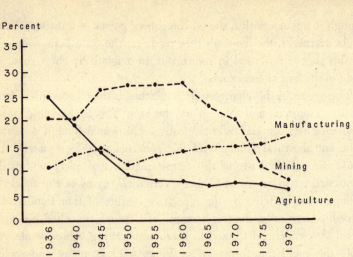

Percent

FIGURE 14: Share of Gross Domestic Product by Economic Activity, 1936-1979 (Table III-5)

minimum of social-overhead capital. The Venezuelan elite also realized that their continued participation in the good life required these investments.

For example, the construction, maintenance, and operation of the petroleum complex required the existence of paved roads, reliable electric service, good health conditions, adequate housing, competent medical care, and the like. Many of these conditions existed within the enclave society focused on the petroleum camps, and the elite proved anxious to duplicate these accomplishments in their own urban environments. This led, in turn, to an impressive building spree of public works in Caracas and other principal cities. While petroleum income was not sufficient to bring all of Venezuela into relative affluence and comfort, it sufficed to bring about dramatic changes in the physical plant and social services in the major cities.

The availability of great wealth also had another interesting effect on the Venezuelans charged with managing the economy and society. It seemed to give them, whether under the rule of Marcos Pérez

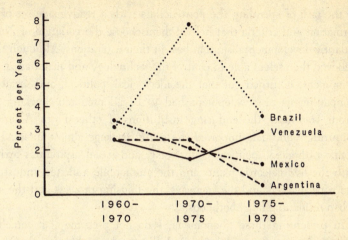

FIGURE 15: Gross Domestic Product Per Capita Growth Rates, 1960-1979, in 1978 US$ (Table III-4)

Jiménez or Rómulo Betancourt, a sense of limitless possibilities, a belief that the time of prosperity and achievement was at hand. As a consequence, these leaders, and the technological elite that followed them, developed an acute sense of impatience when confronted with the complexities of the social and economic transformation they had initiated. This sense of urgency, this unwillingness to plan for results in the next generation, is of course another manifestation of this generation's lack of tradition and its disassociation from the country's past. Because the Venezuela of yesterday held little meaning for the Venezuela of today, these people, from the cab drivers to the bankers to the president of the Republic, acted as if there would be no tomorrow. Impatience is by no means unusual; most activists in underdeveloped countries want their progress today, not tomorrow. Venezuela had the money to buy whatever was believed essential to bring the country up to North Atlantic standards in one generation.

The generation of 1928, whose members provided most of the leadership for the Venezuelan transformation of the 1950s and 1960s, saw the world in a most sophisticated North Atlantic context. They came to the task of spending the petro-dollars with a ready-made set of information and criteria that helped them choose the variation of North Atlantic developmentalism that best fit their aspirations. Although they believed themselves able to control the technology and materials of development, it turned out that the ideological, political, and social accompaniments of development had to be adopted too. Lacking the strong traditions, the enduring institutions of other Latin American countries, Venezuela imported the entire package almost intact. Economic orthodoxy, political controversy, and social aspirations arrived with the hydroelectric plants and the automobile and steel industries, the supermarkets and the freeways, the housing projects and the suburban residential neighborhoods.

In presenting these phenomena, I do not presume that somehow Venezuela was wrong or that this ability to adopt wholesale the North Atlantic model is less virtuous than some imaginable alternative. Not at all. Whatever value we may place on tradition or on alternative development strategies, the Venezuelan decision to import an entire way of life—politics, consumer habits, architectural conventions, economic and social organizations—brought the elite, the middle class, and most of the rest of the country's inhabitants a level of material well-being beyond what most of the rest of Latin America can provide. Furthermore, by importing all the elements of this new society, the Venezuelans have achieved a complete transformation of their world in a generation's time. If self-determination is the measure of authenticity, Venezuela's society is authentically Venezuelan.

For all the intervention and influence from outsiders—from American and European oil companies to United States agents, from Castroite revolutionaries to Soviet or Chinese propagandists, from European socio-political ideologues to French intellectuals—every critical choice since 1936 at least has been made by Venezuelans. There is no evidence that the choices available to Venezuela have been less varied than those available to members of the North Atlantic developed world.

The dependence of Venezuela on this North Atlantic complex is, of course, great in absolute terms. It is inconceivable, for example, that Venezuela should fail to heed the dictates of Euro-American or Japanese technology or the requirements of the World Bank. In relation to the older societies of England, France, Italy, or a more recently developed country such as Canada, Venezuela's independence of action appears considerable. There is no reason to cast the founder of OPEC, the manager of a comprehensive nationalization of the oil industry, and the developer of strong national steel and aluminum industries as a simple-minded dependent on North Atlantic whims. Of course Venezuela, like England, France, and the United States, must conform to a set of norms dictated by North Atlantic trade and complicated by the emergence of Japanese commercial power. But Venezuela's control over its destiny is at least as comprehensive as that of England, the Scandinavian countries, Italy, or Spain.

Venezuela's participation in the North Atlantic system is notable not for its dependent relationship but for its aggressive consumerist approach. If we were to imagine Venezuela as a single individual with a rather generous income and an insistent desire to live the good life, we would have a usable model of this country's behavior. If then we were to see the North Atlantic world as the closest and most familiar department store, we would have little difficulty evaluating Venezuela's consumerism. The country picks and chooses among the various styles of merchandise available, sometimes making frivolous or dangerous purchases, often squandering income on useless or defective items, but rapidly acquiring the ability to buy things that combine well, that give good service, and that require reasonable maintenance. Sales people try to influence these purchases through advertising, bargain prices, discounts, package plans. Distant competitors attempt to lure the Venezuela trade away from this North Atlantic emporium.

The package of goods acquired in this shopping spree responds to a complex psychology of desires, ambitions, and resources, but it is a Venezuelan psychology. Especially convincing is that, while the dominant supplier of Venezuelan things is the United States, the package has a large number of significant items derived from European and Japanese sources, whether automotive products, industrial machinery, artistic styles, or clothing.

This analogy does not imply that the Venezuelan model of develop-

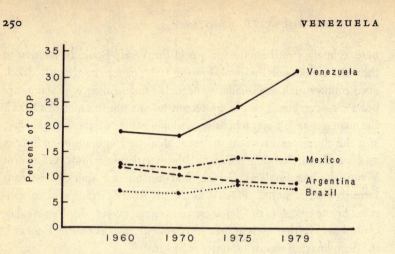

FIGURE 16: Imports as a Percent of Gross Domestic Product, 1960-1979 (Table III-6)

ment has no faults. By importing everything, the country inevitably has many inconsistencies and inefficiencies. The Venezuelans are the first to hold their leaders accountable for the management of the country's resources; for while the transformation of Venezuela from an agriculturally based archaic society to a petroleum-based modern society has been accomplished in two generations, the speed of transformation has not left the population, especially the urban majority, complacent. The elections of 1978 are a case in point.

Although the two principal parties, AD and COPEI, proposed ideological analogues as their platforms, the major issue of this election, as in previous ones, was the efficacy of the incumbent's management of the petroleum bonanza. To present both the government's case and COPEI's challenge, United States advertising teams were imported to engage in a very elaborate electoral campaign, complete with all the paraphernalia characteristic of United States elections. While the spectacle of a Venezuelan election run and managed by United States firms is, at first glance, startling, it is, on further reflection, only natural. This country is now so sophisticated in its technology, political education, and popular participation that only the most expert of electoral manipulators can hope to influence the electorate. In the same

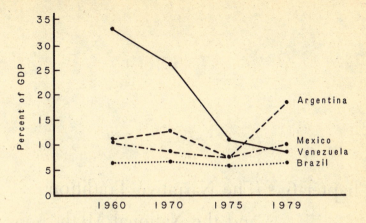

FIGURE 17: Exports as a Percent of Gross Domestic Product, 1960-1979 (Table III-6)

way Venezuela demands the best in industrial machinery, the country demanded the best in election campaigns.

The campaign was a good one, complete with image-making, television blitzes, campaign rallies, and the now traditional Venezuelan presidential election pilgrimage to all corners of the country. But the issue of efficacy, efficiency, and technical competence, for all the hoopla, remained central to the campaign, and the election of the opposition candidate, Luis Herrera Campíns of COPEI, signaled a variety of attitudes in Venezuela's electorate. It indicated the normal tendency for the incumbent to be blamed for the world's ills occurring during his term; it also indicated the decline of the AD rural base, a casualty of a generation of urban-rural migration. It demonstrated the electorate's conviction that, with the immense revenues available, the government ought to be able to produce a better distribution of resources and a more visible sense of progress toward the nirvana of technological sufficiency and the good life.

The performance of the Herrera government through 1980 demonstrates the intractability of many of the country's problems. Inflation, corruption, and inefficiency continue unabated; and the problems engendered by Venezuela's rapid development resist solution.

Chapter 6 • The Narrative Tradition and the National Myth

Venezuela's cultural identity is pre-eminently Hispanic, although the country has benefited from African and Indian contributions as well. The most accessible image of Venezuelan culture is found in the novels and other narrative writings of the region's intellectual and political leaders and in the accounts of some of its more perceptive visitors. In this country, as is the case elsewhere in the Hispanic world, the separation between novelist, historian, and public polemicist is never very clear. Venezuelan novelists also cultivate history and serve as public figures in government. They write poetry and political tracts, novelistic history and historical novels. As a result, the narrative literature is most useful for understanding Venezuela's past.

This is not to ignore the country's rich musical and artistic traditions, but these expressions of thought and feeling belong less uniquely to Venezuela than to the universal worlds of art and music. Since the late colonial period at least, Venezuelan orchestras, bands, chamber ensembles, and choirs have entertained audiences in Caracas and to a lesser extent elsewhere. This has been a constant feature of the Venezuelan cultural milieu, and today the country has an outstanding complement of orchestras in Caracas and in other principal cities. The wealth of petroleum has naturally made the opportunity for musical performance and musical education greater than ever before. Venezuela's musicians travel to the United States and Europe for training and performance and find appreciative audiences everywhere. The most famous of Venezuela's performing artists, the exceptionally talented pianist Teresa Carreño (1853-1917), can stand as a representative of this country's excellent musical tradition.

The music and the plastic arts that flourish in Venezuela serve more to indicate the sophistication and competence of the Venezuelan elite than to illustrate the context of the country's past. To be sure, heroic painters such as Juan Lovera (1778-1841) and Martín Tovar y Tovar (1828-1902) have left evocative portraits of Venezuelan independence and the pageantry and excitement of its warfare. Still, the chronicle, the political tract, the novel, the short story, and the narrative report provide the best insights into the themes presented in this book.

THE NARRATIVE TRADITION

Because Venezuela has spent such a large part of its history in transition—from Indian territory to colonial outpost, to commercial bureaucratic state, and then to the technocratic regimes—the literary focus is also on transitions.

The conquest epic, of much greater grandeur in Mexico and Peru than in Venezuela, nevertheless attracted the attention of Juan de Castellanos (1522-1607), whose epic poem, the *Elegía de varones ilustres de América* (1589), describes his American odyssey on the island of Margarita in the period of the pearl fisheries. He lived there in the 1540s, and his verses about the region indicate the enthusiasm of this young adventurer for the charms of the pearl island. Castellanos traveled everywhere and wrote about everything, demonstrating his extraordinary memory and his facility for mediocre verse, but for our purposes it is the stanzas on the pearl island of Margarita that place him near the beginning of the long line of skillful interpreters of Venezuela's past.

Although Venezuelan letters of the colonial period before the mid-eighteenth century can claim no special distinction, the narrative spirit nevertheless existed in abundance. Both the rough chronicle of the sixteenth-century conquest and settlement by the Franciscan Fray Pedro de Aguado (1538-1590?) or the much more refined classic account by José Oviedo y Baños (1671-1738) some generations later, capture the spirit of these difficult decades of conquest and colonization. Perhaps even more evocative of the conditions and concerns of the Spaniard in Venezuela, the official reports collectively called *Relaciones Geográficas* describe the communities, villages, and problems of the colonial generations. Especially valuable for the mid-sixteenth and the eighteenth century, these accounts prepared at government request can be taken as authentic chronicles of the lives and times of a society in transition. While lacking literary merit, they provide the modern reader with as good a sense of time and place as the more pretentious literary productions of the period.

With the expansion of the economy and the maturation of society that characterized the second half of the eighteenth century and the first decade of the nineteenth century, Venezuela's literary sophistication also increased, although the colony's first printing press arrived only in 1808 and had little impact on colonial letters. Excellent representatives of this eighteenth-century literary style are two foreigners whose descriptions of Venezuela form obligatory parts of a Venezuelanist library. François Depons (1751-1812), a French commercial and semiofficial representative, came to the country with the French exodus from Santo Domingo and stayed to report on conditions in Venezuela and the Caribbean from 1801 to 1804. His greatest contribution turned out to be his fascinating account, published in 1806, of Venezuelan—especially *caraqueño*—society and politics at the close of the colonial period. His contemporary, the famous German naturalist Alexander von Humboldt (1769-1859), also visited Venezuela during the years 1799-1801. His multivolume account, first published in 1814, stands as the definitive contemporary analysis of Venezuela on the eve of independence.

This eighteenth-century enthusiasm for understanding the natural and political habitat reflected the enlightenment passion for useful knowledge. For Spanish-Americans it was this aspect of the European Enlightenment that had the greatest influence and the most lasting effect. Much less taken with the alien notions of political and social liberty, the Spanish-American elite embraced the concepts of experiment and improvement in the utilitarian arts, sciences, industry, and agriculture, if not in the more dangerous domain of politics, religion, and social order. Even the Spanish Church found a new interest in practical knowledge and commissioned an elaborate census of the American parishes in the last quarter of the eighteenth century. Clearly, the Enlightenment drive for useful knowledge coincided with the traditional Spanish mania for information collection. In Venezuela, one of the most remarkable examples of this Spanish passion for knowing and recording is the elaborate inspection tour conducted by Bishop Mariano Martí (1721-92) during the years 1771-84. His Bishopric of Caracas covered most of the central part of Venezuela, and this energetic prelate set out to visit every hamlet, village, and town. The record of his *visita* fills some seven volumes even in somewhat abridged form and stands as a rich account of life at all levels of Venezuelan society.

Venezuelan letters, properly speaking, begin with the independence movement in 1810. This is so not only in a formal sense defined by the political activities of independence but also in a cultural sense defined by the writings of this independence generation. The independence movement turns out to have been the most important Venezuelan cultural and intellectual focus. Independence themes not only were the predominant topics of Venezuelan authors during the first half-century of republican life, but continue to attract attention from writers today.

The independence era authors were romantics, and few symbolized this turn of mind better than the duo of Simón Rodríguez (1771-1854) and Simón Bolívar. In many ways they represented dissimilar social and cultural backgrounds: Bolívar the scion of ancient *caraqueño* aristocracy and Rodríguez a middle-level pedagogue. Both shared that romantic trademark of extravagant excess. Rodríguez's excess tended toward the intellectual and personal. He lived a life of extravagant gesture, traveled widely to the European centers of romantic inspiration, and wrote with similar abandon. His influence would have been small had he not connected with the young Simón Bolívar in 1795-97 as his tutor and then later accompanied him on a walking tour of France and Italy in 1804-6. Bolívar evidently learned much from this idiosyncratic pedagogue, and over the years, his letters to Rodríguez testified to the great impression left by the romantic teacher.

It is Bolívar, however, who is the archetypical Spanish-American romantic, whether in the style of the heroic public person or in the character of the impassioned man of letters. Born to the best of families in 1783, Bolívar acquired all the attributes of success. He had private tutors in Caracas. He traveled to Spain in 1799-1802 to complete his education and to connect with the family's metropolitan network. He traveled to France, then, in 1802, he concluded a well-placed Spanish marriage. From this stylized, elegant, and conventional beginning, Bolívar suffered a tragedy when his bride sickened and died in 1803 soon after their return to Venezuela. This tragedy seems, in retrospect, to have released Bolívar from the obligations of birth and class and to have turned him into the tragic hero of American independence. Bolívar then returned to Europe and spent several years in travels and study in France and Italy, observing the Napoleonic era. It was during this period that Bolívar took his walking tour of those countries with his Venezuelan teacher, Simón Rodríguez.

Although Bolívar's trajectory in Spanish America is well known and often retold, its romantic dimensions deserve emphasis. Bolívar's rejection of all mundane concerns in his pursuit of the grand design for America, his total uninterest in his patrimony and his obligations as the heir of an American fortune, and his disregard for his personal comfort and safety contributed an important dimension to the work of art that was his life. His military and political career added another, with its rapid changes from disaster to triumph to disaster. The brilliant Campaña Admirable in 1813 that gave way to the defeat at the hands of the *llanero* troops of Boves in 1814, the difficult times in Angostura, and the incredibly daring crossing of the Andes in 1819 all led to the triumph and adulation that followed the battle of Boyacá in the same year. Even the campaigns in Peru and Ecuador in 1821-24, the meeting with the Argentine liberator in Guayaquil in 1822, and the Bolivian Constitution in 1826 seemed designed for a romantic tapestry, a heroic novel. Not content with an extravagant public life, Bolívar's personal life was the stuff of fiction. The celebrated love affair in Peru with Manuelita Sáenz, the wife of a British doctor, could have been invented by an overwrought romantic poet.

The conclusion of this epic came with great tragedy in December 1830. In the town of Santa Marta on the road to exile, the hero of Spanish America died, virtually unmourned, in disgrace in both his native land and his adopted countries. Bolívar's legacy to America is the volumes of laws, decrees, proclamations, letters and the like which document better than any historian the life and art he tried to create. This prolific frenzy left Venezuela and Spanish America with an extraordinary vision of the nineteenth-century romantic man of letters and action: a model much cultivated since in the Americas. It is through his writings that Bolívar emerges as one of Venezuela's important literary figures. The letters reveal a cultivated and enlightened intellect, well read and perceptive, filled with idealism, yet laced with a realism born of astute observation. The set pieces, however, are crafted and written with style and skill to impress the intended audience. The famous Jamaica Letter, sent from Kingston in 1815 and aimed at a British audience that might doubt the legitimacy of Spanish America's independence spirit, or the speech at Angostura in 1819 delivered to the wavering Venezuelan legislators of the Congress of Angostura in an effort to stiffen their resolve for the continental assault on the Spanish empire and the creation of a constitution—each of these pieces, along with other classic Bolivariana, qualifies for inclusion in the roster of Venezuela letters.

While Bolívar's contribution to Venezuelan literature looms large because of his domination of its politics, others of this generation provided a more refined literary offering. Don Andrés Bello (1781-1865), whose independence era credentials came from diplomatic service in Europe, contributed a classic poem to Venezuelan literature in the *Silvas Americanas* (1823, 1826). More classic than romantic in inspiration, Bello's fine style glorified the powerful and mysterious American wilderness. Bello, an exceptionally talented individual, traveled to Chile in 1829, where his contributions to education, law, and letters are a monument to his wisdom and intellect.

Given the task of converting Venezuela into an ideal commercial-bureaucratic state, the country's literary talent spent most of its energy on the discussion of public issues during the first independence years. The best writing in the Venezuela of Páez and Monagas can be found in the political tracts, the congressional speeches, and especially in the periodical press. Fermín Toro's (1807-1865) enlightened discussions of the country's agricultural economy in the 1830s and 1840s, for example, represent some of the best and most interesting writing of the time. Perhaps the most intriguing figure of these years, and indeed well into the Federal Wars period, was Juan Vicente González (1810-1866). This skillful, romantic polemicist filled the pages of the press with a never-ending diatribe against the Liberal party and its premier demagogue, Antonio Leocadio Guzmán. González belonged to the Hispanic romantic tradition that emphasized excessive emotion and an extravagant life style. Although his dreams of glory were grandiose, his accomplishments earned him a much smaller reputation. Nevertheless, the *Biografía de José Felix Ribas* (1865) marks the beginning of the historical novel or the novel as history in Venezuela. Its focus on the independence epoch also indicates the work's accurate reflection of the primary Venezuelan theme.

In spite of the excellence of Venezuela's political writings, the period of the postindependence generation through the end of the Federal Wars produced relatively little in the way of memorable literature. Juan Vicente González, never at a loss for words, had an explanation for this phenomenon: "But if literature is a luxury of advanced societies," he said, "it is unlikely to be found amongst those like us who are without leisure to write, inspired by momentary passions, distracted by the noise of catastrophe, saddened by the present, and fearful of the future."

As Venezuela became more involved in the commercial-bureaucratic empire of the North Atlantic, a shift from a focus on the independence and the fascination with romanticized versions of an idealized Venezuelan environment occurred. The novelists and writers of the turn of the century and well into the twentieth century began to examine Venezuela's landscape, customs, traditions, and styles with a much more critical eye. Some, following the fashion of the times, expressed their notions in the modern mode with its emphasis on elegance of style and form. In Venezuela it was Manuel Díaz Rodríguez (1868-1927) who symbolized this modernist style. His *Idolos Rotos* (1901) and *Sangre Patricia* (1902) stand as exceptional examples of the modernist novel in Spanish America.

While the previous generations had focused on the independence epic and expressed great interest in themes of heroic warfare and the creation of nations, the writers of the following generation attempted to explain and portray the remarkable division between the elegant, civilized city and the untamed, barbaric countryside. The civilization and barbarism theme, made famous in Spanish America by the Argentine Domingo F. Sarmiento in *Facundo,* pervades Venezuelan letters until well after the end of the Gómez regime. The theme appeared in many forms, sometimes expressed as a conflict between the aristocracy and the environment. In Manuel Díaz Rodríguez it was this aristocratic temperament that failed to conquer the environment and the reality of Venezuela, although the highly stylized, psychological approach of Díaz Rodríguez distinguishes his work from the more realistic tone of his successors.

The positivists approached the analysis of Venezuela with an entirely different philosophical perspective from that of either the romantics or the modernists, although their thematic focus differed hardly at all. More interested in history and sociology than in novelistic literature, the positivists also saw Venezuela as the scene of a clash between the two worlds of civilization and barbarism. José Gil Fortoul (1861-1942), whose outstanding *Historia constitucional de Venezuela* (1906-7) attempted an explanation of this conflict in a clear and systematic style, saw Venezuelan history as progress toward an orderly and stable society, one increasingly characterized by regular, constitutional forms. Lisandro Alvarado (1859-1929) demonstrated positivist enthusiasm for that Venezuela outside the cities, and beyond the elegant urban domain. His studies of Venezuelan ethnography and linguistics place him as a founder of sociological studies in Venezuela.

Perhaps the most famous positivist of all, Laureano Vallenilla Lanz (1870-1936), brought the theme of civilization and barbarism into sharp focus in his several works analyzing the state of Venezuela's political and social culture. His contribution, the *Gendarme Necesario* or the essential policeman, provided the most coherent and effective justification for authoritarian government and by far the most convincing apologia for the regime of Juan Vicente Gómez. The analysis that led Vallenilla Lanz to recommend the authoritarian policeman in his work *Cesarismo democrático* (1919) is perceptive and informed, and it draws on the symbols of the Spanish colonial system and the heroic period of the independence. The order and progress that Vallenilla Lanz pursued required a forced resolution of the conflict between the civilization of the cities and the barbarism of the countryside. Whatever the merit of Vallenilla Lanz's political solutions, his brilliant analysis of Venezuela clearly places him among the best of the country's historians.

If the Gómez regime generated its intellectual justification, it also produced a literary opposition. The work of José Rafael Pocaterra (1888-1954) gains its reputation not primarily from the powerful indictment of the Gómez oppression in the *Memorias de un venezolano de la decadencia* (1936) but rather from the realistic novels and short stories about the lives of his contemporaries. The series of *Cuentos grotescos* (1922) provide vignettes of Venezuela that excel in an unrelieved portrayal of the inevitability of injustice. In these stories virtue is not usually rewarded, and the protagonists are frequently the least impressive members of a society that shows remarkable indifference to the suffering of its members. Pocaterra did have his heroes, however. In the *Casa de los Abila* (1946) he traced the activities of a middle-class Venezuelan family. This striking novel about the follies and shallow values of the new-rich Venezuelan explores several themes that are central to the country's experience. The family wealth and so-

cial prominence rests on rural properties which the patriarch worked'
himself to death to develop.

The family, however, is a *caraqueño* family that aspires to exhalted
social importance in urban society. Their interest is directed toward
manipulating the connection between Caracas and Europe in order to
impress *caraqueño* society with their social importance. They ignore
their source of wealth in the land and turn instead to commerce and
speculation to increase their closeness to that North Atlantic world.
The family squanders its money on foolish commercial ventures, and
the *casa de los Abila* is sold. But within the family lies salvation in the
person of the youngest son, despised by all because he lacks social
graces. The boy, inspired by his grandfather to hold dear the traditional virtues of agrarian Venezuela, returns to the land and begins to
restore the family fortune. Clearly this novel is an allegory for Venezuela. At the same time that it paints a vivid picture of the sycophantic
Venezuelan society of the early twentieth century, it prescribes the return to the agrarian tradition that was being destroyed by the slavish
imitation of foreign ways.

While this focus on the exterior life and style of a changing society
illustrates the broad dimensions of a country in transition, Venezuela
also had authors capable of portraying the inner conflicts that accompanied these changes. Teresa de la Parra (1898-1936) wrote two novels, *Ifigenia* (1924) and *Memorias de Mamá Blanca* (1927), that provide an extraordinary vision of the social requirements and interior
life of the women of upper-class *criollo* society. Not only are they important as a literary accomplishment, these books give a glimpse into a
world that would soon cease to exist, a world in which domestic traditions governed the aspirations and horizons of Venezuela's women.

For all the intellectual and literary power, all the social commentary
and realistic portraits of a Teresa de la Parra or a José Rafael Pocaterra, it is the work of Rómulo Gallegos (1884-1969) that seems to define the maturity of Venezuelan literature. Gallegos succeeds because
his work has coherence. The cycle of Gallegos novels from *El último
solar* (1920), through *Canaima* (1935), and including *La rebellión*

(1922), *La trepadora* (1925), *Doña Bárbara* (1929), and *Cantaclaro* (1934) touches on each of the typical Venezuelan landscapes, each of the critical problems of Venezuela's past and present, and does this with a clear sense of the true and correct solution. Gallegos, like most of his compatriots in Spanish America, found the clash between the expectations of civilization and the requirements of survival in the native American habitat to be the central contradiction of Venezuelan life. This basic conflict manifests itself in his novels through themes universal in Spanish America but of special concern to Venezuelans, such as unequal marriages and social prejudice derived from artificial distinctions of class, race, and miscegenation; and the power of human passion unrestrained and unchanneled by the best instincts of human compassion and social justice. The novels are rich in detail, powerful in language, and, as a group, help define that cultural and geographical combination that is the Venezuelan variant of Spanish-American culture. Gallegos's reputation for social sensitivity and popular esteem, his renown outside of Venezuela, and his well-known opposition to the Gómez dictatorship made him an ideal choice as standard bearer for the democratic experiment in 1945. Although his political skills proved less impressive than his literary talents, he survived this unhappy experience with his integrity intact.

With the advent of petroleum wealth, Venezuela became a country capable of supporting a wide range of literary and artistic talents. As Venezuela became more a part of the North Atlantic world, the country's artists and authors reflected the whole range of trends and styles current there. Polemical, political, introspective, psychological, existential—whatever the mode, Venezuelans cultivated it with distinction.

Beginning in the 1930s, such authors as Arturo Uslar Pietri (1906-   ) developed new styles and brought new insights to the traditional themes of Venezuelan literature. His *Lanzas coloradas* (1931) is an exciting story set in the era of the War to the Death during the independence. The style is modern, the dialogue vivid, and the scenes impressive, but the themes are those that have intrigued Venezuelan authors since independence: the conflicts of class and race, the tension between civilization and savagery, and the power of the independence war as a national myth. Equally within this tradition is Ramón Díaz Sánchez (1903-1968), whose modernist style and superb reportorial skills outlined both past and present. His work on *Guzmán, Elipse de una ambición de poder* (1950) provides the best view yet of the Antonio Leocadio Guzmán–Antonio Guzmán Blanco careers. His petroleum novels *Mene* (1936) and *Cassandra* (1957) capture first the transformation of the rural countryside in response to the demands of oil production, and second the destruction of a land-based social structure and its replacement by a commercial middle class whose social and moral referents derive from the cultivation of foreign styles. Díaz Sánchez, like Uslar Pietri, continued the Venezuelan themes of his predecessors in spite of his elegant modernity, although the impact of petroleum on values and society is the newest manifestation of the theme of civilization and barbarism.

THE NATIONAL MYTH

This rapid, incomplete, overview of the Venezuelan narrative tradition illustrates important characteristics of the country's cultural landscape. The essence of a national culture is shared myths, and Venezuelans have found it difficult to identify those myths of its past that uniquely define its culture. Because the country's identity is preeminently Hispanic, the Venezuelan variant is difficult to separate from what might be regarded as the Hispanic base. Venezuelan literature fits easily into the categories of Spanish-American literature, so easily, in fact, that it would be hard to identify the specifically Venezuelan component of the country's classic literary works. To be sure, the place names and the geographic referents identify the locales, but the stories, to a large degree, would make almost as good sense with a different set of place names from Colombia or perhaps Argentina.

This helps explain the overwhelming emphasis in Venezuelan letters on the independence period. This period from 1810 to 1830 defines Venezuela and constitutes the country's identifying myth until perhaps the 1950s or 1960s. The independence, with its hero Bolívar, its complex, violent, and prolonged warfare, gave Venezuela the unique-

ness necessary for a national myth. After independence, the struggle to
remake Venezuela in the commercial-bureaucratic mode offered few
heroes who lasted long enough to glorify, and few national triumphs
worthy of commemoration. Páez, whose successes in the independence
and subsequent republican years should have made him a cultural
symbol of considerable power, continued his fight for pre-eminence for
too long. Hence, between 1848 and his death in 1873, Páez's failures
as a military leader of a lost cause left his reputation unfit for national
mythology. The remarkable organizational gifts of Antonio Guzmán
Blanco resisted successful hagiography because the man became so
much a European as to become a foreigner in his own land. The subsequent regimes of Cipriano Castro and Juan Vicente Gómez failed
the test of mythology also, the one because it was too publicly decadent
and lost a contest with the European powers who blockaded Venezuelan ports in 1902-3, the other because its unremitting oppression
and colorless style left little material for hagiographic reconstruction.

Since the petroleum extravaganza has changed much of the style and
some of the content of Venezuelan life, the technocratic elite must discover a new myth for Venezuela's future. The independence and Bolívar seem to be losing their power as symbols of nationalism, not only
because those times seem hopelessly remote to the urban technocrat,
but also because the values of rural Venezuela that they symbolized are
no longer germane to this generation.

Out of the mass media of television and movies, popular magazines
and recorded music, Venezuela is creating a new cultural dimension.
It is still Hispanic in language and structure, but it is rapidly becoming
cosmopolitan to a degree unimaginable at the beginning of the century. Yet beneath the beat of rock music, the incessant torrent of soap
operas, and the innumerable movies made in Hollywood or Europe,
the integrity of Venezuelan culture still remains intact in the Hispanic
structure brought to America in the sixteenth century.

Conclusion

This history identifies a number of unifying processes and themes that have provided Venezuela with the continuity of its national identity. The first of these is the powerful force of language and culture. Derived from the Spanish imperial tradition, this Hispanic cultural focus marked Venezuela as an integral part of the Western world from the sixteenth century onward. Although belonging to a peripheral and dependent economy, the Venezuelans of Tierra Firme who directed and controlled their region never saw themselves apart from the main fashions of North Atlantic culture. Spanish imperial policy, as was true in the rest of Spanish America, insisted that Venezuela become a part of the Western world during the conquest and settlement of America. Independence, in 1810, signified only a rearrangement of governing elites and the reorganization of commercial affairs, not the rejection of a cultural past. Consequently, the developing nations of Spanish America are old, long-term participants in the North Atlantic variant of Western Civilization. The transformations described in this book represent Venezuelans' efforts to create out of the material at hand a prosperous North Atlantic society.

If language and culture provided Venezuelans with a clear sense of their place in the Western hegemony, they failed to define their place within the Hispanic world. This entity we so easily label Venezuela came into existence only after a long search for the administrative and political design appropriate for the territory. In this slow process, Venezuela had no help from a preconquest indigenous society. Unlike Mexico or Peru, for example, Venezuela's urban and administrative structure had to be invented out of the physical and human materials at hand. While the presence of Indians and their willingness to accept Spanish domination certainly had an impact on the arrangement of Venezuela's Hispanic form, these indigenous influences constituted but one element in the complex and deliberate fashioning of Venezuela's Spanish landscape. The primary force in the consolidation of what is Venezuela was the gradual expansion and interconnection of the urban network anchored by the central city of Caracas. Not until the last generation of the colonial period did Venezuela achieve a mature colonial society with a fully articulated central city.

This theme—the invention, maintenance, and development of the urban framework constructed around Caracas—runs throughout the history of Venezuela, for this arrangement of space, power, and resources is Venezuela. The urban network combined with the Hispanic cultural heritage provide from 1780 to 1980 the effective organization and continuity for the country, linking the regimes of the *audiencia* in colonial times, the Páez years of the early nineteenth century, and the Guzmán Blanco years of the late nineteenth century, with the Gómez regime and the subsequent democratic governments of the twentieth century. Across the discontinuities of civil war and political transformations, agricultural and industrial economies, rural life styles and urban agglomerations, Venezuela has functioned through the stable network of towns and cities whose interconnections defined the patterns of control, the directions of resource distribution, and the country's identity. This theme is not unique to Venezuela, but few Latin American countries provide such a clear and unambiguous demonstration of the principles and operation of this Hispanic institutional artifact.

Language and culture, and the urban network provide two of the major themes identifying Venezuela and ordering the country's history. But if the period from conquest to 1800 provided Venezuela with its organization and identity, the subsequent years saw a long and apparently chaotic struggle to invent the political, social, and economic order that would bring the country the progress it required. In the nineteenth and twentieth centuries the alternating succession of regimes and civil wars, political constitutions and rebellions represent not the confused gropings of a disorganized people but a consistent and coherent search for the order that would bring progress. Venezuela, unable until the 1960s to afford the luxury of a Western democracy, used caudillesque violence to serve as the crude but effective mechanism for selecting, confirming, legitimating, and removing leaders. Spending the only currency available, the manpower and technology of a rural society, Venezuelans selected and discarded regimes according to a rough, performance-based criterion. As long as the current order appeared to move the country toward the realization of the dream of progress, the inevitable challenges to authority failed to change the regime. But should the progress falter, change came swiftly, inelegantly, but effectively.

As part of the cultural mainstream of Western and North Atlantic society, Venezuelans found it essential to keep to the forms and styles of North Atlantic political models. Otherwise the discordance created might threaten the integrity of the country's Hispanic heritage. Similarly, every regime, from *audiencia* to populist democracy, operated with and through the Caracas-centered urban network because to do anything else would have weakened the country's structure. Indeed, every regime, whatever its origin or intention, strengthened the bureaucracy and power of Caracas, which in turn reinforced the stability and efficacy of this urban artifact.

What demonstrates this arrangement so dramatically is the abrupt break that occurred at the end of the Gómez years and during the subsequent generations. Venezuela's economic base was transformed from agriculture and stock raising to mining and industry. The political system was transformed from Hispanic caudillism to North Atlantic populist democracy, and the social system was transformed from a land-based, family-oriented hierarchy to an income-based, technocratic meritocracy. Yet Venezuela's structure remained for the most part intact. The urban network continues to function as it did for the Audiencia of Caracas, albeit in much more complex ways, and the Hispanic cultural heritage still offers Venezuelans their primary identity.

Although this book makes the case for the power and strength of the urban network, it is possible that the most recent results of the search for order, the dream of progress, will be enough to disturb this remarkable Hispanic artifact. With only a generation of experience, it is too soon to know whether the force of wealth and technology will be sufficient to remake Venezuela by changing both urban network and cultural heritage. Such might be the price of Venezuela's dream.

Chronology

Prepared by Mary B. Floyd

THE COLONIAL PERIOD

1498   Columbus discovers the coast of Venezuela on his third voy-
            age to America.
1510-40   Period of preliminary exploration and settlement.
            (1510) Nueva Cádiz, on the island of Cubagua, becomes
            the first settlement in Venezuela. (1523) Diego Castellón
            founds Cumaná, the first successful settlement on the main-
            land. (1525) Margarita Island becomes an independent
            province. (1527) Juan de Ampíes founds Coro.
1528-56   Governors sent by the German House of Welser attempt to
            fulfill the concession awarded by Charles V to conquer, settle,
            and explore western Venezuela.
            (1529) Ambrosio Alfinger, the first governor of Venezuela,
            lands at Coro. (1529-30) Alfinger takes an expedition into
            the interior in search of El Dorado. (1530-36) Nicolás Feder-
            man heads two expeditions into the interior. (1531) Coro
            becomes the site of the first bishopric in Venezuela. (1535-
            38) Jorge de Espira, the governor of Coro, leads two expedi-
            tions into the interior. (1541) Felipe de Hutten, as lieuten-
            ant governor of Coro in 1541, and as governor in 1546,
            searches for El Dorado.
1545-89   Period of town foundations.

269

(1545) Juan de Carvajal founds El Tocuyo. (1545-50s) Major *encomienda* period begins after the founding of El Tocuyo. Barquisimeto (1552), Valencia (1555), Mérida (1558), and Trujillo (1558) settled. (1560) A royal *cédula* permits the *cabildos,* in the absence of the local governor, to govern the province of Caracas independently of the Audiencia of Santo Domingo until a new governor arrives. (1567) Caracas is founded by Diego de Losada and Maracaibo by Alonso Pacheco. (1589) Caracas's port town of La Guaira is founded.

1595-1720   Establishment of colonial society.

(1595) The English pirate Amayas Preston attacks and sacks Caracas. (1636) The king approves the transfer of the bishopric for Venezuela from Coro to Caracas. (1652) Philip IV institutes the mission system in Venezuela. (1656) The Bishopric of Coro is re-established as the Bishopric of Caracas in Caracas. The Franciscans (1656) and the Capuchins (1657) begin their missions in Píritu. (1658) The Capuchins also establish a mission in the province of Caracas. (1673) The Seminary of Santa Rosa is founded in Caracas. (1676) A royal decree confirms the authority of the Caracas *cabildo* to govern the province in the absence of a governor.

1721-1808   Consolidation of a mature colonial society.

(1721) The crown elevates the Seminary of Santa Rosa to the status of a university, and in 1725 it becomes the Real y Pontífica Universidad de Caracas. (1728-84) The period of the Caracas Company. (1749-51) Juan Francisco de León leads armed rebellions protesting the policies of the Caracas Company. (1767) The king expells the Jesuits from Latin America including Venezuela. (1776) The king creates the institutions of the Intendencia del Ejército y Real Hacienda, and in 1777 the Gran Capitanía General de las Provincias Unidas de Venezuela; the crown also approves the creation of the Bishopric of Mérida de Maracaibo (Maracaibo, Coro, Trujillo, Mérida) and extends the royal tobacco monopoly to Venezuela. (1785) A seminary is founded in Mérida. (1786) The Audiencia of Caracas is created. (1788) The Colegio de Abogados opens. (1789) The crown extends free-trade system to Venezuela. (1790) The Bishopric of Guayana (Trinidad, Margarita, Cumaná, and Guayana) is created. (1793) The Real Consulado de Caracas (merchants' guild) is approved. (1797) Manuel Gual and José María España escape to Trinidad after their plot to foment revolution in Venezuela fails. (1804) The See of Caracas is elevated to an archbishopric and takes jurisdiction over the bishoprics of Guayana and Mérida de Maracaibo. (1806) Francisco de Miranda lands in Coro. Venezuelan troops rout his forces. His earlier expedition that year to Puerto Cabello had also failed. (1807) Juan de Casas arrives in Caracas as captain general.

THE INDEPENDENCE PERIOD

1808-10   The declaration of independence.
(1808) The Napoleonic invasion of Spain forces the abdication of Charles IV in March. In September the Supreme Central Junta, in opposition to Bonaparte, meets in Aranjuez to govern in the name of the captive king, Ferdinand VII. The Junta Central moves to Seville in November. The *Gaceta de Caracas,* Venezuela's first newspaper, begins publication. (1809) Vicente de Emparán governs as captain general from May to April 1810. (1809) The Spanish Junta Central moves from Seville to Cádiz. Within two months, the junta dissolves itself in favor of a five-member Regency Council. (1810) On April 19 the Caracas Cabildo holds an open session (*cabildo abierto*), ousts the captain general, and organizes a Junta Conservadora de los Derechos de Fernando VII. The slave trade to Venezuela is prohibited.

1811-12   The First Republic or Patria Boba.
(1811) General Congress of the United Provinces of Venezuela convenes in March, passes a Bill of Rights in July, and declares Venezuela's independence from Spain on July 5, 1811. Miranda, in charge of Venezuelan forces, subdues the royalist sympathizers in Valencia. In December Congress approves a Federal Constitution. (1812) In Spain, the Cortes at Cádiz approves a liberal constitution in March. In July Miranda surrenders to Monteverde, and the patriots arrest Miranda and turn him over to the Spanish captain.

1813-14   The Second Republic.
(1813) Margarita and the eastern part of the Republic are controlled by patriots. Bolívar enters Venezuela in April, completing the Campaña Admirable. During the campaign he issues the decree of War to the Death in June. Between April

and August the Campaña Admirable brings Mérida, Trujillo, Barquisimeto, and Valencia under patriot control. The Mérida town council confers the title of Liberator on Bolívar in June, and after Caracas falls to the patriots on August 6, it is confirmed in that city in October. In November José Tomás Boves declares a war to the death against patriots in his Proclamation of Guayabal. (1814) Bolívar receives supreme power from the assembly in January. Boves routs Bolívar and Santiago Mariño in the Battle of La Puerta on June 14, enters Valencia on July 10, and enters Caracas on the 16th. Bolívar is forced to leave Venezuela for Cartagena in September. Boves dies from wounds received in the Battle of Urica, which his army wins. (1815) Pablo Morillo arrives in Venezuela with over 10,000 troops. In May Morillo enters Caracas. Bolívar explains his political philosophy in the Jamaica Letter—Reply of a South American to a Gentleman of this Island.

1816-19   The Third Republic.
(1816) Haitian President Alexandre Petión sponsors Bolívar's first attempt to invade Venezuela in May-August. In July Bolívar issues a proclamation on the liberty of slaves. A second invasion succeeds when Bolívar lands in Barcelona and begins a march to Guayana in December. Bolívar inaugurates the Third Republic. (1817) Patriot forces, led by Manuel Piar and later Bolívar, lay siege to Angostura in April, and the royalists withdraw in July. The patriots condemn Piar as a conspirator, rebel, and deserter and execute him in October. (1818) Bolívar establishes the *Correo de Orinoco* to speak for the patriots. (1819) The second national Congress meets in Angostura and Bolívar delivers the opening address. In February the Congress elects him president of Venezuela. Bolívar then crosses the Andes and in August defeats the royalists at Boyacá, thereby liberating New Granada. In August the congress sanctions the Constitution of Angostura. The Congress creates the Republic of Colombia from the provinces of Ecuador, New Granada, and Venezuela and, in December, elects Bolívar president of Colombia.

1820-30   The Achievement of Independence.
(1820) In Spain, the Liberals curb the power of Ferdinand VII in January, and the king is forced to recognize the Constitution of 1812. Morillo is ordered to negotiate with the patriots. Bolívar and Morillo sign an armistice in November.

(1821) In January the patriots break the truce by seizing Maracaibo. Between May and July the Congress of Cúcuta ratifies the formation of the Republic of Colombia, sanctions a liberal constitution, and decrees a manumission law. Bolívar, supported by Mariño and Páez, defeats the royalists in June at the Battle of Carabobo. Puerto Cabello surrenders to the patriots in November. (1822) In April Bolívar, supported by General Pedro León Torres, defeats the royalists in the Battle of Bomboná. The United States recognizes the Republic of Colombia. In July Bolívar meets with General José de San Martín in Guayaquil. (1823) Admiral Padilla ousts the royalist forces from Maracaibo, and in November Páez frees Puerto Cabello from royalist control, thus ending the military phase of independence. Bolívar, authorized by the congress of Colombia, arrives in Lima in December to help with the independence of Peru. (1824) The Colombian congress decrees the Law of Ecclesiastical Patronage, establishing civil control over the Church. Bolívar defeats the royalists at the Battle of Junín in August. Sucre liberates Peru with his defeat of the royalists in December at Ayacucho, and Bolívar confers the title of Gran Mariscal de Ayacucho on Sucre. (1825) In December General Páez calls on the local militia to enforce order in the Republic, precipitating a conflict with the central government in Bogotá. (1826) Páez is relieved of his command and ordered to Bogotá. Páez refuses, and becomes the civil and military chief of Venezuela. In November Bolívar returns to Bogotá from Peru to help curtail the separatist rebellion in Venezuela. (1827) Bolívar issues a general amnesty to the Venezuelan rebels and Páez submits to Bolívar's authority. From January to June Bolívar governs Venezuela in Caracas and returns to Bogotá in July, assuming the presidency in September. (1828) The Convention of Ocaña opens in April. The meeting fails and Bolívar becomes the dictator of Colombia. (1829) In November Páez supports another separatist rebellion in Venezuela and leads the country out of Colombia.

THE CONSERVATIVE OLIGARCHY

1830-48   Páez presides over a Conservative oligarchy that controls Venezuelan politics for these years.

(1830) A constituent congress meets in Valencia in May,

and Páez assumes a provisional presidency. In September the congress passes a semifederalist constitution that remains in force for twenty-seven years. In November the Archbishop of Caracas, Ramón Ignacio Méndez, and the bishops of Mérida and Guayana refuse to take the oath to support the constitution. The government issues an order of exile. Símon Bolívar dies in December in Santa Marta, Colombia.

1831-35   The administration of President José Antonio Páez.
           (1831) Páez suppresses a military revolt against his government led by Generals José Tadeo and José Gregorio Monagas. (1832) The Archbishop of Caracas and the Bishop of Mérida return from exile and take the oath supporting the constitution. (1833) Congress recognizes the 1824 Law of Patronage in March, and in April Congress passes a law abolishing the tithe. (1834) In February Congress grants the right of freedom of worship. The Credit Law of April 10, 1834, favors creditors and becomes a focal point for debtor opposition to the government.

1835-36   The administration of Dr. José María Vargas, Venezuela's first civilian president.
           (1835) Páez defeats General Santiago Mariño and other independence-era generals who attempt to take over the government and force constitutional reforms (The Revolution of the Reforms). (1836) Vargas resigns office in April after failing to secure severe punishment for the leaders of the rebellion.

1836-39   Vice-Presidents Dr. Andrés Narvarte (1836-37) and General Carlos Soublette (1837-39) govern Venezuela.
           (1836) The government exiles Archbishop Méndez in November for his refusal to recognize the civil jurisdiction of the state.

1839-43   The second administration of General José Antonio Páez.
           (1839) The Banco Colonial Británico, a branch of the Colonial Bank of London, becomes the first bank established in the Republic. (1840) In August the opposition Liberal party takes shape. (1841) Congress establishes the Banco Nacional de Venezuela.

1843-47   The administration of General Carlos Soublette.
           (1845) President Soublette vetoes a bill to establish the Institute of Territorial Credit, a land bank. (1846) A popular uprising against the government led by Rangel and Ezequiel Zamora fails.

1847-51   The administration of General José Tadeo Monagas.
            (1847) Monagas grants amnesty to Liberals convicted of
            treason and conspiracy which causes the conservatives to
            withdraw their support from the government. (1848) A
            popular uprising in January provides Monagas with an excuse
            to dissolve Congress. Páez attempts to overthrow Monagas
            but fails.

1851-55   The administration of General José Gregorio Monagas,
            brother of José Tadeo Monagas.
            (1854) Congress passes the first national mining code in
            March, and Monagas signs the law abolishing slavery in the
            same month. (1855) A new mining code reaffirms the Span-
            ish rule that subsoil rights belong to the nation.

1855-58   The second administration of General José Tadeo Monagas.
            (1856) A telegraph line is installed between Caracas and
            La Guaira. (1857) The constitution of 1857 expands execu-
            tive powers and reduces the power of the provinces or states.
            (1858) A rebellion in March against the abuse of power by
            Monagas forces him to resign the presidency.

THE FEDERAL WARS

1858-59   The provisional presidency of General Julián Castro.
            The Valencia Convention meets between July 1858 and
            January 1859 to debate the future of the Republic. The
            Constitution of 1858, approved in December 1858, attempts
            to reconcile federalist and centralist ideas.

1859-61   The administration of Dr. Manuel Felipe Tovar.
            (1859) The Federal Wars begin. The Federalists, led by
            General Ezequiel Zamora, win a major victory in December
            at Santa Inés. (1860) General Ezequiel Zamora is assassi-
            nated. Government troops defeat the Federalist forces at
            Coplé, temporarily disrupting the Federalist war effort.

1861   The administration of Dr. Pedro Gual, from May to
            September.

1861-63   The dictatorship of General José Antonio Páez.
            (1861) Merchants form the Banco de Venezuela (1861-62)
            to support Páez's government. (1863) The Conservatives
            lose the Federalist Wars and the Treaty of Coche in May
            ends the wars.

1863-64   A constituent assembly meets from December 1863 to April 1864 to establish Federalist priorities and to draft a new constitution. The assembly elects General Falcón provisional president and General Antonio Guzmán Blanco vice-president.

THE FEDERAL EXPERIMENT

1864-65   The provisional presidency of General Juan C. Falcón.
          The Federal District of Caracas is created from three departments in the state of Bolívar. A Federalist constitution is approved.

1865-68   The administration of General Juan C. Falcón.
          Continuous disturbances in the states undermine the administration's efforts to create a stable government. (1867-68) A revolution joins Liberals and Conservatives in a coalition to overthrow the Federalists. General José Tadeo Monagas assumes leadership of the revolution. (1868) Falcón resigns the presidency and leaves the country in April.

1868-70   The coalition takes over the government in June 1868, retains the 1864 constitution, and attempts to bring the states under the purview of the central government.
          (1868) Former Federalist vice-president General Antonio Guzmán Blanco becomes the leader of the Liberal Union opposition to the coalition. (1870) Guzmán Blanco, supported by Federalists and Liberals, leads a revolution to overthrow the government. After a three-day siege in April, Guzmán Blanco occupies Caracas.

THE GUZMANATO

1870-77   The Septenio: The first administration of Antonio Guzmán Blanco.
          (1870) In June Guzmán Blanco issues a decree making education free and obligatory. Conflicts between the government and the Church result in the expulsion of Archbishop Silvestre Guevara y Lira in September. (1872) A rebellion led by General Matías Salazar fails. In an unprecedented reprisal, Salazar is executed. Guzmán Blanco closes seminaries and the university is given jurisdiction over religious studies. (1873) Guzmán Blanco establishes civil marriages and a civil registry. (1874) A new constitution requires voters to sign votes,

eliminates the office of vice-president, reduces the presidential period to two years, and prohibits the immediate re-election of the president. Convents and other religious communities are closed. (1874-75) Generals León Colina and José Ignacio Pulido fail in the only large-scale uprising against Guzmán Blanco.

1877-78   The administration of General Francisco Linares Alcántara, Guzmán Blanco's hand-picked successor.

(1877) Critics of the Septenio almost immobilize the government. (1878) Manuel Antonio Pulido forms the Táchira Petroleum Company to exploit a fifty-year concession in that state. Alcántara's death in November 1878 intensifies the civil conflict. (1879) A revolution led by Generals Gregorio Cedeño and Joaquín Crespo overthrows the government. Guzmán Blanco proclaimed the Supreme Director of the Republic and returns to power.

1879-84   The Quinquenio: The second administration of Antonio Guzmán Blanco.
Public works and railroad schemes dominate politics.

1880-82   The administration of Antonio Guzmán Blanco.
(1881) A new constitution reduces the number of states and places the election of the president in the hands of a Federal Council. (1882) The Federal Council elects Guzmán Blanco president.

1882-84   The administration of Antonio Guzmán Blanco.
1884-86   The administration of General Joaquín Crespo.
1886-88   La Aclamación: The third administration of Antonio Guzmán Blanco.
Political differences between Guzmán Blanco and Crespo remain unresolved, and Guzmán Blanco's repressive politics causes widespread reaction. (1887) Guzmán Blanco turns over the government to General Hermógenes López, President of the Federal Council, and leaves for Europe in August.

FROM GUZMÁN BLANCO TO GÓMEZ

1888-90   The administration of Dr. Juan Pablo Rojas Paúl, the first civilian president elected to office since 1834.
Crespo fails in a bid to overthrow the government. Rojas Paúl dissociates himself from the politics of Guzmán Blanco.

1890-92   The administration of Dr. Raimundo Andueza Palacio.

(1891) Seeking a second term in office, Andueza calls for constitutional reform to alter the system of presidential election and to expand the presidential term. (1892) Andueza dismisses Congress and convokes a Constituent Assembly in March. Crespo leads his army against the government in the Legalist Revolution. In June Andueza abandons the presidency after the defeat of government troops. An economic crisis as well as a state of civil war continues. Crespo assumes power in October.

1892-97   The second administration of General Joaquín Crespo.
(1893) A National Assembly reforms the constitution, returning to many of the principles of the 1864 constitution. (1894) Congress verifies Crespo's election as president. (1895) Economic crisis paralyzes commerce, and 3,000 workers and artisans protest the lack of jobs. (1896) The conflict with Great Britain over the Guayana boundary intensifies. President Cleveland of the United States demands an arbitration of the issue. The first Congress of Workers meets in Caracas to form a Popular Party, improve education of workers, and establish cooperatives.

1898-99   The administration of General Ignacio Andrade.
(1899) A constitutional revision re-establishes the states recognized in the 1864 constitution. Congress authorizes Andrade to name provisional presidents of states. The Paris Tribunal declares in favor of Great Britain in the boundary dispute. Andrade succumbs to the Liberal Revolutionary Restoration of General Cipriano Castro and abandons the presidency in October.

1899-1908   The dictatorship of General Cipriano Castro.
Castro's government represents the beginning of Andean prominence in Venezuelan politics. (1902-3) A revolution led by General Manuel Antonio Matos, supported by European interests, attempts to overthrow Castro. Castro's refusal to pay European creditors leads to a blockade of Venezuelan ports by English, German, and Italian warships. (1903) The Washington Protocol, which ends the blockade, requires Venezuela to allocate 30 percent of its customs duties to the payment of European claims. (1904) A new mining code includes regulations for hydrocarbons.

1905-8   The administration of General Cipriano Castro.
Castro named president and General Juan Vicente Gómez named vice-president for the period 1905-11. (1905) A

mining law allows concessions for up to fifty years. (1906)
New regulations issued for the 1905 law which reaffirms
presidential right to grant and administer concessions without
congressional consent. (1908) General Juan Vicente Gómez
successfully deposes Castro on December 19 while Castro is
in Europe.

THE ERA OF JUAN VICENTE GÓMEZ

1909-10   The provisional presidency of Juan Vicente Gómez.
           Congress sanctions a new constitution. (1910) Congress
           names Gómez president. Dr. Emilio Constantín Guerrero
           serves as provisional president.

1910-14   The administration of Juan Vicente Gómez.
           (1913) A political crisis arises over Gómez's intention to re-
           main in the presidency after 1914. Gómez suspends constitu-
           tional guarantees and imprisons opposition leaders. (1913)
           Dr. José Gil Fortoul, president of the Government Council,
           exercises executive powers for eight months. (1914) Dr.
           Victorino Márquez Bustillos governs as provisional president.
           The Caribbean Petroleum Company, a subsidiary of Royal
           Dutch Shell, begins commercial production with the Zu-
           maque-I oil well in the Mene Grande field, Lake Maracaibo
           Basin. General Emilio Arévalo Cedeño leads the first of three
           unsuccessful attempts to overthrow Gómez. The second and
           third occur in 1918 and 1921.

1915-22   The administration of Juan Vicente Gómez.
           Congress re-elects Gómez and Márquez Bustillos continues in
           executive office as provisional president for the entire period.
           (1917) The Caribbean Petroleum Company establishes two
           pipelines from the Mene Grande field to San Lorenzo, where
           the first oil refinery in Venezuela opens. Petroleum exports
           begin. (1918) Political prisoners stage an uprising in the
           Castillo of Puerto Cabello. A new mining law declares that
           concessionaires have exploration rights only, not ownership
           of the deposits. (1919) A military plot to overthrow Gómez
           is uncovered. Many conspirators are tortured and imprisoned.
           (1920) Congress sanctions the Republic's first hydrocarbons
           law. (1921) Gómez allows the oil companies to participate
           in the drafting of a new hydrocarbon law favorable to the
           operating companies. (1922) Congress re-elects Gómez.

1922-29   The administration of Juan Vicente Gómez.

(1922) The third hydrocarbons law increases size of parcels and extends exploitation period. The law also provides benefits to workers. With only minimal alterations in 1925 and 1928, the law remains in force for over two decades. (1923) Gómez creates the CVP (Venezuelan Petroleum Company) through which he pursues his policy of awarding concessions. (1924) American companies begin purchasing concessions from the CVP. (1925) Oil workers in the Bolívar fields protest against the high cost of living. Government troops end the strike. (1926) Petroleum becomes Venezuela's chief export, exceeding coffee in value. (1928) Student protest of dictatorship during Student Week leads to arrest of student leaders, a sympathy strike in Caracas, and riots. Young military officers, in league with student leaders, fail in a barracks revolt. Gómez closes the UCV and the Military Academy. The government approves the Republic's first labor law which permits unions, requires accident compensation, death benefits, and a nine-hour work day. The law remains unenforced until after 1935. (1929) Congress appoints Gómez Chief of the Army, and makes Dr. Juan Bautista Pérez, who was president of the Federal Court, president of the Republic. Gómez continues to govern from Maracay.

1929-31   The administration of Juan Bautista Pérez.
(1929) Anti-government rebels fight the dictatorship in various states in June and August. Venezuela becomes the world's largest oil exporter. (1931) Congress asks for the resignation of Dr. Juan Bautista Pérez, reforms the constitution for the seventh time, and re-elects Gómez as president.

1931-35   The administration of Juan Vicente Gómez.
(1931) Dr. Itriago Chacín, Minister of Foreign Relations, occupies the presidency for Gómez. The PCV (Venezuelan Communist Party) is founded but the government refuses to grant it legal status. (1935) On December 17, Gómez dies of natural causes.

FROM GÓMEZ TO THE TRIENIO

1935-36   The provisional government.
General Eleazar López Contreras, Minister of War and Navy, temporarily assumes executive powers in December 1935. During 1936 several political parties appear: FEV (Federa-

tion of Venezuelan Students), UNR (National Republican Union, PRP (Progressive Republican Party), and ORVE (Movement of Venezuelan Organization). General López Contreras announces a plan for legalizing the government in his February Program. He turns the government over to Dr. Antonio Borjas, President of the Supreme Court, in February. The Oil Workers' and Employees' Syndicate of Cabimas (Zulia) becomes the first labor union of the oil industry. UNR, PRP, and ORVE create the Bloque de Abril to oppose López Contreras.

1936-41   The administration of General Eleazar López Contreras. The government institutes a three-year program of domestic improvements. (1936) A widespread strike fails to persuade the government to enact democratic reforms. Several leftist political groups—ORVE, PRP, and others—join forces to form the PDN (National Democratic Party), the forerunner of AD (Acción Democrática). This party fails to gain legal recognition from the government. (1936-37) The oil workers, supported by the PDN, strike for better housing and work facilities and salary increases. (1937) López Contreras grants oil workers a wage increase of one Bolívar, issues back-to-work order, dissolves the petroleum workers' union, suspends activities of the PDN member groups, and exiles the leaders. (1938) López Contreras inaugurates a three-year plan of domestic improvements. The new hydrocarbons law, unlike previous laws, favors government control. (1939) The BCV (Venezuelan Central Bank) begins operations with a responsibility to control foreign exchange and function as Venezuela's central bank. A social security law is enacted. (1941) Venezuela signs a boundary treaty with Colombia. Congress elects General Isaías Medina Angarita, Minister of War and hand-picked successor of López Contreras.

1941-45   The administration of General Isaías Medina Angarita. (1941) AD, following recognition by the government in July, holds its first public assembly in September. (1942) The government issues the first income tax law, effective January 1, 1943. (1943) A new hydrocarbons law represents the first real expression of nationalistic self-interest. In response to the growing popularity of AD, the government sponsors the formation of a political party, PDV (Venezuelan Democratic Party). (1944) UPV (Venezuelan Popular

Union), a communist splinter-group from the PCV, organizes to oppose Medina. FEDECAMARAS (Federation of Chambers of Commerce and Industry) is formed to coordinate economic groups and policy and to bridge the gap between private and public sectors. (1945) A constitutional reform retains indirect electoral system for the election of the president, establishes direct vote for congressional deputies, and eliminates the prohibition on communist activities. Congress also passes an Agrarian Reform Law designed to distribute government land to peasants. Medina grants the PCV legal status. In the October Revolution, AD and a group of young military officers, the Unión Patriótica Militar, overthrow the government.

FROM THE TRIENIO THROUGH PÉREZ JIMÉNEZ

1945-48   The Trienio. AD and the Junta Revolucionaria de Gobierno. (1945) Rómulo Betancourt presides over a seven-man civil-military council called the Junta Revolucionaria de Gobierno. The junta suspends constitutional guarantees, creates a Ministry of Labor, dissolves the PDV, and exiles Medina Angarita and López Contreras. URD (Democratic Republican Union) receives legal recognition. The junta repeals the Agrarian Reform Law and decrees an oil company earnings tax in order to gain a true 50-50 profit split between the government and the companies. (1946) COPEI (Committee for Political Organization and Independent Election), a Christian Democratic group, receives government recognition as a legal political party. A new election law provides for the direct election of the president and delegates to the National Constituent Assembly. (1946) FEDEPÉTROL (Federation of Petroleum Workers) is founded in March. AD wins a majority of National Constituent Assembly seats in the October elections. The National Constituent Assembly assumes power from the junta in December 1946. The government suppresses an army revolt and the SN (National Security Police) is established. (1947) The government decides to market part of the 1948-49 royalty oil. A constitution approved by the Assembly allows universal suffrage and lowers the voting age to 18. The CTV (Confederation of Venezuelan Workers) is organized. In December Rómulo Gallegos, the AD candidate, becomes the first president elected by popular election.

1948   The administration of Rómulo Gallegos (February-November).

Congress passes an agrarian reform law that calls for the expropriation of private land with compensation. The IAN (National Agrarian Institute) is created to administer the reform law. Congress also passes a new income tax law guaranteeing the government 50 percent of industry profits. In November military officers meet with Gallegos to discuss the government's liberal policies. Within days of the meeting a military coup deposes Gallegos.

1948-52   The government of the Junta Militar de Gobierno headed by Lt. Cols. Carlos Delgado Chalbaud, Marcos Pérez Jiménez, and Luis Felipe Llovera Páez.

(1948) The junta exiles Gallegos and dissolves AD in December. (1949) The petroleum workers in Maracaibo declare a general strike. In February the junta disbands the AD-dominated CTV after the union orders a general strike. (1950) Following difficulties in March and April with oil workers and students, the junta in May dissolves several petroleum unions, suspends class at the UCV, and outlaws the PCV. Junta president Delgado Chalbaud is assassinated in November. Germán Suárez Flamerich, a civilian, heads the government junta in November. (1951) The FEI (Independent Electoral Front) organizes to support Pérez Jiménez for president. Following riots in Caracas and elsewhere and a student strike, the junta suspends classes at the UCV in October and closes the university in November. (1952) Pérez Jiménez voids the November 30 election results after an apparent URD victory and sends the URD leaders into exile. The Armed Forces name Pérez Jiménez provisional president.

1952-58   The dictatorship of Marcos Pérez Jiménez.

This presidency is characterized by a program called the New National Ideal, which relies heavily on extensive public works and political repression. (1953) The National Assembly names Pérez Jiménez president for the 1953-58 period and approves a new constitution. Two private universities are founded in Caracas, the Universidad Católica Andrés Bello and the Universidad Santa María. (1956) After an eleven-year suspension, the government begins to grant new oil concessions. (1957) In May Monsignor Rafael Arias Blanco, Archbishop of Caracas, issues a pastoral letter criticizing labor conditions. The MLN (Movement for National Liberation) is organized by military officers who plot to overthrow the dictator. Pérez Jiménez wins a November plebiscite on his presidency for the period 1958-63. (1958) On January 23 the Air Force leads a rebellion against the dictator. There are popular uprisings and the Patriotic Junta calls for a general strike, which leads to the military overthrow of Pérez Jiménez and his exile to Miami.

THE DEMOCRATIC GOVERNMENTS

1958-59   The government of the Junta de Gobierno, a civil-military group headed by Rear Admiral Wolfgang Larrazábal.
(1958) The exiled leaders of the major political parties return to Caracas. The junta abolishes the National Security Police. In March the junta's Plan de Emergencia calls for unemployed laborers to be compensated by the government. Communist sympathizers and the unemployed disrupt a May visit to Caracas by the U.S. vice-president, Richard Nixon. The leaders of AD, COPEI, and URD agree in November, in the Pact of Punto Fijo, to a common government program to support the winner of the presidential election and to establish a coalition government. Larrazábal leaves the junta to campaign for the presidency and Dr. Edgard Sanabria presides over the junta. Rómulo Betancourt, the AD candidate, wins the November presidential election with 49.2 percent of the vote. A revision of the income tax law raises the government's share of oil company profits to over 60 percent. In December General Pedro Quevedo assumes the leadership of the junta.

1959-64   The administration of Rómulo Betancourt.
(1959) The Ministry of Mines and Hydrocarbons establishes a Coordinating Commission for the Conservation and Commerce of Hydrocarbons to recommend regulations on the marketing of petroleum and on conservation policy. Juan Pablo Pérez Alfonso, Minister of Mines and Hydrocarbons, attends the April meeting of the First Arab Petroleum Congress in Cairo. (1960) A coalition of labor, business, and agricultural interests and political parties sponsor an agrarian reform law. General Jesús María Castro León leads another

unsuccessful uprising in April from western Venezuela. The government establishes the CVP (Venezuelan Petroleum Corporation) to exploit hydrocarbon resources through service contracts with foreign concerns. Dissidents fail in a June assassination attempt on Betancourt. The government charges Rafael Trujillo, dictator of the Dominican Republic, with complicity in this attempt. The MIR (Movement of the Revolutionary Left), the first of three splits in the AD organization, is formed by young radicals in July. Venezuela asks the OAS for support in imposing sanctions against the Dominican Republic. In September Pérez Alfonso takes the lead in forming OPEC. The Universidad de Oriente, designed specifically to offer scientific and technical education in eastern Venezuela, begins classes in October. The URD leaves the government coalition in November. MIR and PCV call for a general strike and a popular rebellion against the government. (1961-67) Ciudad Guayana is built following guidelines set by an urban planning project coordinated by the Joint Center for Urban Studies of MIT and Harvard. (1961) The second OPEC Conference meets in Caracas in January. A new constitution issued in January establishes obligatory voting and universal adult suffrage, and places oil concessions under the authority of Congress. (1962) In January AD loses the support of some party leaders who oppose the government's laxity in implementing reforms. The dissidents form ARS (AD in the Opposition) in January. Leftist-associated military rebellions in Carúpano in May and Puerto Cabello in June are suppressed by the government. In May the government suspends the activities of the PCV and the MIR. Former members of the MIR form the FDP (Popular Democratic Force) in August. The FALN (Armed Forces for National Liberation), a group of leftist dissidents, turns to armed rebellion to prevent the 1963 elections. (1963) Leftist terrorists engage in violent protests against the government throughout the year. The government discovers an arms cache which later proves to have been sent from Cuba for the Venezuelan subversives. This leads to a request for an OAS meeting of consultation and the breaking of relations with Cuba (November). In the December elections Dr. Raúl Leoni, the AD candidate, is elected president with 33 percent of the vote.

1964-69   The presidency of Dr. Raúl Leoni.

(1964) The FND (National Democratic Front), a right-of-center group, becomes a legal political party in March. A July meeting of OAS foreign ministers in Washington agrees to impose sanctions on Cuba. Leoni decrees a new system for domestic distribution of petroleum products and transfers a number of private gasoline stations to the CVP. URD and the FND form a coalition with AD to create a broad-based government in November. (1965) The CNC (National Civic Crusade), a right-wing group including followers of Pérez Jiménez, receives legal recognition from the government in October. (1966) The AD-FND-URD coalition ends in March. The government declares a state of emergency following the discovery of a plot to overthrow the government in April. Leoni signs the Treaty of Montevideo of the LAFTA (Latin American Free Trade Association). In December a new income tax law places higher rates on private and corporate income and creates a system of reference prices for oil to be used for tax purposes. Leftist activity against the government leads to the December suspension of constitutional guarantees, the first such suspension since 1962. The Geneva Accord with Great Britain recognizes Venezuela's position on the Guayana boundary dispute. (1967) Leoni attends the April meeting in Punta del Este on Latin American economic integration. Dr. R. Leandro Mora temporarily takes charge of the presidency. Congress amends the 1943 Hydrocarbons Law to allow the CVP or the Ministry of Mines and Hydrocarbons to negotiate service contracts. The governments of Venezuela, Colombia, Chile, Ecuador, and Peru agree in Caracas in August to form a regional common market. MEP (People's Electoral Movement) is established by adherents of democratic socialism who leave AD to form this political party. (1968) The Supreme Court of Justice convicts ex-dictator Marcos Pérez Jiménez of illicit enrichment in public office. In December Rafael Caldera, the COPEI candidate, wins the presidential election with 29 percent of the vote.

1969-74 The presidency of Dr. Rafael Caldera.
(1969) AD opposition to the government creates a legislative stalemate. In March Caldera lifts the ban on the PCV. The Supreme Court of Justice annuls the election of Pérez Jiménez as senator from the Federal District. (1970) Caldera visits the United States in June, and the minister of Interior Relations,

Lorenzo Fernández, takes charge of the executive office. Congress votes to end university autonomy. OPEC ministers meet in Caracas in December. The income tax law sanctions a tax increase on oil profits. (1971) MAS (Movement toward Socialism) is created out of a splinter group from the PCV in January. Congress passes a Hydrocarbons Reversion Law in July which prepares for the eventual control of existing concessions when they expire. The government nationalizes the natural gas industry in July. (1973) The government lifts an eleven-year suspension of activities against the MIR. Carlos Andrés Pérez, the AD candidate, wins the presidential election with 49 percent of the vote. Venezuela formally joins the Andean Pact.

1974-79   The administration of Carlos Andrés Pérez.
(1974) Pérez announces the nationalization of the iron industry in April. Venezuela's Declaration of Guayana pledges the country to help finance efforts by Central American coffee producers to withhold coffee from the market until prices recover. Venezuela and Cuba agree to restore diplomatic relations. (1975) The Orinoco Mining (U.S. Steel) and Iron Mines Company (Bethlehem Steel) come under government control in January and an income tax reform raises the levy on foreign oil companies from 63.5 percent to 70 percent. In August Pérez signs the law nationalizing the petroleum industry. The government begins incorporating the state holding company, PETROVEN (Venezuelan Petroleum) to supervise and control the operations of the companies. The administration begins (October) to investigate the charges that Occidental Petroleum executives had bribed government officials to obtain oil concessions from 1961 to 1972. (1976) PETROVEN takes control of the petroleum companies in January. Pérez visits Moscow to discuss economic and industrial cooperation with the USSR. (1977) In November, guerrillas and government troops clash in Barcelona. Luis Herrera Campíns, the COPEI candidate, wins the presidential election with 46 percent of the vote.

1979-   The administration of Luis Herrera Campíns.
COPEI wins an overwhelming victory in the nationwide June municipal elections with 50 percent of the vote. The selection of a new AD general secretary causes a rift in the party leadership.

Bibliographic Essay

INTRODUCTION

The sources for the study of Venezuelan history are many and varied. Because of the organization of the publishing industry and the scholarly traditions of Venezuela, the country's voluminous literature on history, culture, and the social sciences tends to be fragmentary in coverage and uneven in depth. The reference tools available to guide scholars through the field reflect this same tradition. Many excellent bibliographies on selected topics exist, but general reference works are few and uneven in coverage. Similarly, it has been relatively difficult to keep track of current publications, especially given the substantial publishing activity of banks, government agencies, foundations, and corporations in the areas of history and the social sciences.

In recent years, however, the Venezuelans have made remarkable progress in the sustained effort to bring their country's unruly bibliography under control. For example, in collaboration with the Biblioteca Nacional, the Fundación para el Rescate de Acervo Documental Venezolano has sponsored an ambitious project to collect and bring under bibliographical control everything in the western world on, about, or by Venezuela and Venezuelans. This extraordinary effort, designed and implemented for United States items at the Northwestern University Library, promises in the near term a computer-based, interactive bibliographical catalog kept current by the Biblioteca Nacional. As soon as this catalog, in effect a world-wide union catalog on Venezuela, becomes generally available to scholars, research on Venezuelan topics will be made significantly easier.

Meanwhile, the traditional bibliographical tools will have to suffice. This chapter is designed to indicate some of the significant, useful, and representative items from Venezuela's historical bibliography to serve as an introduction to the field, and it obeys a set of criteria governing the selection and inclusion of items. Given the limitations of space in a book of this kind, and in light of the large scope of its concerns, this essay attempts to be neither complete nor exhaustive. Rather, the primary function of this discussion of books about Venezuela is to introduce the interested student to the wide range of materials available and provide a starting place for the examination of themes and issues presented in the preceding text.

Inclusion or exclusion of individual works is governed by judgments of quality, utility, and representativeness. Similar to most national historiography, Venezuela's flow of books about the past can be sampled here and there along its course from the colonial period to the 1980s to provide a reasonable understanding of the main currents, the deep pools, and even the stagnant waters characteristic of the stream. Students in pursuit of more extensive information on Venezuela's past will find in these remarks a practical guide to the literature. Experts will discover many important works in their specialty missing, but, of course, this essay is not prepared for them.

In an effort to provide a bibliographical counterpoint to the analysis of the preceding chapters, this essay roughly parallels the organization of the text. Since most Venezuelan publishing occurs in Caracas, only cities other than Caracas are cited with the date. A few special characteristics of Venezuelan publishing practice deserve mention. For a variety of reasons Venezuela has sponsored innumerable reprintings, re-editions, and revisions of standard, classic, and popular works. Hence, the date of publication given here is a poor guide to the date of first issue. Similarly, the designation of edition number, such as 2nd ed. or 3rd ed., frequently, although not always, indicates simply a reprinting or reissuing of the original text without changes, although sometimes with updated introductory remarks. The introductions to re-editions of classic works or to documentary publications are often more valuable than the work itself. Because the format of this essay does not permit the citation of publishers, it may help to recognize here the wide range of scholarly publishers in the Venezuelan context. Banks, race tracks, all branches and levels of government, foundations, and individuals, in addition to university and commercial presses, are in the historical book business. In Venezuela it is perfectly reasonable for the national race track to publish nineteenth-century travel accounts, or for the central bank to publish a historical series, many of whose volumes have nothing to do with economics or banking.

This enthusiasm for the publication of historical documents represents the Venezuelan belief in the appropriateness of historical publication as a form of patriotic display. It also reflects the primitive organization of the domestic publishing industry that prevailed until recent years. This penchant for official and ceremonial publication has led to a reluctance to engage in contemporary history or revisionist history. Official publishers, whose goals often appeared more closely attuned to public relations than to scholarly inquiry, preferred colonial and independence themes and the publication of documentary collections to the pursuit of controversial interpretations. Hence, Venezuela is unusually well endowed with published documents in the colonial and early independence periods, although less well served for the twentieth century.

In like fashion, the density of historiography is uneven, obeying much the same logic as the documentary publications. The independence period and the life of Bolívar have been pursued to an almost infinite depth but in a selective fashion. Some periods of Venezuelan history, such as the Federal Wars and the era of Antonio Guzmán Blanco in the second half of the nineteenth century, are only thinly covered. But the advent of the petroleum economy and the post-1935 enthusiasm for the standards and norms of the industrialized west have brought new vigor to the writing and publishing of Venezuelan history. More attention to contemporary affairs, revisionism, and higher standards of scholarship are all visible products of the new generations of historians. Their enthusiasm and rigor has also helped the traditionalists of the Venezuelan historical establishment to expand their horizons and revitalize their institutions. To be sure, much controversy and some intemperate displays of academic ego have accompanied this transformation, and this healthy state of affairs makes some historians wish for the somnolent quiet of earlier generations.

GENERAL REFERENCE AND DOCUMENT COLLECTIONS

Although the primary characteristic of Venezuelan bibliography has been the cultivation of specialized bibliographic studies focused on a restricted theme or chronological period, there are a number of useful guides to longer periods and broader topics. Because of the interest in documentary collections and the publication of documents, the country's archival resources are relatively well known and surveyed, if incompletely cataloged. Lino Gómez Canedo, *Los archivos históricos de Venezuela* (Maracaibo, 1966), provides a fine introduction to these resources, and Mario Briceño

Perozo, *Archivos venezolanos* (1970), complements it. Further assistance in archival study can be gleaned from Agustín Millares Carlo, *Estudio bibliográfico de los archivos venezolanos y extranjeros de interés para la historia de Venezuela* (1971); Joaquín Gabaldón Márquez et al., *Misiones venezolanas en los archivos europeos* (Mexico, 1954); and José Luciano Franco, *Documentos para la historia de Venezuela existentes en el Archivo Nacional de Cuba* (Havana, 1960).

Several institutions, in addition to the Archivo Nacional, maintain archives of national importance. For example, the extraordinarily rich collection of materials in the Church archives have been surveyed in Jaime Suriá, *Catálogo del Archivo Arquidiocesano de Caracas* (Madrid, 1964). Unfortunately, the similarly valuable Archivo del Registro Principal de Caracas is without a comparable guide. The Academia Nacional de la Historia, the Archivo General de la Nación, the Sociedad Bolivariana, and the Archivo Histórico de Miraflores all publish periodicals with articles about their documentary resources. The *Boletín de la Academia Nacional de la Historia* (1912-) has an *Índice general del Boletín de . . . 1912-1914, nos. 1-188* (1966), and the *Revista de la Sociedad Bolivariana de Venezuela* (1939-) has an *Índice de la Revista. . . . 1939-1955* (1959), but the *Boletín del Archivo General de la Nación* (1923-) and the *Boletín del Archivo Histórico de Miraflores* (1959-) unfortunately do not.

In addition to these official agencies, the Fundación John Boulton maintains an extensive archive and library and publishes the *Boletín histórico* (1962-). The Fundación Boulton has also issued a guide to a major portion of its archive in *Sección venezolana del Archivo de la Gran Colombia. Índice sucinto* (1960). A number of other useful guides to specialized collections will be discussed later on in this essay. If the quantity of material on these archival resources appears impressive, it nonetheless must be emphasized that these guides and journals are neither completely systematic nor at all comprehensive, but they indicate the richness of the archives and alert the student to the variety and quality of material available.

Much the same caution applies to the large-scale bibliographical guides to Venezuelan historical topics. The most recent guide to Venezuelan history is John V. Lombardi et al., *Venezuelan History: A Comprehensive Working Bibliography* (New York, 1977). The emphasis in that work is on the inclusion of as many titles on Venezuelan history as possible without attempting an exhaustive compilation. It is what its title suggests, a working bibliography, a place to begin serious scholarly work on Venezuelan history. The classic Venezuelan bibliography is the older work by Manuel Segundo Sánchez published in his *Obras* (2 vols., 1964). Another important general guide is Angel Raúl Villasana, *Ensayo de un repertorio biblio-*

gráfico venezolano (años 1808-1950) (4 vols., 1969-70), and the section
in Charles C. Griffin, *Latin America. A Guide to the Historical Literature*
(Austin, 1971), which has helpful annotations. Because of the volume of
new historical work constantly appearing in Venezuela, the publication of
Bibliografía venezolana, issued by the Biblioteca Nacional since 1970, is
most useful to researchers.

In addition to these broad-based sources, there are a number of more
narrowly focused bibliographical guides of general interest. For example,
the two volumes of Ricardo Archila, *Bibliografía médica venezolana,
1952-58* (3rd ed., 1960), and *1959-61* (1967), and the volumes of Victor
M. Badillo and Celestino Bonfanti, *Indice bibliográfico agrícola de Venezuela* (1957, and supplements, Maracay, 1962 and 1967), provide important assistance on these broad themes. The guide to the Biblioteca de los
Tribunales del Distrito Federal Fundación Rojas Astudillo, entitled *Material bibliográfico de la biblioteca* (1963), illustrates the legal literature
available as does the earlier item by Helen Lord Clagett, *Guide to the Law
and Legal Literature of Venezuela* (Washington, 1947). María Luisa
Ganzenmuller de Blay, *Contribución a la bibliografía de viajes y explora-
ciones de Venezuela, colección de 467 fichas* (1964), is a good place to
begin a search for travelers' accounts on most periods of Venezuelan
history.

Although many of the interesting and important documentary publications on specialized topics will be discussed later in this essay, a number of
extensive collections deserve mention here, either because of their extent or
because they represent a category of special note. For example, the premier
publisher of Venezuelan historical materials is, and has been throughout the
twentieth century, the Academia Nacional de la Historia. Officially charged
with the duty to preserve and promote the nation's past, the Academia
has a distinguished record of publication. From one of its earliest series, the
*Documentos para los anales de Venezuela desde el movimiento separatista
de la unión colombiana hasta nuestros días* (11 vols., 1899-1912), to its
more recent series, *Fuentes para la historia republicana* (20 vols., 1973-),
the Academia documentary publications provide essential raw material for
students of Venezuela's past. The Academia's current primary documentary
series, which includes 53 volumes on the independence period and over
150 volumes on the colonial period, continues to grow steadily. These valuable items often are prefaced with extensive monographic studies, and in
recent years more and more of the items published are scholarly works in
their own right rather than documents preceded by scholarly introductions.
Many items from these series are mentioned individually below. The
chronological focus of the Academia publications mirrors, of course, the

general enthusiasm for the colonial and independence years and the relative neglect of other periods.

Fortunately, other documentary series have attempted to fill the gaps in the published documents. The exceptionally well done collection prepared by Pedro Grases and Manuel Pérez Vila and published by the Presidencia de la República, *Pensamiento político venezolano del siglo XIX. Textos para su estudio* (15 vols. 1960-62), provides a careful selection of basic texts for the political and economic history of the nineteenth century. Somewhat more specialized, the digest by Francisco José Parra, *Doctrinas de la cancillería venezolana. Digesto* (7 vols., New York, 1952-1972), illustrates Venezuelan foreign policy positions, and the collection of documents on *Las fuerzas armadas de Venezuela en el siglo XIX. Textos para su estudio* (12 vols., 1963-) provides information on the origins of Venezuela's military traditions. These collections give a reasonable glimpse of the extraordinary richness of the published primary material available.

A number of other reference works deserve mention in a general introduction of this kind. David P. Henige, *Colonial Governors from the Fifteenth Century to the Present: A Comprehensive List* (Madison, 1970), includes a list for Venezuela. Miguel Llorens Izard, *Series estadísticas para la historia de Venezuela* (Mérida, 1970), includes statistics compiled from a variety of sources on population and economics from the colonial period to the mid-twentieth century. A number of publications attempt to provide complete information on notable Venezuelans. For example, there is Ramón Armando Rodríguez, *Diccionario biográfico, geográfico e histórico de Venezuela* (Madrid, 1957); the *Valores humanos de Venezuela (Quién es quién)* (Bogotá, 1965); Donna Keyse and G. A. Rudolph, *Historical Dictionary of Venezuela* (Metuchen, N.J., 1971); and the *Diccionario biográfico de Venezuela* (Madrid, 1953).

GENERAL HISTORIES

While documentary collections and bibliographies are essential tools for those interested in pursuing special topics in Venezuelan history, most students should begin with a general history of the country to get a sense of the issues, controversies, and context of its past. In English, Edwin Lieuwen, *Venezuela* (2nd ed., London, 1965), has long been the standard survey, replacing the somewhat longer history by William David and Amy L. Marsland, *Venezuela Through Its History* (New York, 1954). Three other books in English are quite helpful. David E. Blank, *Politics in Venezuela. A Country Study* (Boston, 1973), and Raymond E. Crist and Edward P. Leahy, *Venezuela. Search for a Middle Ground* (New York,

1969), are useful short introductions to the country's modern political system, and Robert L. Gilmore, *Caudillism and Militarism in Venezuela, 1810-1910* (Athens, Ohio, 1964), provides essential background and some provocative hypotheses for understanding the nineteenth century.

Several classic histories of Venezuela are required reading for any serious student of the country's past. This is not only because these works are informative, but because their perspectives have helped determine the language and structure of historical studies in Venezuela for several generations. Francisco González Guinán, *Historia contemporanea de Venezuela* (15 vols., 1954), is an extraordinarily detailed chronicle of Venezuela's past from the independence period into the last decades of the nineteenth century. The 15-volume edition published in 1954 is accessible and has a very useful index. José Gil Fortoul, *Historia constitucional de Venezuela* (5th ed., 3 vols., 1967), is much less detailed but much better organized. From a legalistic, constitutionalist perspective, Gil Fortoul's account of Venezuela's past is quite helpful in orienting beginning scholars to the field.

Two historiographical works by Germán Carrera Damas are essential for an understanding of Venezuelan historians and their works. The *Historia de la historiografía venezolana. Textos para su estudio* (1961) displays, with insightful notes, examples of the various historiographical styles characteristic of the Venezuelan tradition. *Historiografía marxista venezolana, y otros temas* (1967) also focuses on historiographical issues related to the writing on and the conceptions of Venezuela's past. Also, see the very thorough *Historiografía colonial de Venezuela* (1977) by Angelina Lemmo B.

For a thorough, standard interpretation it would be difficult to find a better introduction to Venezuelan history than José Luis Salcedo Bastardo, *Historia fundamental de Venezuela* (7th ed., 1977). Several other prominent Venezuelan historians have attempted grand syntheses of their country's past, although with less satisfactory results. Federico Brito Figueroa, *Historia económica y social de Venezuela. Una estructura para su estudio* (2 vols., 1966), proposes a quasi-materialist interpretation that excells at hypothesis. Guillermo Morón, *Historia de Venezuela* (5 vols., 1971), is a luxurious edition with heavy emphasis on the colonial and independence periods that has generated considerable controversy, a representative sample of which is in Angelina Lemmo B., *De como se desmorona la histora. Observaciones a la "Historia de Venezuela" de Morón* (1973).

Although not properly complete treatments of Venezuela's past, several extensive views of broad themes provide excellent introductions. For example, Juan B. Fuenmayor, *Historia de la Venezuela política contem-*

poranea, 1899-1969 (5 vols. in 6, 1975-79); Manuel Vicente Magallanes, *Historia política de Venezuela* (3 vols., Madrid, 1972); and Augusto Mijares, *La evolución política de Venezuela, 1810-1960* (Buenos Aires, 1967), give considerable insight into post-independence political history. The classic, extremely perceptive, and influential work by Laureano Vallenilla Lanz, *Cesarismo democrático: Estudios sobre las bases sociológicas de la constitución efectiva de Venezuela* (4th ed., 1961), is a required part of every Venezuelanist library.

Finally, it is important to recognize the category of multi-author histories which have proved popular in Venezuela. For example, Ramón J. Velásquez et al., *Venezuela moderna. Medio siglo de historia, 1926-1976* (2nd ed., revised, 1979), is by far the best introduction to this period, especially the exceptional extended essay by Velásquez. Similarly, Mariano Picón Salas et al., *Venezuela independiente, 1810-1960* (1962), is a useful introduction as is the work *Política y economía en Venezuela, 1810-1976*, published by the Fundación John Boulton in 1976. The *Area Handbook for Venezuela* (Washington, 1977) by Howard I. Blutstein et al., is also helpful.

However, even with the guidance of these works, it is clear that much careful synthesis remains to be written if many portions of Venezuela's past are to be made clear.

GEOGRAPHY

Because of Venezuela's petroleum interest, a considerable amount of scholarly work is available on the country's geography. Moreover, since the Spanish imperial philosophy of information collection emphasized geographic data and description, the modern enthusiasm for geographic exploration in search of petroleum reinforced a strong traditional concern for this area of knowledge.

Among the many books available, two items provide the best introductions. The first is the extensive survey of Venezuela geography by Pablo Vila et al., *Geografía de Venezuela* (2 vols., 1960-65). This work has chapters covering everything imaginable in physical, human, plant, and animal geography. The chronological scope of this work extends from the period of discovery and conquest. It is an unusually useful if sometimes uneven work. The second essential item is the *Atlas de Venezuela* published by the Venezuelan Dirección de Cartografía Nacional in 1971. This *Atlas* is very well done, with a wide variety of maps, including analytical maps of social and economic data. This is indispensable for serious students of Venezuela.

In addition to these basic sources, a number of other works provide valuable information. For example, see Luis Fernando Chaves Vargas, *Geografía agraria de Venezuela* (1963). Antonio Arraiz and Luis E. Egui, *Geografía económica de Venezuela* (1950), is dated but useful. Alfredo Jahn, *Aspectos geográficos de Venezuela* (1941), is an example of work by one of the country's outstanding geographers. The extensive series of volumes on *Aspectos físicos (geográficos) de. . . . [state name]* prepared by Marco Aurelio Vila since 1952 contains a wealth of information.

For historical topics, there are a number of useful sources. On the cartographic resources for historical geography see *Cartografía histórica de Venezuela, 1635-1946. Selección de los principales mapas publicados hasta la fecha* (1946); Ivan Drenikoff, *Mapas antiguos de Venezuela. Grabados e impresos antes de 1800 con la reproducción del primer mapa impreso en Venezuela y de mapas antiguos* (1971); Francisco Morales Padrón and José Llavador Mira, *Mapas, planos y dibujos sobre Venezuela existentes en el Archivo General de Indias* (2 vols., Seville, 1964-65); and Julio González, *Catálogo de mapas y planos de Venezuela* (Madrid, 1968). Also very helpful are the two works by Marco Aurelio Vila, *Nomenclator geohistórico de Venezuela, 1498-1810* (1964), and his *Antecedentes coloniales de centros poblados de Venezuela* (1978). Similarly useful for determining what is where is the *Recopilación de leyes de división territorial de la República* (1959). There is also a wealth of historical information on colonial geography in the missionary accounts, *Relaciones geográficas,* and similar sources of the early colonization period, which will be mentioned below.

A comparable amount of scholarship exists on the human resources of Venezuela, although complete comprehensive treatments of most themes in this category are rare. Modern studies of demographic issues are many, for example, Eduardo E. Arriaga and Julio Páez Celis, *Venezuela. Distribución geográfica de la población y migraciones internas* (Santiago, 1974), and Arriga, *Venezuela. Proyección de la población económicamente activa, 1950-1975* (Santiago, 1965), are exceptional. See also the work of Chi Yi Chen, *Movimientos migratorios en Venezuela* (1968), and *Distribución espacial de la población venezolana. Diagnóstico y perspectiva* (1973). Also helpful is Ramón A. Tovar, *La población de Venezuela* (1968), and the older work by José A. Vandellos, *Ensayo de demografía venezolana* (1938). Also helpful on these issues are Aníbal Buitrón, *Causas y efectos del éxodo rural en Venezuela* (Washington, 1955); George William and Ruth Oliver Hill, *La inmigración y colonización en Venezuela. Bases sociales y económicas* (1960); José Eliséo López, *La expansión demográfica de Venezuela* (Mérida, 1968).

In addition to these more general works, some specialized topics have also been explored. Nicolás Perazzo, *La inmigración en Venezuela, 1830-1850* (1973), and Miguel Acosta Saignes, *Historia de los portugueses en Venezuela* (1959), are examples of this genre. In addition see also Vicente de Amézaga Aresti, *El elemento vasco en el siglo XVIII venezolano* (1966), and Pedro Manuel Arcaya, *Población de origen europeo de Coro en la época colonial* (1972). Ricardo Archila, *Orígenes de la estadística vital en Venezuela* (1949), is also useful.

Outstanding works on Venezuelan immigration are by Susan Berglund T. and Humberto Hernández Calimán, *Estudio analítico de la política inmigratoria en Venezuela* (1977), and Susan Bergland T., "The 'Musiues' in Venezuela: Immigration Goals and Reality, 1936-1961" (Ph.D. diss., U. Massachusetts, 1980). Also helpful is Aníbal Buitrón, *Las inmigraciones en Venezuela. Sus efectos económicos y sociales* (Washington, 1956).

CONQUEST AND SETTLEMENT

The conquest and settlement of Venezuela as part of the general Hispanic expansion in the New World are discussed in many studies of the conquest in general. For a guide to those works see the Griffin, *Guide,* cited above. The tale of the German episode of the sixteenth century is told in Juan Friede, *Los Welser en la conquista de Venezuela* (1961). But the largest body of literature on the conquest and settlement of Venezuela relates to two themes. The first is the work of the missionaries, extending from the earliest times well into the eighteenth century, and the second is the process of city foundation.

For the religious conquest the following volumes will provide a representative set of documents and discussions of the work of the various orders. Alberto E. Ariza S., *Los Dominicos en Venezuela* (Bogotá, 1971); Father Buenaventura de Carrocera, *Misión de los Capuchinos en los Llanos de Caracas* (3 vols., 1972), and his *Misión de los Capuchinos en Cumaná* (3 vols., 1968); Fernando Campo del Pozo, *Historia documentada de los Agustinos en Venezuela durante la época colonial* (1968), and his *Los Agustinos en la evangelización de Venezuela* (1979); Lino Gómez Canedo, *Las misiones de Píritu. Documentos para su historia* (2 vols., 1967), and his *La provincia franciscana de Santa Cruz de Caracas. Cuerpo de documentos para su historia* (1513-1837) (3 vols., 1974), round out the work of the orders other than the Jesuits. On the Jesuits in Venezuela, see Manuel Aguirre Elorriaga, *La Compañía de Jesús en Venezuela* (1941); José Cassani, *Historia de la Provincia de la Compañía de Jesús del*

Nuevo Reyno de Granada en la América (1967); José del Rey Fajardo, *Misiones jesuíticas en la orinoquia* (vol. I, 1977), *Bio-bibliografía de los jesuitas en la Venezuela colonial* (1974), and his *Documentos jesuíticos relativos a la historia de la Compañía de Jesús en Venezuela* (3 vols., 1974). Also useful is Joseph Gumilla, *El Orinoco ilustrado y defendido* (1963).

For information on the work of the secular clergy, see Francisco Armando Maldonado, *Analectas de historia eclesiástica venezolana. Seis primeros obispos de la iglesia venezolana en la época hispánica, 1532-1600* (1973); Diego de Baños y Sotomayer, *Constituciones sinodales del Obispado de Venezuela, y Santiago de León de Caracas. Hechas en la Santa Iglesia Cathedral de dicha ciudad de Caracas . . . 1687* (1848); Nicolás Eugenio Navarro, *Anales eclesiásticos venezolanos* (2nd ed., 1951); Manuel Pérez Vila, *Ensayo sobre las fuentes para la historia de la Diócesis de Guayana durante los períodos de la colonia y la independencia* (1969); and the *Actas del Cabildo Eclesiástico de Caracas. Compendio cronológico, 1580-1808* (2 vols., 1963).

The literature on town foundations and the colonial settlement of urban centers is voluminous. The items listed below give only a taste of the feast available. José Antonio de Armas Chitty has three books of interest here. His *Caracas. Origen y trayectoria de una ciudad* (2 vols., 1967) is useful and his *Tucupido, formación de un pueblo del llano* (1961) is exceptional, as is the similar work on Zaraza. *Biografía de un pueblo* (1949). Ambrosio Perera, *Historia de la organización de pueblos antiguos de Venezuela. Génesis, desarrollo y consolidación de pueblos venezolanos, pueblos coloniales de Barquisimeto, . . .* (3 vols. in 1, Madrid, 1964), is very detailed. Other helpful items on individual places are Brother Nectario María, *Historia documental de los orígenes de Acarigua* (Madrid, 1964); Ermila Troconís de Veracoechea, *Historia de El Tocuyo colonial. Período histórico, 1545-1810* (1977); and the index of place names of Marco Aurelio Vila, *Antecedentes coloniales de centros poblados de Venezuela* (1978). Especially interesting is the work on the first European settlement of consequence by Enrique Otte, *Las perlas del Caribe. Nueva Cádiz de Cubagua* (1977). Otte has also published 8 volumes of royal decrees on Venezuela in the sixteenth century under the general titles of *Cedularios de la monarquía española . . .* and *Cédulas de la . . .* (8 vols., 1959-67).

The extensive literature on town foundations, only a sample of which is included above, has a strong concentration on the case of Caracas, Venezuela's central city. The following items provide an introduction to the field and a sense of the genre. Brother Nectario María, *Historia de la fundación de Caracas* (1966); Demetrio Ramos Pérez, *La fundación de*

Caracas y el desarrollo de una fecunda polémica. Cauces jurídico-consuetu-
dinarios de la erección de las ciudades americanas (1967); María Teresa
Bermejo de Capdevila, *Análisis de documentos para el estudio de la funda-*
ción de Caracas (1967); Graziano Gasparini, *Caracas colonial* (Buenos
Aires, 1969); and Irma de Sola Ricardo, *Contribución al estudio de los*
planos de Caracas. La ciudad y la provincia, 1567-1967 (1967). The con-
fluence of publication dates around the 400th anniversary of the foundation of Caracas is more than coincidental.

There is also much to be learned from the *Actas del Cabildo de Caracas,*
1573-1629 (11 vols., 1943-1969), and from general works on the colonial
period such as Eduardo Arcila Farías, *Economía colonial de Venezuela*
(2nd ed., 2 vols., 1973). For a good view of the physical and social organization of the city see Kathleen Waldron, "A Social History of a Primate
City: The Case of Caracas, 1750-1810" (Ph.D. diss., Indiana U., 1977).
Some of the many specialized document collections provide insight into
this era, for example, Carmela Bentivenga de Napolitano, *Cedulario in-*
dígena venezolano, 1501-1812 (1977), and Héctor García Chuecos,
Derecho colonial venezolano. Indice general de las reales cédulas que se
contienen en los fondos documentales del Archivo General de la Nación
(1952).

On the administrative reorganization of the late eighteenth century the
following items are especially helpful. Caracciolo Parra Pérez, *El régimen*
español en Venezuela. Estudio histórico (2nd ed., Madrid, 1964); José L.
Sucre Reyes, *La capitanía general de Venezuela* (Barcelona, 1969); Manuel Nunes Dias, *El real Consulado de Caracas (1793-1810)* (1971); *Doc-*
umentos para la historia de la iglesia colonial en Venezuela (2 vols., 1965);
and Nicolás Eugenio Navarro, *Anales eclesiásticos venezolanos* (2nd ed.,
1951). Also helpful is Guillermo Boza, *Estructura y cambio en Venezuela*
colonial (1973). The classic account of the Caracas Company is still
Roland D. Hussey, *La Compañía de Caracas, 1728-1784* (1962). Eduardo
Arcila Farías, *El Real Consulado de Caracas* (1957), *El régimen de la*
encomienda en Venezuela (2nd ed., 1966), *Comercio entre Venezuela y*
México en los siglos XVI y XVII (1950), and his *Historia de un monopolio.*
El estanco del tabaco en Venezuela (1779-1833) (1977), are excellent.
See also Mercedes M. Álvarez F., *El Tribunal del Real Consulado de*
Caracas (2 vols., 1967).

An interesting study of artisanry is Carlos F. Duarte, *Los maestros*
fundidores del período colonial en Venezuela (1978). Ildefonso Leal, *His-*
toria de la Universidad de Caracas (1721-1827) (1963), and his *La cul-*
tura venezolana en el siglo XVIII (1971), are useful analyses of colonial
higher education and culture. Ermila Troconís de Veracoechea, *Las Obras*

Pías en la iglesia colonial venezolana (1971); her *La tenencia de la tierra en el litoral central de Venezuela* (1979); and her *Documentos para el estudio de los esclavos negros en Venezuela* (1969) provide considerable insight on these important topics.

Other items for social history are Miguel Acosta Saignes, *Vida de los esclavos negros en Venezuela* (1967); Carlos Siso Maury, *La formación del pueblo venezolano. Estudios sociológicos* (2 vols., Madrid, 1953); Pedro Manuel Arcaya, *Insurrección de los negros de la serranía de Coro* (1949); Federico Brito Figueroa, *Las insurrecciones de los esclavos negros en la sociedad colonial venezolana* (1961); and Stephanie B. Blank, "Patrons, Clients, and Kin in Seventeenth Century Caracas. A Methodological Essay in Colonial Spanish American Social History," *Hispanic American Historical Review*, 54 (1974), 260-83. An especially interesting study that revises our understanding of colonial Venezuelan society and illustrates the complexity of social organization and its economic basis is Robert J. Ferry, "Essays in the Society and Economy of Colonial Caracas, 1580-1810" (Ph.D. diss., U. Minnesota, 1980).

On colonial demography, the information available is at best fragmentary. The most frequently used sources are Alexander von Humboldt's estimates in *Viaje a las regiones equinocciales del nuevo continente . . . 1799-1804* (2nd ed., 5 vols., 1956), but the information in Mariano Martí's records of his episcopal visita in the last quarter of the eighteenth century is much more specific, *Documentos relativos a su visita pastoral de la diócesis de Caracas, 1771-1784* (7 vols., 1969). Some more systematic estimates are available in John V. Lombardi, *People and Places in Colonial Venezuela* (Bloomington, Indiana, 1976).

Another vision of Venezuela, both before the eighteenth-century consolidation and after can be gleaned from the *Relaciones geográficas de Venezuela* (1964) published by Antonio Arellano Moreno and those published by Angel de Altolaguirre y Duvale, *Relaciones Geográficas de la Gobernación de Venezuela* (1767-68) (1954), and in the contemporary histories by Antonio Caulín, *Historia de la Nueva Andalucía* (2 vols., 1966), and José Oviedo y Baños, *Historia de la conquista y población de la provincia de Venezuela* (1967).

INDEPENDENCE

Of all periods of Venezuelan historiography, the independence era has generated the largest volume of material. These items fall into two general categories: those about independence and those about Bolívar.

Although mentioned earlier, it is important to stress the usefulness of

the 53 volumes of the Academia Nacional de la Historia's series on independence. Especially helpful from those books are Caracciolo Parra Pérez,
Historia de la Primera República de Venezuela (2nd ed., 2 vols., 1959),
and his *Mariño y la independencia de Venezuela* (5 vols., Madrid 1954-
57). See also the fascinating *Causas de infidencia* (2 vols., 1960). For a
discussion of the royalist activities see Steven K. Stoan, *Pablo Morillo and
Venezuela, 1815-1820* (Columbus, Ohio, 1974), and the *Anuario del
Instituto de Antropología e Historia*, UCV, 1967-1969 (2 vols., 1971).
Germán Carrera Damas, "La crisis de la sociedad colonial," in that *Anuario*
(vol. 1, pp. xv-lxxxix), is very good. Carrera Damas's revisionist examination of one of the royalist caudillos, *Boves. Aspectos socioeconómicos de la
guerra de independencia* (3rd ed., 1972), has had considerable success in
modifying traditional views of the royalist guerrillas. Also relevant to this
topic is Charles C. Griffin, *Ensayos sobre historia de America* (1969). An
excellent analysis of the independence movement from a continent-wide
perspective is in John Lynch, *The Spanish-American Revolution, 1808-
1826* (New York, 1973).

On some other topics of independence interest see Carlos Felice Cardot,
La Iglesia y el estado en la Primera República (Madrid, 1962), and
Miguel Batllori, *El Abate Viscardo. Historia y mito de la intervención de
los jesuitas en la independencia de Hispanoamérica* (1930).

Independence bibliography is well covered through the early 1960s in
Pedro Grases and Manuel Pérez Vila, "Gran Colombia. Referencias rela-
tivas a la bibliografía sobre el período emancipador en los países granco-
lombianos (desde 1949)," *Anuario de estudios americanos*, 21 (1964),
733-77, and subsequent publications by Pedro Grases, *Investigaciones
bibliográficas* (1968), and his *Temas de bibliografía y cultura venezolana*
(2nd ed., 2 vols., 1973). Grases has also published an important analysis
of *La conspiración de Gual y España y el ideario de la independencia*
(1949). On some of the heroes of independence other than Bolívar, see
William Spence Robertson, *La vida de Miranda* (1967); Francisco de
Miranda, *Archivo del General Miranda* (24 vols., 1929-50); and the
Indice del Archivo del General Miranda (1927). On Sucre see John P.
Hoover, *Sucre, Soldado y revolucionario* (Cumaná, 1975), and Grases,
*Bibliografía de Antonio José de Sucre, Gran Mariscal de Ayacucho, 1795-
1830* (1974).

Of course, it is Bolívar who has captured the imagination of generations
of Venezuelan historians. This fascination with the Bolivarian legend is
dissected in Carrera Damas, *El culto a Bolívar. Esbozo para un estudio de
la historia de las ideas en Venezuela* (2nd ed., 1973), although this revisionist approach is much deplored by the guardians of the faith. Much

attention has been given to Bolívar's writings in various collections. Grases' discussion of *El archivo de Bolívar: manuscritos y ediciones* (1978) is an excellent introduction to these publications. One of the earliest efforts to publish the Bolivarian texts is José Félix Blanco, *Documentos para la historia de la vida pública del libertador de Colombia, Perú y Bolivia, . . .* (14 vols., 1875-78). The standard edition of Bolívar's letters is Simón Bolívar, *Cartas del Libertador* (2nd ed., 8 vols., 1964-70). The major decrees of the Liberator are in *Decretos del Libertador* (3 vols., 1961). The definitive collection of Bolívar's writings, still in process, is *Escritos del Libertador* (15 vols., 1964-   ). An English language edition of Bolívar's major writings has been compiled by Vicente Lecuna in *Selected Writings* (2nd ed., 2 vols., New York, 1951).

With the thoroughness characteristic of national hagiography, every Bolivarian note or comment has been saved and published. See for example Manuel Pérez Vila, *Los borradores del discurso de Angostura* (1969), and his *Acotaciones bolivarianas. Decretos marginales del Libertador, 1813-1830* (1960). Also some independence heroes shine in reflected glory, as in the *Testimonios Peruanos sobre el Libertador* (1964) and Antonio José de Sucre, *Cartas de Sucre al Libertador* (1820-1830) (2 vols., Madrid 1919). Other associates of the Liberator have been studied in the works by Paul Verna, *Petión y Bolívar. Cuarenta años* (1790-1830) *de relaciones Hatián Venezolanas y su aporte a la emancipación de Hispanoamérica* (1969), and Robert Sutherland, *Un amigo de Bolívar en Haití. Contribución al estudio de los destierros del Libertador en Haití, y sus expediciones de Los Cayos y de Jacmel* (1966).

This interest in Bolivarian themes has led to the development of a sophisticated scholarly critique of those who might attribute falsely or interpret wrongly. For example, see Vicente Lecuna, *Catálogo de errores y calumnias en la historia de Bolívar* (3 vols., New York, 1956); Marcos A. Osorio Jiménez, *Bibliografía crítica de la detracción bolivariana* (1959); and Manuel Pérez Vila, *Documentos apócrifos atribuidos al Libertador, 1809-1812* (1968). Similarly, the incident between the Argentine San Martín and Bolívar in Guayaquil has generated its share of defense and attack. The classic Venezuelan case is in Vicente Lecuna, *La entrevista de Guayaquil* (4th ed., 2 vols., 1961-63).

Full-scale biographies and major interpretations of Bolívar's life and times provide an important context for understanding the Bolivarian phenomenon. The volume by Gerhard Masur, *Simón Bolívar* (rev. ed., Albuquerque, 1969), is the best in English. Augusto Mijares, *El Libertador* (5th ed., 1969), is a very balanced traditional treatment. Salvador de Madariaga has an unusual interpretation in his *Bolívar* (New York, 1969) which has been extensively refuted in Victor Andrés Belaunde et al., *Estudios sobre el "Bolívar" de Madariaga* (1967), and in Joaquín Gabaldón Márquez, *El Bolívar de Madariaga y otros Bolivares* (1960). Various Venezuelan presidents have found intellectual stimulation in the life of Bolívar, Antonio Guzmán Blanco, *El Libertador de la América del Sur* (London, 1885), and Eleazar López Contreras, *Temas de historia bolivariana* (Madrid, 1954), for example.

Because of the importance of Bolivarian ideology in the Venezuelan context there have been a number of analyses of his education and intellectual range. His tutor, Simón Rodríguez, for example, can be approached through his collected writings in Simón Rodríguez, *Escritos. Compilación y estudio bibliográfico por Pedro Grases* (3 vols., 1954-58). See also Alfonso Rumazo González, *Simón Rodríguez, Maestro de América: Biografía* (1976). On Bolivarian thought in general see Manuel Pérez Vila, *La formación intelectual del Libertador* (1971); Armando Rojas, *Ideas educativas de Simón Bolívar* (2nd ed., 1955); Nicolás Eugenio Navarro, *La política religiosa del Libertador* (1933); Víctor Andrés Belaunde, *Bolívar and the Political Thought of the Spanish American Revolution* (Baltimore, 1938); Mario Briceño Perozo, *Reminiscencias griegas y latinas en las obras del Libertador* (1971).

Some other representative pieces on a variety of themes are Alfredo Bolton, *Los retratos de Bolívar* (2nd ed., 1964); Rufino Blanco Fombona's discussion of a controversial episode in the independence wars, *Bolívar y la Guerra a Muerte. Epoca de Boves. 1813-1814* (1942); the account of Bolívar's most perceptive assistant, Daniel Florencio O'Leary, *Bolívar and the War of Independence* (Austin, 1970). José Luis Salcedo Bastardo, *Visión y revisión de Bolívar* (4th ed., 1960), attempts to place Bolívar within the context of Venezuelan history. Finally, the discussion of the Bolivarian bibliography cannot end without mention of the excellent and exhaustive works by Vicente Lecuna, especially his *Crónica razonada de las guerras de Bolívar* (2nd ed., 3 vols., 1960), and *Bolívar y el arte militar* (New York, 1955).

THE NINETEENTH CENTURY

Venezuelan historiography of the nineteenth century is substantial but most uneven. While a considerable quantity of material is available on the Páez era through the 1848-1854 period, the subsequent decades until Guzmán Blanco and Cipriano Castro are quite sparsely populated with historical studies. Nevertheless, enough exists to give a student a reasonable start on the major events of the period. Furthermore, some of the best available information is contained in the general treatments mentioned earlier in this essay.

On the years before the Federal Wars, which include the periods of Páez and Monagas, a number of monographs and documentary collections exist to help the scholar. The *Pensamiento político venezolano* cited above remains the fundamental collection of basic documents for the political controversies of the period. Also valuable is Antonio Arellano Moreno, *Las estadísticas de las provincias en la época de Páez* (1973), and the volumes of Tomás Enrique Carrillo Batalla, *Historia de las finanzas públicas en Venezuela, 1830-1857* (1969-   ). For excellent overviews of the state of the nation during the Páez era see José Rafael Revenga, *La Hacienda Pública en Venezuela, 1828-1830* (1953); *Sociedad Económica de Amigos del País, Memorias y estudios, 1829-1839* (2 vols., 1958); and the fine geography by Giovanni Battista Agostino Codazzi in his *Obras escogidas* (2 vols., 1961). Additionally, much useful information is in the *Fuentes para la historia republicana de Venezuela* (15 vols., 1957-60), and on military matters see *Las fuerzas armadas de Venezuela en el siglo XIX* (12 vols., 1963-   ). Finally, the somewhat specialized but very valuable collection published by the Universidad Central under the title *Materiales para el estudio de la cuestión agraria en Venezuela* (1800-1830) (vol. I, 1964) is essential as is the subsequent volume in the series on *Materiales . . . (1810-1865). Mano de obra: Legislación y administración* (vol. I, 1979) with the excellent introductory study by Antonieta Camacho, "Aportes para el estudio de la formacion de la mano de obra en Venezuela: Esclavos y libres (1810-1865)," pp. vi-lix.

For insight into the personalities and issues of the period see Ramón Díaz Sánchez, *Guzmán. Elipse de una ambición de poder* (5th ed., 2 vols., 1968), and the analysis of a British diplomat in Sir Robert Ker Porter's *Caracas Diary, 1825-1842. A British Diplomat in a Newborn Nation* (1966). Carmen Gómez R. has an important study on "Política de enajenación y arrendamiento de tierras baldías (1830-1858)" in *Materiales para el estudio de la cuestión agraria en Venezuela* (1829-1860) (vol. I., pp. vi-lxxii, 1971). Robert D. Matthews, Jr., *Violencia rural en Venezuela, 1840-1858* (1977), analyzes one of the most interesting features of the political environment. John V. Lombardi, *The Decline and Abolition of Negro Slavery in Venezuela, 1820-1854* (Westport, Conn., 1971), describes abolition within the political and economic context of the Páez-Monagas years. The Venezuelan scholar, litterateur, and statesman Andrés Bello has been the subject of considerable scholarship. Although more will be listed below, Pedro Grases, *Vida y obra de Don Andrés Bello* (1970), is an excellent starting point for this extraordinary Venezuelan figure. Fernando Ignacio Parra Aranguren, *Antecedentes del derecho del trabajo en Venezuela, 1830-1928* (Maracaibo, 1965), is quite valuable for this entire century.

Although there has yet to appear a really definitive biography of José Antonio Páez, his life can be approached through his *Autobiografía del General* . . . (2 vols., 1973), his *Archivo del General* . . . (1818-1823) (2 vols., 1973), and Robert B. Cunninghame Grahame, *José Antonio Páez* (London, 1929). The outstanding work by Caracciolo Parra Pérez on *Mariño y las guerras civiles* (3 vols., Madrid, 1958-60) is indispensable.

The Federal Wars (1858-63) have long been regarded as similar to the independence epic in terms of civil warfare and the disruption of social and material conditions. But the resolution of the myriad historiographical questions relating to that period is most difficult, given the lack of systematic study. Lisandro Alvarado, *Historia de la revolución federal en Venezuela* (1956), is one of the few to explain these years. A number of scholars have made contributions to the study of various aspects of the period: Ezequiel Zamora has been analyzed by Federico Brito Figueroa, *Ezequiel Zamora. Un capítulo de la historia nacional* (1951), and by Laureano Villanueva, *Vida del valiente ciudadano General Ezequiel Zamora* (1898). José Santiago Rodríguez, *Contribución al estudio de la Guerra Federal en Venezuela* (2 vols., 1960), is helpful as is the *Bosquejo histórico de Venezuela. Primera parte, 1830-1863* (Paris, 1888) by José María Rojas. Dolores Bonet de Sotillo has a useful compilation in *Crítica de la Federación. Campañas de prensa. 1863-1870* (4 vols., 1964-68) which reflects the results of that war.

The principal leader on the winning side was Juan C. Falcón whose *Archivo del Mariscal Juan Crisóstomo Falcón* (5 vols., 1957-60) is an important source. There is also a *Biografía del Mariscal Juan C. Falcón* (2nd ed., 1960) by Jacinto R. Pachano. For this period, and the century as well, Gilmore, *Caudillism and Militarism in Venezuela, 1810-1910*, is most helpful.

Antonio Guzmán Blanco is another of those towering Venezuelan figures about whom much research remains to be done. Some works such as Manuel Briceño, *Los "Illustres." O, la estafa de los guzmanes* (1954?), are highly partisan and others are valuable for parts of the Guzmán Blanco epic, for example Julián Nava, "The Illustrious American. The Development of Nationalism in Venezuela under Antonio Guzmán Blanco," *Hispanic American Historical Review*, 45, 4 (1965), 527-43, which focuses on society and culture. Rafael Angel Rondón Márquez, *Guzmán Blanco, "El Autócrata Civilizador." Parábola de los partidos políticos tradicionales en la historia de Venezuela* (2 vols., 1944), and George S. Wise, *Caudillo. A Portrait of Antonio Guzmán Blanco* (New York, 1951), are standard works. Ramón J. Velásquez tells more about the period in his discussion of *La caída del liberalismo amarillo. Tiempo y drama de Antonio Paredes* (2nd ed., 1973) than most other sources. The collection published by the Fundación John Boulton, *Política y economía en Venezuela, 1810-1976* (1976), has a couple of good articles on Guzmán Blanco. Graziano Gasparini, *Caracas. La ciudad colonial y guzmancista* (1978), is an exceptional visual display. Also revealing is Rafael Ramón Castellanos, *Guzmán Blanco íntimo* (1969), and Armando Rojas, *Las misiones diplomáticas de Guzmán Blanco* (1972). Especially helpful on the urban dimensions of the Guzmán Blanco era is Robert H. Lavenda, "The First Modernizing Attempt: Modernization and Change in Caracas, 1870-1908" (Ph.D. diss., Indiana U., 1977). For insight into the operation of his political regime see Mary B. Floyd, "Antonio Guzmán Blanco: The Evolution of Septenio Politics" (Ph.D. diss., Indiana U., 1981).

Similarly, Luis Level de Goda, *Historia contemporánea de Venezuela. Política y militar, 1858-1886* (vol. I, 1954), has some useful material, and the documents on the conflict between Church and State are presented by Nicolás Eugenio Navarro, *El Arzobispo Guevara y Guzmán Blanco. Documentación relativa al conflicto entre la Iglesia y el Estado habido en Venezuela . . . 1870-1876* (1932). The publication of Francisco Pimentel y Roth, *Historia del crédito público en Venezuela* (1974), is helpful in understanding the complex credit policy under Guzmán Blanco, and Ricardo Archila, *Orígenes de la estadística vital en Venezuela* (1949), provides insight into Guzmán Blanco's fascination with modern statistics.

If Guzmán Blanco has failed to receive the detailed treatment that is his due, much the same can be said of the more controversial, although probably less significant figure of Cipriano Castro. Mariano Picón Salas, *Los días de Cipriano Castro. Historia venezolana del 1900* (1958), and Enrique Bernardo Núñez, *El hombre de la levita gris. Los años de la restauración liberal* (1953), are good places to begin. See also Antonio Paredes, *Como llegó Cipriano Castro al poder* (2nd ed., 1954). Carlos Brandt, *Bajo la tiranía de Cipriano Castro* (1952), is also well known. Castro's own archive is published in *Documentos del General Cipriano Castro* (6 vols., 1903-1908). See also Castro, *Epistolario presidencial (1899-1908)* (1974).

A number of other works treat a variety of themes of importance for this period not restricted to either the Guzmán Blanco or later presidencies. For example, Luis Beltrán Guerrero, *Introducción al positivismo venezolano* (1956); Douglas Carlisle, *Venezuelan Foreign Policy. Its Organiza-*

tion and Beginning (Washington, 1978); Benjamin A. Frankel, *Venezuela y los Estados Unidos, 1810-1888* (1977); and Sheldon B. Liss, *Diplomacy and Dependency. Venezuela, the United States, and the Americas* (Salisbury, N.C., 1978), have much of interest. Similarly, Francisco J. Parra, *Doctrinas de la cancillería*, and Ulises Picón Rivas, *Indice constitucional de Venezuela*, both cited above, are essential. Antonio Ramón Silva, *Documentos para la historia de la diócesis de Mérida* (6 vols., Mérida and Caracas, 1906-27), has much from this period as do the *Anales diplomáticos de Venezuela. Relaciones con la Santa Sede* (5 vols., 1975); George Edmund Carl, *First among Equals: Great Britain and Venezuela, 1810-1910* (Syracuse, N.Y., 1980); and Mary Watters, *A History of the Church in Venezuela, 1810-1930* (New York, 1933). In addition, many of the travelers' accounts published by nineteenth-century visitors are valuable sources. Pascual Venegas Filardo, *Viajeros a Venezuela en los siglos XIX y XX* (1973), is a good place to begin surveying them.

VENEZUELA IN THE TWENTIETH CENTURY

The twentieth-century historiography on Venezuela is by any measure voluminous, in part because the line between what ought to be thought of as history and what ought to be regarded as properly economics or contemporary affairs is hard to draw. Nevertheless, the items mentioned in the following remarks have been selected to illustrate the range of materials available and suggest the richness of these sources. It would be impossible, of course, to provide a comprehensive listing on petroleum, for example, or on the political activities of the country's many political parties and groups, but the items mentioned here will provide access to the literature.

The twentieth century began with Juan Vicente Gómez whose regime conditioned much of what has followed. Not too surprisingly, the authors who have published since the end of the Gómez years have been critical of this most successful and ruthless Venezuelan president. Daniel J. Clinton (pseud. Thomas Rourke), *Gómez, Tyrant of the Andes* (New York, 1941), and José Rafael Pocaterra, *Archivo de . . . La oposición a Gómez* (2 vols., 1973) and his *Memorias de un venezolano de la decadencia* (2 vols., 1937), give a sense of the opposition. Pedro M. Arcaya, *The Gómez Regime in Venezuela and Its Background* (Baltimore, 1936), and Gómez's papers, published in *El General J. V. Gómez. Documentos para la historia de su gobierno* (1925), illustrate the official *gomecista* perspective on the regime. Mario Briceño Iragorry's novel *Los Riberas* (1957) provides fascinating insights into the spirit of the oil bonanza under Gómez. See also Carrera Damas' discussion of the novel in "Proceso de la formación de la burgesía venezolana," *Tres temas de historia* (2nd ed., 1974).

Others have written on Gómez as well: see, for example, Pablo Emilio Fernández, *Gómez el rehabilitador* (1956), and John Lavin, *A Halo for Gómez* (New York, 1954). Angel Ziemes has a fascinating discussion of *El gomecismo y la formación del ejército nacional* (1979). Elías Pino Iturrieta, *Positivismo y gomecismo* (1978), explores the relationship between ideology and the Gómez regime, while Domingo Alberto Rangel reinvents Gómez through the notion of an Andean neo-populist mystique in *Gómez. El amo del poder* (1975). This approach is an echo of themes originally begun in Rangel's discussion of *Los andinos en el poder. Balance de una hegemonía, 1899-1945* (1965). Both books have had wide popular appeal and have generated significant historiographical controversy.

Perhaps most interesting of the Gómez books is the set of imaginary conversations invented by Ramón J. Velásquez, *Confidencias imaginarias de Juan Vicente Gómez* (5th ed., 1980). A publishing phenomenon in its own right, this work permits Velásquez to project a vision of what Gómez must have been like when seen by a more or less sympathetic but not sycophantic intimate. It is an extraordinarily evocative performance and required reading for anyone interested in the man and his times.

The subsequent period of political history has received extensive treatment in a number of places. Robert J. Alexander, *The Venezuelan Democratic Revolution. A Profile of the Regime of Rómulo Betancourt* (New Brunswick, New Jersey, 1964), provides a sympathetic profile of the rise of one of the country's great populist leaders. Alexander, *The Communist Party of Venezuela* (Stanford, 1969), is much less sympathetic in his view of that political group. These studies of the Venezuelan political system have been expanded and developed in a number of useful works. Charles D. Ameringer, *The Democratic Left in Exile. The Antidictatorial Struggle in the Caribbean, 1945-1959* (Coral Gables, Florida, 1974); Winfield J. Burggraff, *The Venezuelan Armed Forces in Politics, 1935-1959* (Columbia, Missouri, 1972); and Philip B. Taylor, Jr., *The Venezuelan Golpe de Estado of 1958. The Fall of Marcos Pérez Jiménez* (Washington, 1968), provide valuable information on those topics. Judith Ewell, "The Extradition and Trial of Marcos Pérez Jiménez, 1959-1968: A Case Study in the Enforcement of Administrative Responsibility" (Ph.D. diss., U. of New Mexico, 1972), is a most interesting analysis of the dictator's post-1958 presence in Venezuela seen through the lens of his extradition and trial for financial misdeeds. Betancourt, *Venezuela, política y petróleo* (Mexico, 1956), is essential background reading for the post-Gómez political transformation as is Eleazar López Contreras' defense of his *Gobrierno y administración, 1936-1941* (1966), and Harrison Sabin Howard, *Rómulo Gallegos y la revolución burguesa en Venezuela* (1976).

A number of books take a broader or longer look at this political environment and process. See for example Juan B. Fuenmayor, *Historia de la Venezuela política contemporanea, 1899-1969* (5 vols., in 6, 1975-79); Manuel Vicente Magallanes, *Historia política de Venezuela* (3 vols., Madrid, 1972); and Naudy Suárez Figueroa, *Programas políticos venezolanos de la primera mitad del siglo XX* (2 vols., 1977). Essential for the understanding of this period are the following works by American political scientists who have been especially fascinated by the democratic system emerging in Venezuela. Daniel H. Levine, *Conflict and Political Change in Venezuela* (Princeton, New Jersey, 1973); John D. Martz and Enrique A. Baloyra, *Electoral Mobilization and Public Opinion. The Campaign of 1973* (Chapel Hill, North Carolina, 1976); John Duncan Powell, *The Political Mobilization of the Venezuelan Peasant* (Cambridge, Mass., 1971); and Talton F. Ray, *The Politics of the Barrios of Venezuela* (Berkeley, 1969), are very good on their topics.

In addition, John D. Martz, *Acción Democrática. Evolution of a Modern Political Party in Venezuela* (Princeton, New Jersey, 1966), gives the standard introduction to the operation of Venezuela's democratic political system and the behavior of its largest party. Two collections of articles provide excellent introductions to modern Venezuelan affairs. John D. Martz and David J. Myers, eds., *Venezuela. The Democratic Experience* (New York 1977), is especially good on recent developments and the economy, and Ramón J. Velásquez, ed., *Venezuela moderna. Medio siglo de Historia, 1926-1976* (2nd ed., revised, 1979), is best on politics, primarily because of the outstanding essay by Velásquez on political parties and behavior. On the most recent election in 1978 see José Agustín Silva Michelena and Heinz Rudolf Sonntag, *El proceso electoral de 1978. Su perspectiva histórica estructural* (1979). A valuable work on politics and the labor movement is Steve Ellner, *Los partidos políticos y su disputa por el control del movimiento sindical en Venezuela, 1936-1948* (1980).

After politics, the economy and especially the petroleum economy have been the favorite topics of commentators and analysts of Venezuela's post-Gómez affairs. Although the literature on the Venezuelan economy in general is extensive, the following series of items should provide a reasonable introduction into the field. Loring Allen, *Venezuelan Economic Development* (Grenwich, Conn., 1977), and Edward I. Altman and Ingo Walter, *Venezuelan Economic Development. A Politico-economic Analysis* (St. Louis, 1977), are useful. The summary published by the Banco Central de Venezuela, *La economía venezolana en los últimos treinta años*

(Caracas, 1971), is exceptionally valuable. John Friedmann, *Regional Development Policy. A Case Study of Venezuela* (Cambridge, Mass., 1966), is good on Venezuela's first efforts at comprehensive regional planning as is Fred D. Levy, *Economic Planning in Venezuela* (New York 1968). D. F. Maza Zavala, *Hacia la independencia económica* (1975), illustrates the critical view from the left. For an international economic perspective see the report sponsored by the International Bank for Reconstruction and Development, *The Economic Development of Venezuela* (Baltimore, 1961).

On somewhat more specialized topics see Tomás Enrique Carrillo Batalla, *Crisis y administración fiscal* (1964); Fondo de Inversiones de Venezuela, *Evolución de la deuda pública de Venezuela* (1979); Mostafa Fathy Hassan, *Economic Growth and Employment Problems in Venezuela. Analysis of an Oil-Based Economy* (New York, 1975); Héctor Malavé Mata, *Estructura, superestructura, sistema* (1969); Carl S. Shoup et al., *The Fiscal System of Venezuela* (Baltimore, 1959); and Alcides Villalba, *El Bolívar flotante. Consideraciones sobre una política cambiaria para Venezuela* (1978).

But when all is said and done, it is petroleum that makes Venezuela's economy the fascinating phenomenon that it is. As anyone would expect, the books on the subject of petroleum are legion. The classic history of Venezuela's oil is Edwin Lieuwen, *Petroleum in Venezuela. A History* (Berkeley, 1954). Much of course has happened since 1954, and Franklin Tugwell, *The Politics of Oil in Venezuela* (Stanford, 1975), provides an excellent analysis of the major issues. The legal aspects of petroleum in Venezuela can be approached through Germán Acedo Payárez, *Jurisprudencia petrolera venezolana, 1918-1971* (1973), and Salvador de la Plaza et al., *Breve historia del petróleo y su legislación en Venezuela* (1973).

The nationalization of Venezuela's oil industry naturally attracted considerable interest, as is evidenced in the following selection. Manuel R. Egaña et al., *Nacionalización petrolera en Venezuela* (1971); *Nacionalización del petróleo en Venezuela. Tesis y documentos fundamentales* (1975); James F. Petras et al., *The Nationalization of Venezuelan Oil* (New York, 1977); and José A. Silva Michelena and Felix Soublette, *Nacionalización petrolera. Recursos humanos* (1976).

Other useful work on the relationship of petroleum to the realization of the Venezuelan dream of progress is illustrated by the following items. Rómulo Betancourt, *Venezuela's Oil* (Winchester, Mass., 1978); Eduardo Machado, *Petróleo en Venezuela* (1958); Héctor Malavé Mata, *Petróleo y desarrollo económico de Venezuela* (Havana, 1964); Aníbal R. Martínez, *Una política energética* (1974); Juan Pablo Pérez Alfonzo, *Política petro-*

lera (1962), and *Petróleo y dependencia* (1971); Jorge Salazar Carillo, *Oil in the Economic Development of Venezuela* (New York, 1976); and Pedro R. Tinoco, *Petróleo. Factor del desarrollo* (1968).

The extraordinary economic boom brought to the country by the petroleum economy has produced many problems of adjustment and organization. Educational ferment at all levels is one of the consequences of the changes a democratic and wealthy government has wrought. At the university level some examples can be seen in Robert F. Arnove, *Student Alienation. A Venezuelan Study* (New York, 1972); Manuel Caballero, *Sobre autonomía reforma y política en la Universidad Central de Venezuela, 1827-1958* (1974); Germán Carrera Damas, *Sobre la teoría y la práctica de la enseñanza de la historia en una era de cambios* (1966); Luis Beltrán Prieto Figueroa, *De una educación de castas a una educación de masas* (Havana, 1951); Darcy Ribeiro, *Universidad Central de Venezuela, propuestas acerca de la renovación* (1970); René de Sola, *La universidad y la profesión de abogado* (1968). For secondary education and educational problems in general the following items will give a sense of the interest provoked by this topic. For example, Orlando Albornoz, *Sociología de la educación* (2nd ed., 1972); Ceferino Alegría M., *Historia de la medicina y su enseñanza en Venezuela* (2nd ed., 1967); Carlos Felice Cardot, *Décadas de una cultura. Origen y evolución de la educación secundaria en El Tocuyo* (2nd ed., 1974); Arnoldo Gabaldón, *La sanidad y la educación desde el punto de vista político, económico y social* (1965); Martín García Villasmil, *Escuelas para formación de oficiales del ejército. Origen y evolución de la escuela militar* (1964); Thomas J. La Belle, *The New Professional in Venezuelan Secondary Education* (Los Angeles, 1973); and George I. Sanchez, *The Development of Education in Venezuela* (Washington, 1963).

With the emphasis on petroleum development and industrialization, Venezuela's agricultural base suffered considerably during the century. Land reform, a high priority in most political propaganda, failed to achieve productivity levels adequate to supply Venezuela with its domestic needs. On the problem of land reform and agricultural development see the following representative items: Miguel Acosta Saignes, *Latifundio* (Mexico, 1938); Ramón Fernández y Fernández, *Reforma agraria en Venezuela* (1948); Louis E. Heaton, *The Agricultural Development of Venezuela* (New York, 1969); Oscar David Soto, *La empresa y la reforma agraria en la agricultura venezolana* (2nd ed., Madrid, 1978); and James W. Wilkie, *Measuring Land Reform* (Los Angeles, 1974).

Similarly, the success of petroleum-fueled industrialization brought difficulties in administration and urbanization as Venezuelans rushed to take advantage of the opportunities available after Gómez and again after Pérez Jiménez. Some of these problems are explored in Carlos Raúl Villanueva et al., *La vivenda popular en Venezuela, 1928-1952* (1953); Allan R. Brewer Carías, *Estudios sobre la regionalización de Venezuela* (1977), and his *Problemas institucionales del área metropolitana de Caracas y del desarrollo regional y urbano* (1971); Luis Fernando Chaves Vargas, *Estructura funcional de las ciudades venezolanas* (Mérida, 1973); *Estudio de Caracas* (15 vols., 1967-   ); David J. Gould, *Report. The Venezuelan Public Administration Education System* (1972); Kenneth L. Karst et al., *The Evolution of Law in the Barrios of Caracas* (Los Angeles, 1973); Rodolfo Quintero, *Sindicalismo y cambio social en Venezuela* (1966); Lloyd Rodwin et al., *Planning Urban Growth and Regional Development. The Experience of the Guayana Program of Venezuela* (Cambridge, Mass., 1969).

LITERATURE, THE ARTS, AND FOLKLORE

This book does not explore in depth the rich cultural heritage and accomplishments of Venezuelans, but in this bibliographical essay it is important to mention some of the sources of information on this fascinating dimension. Most of the items mentioned here are included because they can help the beginning student gain access to the cultural history of Venezuela, but no effort is made to include a representative sample of Venezuelan authors, novelists, or poets.

The obvious place to begin is with the specialized bibliographies focused on literature. For example, Horacio Jorge Becco, *Bibliografía de bibliografías venezolanas: Literatura* (1968-1978) (1979); the *Bibliografía de la novela venezolana* published by the Centro de Estudios Literarios of the Universidad Central (1963); or the *Diccionario general de la literatura venezolana. Autores* (Mérida, 1974), provide useful lists. Also there is the *Bibliografía de la novela venezolana,* edited by José Fabbiani Ruiz (1963), and the series of bibliographies on major Venezuelan authors such as Enrique Bernardo Núñez, Fernando Paz Castillo, Luis Manuel Urbaneja Achepohl, Ramón Díaz Sánchez, and Rómulo Gallegos, among others, published by the Universidad Católica Andrés Bello through the Seminario de Literatura Venezolana under the series title of *Contribución a la bibliografía de . . .* (1967-   ). Anthologies and general discussions of the Venezuelan literary and cultural mileu are also excellent introductions, such as are provided in the *Antología de costumbristas venezolanos del siglo XIX* (1964); Pedro Pablo Barnola, *Altorrelieve de la literatura venezolana* (1970); and Pedro Díaz Seijas, *Literatura venezolana. Tesis y antología* preparados de acuerdo con el programa oficial (4 vols., 1950). Further assistance is available in Juan Liscano V., *Panorama de literatura venezolana actual* (Washington, 1973), and Mariano Picón Salas, *Formación y proceso de la literatura venezolana* (1940). The general surveys in the *Historia de la cultura en Venezuela* (2 vols., 1955-56) and the historical perspective in Mario Briceño Iragorry, *Tapices de historia patria. Esquema de una morfología de la cultura colonial* (4th ed., 1956), are useful.

Somewhat more specialized information is available in Rafael Caldera Rodríguez' study of *Andrés Bello* (4th ed., revised, 1973), and Pedro Grases, *Antología de bellismo en Venezuela* (1969). For the clarification of names and pseudonyms see Lubio Cardozo and Juan Pito, *Seudonimia literaria venezolana (con un apéndice de José E. Machado sobre seudónimos de escritores y políticos venezolanos)* (Mérida, 1974). On philosophical thought in Venezuela see Juan David García Bacca, *Antología del pensamiento filosófico venezolano (siglos XVII-XVIII). Introducciones sistemáticas y prólogos históricos* (3 vols., 1954). On the language of Venezuelans see Angel Rosenblat, *Buenas y malas palabras en el castellano de Venezuela* (2 vols., 1960), and Francisco Tamayo, *Léxico popular venezolano* (1977).

Painting and sculpture, architecture, and the artisan crafts have all been cultivated with enthusiasm and success in Venezuela. Alfredo Boulton, *Historia de la pintura en Venezuela* (3 vols., 1964-72), is excellent as is the work by Boulton et al., *Arte de Venezuela* (1977). Graziano Gasparini's excellent *La arquitectura colonial en Venezuela* (1965) is a fine introduction with exceptional photographs, and his and Juan Pedro Posani, *Caracas a través de su arquitectura* (1969), is outstanding. Pedro Briceño and Rafael Angel Díaz Sosa (Pseud. Rafael Pineda), *La escultura en Venezuela* (1969), is helpful also. For the substantial musical accomplishments of Venezuelan artists see José Antonio Calcaño, *La cultura musical en Venezuela* (1959), and Juan Bautista Plaza, *Música colonial venezolana* (1958). Fernando Paz Castillo and Pablo Rojas Guardia, *Diccionario biográfico de las artes plásticas en Venezuela, siglos XIX y XX* (1973), makes access to these arts possible.

In between the high culture described in the works above and the peasant and folk craftsmen exist a category of artisans whose work graces the artifacts of elite society. In the work of Carlos F. Duarte, some of these masters and their work have been saved from the anonymity that is their normal fate. In *Historia de la orfebrería en Venezuela* (1970); *Domingo Gutiérrez, El Maestro del Rococo en Venezuela* (1977); *El orfebre Pedro J. Ramos* (1977); *Los maestros fundidores del período colonial en Vene-*

zuela; and *Pintura inconográfica popular de Venezuela* (1978), Carlos F. Duarte has highlighted the conditions and accomplishments of these extraordinary craftsmen.

Finally, there is a considerable literature on the folklore and ethnology of Indian, African, and European sub-communities in Venezuela. Miguel Acosta Saignes, *Gentilícios africanos en Venezuela* (1956), for example, or Isabel Aretz de Ramón y Rivera, *Manual de folklore venezolano* (2nd ed., revised, 1969); the work on *Arte prehispánico de Venezuela* (1971), along with Lubio Cardozo, *Bibliografía de la literatura indígena venezolana* (Mérida, 1970), provide a glimpse into this field. Also important to the topic are: Adelaida G. de Díaz Ungría, *El poblamiento indígena de Venezuela a través de la genética* (1963); Helmuth Fuchs, *Bibliografía básica de etnología de Venezuela* (Seville, 1964); Luise-Maria M. Suárez Margolies, *Historia de la etnología contemporánea en Venezuela* (1978); Johannes Wilbert, *Survivors of El Dorado. Four Indian Cultures of South America* (New York, 1972); Angelina Pollak Eltz, *Vestigios africanos en la cultura del pueblo venezolano* (1972); and her *Aportes indígenas a la cultura del pueblo venezolano* (1978).

Statistical Supplement

No discussion of Venezuela's past would be complete without some reference to the statistical information available. Indeed, throughout this book many themes and hypotheses have been presented in terms of changes in quantities, relative magnitudes, and specific amounts. Although expressed for the most part in prose, these quantities have a numerical foundation, some of which is presented in this Statistical Appendix. The tables also provide the numbers for the graphs and charts in the text.

In the best of all possible worlds, such a series of tables ought to be able to stand alone, requiring no explanations or caveats. But the world of international statistics is not such a case, so a modest explanation of the following numbers is essential. In general, I have tried to extract as much information as possible from standard sources such as the *Statistical Abstract of Latin America* or the OAS *Statistical Bulletin* because the data permit some comparisons between Venezuelan numbers and those for other countries in the region.

The editors of the *Statistical Abstract* and the OAS *Bulletin* make heroic efforts to verify and standardize the information presented there, but such techniques have not been applied to some of the other data sources cited in the following pages. For example, Miguel Izard, *Series estadísticas,* collects the information as-is from a wide range of Venezuelan sources, some reliable, some not. Of course, data from the colonial and nineteenth centuries are not likely to be as reliable as subsequent twentieth-century sources.

The purpose of these tables in the Statistical Supplement is not to provide a standard reference of statistical information on Venezuela. Instead, the data are included to indicate the relative orders of magnitude of Venezuelan affairs, to demonstrate the dramatic changes in these orders of magnitude that are discussed in the text, and to show how Venezuela compares to such Latin American countries as Argentina, Brazil, and Mexico.

Given this perspective, it is obvious that the precision of the numbers is less important than the trends, continuities, discontinuities, and relative positions that they show. For such purposes these numbers will serve. Students interested in the development of more sophisticated statistical arguments, especially those related to population and economics, should pursue those topics in the specialized literature, some of which is cited in the Bibliographical Essay.

The three general areas of geography, population, and economics lend themselves especially well to statistical treatments, and the following tables are arranged accordingly.

GEOGRAPHY

In this book I have given considerable weight to the geographic dimensions and context of Venezuela's historical development, including a detailed discussion of the country's principal regions. The first part includes the basic geographic information for Venezuela, including longitude and latitude, administrative regions, and individual tables for each of the seven geographic regions discussed in the text. This data is taken, for the most part, from the remarkable *Atlas de Venezuela,* an indispensable source of information on Venezuela. The regional tables refer as well to the series of regional maps in Chapter I.

POPULATION

I have also emphasized the differential growth of the various regions of Venezuela, both in economic and especially in demographic terms. This second part of the Statistical Appendix includes eleven tables illustrating a variety of population topics. Three principal subcategories encompass most of these tables.

General population estimates including growth rates are important indices of Venezuela's demographic profile and are displayed in two of the tables. The urban context of Venezuelan history is another theme stressed in the text, and three tables focus on city size, urban population, and Caracas. Finally, because of the importance of immigration in the development of Venezuela's population in the last half of the twentieth century, three tables focus on this topic.

ECONOMICS

Economics is, of course, the most statistical of social sciences. To reflect that character I have included thirteen tables focusing on a few of the many possible indices of economic development.

The first tables provide dramatic evidence of the size and the growth of Venezuela's economy since 1960 in terms of gross national product and per capita gross national product.

Venezuela, as is the case with all of Latin America, has always been closely tuned to the rhythms of international trade. Hence, these tables display some of the dimensions of that activity in the twentieth century. The percentage of exports and imports to four countries documents the preponderance of United States commerce in Venezuelan trade. The table of exports as a percent of GDP shows the importance of these exports within Venezuela's economy and indicates that no other Latin American country is as dependent on exports. This same message is even more graphically displayed by the table showing the concentration of exports, for Venezuela is not only dependent on exports but especially on the export of petroleum. Given the importance of oil in the modern history of Venezuela, the table on petroleum production since 1920 illustrates the growth of this extractive industry.

Venezuela's economic strength has made it an exceptional credit risk, and the country is one of the largest payers of public debt service in Latin America. Even so, Venezuela's external public debt service is only a small percentage of the value of exports.

Most one-export economies are especially sensitive to changes in the price paid for the principal export. Venezuela is no exception, but unlike most such economies, the price of Venezuela's export has done nothing but rise in recent years, spectacularly since 1974. Yet as the table on wholesale prices indicates, the domestic economy managed to escape the catastrophic inflationary pressures that unbalanced other Latin American economies, although the recent jump in inflation is a matter of considerable concern.

Any economic analysis that attempts to measure standard of living is doomed to interminable controversy. I have nevertheless included a table on energy consumption per capita and on the percent of the population supplied with electric lighting as a demonstration. The tables clearly show Venezuela's rapid advance within Latin America in recent decades. These tables take the place of any number of other tables that could have been included to show the same rapid advance in standard of living. While energy and electric lighting are not necessarily the best indicators of an advanced material culture, they correlate well with a host of similar measures.

CONCLUSION

These tables, then, provide a glimpse into the statistical forest that stands ready to be harvested by those interested in numerical explanations of the country's past. But these numbers must always be viewed with skepticism, for the experts have shown that their accuracy and reliability in detail leave much to be desired. They have been presented here to illustrate, to draw attention to some trends, and to provide some comparative references.

Tables

DATA SOURCES FOR THE TABLES

Anuario estadístico. Dirección General de Estadística y Censos Nacionales,
v. 1 (1972).

Atlas de Venezuela. Dirección de Cartografía Nacional (1971).

Susan Bergland T. and Humberto Hernández Calimán. *Estudio analítico
de la política inmigratoria en Venezuela* (1977).

IMF. *Direction of Trade, Annual,* 1979.

Miguel Llorens Izard. *Series estadísticas para la historia de Venezuela*
(Mérida, 1970).

Oil and Gas Journal, 1981.

OAS. *Statistical Bulletin,* v. 1-3 (Washington, D.C., 1980).

James W. Wilkie, ed. *Statistical Abstract of Latin America,* v. 19-20 (Los
Angeles, 1978-1980).

James W. Wilkie, ed. *Statistics and National Policy* (Los Angeles, 1974).

PART I GEOGRAPHY

Table 1. Geographic Location

LONGITUDE: 59 45′ 49″ TO 73 11′ 49″
LATITUDE: 0 45′ 00″ TO 12 11′ 46″

NORTH-SOUTH DISTANCE: 789 Miles
EAST-WEST DISTANCE: 927 Miles

ADMINISTRATIVE REGIONS IN 1971

1. CAPITAL REGION
   Metropolitan area of Caracas, Federal District, Miranda State, Federal Dependencies.

2. CENTRAL REGION.
   States of Aragua, Carabobo, Cojedes, and Guárico.

3. CENTER-WEST.
   States of Falcón, Lara, Portuguesa, and Yaracuy (Less District of Sucre and the Municipality of Guanare).

4. ZULIA.
   State of Zulia.

5. ANDES.
   States of Barinas, Mérida, Táchira, and Trujillo (Plus the Municipality of Guanare, the District of Sucre, and the District of Páez).

6. SOUTH.
   State of Apure (Less the District of Páez), the District of Cedeño, and the Amazonas Federal Territory.

7. NORTHEAST.
   States of Anzoátegui, Monagas, Nueva Esparta, and Sucre.

8. GUAYANA.
   State of Bolívar (Less the District of Cedeño), and the Delta Amacuro Federal Territory.

Source: Anuario estadístico, 1971, pp. 3-4. (Converted from kilometers to miles.)

Table 2. Surface Area of Venezuelan Regions
(See Map, p. 11)

REGION	AREA (SQ MI)	% OF TOTAL AREA
Coast	58,950	16.6
Segovia Highlands	9,344	2.6
Andes	20,803	5.9
Coastal Range	11,367	3.2
Llanos	91,614	25.8
Guayana	163,320	46.0
Total	355,398	100.0

Source: Atlas de Venezuela, pp. 123-24.

Note: The source for this and the rest of the tables in this section is the *Atlas de Venezuela*. The Coast excludes the Continental Platform and Lake Maracaibo and includes the islands and the Orinoco Delta. Percentages may not total 100.0 because of rounding. Totals may not add because of conversion from kilometers to miles. The area reported in the *Atlas* is slightly different from the area reported in the *Anuario*.

Table 3. Surface Area of the Coast
(See Map, p. 13)

SUBREGION	AREA (SQ MI)	% OF REGION
Orinoco Delta	22,973	39.0
Cariaco-Araya-Paria	1,653	2.8
Unare Basin	9,846	16.7
Central Coast	479	0.8
Chichiriviche Coastal Plain	6,116	10.4
Coro Coastal Plain	4,409	7.5
Maracaibo Basin	12,780	21.7
Islands	695	1.2
Total	58,950	100.0

Table 4. Surface Area of the Segovia Highlands
(See Map, p. 19)

SUBREGION	AREA (SQ MI)	% OF REGION
Northern Mountains	1,050	11.2
Plains of Falcón	1,544	16.5
Barbacoas Mountains	2,008	21.5
Baragua Mountains	1,822	19.5
Lara Depression	1,544	16.5
Lara Mountains	1,375	14.7
Total	9,344	100.0

Table 5. Surface Area of the Andes
(See Map, p. 19)

SUBREGION	AREA (SQ MI)	% OF REGION
Andes	13,931	67.0
Perijá Mountains	2,888	13.9
Plains of Zulia	3,985	19.2
Total	20,803	100.0

Table 6. Surface Area of the Coastal Mountains
(See Map, p. 22)

SUBREGION	AREA (SQ MI)	% OF REGION
Central Coastal Range	8,386 (100.0%)	73.8
Nirgua-Tinaquillo Hills	1,452 (17.3%)	12.8
Central Littoral Mountains	1,853 (22.1%)	16.3
Valencia Basin	494 (5.9%)	4.3
Interior Valleys	1,375 (16.4%)	12.1
Central Interior Mountains	3,212 (38.3%)	28.3
Eastern Coastal Range	2,981 (100.0%)	26.2
Eastern Littoral Mountains	819 (27.5%)	7.2
Eastern Interior Mountains	2,162 (72.5%)	19.0
Total	11,367	100.0

Table 7. Surface Area of the Llanos
(See Map, p. 25)

SUBREGION	AREA (SQ MI)	% OF REGION
Llanos of Barinas-Portuguesa	19,768	21.6
Llanos of Apure	28,764	31.4
Baúl Massif	263	0.3
Llanos of Calabozo	27,568	30.1
Llanos of Maturín	15,251	16.6
Total	91,614	100.0

Table 8. Surface Area of Guayana
(See Map, p. 28)

SUBREGION	AREA (SQ MI)	% OF REGION
Plains of the Orinoco	42,394	26.0
Plains of the Casiquiare Channel	9,459	5.8
Amazon Basin	9,073	5.6
Itamaca Mountains	6,641	4.1
Plains of Guayana	28,185	17.3
Pacaraima Mountains	25,869	15.8
Parima Mountains	41,699	25.5
Total	163,320	100.0

PART II   POPULATION

Table 1. Surface Area and Population Density by States
1941-1971

STATE	AREA SQ MI	DENSITY OF POPULATION/SQ MI				% CHANGE 1941-71
		1941	1950	1961	1971	
Federal District:	745	510.0	952.3	1687.6	2504.5	391
States:						
Anzoátegui	16,718	9.3	14.5	22.8	30.3	225
Apure	29,537	2.3	3.1	3.9	5.7	144
Aragua	2,708	51.8	71.0	117.3	200.5	287
Barinas	13,591	4.7	6.0	10.4	17.1	267
Bolívar	91,892	1.0	1.3	2.3	4.1	300
Carabobo	1,795	113.4	144.0	226.4	367.3	224
Cojedes	5,714	8.8	9.1	12.7	16.6	88
Falcón	9,575	24.3	26.9	35.5	42.5	74
Guárico	25,091	5.4	6.5	9.8	12.7	133
Lara	7,645	43.5	48.2	64.0	87.8	102
Mérida	4,363	44.3	48.4	62.2	79.5	80
Miranda	3,069	74.1	89.9	160.3	278.9	277
Monagas	11,158	10.9	15.8	22.0	26.7	145
Nueva Esparta	444	155.9	170.9	201.5	267.5	72
Portuguesa	5,869	14.8	20.7	34.7	50.5	242
Sucre	4,556	64.0	73.3	88.3	102.8	61
Táchira	4,286	57.2	71.0	93.2	119.4	109
Trujillo	2,857	92.5	95.8	114.2	133.4	44
Yaracuy	2,741	46.4	48.2	64.0	81.6	76
Zulia	24,363	17.9	28.7	47.8	53.4	199
Federal Territories:						
Amazonas	67,857	a	0.3	0.3	3.1	5900
Delta Amacuro	15,521	1.8	2.1	2.1	3.1	71
Federal Dependencies:	46	18.4	16.8	18.6	10.1	—45
VENEZUELA	352,143	11.1	14.5	21.8	30.6	174

Source: Anuario Estadístico, 1971, p. 11. Converted from kilometers to miles.

Note: Includes area of Lakes Valencia and Maracaibo in AREA but not in DENSITY.

Totals may not add because of rounding in conversion of kilometers to miles.

a = less than 0.3

Table 2. Population Estimates 1780-2000

YEAR	MILLIONS OF INHABITANTS
1780	.33
1800	.78
1820	.76
1840	1.14
1860	1.66
1880	2.08
1900	2.45
1910	2.60
1920	2.82
1930	3.12
1940	3.71
1950	4.97
1960	7.35
1970	10.40
1980	13.81
1990	22.20
2000	25.71

Source: 1780-1880: Izard, Table 1.1.1, p. 9.
1900-2000: Wilkie, Table 620, 625, v. 20.

Table 3. Population Growth Rate 1900-1990
Annual Percentage Growth Rate Estimates

DECADES	ARG	BRAZIL	MEX	VEN
1900-10	4.3	2.2	1.0	0.6
1910-20	2.9	2.1	—.6	0.8
1920-30	3.1	2.0	1.5	1.0
1930-40	1.6	2.0	1.7	1.7
1940-50	1.9	2.4	2.8	3.1
1950-60	1.5	3.1	3.2	4.3
1960-70	1.7	3.0	3.5	3.8
1970-80	1.3	3.0	3.5	3.6
1980-90	1.0	2.8	3.6	3.2

Source: Wilkie, Table 625, v. 20.

Table 4. Population of Principal Cities 1976

CITY	POPULATION $\times$ 100,000
Caracas D.F.	21.8
Maracaibo	6.5
Valencia	3.7
Barquisimeto	3.3
Maracay	2.6
San Cristóbal	1.5
Cabimas	1.2
Ciudad Bolívar	1.0

Source: Wilkie, Table 631, v. 20.

Table 5. Percent of Total Population in Urban Areas of 20,000 or More and Percent of Total Population in Most Populated City 1950-1975

YEAR	COUNTRY	20,000+	100,000+	MOST POPULATED CITY
1950	Argentina	52.4%	44.0%	33.0%
1975	Argentina	69.8	57.9	37.0
1950	Brazil	20.3	13.3	8.2 (1)
1975	Brazil	45.0	32.5	10.3 (1)
1950	Mexico	23.6	15.2	11.1
1975	Mexico	38.7	16.2	18.7
1950	Venezuela	31.0	16.6	9.8
1975	Venezuela	63.7	46.4	9.1

Source: Wilkie, Table 631, v. 20.

Note: (1) = Río plus São Paulo.

Table 6. Percent of Urban Population in Urban Areas of 100,000
or More and Most Populated City as a Percent of Urban Population
in Areas over 100,000
1975

YEAR	COUNTRY	% IN 100,000	MOST POPULATED CITY AS A % OF URBAN AREAS OVER 100,000
1950	Argentina	84.0%	61.1%
1975	Argentina	83.0	53.0
1950	Brazil	65.6	40.5 (1)
1975	Brazil	72.1	22.8 (1)
1950	Mexico	64.3	47.0
1975	Mexico	67.7	48.2
1950	Venezuela	53.6	31.7
1975	Venezuela	72.8	14.2

Source: Wilkie, Table 631, v. 20.

Note: (1) = Rio plus São Paulo.

Table 7. Gain or Loss from Immigration 1936-1975

YEAR	AVERAGE GAIN/YR × 1,000	TOTAL GAIN/PERIOD × 1,000	ENTERING × 1,000	LEAVING × 1,000
1936-47	1.7	19.9	203.7	183.8
1948-59	34.4	412.5	1,303.2	890.8
1960-63	(−.7)	(−2.9)	447.4	450.3
1964-69	13.6	81.8	981.6	899.8
1970-75	29.7	178.1	2,275.2	2,097.1

Source: Bergland T. and Hernandez Calimán, pp. 44, 51, 67, 68.

Table 8. Distribution of Major Immigrant Groups by Nationality
1948-1961

NATIONALITY	1948	1951	1955	1958	1961
Italian	27.5	35.5	34.3	16.2	18.3
Spanish	16.0	33.4	37.2	41.2	26.1
Colombian	4.9	4.2	1.3	7.6	12.8
Portuguese	4.4	5.5	12.2	9.0	9.0

Source: Bergland T. and Hernandez Calimán, p. 128.

Table 9. Foreign Population in 1971

NATIONALITY	NUMBER ✕ 1,000	PERCENT OF FOREIGN POPULATION
Spanish	149.7	25.1
Italian	88.2	14.8
Portuguese	60.4	10.1
Colombian	180.1	30.2
Other	118.2	19.8
Total	596.8	100.0

Source: Bergland T. and Hernandez Calimán, p. 158.

PART III   ECONOMICS

Table 1. Gross Domestic Product 1960-1979 ✕ 100 Million US$ at 1978 Prices

COUNTRY	1960	1965	1970	1975	1979
Argentina	27.1	33.5	41.3	45.0	53.6
Brazil	40.4	50.3	72.8	121.8	156.7
Mexico	26.7	37.6	52.5	69.1	84.3
Venezuela	11.5	16.4	20.5	26.0	32.8

Source: OAS, Table A-2, v. 2, No. 1-2, 1980.

Table 2. Gross Domestic Product Growth Rates 1960-1979 % Per Year

COUNTRY	1960-70	1970-75	1975-79
Argentina	4.32	3.89	1.74
Brazil	6.07	10.84	6.50
Mexico	7.02	5.64	5.08
Venezuela	5.95	4.81	6.04

Source: OAS, Table A-2, v. 2, No. 1-2, 1980.

Table 3. Gross Domestic Product Per Capita 1960-1979
US$ at 1978 Prices

COUNTRY	1960	1970	1979
Argentina	1358	1739	2004
Brazil	580	787	1321
Mexico	740	1037	1215
Venezuela	1566	1997	2428

Source: OAS, Table A-3, v. 2, No. 1-2, 1980.

Table 4. Gross Domestic Product Per Capita Growth Rates 1960-1979
1978 US$ in Percent/Year

COUNTRY	1960-70	1970-75	1975-79
Argentina	2.5	2.5	0.4
Brazil	3.1	7.8	3.6
Mexico	3.4	2.1	1.4
Venezuela	2.5	1.6	2.9

Source: OAS, Table A-3, v. 2, No. 1-2, 1980.

Table 5. Gross Domestic Product by Economic Activity 1936-1979

YEAR	AGRICULTURE	MINING	MANUFACTURING
1936	25.1%	20.4%	10.7%
1940	19.2	20.3	13.6
1945	13.8	26.4	14.6
1950	9.2	27.3	11.2
1955	8.1	27.3	13.1
1960	7.9	27.5	14.0
1965	7.1	23.1	14.9
1970	7.5	20.0	15.0
1975	7.2	10.4	15.3
1979	6.1	8.0	16.7

Source: Wilkie, Table 2223, v. 20. OAS, Table B-67, v. 2, No. 1-2, 1980.

Table 6. Imports and Exports as a Percent of Gross Domestic
Product 1960-1979

COUNTRY	1960 IM—EX		1970 IM—EX		1975 IM—EX		1979 IM—EX	
Argentina	12.5	11.3	10.5	12.8	9.5	7.6	8.9	18.3
Brazil	7.3	6.7	7.0	6.6	9.2	6.0	7.7	6.7
Mexico	12.6	10.3	11.9	8.7	13.8	7.6	13.6	10.0
Venezuela	19.2	33.1	18.2	26.2	24.1	10.9	31.2	8.6

Source: OAS, Table A-4c, v. 2, No. 1-2, 1980.

Table 7. Exports to and Imports from Four Countries
Percent of Total 1912-1979

YEAR	U.S. EX	IM	GERMANY EX	IM	U.K. EX	IM	JAPAN EX	IM	TOTAL EX	IM
1912	39	33	16	16	6	22	a	a	61	71
1920	49	59	b	b	7	24	a	a	56	83
1925	14	50	6	8	4	20	a	a	23	78
1930	5	50	3	12	1	11	a	a	9	73
1935	2	35	2	8	2	9	a	1	6	53
1940	5	75	a	a	a	8	a	3	5	86
1945	81	21	a	a	3	3	a	a	84	24
1950	30	69	1	3	8	11	a	2	47	85
1955	38	59	1	9	4	8	a	2	43	78
1960	44	52	1	9	8	6	a	4	53	71
1965	30	53	2	8	8	5	2	6	42	72
1970	35	47	3	9	4	5	1	8	43	69
1975	43	46	4	9	2	4	a	7	50	65
1979	38	43	2	7	2	3	1	9	43	62

Note: a = less than 1%
      b = no data, presumed nil.

Source: Wilkie, Statistics and National Policy (1974), p. 290.
Wilkie, Table 2705, v. 19, 1978.
Wilkie, Table 2770, v. 20, 1980.
IMF. Direction of Trade, Annual, 1979.

Table 8. Principal Export Commodities as a Percent of Total Exports 1979

COUNTRY PRODUCT	VALUE MILLIONS $	% OF TOTAL EXPORTS
Argentina Meat	781 (1)	12%
Brazil Coffee	1,893	12
Mexico Petroleum	3,790	42
Venezuela Petroleum	13,463	95

Source: OAS, Table A-11, v. 2, No. 3, 1980.
Note: (1) Value for 1978.

Table 9. Petroleum Production 1920-1980
Millions of Barrels

DATE	MILLIONS OF BARRELS
1920	.49
1925	15.82
1930	139.29
1935	152.61
1940	190.43
1945	321.60
1950	540.63
1955	784.50
1960	1036.63
1965	1265.93
1970	1348.51
1975	847.72
1980	790.96

Source: 1920-70. Anuario estadístico (1972), p. 159.
    1975. Wilkie, Table 2002, v. 20, 1980.
    Oil and Gas Journal, May 2, 1981.
Converted from metric tons to barrels at 6.94 barrels/metric ton.

Table 10. External Public Debt Service Payments as a Percent
of Total Exports 1961-1980

COUNTRY	1961	1965	1970	1975	1980
Argentina	22.3	20.5	21.7	22.0	27.6
Brazil	29.3	28.9	14.3	16.1	28.5
Mexico	14.3	24.6	24.1	25.6	59.5
Venezuela	4.9	1.8	2.9	5.8	7.5

Source: OAS, Table AE-8, v. 2, No. 1-2, 1980.

Table 11. Wholesale Price Index 1975-1979
1975 = 100

COUNTRY	1977	1978	1979	GROWTH RATE 1975-1979
Argentina	1494	3676	9163	209.4%
Brazil	204	281	438	44.7
Mexico	173	200	236	24.0
Venezuela	119	128	139	8.6

Source: OAS, Table A-17, v. 2, No. 3, 1980.

Table 12. Energy Consumption Per Capita 1929-1976
Lb/Inhabitant Coal Equivalent

COUNTRY	1929	1950	1960	1970	1976
Argentina	1499	1675	2381	3754	3977
Brazil	220	485	743	1054	1612
Mexico	661	1250	1698	2308	2705
Venezuela	507	1698	5783	5417	6257

Source: Wilkie, Table 2001, v. 20, 1980. Converted from kg/inhabitant.

Table 13. Electric Lighting, Percent of Population Supplied
1960-1973

COUNTRY	1960	1970	1973
Argentina	69.0	76.0	78.5
Brazil	38.7	47.5	51.0
Mexico	45.0	59.6	63.1
Venezuela	58.0	76.2	83.1

Source: Wilkie, Table 908, v. 20, 1980.

Index

Abogados, Colegio de, 106
Abolition of slavery, 176–77, 186.
　See also Blacks
Acarigua, on map, 25, 41
Acción Democrática: during 1945–58,
　223–25; after 1958, 229, 239–41;
　and land reform, 235–36; elections
　of 1978, 250–51
Achaguas, on map, 25, 41, 111
Administration, colonial jurisdictions,
　84
Africans. See Blacks
Agriculture: as a major colonial in-
　dustry, 33–34; loses relative value
　to petroleum, 35; and petroleum
　during Gomez period, 210; agrar-
　ian reform laws under Medina
　Angarita, 223
Aguado, Fray Pedro de, 254
Aguasay, on map, 25
Alfinger, Ambrosio, 64, 65–66
Altagracia de Orituco, on map, 41
Altos de Platillón: 23; on map, 22
Alvarado, Lisandro, 259–60
Amacuro River, on map, 41

Amazonas State, on map, 41
Ampíes, Juan de, 64
Andean Pact, 54
Andes Region: 8, 10; description,
　18–20; on map, 11, 19
Angel Falls, on map, 9, 41
Angostura, Congress of: 151; Bolívar's
　1819 speech to, 257
Antímano, on map, 41
Anzoátegui State, on map, 41
Apure Llanos Subregion, on map, 25
Apure River, on map, 9, 13, 22, 25,
　28, 41
Apure State, on map, 41
Apurito, on map, 41
Aragua State, on map, 41
Aragua de Barcelona, on map, 13, 41
Aragua de Maturín, on map, 25
Aragua: Indians, 43, conquest of
　valley of, 69–70
Aragua-Tuy Valleys, 21
Arauca River, on map, 9, 25, 28, 41
Araure, on map, 25, 41
Araya fortress, 73–74, 78
Araya Peninsula: 23; description, 14

Araya, Salinas de, 12–14, 32
Araya-Cariaco-Paria Coast Subregion, on map, 13
Archbishopric of Venezuela, 106
Argentina, 50
Army: professionalization of, 194; expanded role during Gómez regime, 208, 209–10; participation in coup d'etat, 223, 225, 227; and post-1935 politics, 218, 234, 237–38, 242
Aroa: copper mines, 32; on map, 13
Aruba, on map, 41
Asunción: 63; on map, 41
Atlantic, North: colonial participation in, 94, 95, 103–4; and Venezuelan elites, 159, 183–84; Venezuela within tradition of, 212, 265–66; as source of post 1958-political models, 243
Audiencia, 104–5
Augustinian missions, 90
Authority: within colonial government, 114; failure of in First Republic, 127–30; political in independence, 142–47; establishment of after independence, 157–58
Aves, Islas las, on map, 9
Ayacucho, battle of, 154
Aztec empire, 61

Banditry: and Páez regime, 165–66; and Monagas regimes, 183
Banks: operations in nineteenth-century Venezuela, 173; in 1936–41, 220–21
Baragua Mountains Subregion, on map, 19
Barbacoas Mountains Subregion, on map, 19
Barcelona: colonial trade through, 78; flight to in 1814, 142; on map, 9, 11, 13, 22
Barinas State, on map, 41

Barinas, Province, on map, 111
Barinas, on map, 9, 19, 25, 41, 111
Barinas-Portuguesa Llanos Subregion, on map, 25
Barquisimeto: as source of exploration, 18; and Buría gold mines, 32; founded, 68; on map, 9, 11, 19, 25, 41, 111
Barrancas, on map, 13
Basques: in Caracas Company, 32; in colonial population, 47. See also Caracas Company
Baúl Massif Subregion, on map, 25
Baúl Massif, 24
Bello, Andrés: in England, 125; literary contribution, 257–58
Betancourt, Rómulo: as symbol of generation of 1928, 222; and AD, 239–40
Biografía de José Felix Ribas, 258
Bishopric of Caracas, 93–94
Bishoprics, Mérida-Maracaibo, Guayana-Cumaná, consolidated, 106
Blacks: 48; as major population group, 44–46; African ethnic origins, 45. See also Race, Slaves
Blanquilla, Isla la, on map, 9, 41
Blockade of Venezuela during Castro regime, 202
Boca Grande, on map, 41
Boconó, on map, 19, 41
Bolívar State, on map, 41
Bolívar, Pico, on map, 9, 19
Bolívar, Simón: in England, 125; and the fall of Puerto Cabello, 130; in New Granada, 134, 137, 139; profile of special characteristics, 137–39; expelled from Caracas by Boves, 141; in Haiti, 148–49; in Angostura, 151; death, 155; as a romantic figure, 255–57; background of, 256–57; literary legacy, 257; importance to national myth, 263–64

Bolívar family copper mine at Aroa, 32

Bolívar. *See* Cerro Bolívar, Ciudad Bolívar

Bonaire, on map, 41

Borburata, founded, 67

Boundaries: dispute in Guayana, 28–29; expanded by colonial missionaries, 89, 91; establishment during Páez regime, 166–67

Bourbon, Spanish regime, 95–110; 115

Boves, José Tomás: as royalist leader, 131–32; dies in battle of Urica, 148

Boyacá, battle of, 151

Brazil: 50; on map, 9, 11, 28, 41, 111

Brazo Casiquiare, on map, 9, 28, 41

British Guiana, boundary, 29

Bureaucracy: Spanish colonial and the empire, 113–14; transition to republic of, 159; role in Guzmán Blanco regimes, 192–95; need for technical competency, 233

Buría: 30, 32, 62; on map, 25

COPEI: origins and policy, 224; under Pérez Jiménez regime, 226; party profile after 1958, 239; and elections of 1978, 250–51

Cabildo: importance of Caracas for colonial elite, 81–85; loses power in eighteenth century, 106–7; in the independence, 122–24

Cabildo abierto: against the Caracas Company, 98–99; April 19, 1810, 123–24

Cabimas, on map, 13, 19, 41

Cacao: 32–33; as major colonial export, 32; and the Caracas Company, 95–103; replaced by coffee, 172. *See also* Economy

Cagua, on map, 41

Caicara, on map, 25, 28

Cajigal, Juan Manuel, 134

Calabozo, on map, 9, 11, 25, 41, 111

Calabozo Llanos Subregion, on map, 25; description, 14

Caldera, Rafael: and COPEI, 226–27, 239

Calza Hills, 23

Campaña Admirable, 139–40

Canaima, 261

Canary Islands, 47

Candelaria Parish, 47

Cantaura, on map, 41

Cape Codera, on map, 13, 22

Capitulaciones, 60–61

Captaincy General of Venezuela, 104–5

Capuchin missions, 89–90

Caraballeda: founded, 70; on map, 13

Carabobo State, on map, 41

Carabobo, battle of, 152

Caracas Company, 32, 47; and transportation system, 34; history of, 95–103; and Caracas as a central city, 108–9

Caracas Valleys Subregion, 21–23

Caracas: as a central city, 5, 20, 21, 37, 71, 79–84, 103, 107–10, 158–62; and search for gold, 32; in colonial transportation system, 34; population, 37, 39; Indians, 43, 68; town council's role in colonial elite, 47–48; conquest of, 61, 69–70; founded, 70; province, 81–82, 93, on map, 111; Bishropric of, 93–94; resistance to consolidation of power in, 106–7; in independence, 110–11, 127–30; 140–44; discontent with Gran Colombia, 153–54; in structure of republican government in nineteenth century, 170–72; expansion during Páez regime, 177–78; strengthened by Federal Wars, 188–89; role in government of Guzmán Blanco, 193–95; role during the Gómez regime, 206–8; rapid expansion after 1935, 213–14; on map, 9, 11, 13, 22, 25, 41

Cariaco, on map, 13, 22

Cariaco-Araya-Paria Subregion, 14

Caribbean, focus of Venezuelan colonial activity, 94

Caripe, on map, 22

Caroní River: 26; on map, 9, 22, 25, 28, 41

Carora, on map, 19, 41

Carreño, Teresa, 253

Carúpano, on map, 13, 41

Carvajal, Juan de, 66

Casa de los Abila, 260–61

Casas, Juan de, 122

Casiquiare, Brazo, on map, 9, 28, 41

Cassandra, 263

Castro, Cipriano, 197, 201–5

Castro, Fidel, 234–35

Catatumbo River, on map, 9, 13, 19

Cattle, as a colonial enterprise, 27, 32, 33, 63

Caucagua, on map, 22, 41

Caudillos: as source of legitimacy in government, 158–71; and the Federal Wars, 188; and Guzmán Blanco, 192–93; reduction of power after Guzmán Blanco, 196; and new technology, 203

Caura River: 26; on map, 28, 41

Cesarismo democrático, 260

Census, eighteenth century, 255

Central Coast, 23

Central Coastal Plain Subregion, on map, 13

Central Coastal Range Subregion, 20

Central Interior Mountains Subregion: 21, 23; on map, 22

Central Littoral Mountains Subregion: 21, 23; on map, 22

Cerro Bolívar: 27; on map, 9, 28, 41

Cerro Roraima, on map, 9, 41

Chama River, on map, 9, 19

Charles IV and the independence, 118–19

Chichiriviche Coastal Plain Subregion: 41; description, 15–16; on map, 13

Chivacoa, on map, 41

Chronicles, colonial, 254

Ciudad Bolívar, on map, 9, 11, 25, 28, 41, 111

Ciudad Guayana: as planned city, 37; on map, 13, 28, 41

Ciudad Ojeda, on map, 41

Civil war, during independence, 144–47

Clarines, on map, 41

Climate of Caracas, 79–80

Coast Region: 10; description, 12–17; on map, 11, 13

Coastal Ranges Region: 10; description, 20–23; on map, 11

Coche, Isla, on map, 9, 13, 22, 41

Coffee: replaces cacao, 32, 172; and labor during Páez regime, 176–77

Cojedes River, on map, 9, 22, 25, 41

Colombia: Venezuela and Gran Colombia, 151–54; on map, 9, 11, 13, 19, 25, 28, 41

Colonia Tovar, 50

Columbus, Christopher, 61, 64

Commerce, contraband, 74–76

Commercial network, colonial, 5, 108

Compañía Guipuzcoana. *See* Caracas Company

Congress of Valencia in 1830, 164

Conquest: 59–71; compared to Mexico and Peru, 61–62, 68–69; by conquistadors and missionaries compared, 91

Conservative Party, 179

Consolidation: of colonial subsystems, 71, 72, 94–95; of regional economies, 77–78; of Venezuela around Caracas, 79–84; and the Caracas Company, 95–103; by colonial government agencies, 103–9; of colonial government in Caracas, 108–

10; reasons for failure of Colombian, 154

Constitution of 1830, 164–65

Constitution, Spanish of 1812, 120

Constitution: first, 127; reform of 1857, 183; function of in Venezuela, 198–201

Consulado, creation of, 104–6

Contraband: trade, 15; commerce, 74–76; and the Caracas Company, 95–103

Coporito, on map, 41

Copper, in Aroa, 32

Coro Coastal Plain Subregion: description, 16; on map, 13

Coro: and Spanish exploration, 16, 61, 66–67; as a source of Indian slaves, 64; in German period, 65–66; and colonial trade through, 77; on map, 9, 11, 13, 19, 41, 111

Correo del Orinoco, 151

Corruption, in post-1958 period, 233, 251

Credit: April 10, 1834, law, 173–74; during Páez regime, 173–75, 180; changes in laws under Monagas, 182–83

Creoles, in independence, 121–24

Cúa, on map, 22, 41

Cuba: 63; as source of exploration, 61; as market for Indian slaves, 64

Cubagua, Isla: 61–62; on map, 9, 13, 22, 41

Cúcuta, government of Colombia in 1821, 152

Cuentos grotescos, 260

Cultural identity, 252, 264

Cumaná: in colonization, 61–62, 63–64; colonial trade through, 78; Franciscan convent in, 86; governors and Franciscan missions, 88; province of, 93; on map, 9, 11, 13, 22, 41, 111

Cumanacoa, on map, 41

Cumbes, 57

Curaçao, 64; on map, 41

Curiapo, on map, 13

Cuyuni River, on map, 9, 28, 41

De León, Juan Francisco, 98–99

De la Parra, Teresa, 261

Defense: Venezuela as part of Caribbean, 70, 72–73; and the Caracas Company, 95–103; and Caracas as a central city, 109

Delta Amacuro State, on map, 41

Democracy: influence of Western on Venezuelan policies, 221; since 1958, 241–43

Dependence on North Atlantic world after 1958, 217, 248–49

Depons, François, 254

Depression of Tachira, 20

Development: 38; plans based on petroleum wealth, 230–31; Venezuelan model of, 249–50

Díaz Rodríguez, Manuel, 259–60

Díaz Sánchez, Ramón, 263

Diplomacy: during independence, 125, 140; foreign claims on Castro government, 201–2

Distrito Federal, on map, 41

Dominicans, missions, 90

Doña Barbara, 262

Dragon's Mouth, on map, 41

Dutch interest in salt on Araya Peninsula, 32

Eastern Interior Mountains Subregion: 23; on map, 22

Eastern Littoral Mountains Subregion: 23; on map, 22

Eastern Llanos, description, 14

Economy: colonial of Venezuela, 72, 75–77, 84; and eighteenth-century reforms, 95; during Páez regime, 172–80; modern and archaic compared, 185–86; increased foreign

Economy: (*Cont.*)
penetration, 204–5; changes in Gómez period, 209; development theories of, 216; expectations as a result of petroleum wealth, 248

Ecuador competes for cacao trade, 75–76

Education: and Franciscans, 86–87; need for technical, 233

El Baúl, on map, 25, 41

El Callao, on map, 41

El Dorado, as part of conquest mystique, 18, 59–60, 64–67

El Pao, on map, 25

El Pao de Barcelona, on map, 25

El Sombrero, on map, 25, 41

El Tigre: 24; on map, 25, 41

El Tocuyo: foundation of, 66; on map, 19, 41

El último solar, 261

El Venezolano, 179

Election: of 1952, 227; of 1958, 229; of 1978, 250–51

Elites: in colonial period, 34, 45–46; in colonial Caracas, 81–85; and the Juan Francisco de León revolt, 98–99; and independence, 112–13, 118, 121–26, 135–36; compete to control North Atlantic connection, 160; of Caracas and the Páez regime, 167–68; and republican government in nineteenth-century, 170–71; behavior since independence, 183–84; agreement of foreign and national, 202; oppose democratic regimes after 1958, 233–34; and transformation of Venezuela, 245–46

Emparán, Vicente, 123–24

Encomienda, 43, 66

England: in Guayana boundary dispute, 29; attitude toward independence, 125

Enlightenment in Venezuela, 254–55

Escalante, Diógenes, 223

Essequibo River: 26; in Guayana boundary dispute, 28–29; on map, 41

Espira, Jorge, 65–66

Ethnic Labels, function in colonial society, 48

Ethnic conflict, 56–58

Europe: trade through Orinoco, 12; and interlopers, 72–73

Exploration: 59–71; from Segovia Highlands, 18; Indian hostility to, 43–44; from Caribbean, 61

Facundo, 259

Falcón, Juan C., 190

Falcón State, on map, 41

Federal Wars, 186–90

Federmann, Nicolás, 65–66

Ferdinand VII, and independence of Spanish America, 119–20

Fila Maestra: 23; on map, 22

First Republic, 121, 127–30

Fleet, Spanish, 72–73, 74

Foreign: community's importance in Venezuelan society, 54–56; intervention in Venezuela, 204; influence in 1958 coup d'etat, 227–28

Fortoul, José Gil, 259

Franciscan mission, 85–87, 88–89

Gallegos, Rómulo: political action in 1945–48, 223–24; literary contributions, 261–62

Gendarme necesario, 260

Generation of 1928: 222; sources of political models, 243

Geography: changing value over time, 8; major regions, 8–11; economic in seventeenth century, 78–79

Godoy, Juan Manuel, 118

Gold: 30; in Guayana, 28; in Andes, 32; in Buría, 32; as impetus for conquest of Caracas, 69–70

Golfo Triste, on map, 22

Gómez, Juan Vicente: in Castro regime, 203; regime of, 205–12,
  218–19; literary opposition to re-
  gime of, 260; failure to become
  national symbol, 264
González, Juan Vicente, 258
Government: establishment after in-
  dependence, 157; characteristics in
  1830, 165; structure of republican
  in nineteenth century, 169–72; in-
  stability explained, 185–86; style
  since 1958, 229–30
Gracias al sacar, 57
Gran Colombia. See Colombia
Gran Sabana, on map, 9
Grenada, on map, 41
Guaire River, on map, 41
Guajira Peninsula, on map, 13, 41
Gual y España, 118
Guanare River, on map, 9, 22, 25, 41
Guanare Viejo River, on map, 41
Guanare: Franciscan convent in, 86;
  on map, 9, 19, 25, 41, 111
Guanipa River, on map, 9, 13, 22, 25
Guarenas, on map, 22, 41
Guárico River, on map, 9, 22, 25
Guárico State, on map, 41
Guasdualito, on map, 25, 41
Guatire, on map, 22, 41
Guayana Llanos Subregion, on map,
  28
Guayana Massif, on map, 9
Guayana Plains, 27
Guayana Province, on map, 111
Guayana Region, 10; description, 26–
  29; frontier, 26; on map, 11, 28;
  Franciscans in, 86
Guayana, boundary dispute, 167
Guerrillas against post-1958 govern-
  ments, 234–35
Gulf of Paria, on map, 9, 13, 22, 41
Gulf of Venezuela, on map, 9, 13,
  19, 41
Guyana, on map, 9, 11, 13, 28, 41,
  111

Guzmán Blanco, Antonio: and trans-
  portation system, 34; in Federal
  Wars, 190; regimes of, 190–96
Guzmán, Antonio Leocadio, 179, 181
Guzmán, elipse de una ambición de
  poder, 263

Haiti, influence on Independence,
  118
Herrera Campíns, Luis, 251
High Plains of Zulia Subregion, on
  map, 19
Higuerote, on map, 13
Hispanic culture in modern Vene-
  zuela, 252, 263–64, 266
Hispaniola, 61, 63
Historia constitucional de Venezuela,
  259
Hueque River, on map, 13, 19
Humboldt, Alexander von, 254
Hutten, Felipe, 66
Hydroelectric power, 37

Idolos rotos, 259
Ifigenia, 261
Illustrious American. See Guzmán
  Blanco, Antonio
Immigration: European, 42; desire
  for white, 50; from Spanish Civil
  War, 51; post-WW II, 51–54; of
  Colombians in 1970s, 52–54; unwillingness of Europeans in nineteenth century, 50
Imports, of basic foodstuffs, 36
Inca empire, 61
Independence: challenge to colonial
  social structure, 49–50; and missions, 87, 89, 91; and the consolidation of Venezuela, 107; and
  the central city of Caracas, 110;
  general chronology of origins, 111–
  12; of US and Spanish America
  compared, 115–16; of Spanish
  America, 115–56; styles of conflict, 120–53; impact of events in

Independence: (*Cont.*)
Spain, 120, 123; ending date in 1830, 122; first period, 1808–1812, 122–30; Caracas leadership in, 125–26; second period, 1812–1814, 130–46; activities in 1813, 136–37; heroes and Páez regime, 167–68; literature of, 255–63; importance to national myth, 263–64
Indians: 48; in Andes, 20, 31; resistance to settlement, 20; resistance in Guayana, 26; as natural resources, 30; in Guayana, 31; Venezuela, Mexico, Peru compared, 31; as major population group, 40; at time of conquest, 42–44, 59, 62–63; slave raids, 31, 43, 61–62; heritage, 44; role in conquest and settlement, 68–69; numbers in Caracas valley, 71; resistance to missions, 85; tribute abolished, 125. *See also* Race
Institutions: failure of during First Republic, 128–30; development after 1958, 248
Intendency, 104
Interior Valleys Subregion, on map, 22
Interlopers, Dutch, French, English, 72–73
Investment, government, in Ciudad Guayana, 37
Iron industry in Guayana, 27
Isla Coche, on map, 9, 13, 22, 41
Isla Cubagua, on map, 9, 13, 22, 41
Isla La Tortuga, on map, 9, 13, 22, 41
Isla Margarita, on map, 9, 13, 22, 41
Isla la Blanquilla, on map, 9, 41
Isla la Orchila, on map, 9, 13, 41
Islands Subregion: description, 17; on map, 13
Islas las Aves, on map, 9
Islas las Roques, on map, 9, 13, 41
Italian immigrants, 51–52

Jamaica Letter, Bolívar's, 148, 257
Jesuit missions, 90–91
José I, King of Spain, 120
Junín, battle of, 154
Junta: Central in Spain during Napoleonic invasion, 119; in Caracas in 1810, 122–24; in independence of Venezuela, 125
Justice, insecurity of during and after independence, 157–59

King, role within colonial structure, 114

La Gran Sabana, on map, 41
La Guaira: as main port for Venezuela, 15; in colonial transportation system, 34; on map, 13, 22, 41
La Vela: as port for Coro, 16; on map, 13, 19
La Victoria, on map, 41
La rebellión, 261–62
La trepadora, 262
Labor: shortage in colonial period, 76–77; shortages during Páez regime, 176–77
Lake Cagua, on map, 41
Lake Maracaibo: 35; on map, 9, 13, 19, 41
Lake Valencia, on map, 41
Land reform: 38; after 1958, 235
Lanzas coloradas, 262
Lara Depression Subregion, on map, 19
Lara Mountains Subregion, on map, 19
Lara State, on map, 41
Las Casas, Bartolomé, peaceful conquest near Cumaná, 90
Larrazabal, Wolfgang, 229
Left-wing political parties and programs, 234–37
Legitimacy: political, derived from king, 114; political in indepen-

dence, 142–47; of government after independence, 157–58

Lezama, on map, 25

Liberal Party, 179

Libraries, Franciscan, 86–87

Literary tradition, 253–65

Llaneros: as colonial cowboys, 33; Indians as part of, 43; in the Independence, 131–33; and José Tomas Boves, 141–42

Llanos Region: 10; detailed description, 24–26; conquest of, 70; on map, 9, 11, 25, 41

Llanos of Barinas-Portuguesa Subregion, 24

Llanos of Calabozo Subregion, 24

Llanos od Maturín Subregion, 24

Loans, government, and Guzmán Blanco, 192

López Contreras, Eleazar, 219–22

Los Altos Hills, 23

Los Teques, on map, 22, 41

Losada, Diego, 70

Lovera, Juan, 253

Maiquetía, on map, 41

Manganese in Guayana, 28

Mantuanos: white elite group, 47–48; as leaders of independence, 122–23

Manzanares River, on map, 22

Maracaibo: founded, 68; in German period, 65–66; colonial trade through, 77; on map, 9, 11, 13, 19, 41, 111

Maracaibo, Lake: 35; on map, 9, 13, 19, 41

Maracaibo Bar, as impediment to colonial shipping, 79

Maracaibo Basin Subregion: description, 16–17; as a gateway into Venezuela, 78–79; on map, 13

Maracay, on map, 9, 22, 41

Margarita, Isla: in colonization, 61–63; on map, 9, 13, 22, 41

Mariño, Santiago: as a patriot leader, 142–43; and separatist revolt, 166

Maroa, on map, 41, 111

Martí, Mariano, 255

Maturín Llanos Subregion, on map, 25

Maturín, on map, 9, 13, 25, 41

Medina Angarita, Isaías, 222–

Memorias de Mamá Blanca, 261

Memorias de un venezolano de la decadencia, 260

Mene Grande, on map, 41

Mene, 263

Merchants: and the consulado, 104–6; during Páez regime, 173

Mérida: 20; on map, 9, 11, 19, 25, 41, 111

Mérida de Maracaibo: bishopric, 106; province, on map, 111

Mérida State, on map, 41

Meta River, on map, 9, 13, 25, 28, 41

Mexico: market for cacao, 32; as a market for wheat, 34; as protected market for cacao, 75–76

Middle class, during Gómez regime, 210

Migration to the cities, 37

Mineral resources in Guayana, 27

Mining in colonial period, 30

Miranda State, on map, 41

Miranda, Francisco: expedition of 1806, 118; surrenders to Monteverde, 130

Missionaries in Guayana, 26

Missions, 84–92

Modernism, 259

Monagas State, on map, 41

Monagas, José Gregorio, 183

Monagas, José Tadeo, 182–86

Montalbán, on map, 22

Monteverde, Domingo, 127–30, 134

Morillo, Pablo, 148, 152

Musical traditions, 253

Myth, development of national, 263–64

Naiguatá, Pico, 23; on map, 9, 22
Naiguatá, on map, 13, 41
Napoleon and the invasion of Spain in 1808, 119
Nationality: the problem of during independence, 129; and decree of War to the Death, 140
Natural resources, 30–40
Negro River, on map, 28, 41
Netherlands Antilles, on map, 41
Neveri River, on map, 22
New Granada: as market for early colonial towns, 67; as focus of Venezuelan colonial activity, 94; in independence, 133–34
Nirgua, on map, 22
Nirgua-Tinaquillo Hills Subregion: 21; on map, 22
North Atlantic. See Atlantic, North
Northern Mountains Subregion, on map, 19
Neueva Andalucía. See Cumaná, province of
Nueva Esparta State, on map, 41

OPEC, 40
Ocumare del Tuy, on map, 22, 41
Orchila, Isla la, on map, 9, 13, 41
Order, search for, 267–68
Organizational modes of Venezuela, 3–6
Orinoco Delta: Subregion, 24, description 12; in Guayana boundary dispute, 29; on map, 13, 41
Orinoco River: 26, 35; as a gateway into Venezuela, 78–80; Franciscans in, 88; on map, 9, 13, 22, 25, 28, 41
Orituco River, on map, 25
Ortiz, on map, 25
Oviedo y Baños, José, 254

Pacaraima Mountains Subregion, on map, 28

Pacaraima, Sierra de, on map, 9
Páez, José Antonio: compared to Boves, 132; in the independence, 149–51; and dissolution of Gran Colombia, 154–55; description of regime, 162–82; and Vargas regime, 169; revolt against Monagas regime, 182; in the Federal Wars, 190; weakness as national symbol, 264
Painting, 253
Pampatar, as early settlement, 63
Paragua River, on map, 9, 25, 28, 41
Paraguaná Peninsula, on map, 9, 13, 41
Pardos: basis of identification as, 48; in cabildo on April 19, 1910, 124. See also Race
Paria Peninsula: 23; description, 12–14; on map, 9, 13, 22, 41
Paria, Gulf of, on map, 9, 12, 22, 41
Parima Mountains Subregion, on map, 28
Parima, Sierra, on map, 9, 41
Partido Democrático Nacional, 221
Patria Boba, 121, 127–30
Patriotic Society for Agriculture and Commerce, 125
Patrons, clients, middlemen in Caracas elite, 82–83
Paz Galárraga, Jesús Angel, and AD party split in 1967–68, 240
Pearl fisheries: 31–32, 64; and exploration and settlement, 62–63, 67
Pedregal, on map, 19
Pérez Jiménez, Marcos: immigrants and regime of, 52; regime, 225–28; as conservative symbol after 1958, 234
Pérez, Carlos Andrés, 241
Perijá Mountains, 20; Subregion, on map, 19
Petare: 23, on map, 22, 41
Petión, Alexandre, 148–49

Petroleum: and organization of Venezuela, 5–6; changes economic goals of Venezuela, 36; changes relative value of agriculture, 35; industry, 39–40; foreign personnel from companies, 55; in the Gómez regime, 205–6, 209, 212; impact on post-1935 Venezuela, 213, 230; taxes, 222; and technical requirements for, 244–45; and democracy, 243–44

Pico Bolívar, on map, 41

Pico Naiguatá: 23; on map, 9, 22

Pico Platillón, on map, 9

Pirates: in Lake Maracaibo, 16; attack Venezuelan coast, 72–73. See also Interlopers

Píritu: Franciscan missions of, 87–89; on map, 13, 41

Plains of Falcón Subregion, on map, 19

Plains of Guayana, 27

Plains of Zulia, 20

Plastic Arts, 253

Platillón, Pico, on map, 9

Pocaterra, José Rafael, 260–61

Point Araya, 12–14

Political: parties, and racial conflict, 58; development, of colonial Caracas, 81–85; instability in nineteenth century, 162; organization, stability of, 198–99; in the Gómez regime, 206–9; discontinuity as end of Gómez regime, 211; policies of López Contreras, 220; organization in 1936–41, 221–22; leadership during Pérez Jiménez regime, 229; compromise after 1958, 232; parties, system of after 1958, 238–40, 241–43; tracts in the nineteenth century, 258

Population, composition, 42

Porlamar, on map, 41

Port of Spain, on map, 41

Portobelo, as a market for wheat, 34

Portuguesa River, on map, 9, 22, 25, 41

Portuguese immigration, 51–52

Positivism, 259–60

Prieto Figueroa, Luis Beltrán, and AD party split in 1967–68, 240

Primate city. See Consolidation, Caracas

Processions and colonial social organization, 49

Progress, dream of, 267–68

Provinces: colonial, 93–94; consolidation in eighteenth century, 103–9; resistance to preeminence of Caracas, 106–7

Puerto Ayacucho, on map, 28, 41

Puerto Cabello, on map, 13, 41

Puerto Cumarebo, on map, 41

Puerto La Cruz, on map, 41

Puerto Ordaz, 27; on map, 28, 41

Puerto Rico, 63

Punta Penas, on map, 41

Punta de Mata, on map, 41

Quayaquil, 75–76

Quibor, on map, 41

Quilombos, 57

Quiriquire, on map, 41

Race: in colonial period, 48–49; Venezuelan attitude toward, 50; conflict, 56–58; during independence, 118, 136; war feared in 1840s, 180–81

Railroad, Caracas-La Guaira, 35

Ramos Jiménez, Raúl, and AD party split in 1961, 240

Recopilación de leyes de Indias, 113

Regionalism: and Páez regime, 165–67; in independence, 130–31; and the Federal Wars, 188

Relaciones geográficas, 254

Religious Brotherhoods, 49

Religious Orders, 84–92

Resources, human, 40–58

Revolt: separatists and Páez regime, 166; during Vargas regime, 168–69; of Páez against Monagas, 182

Revolucion de las Reforms, La, 168–69

Revolution, social, during independence, 50, 57

Rio Chico, on map, 41

Rodríguez, Simón, 255–56

Romanticism, 255–56

Roques, Islas las, on map, 9, 13, 41

Roraima, Cerro, on map, 9, 41

Rosario: 20; on map, 19

Rubio, on map, 41

Ruíz, Francisco, 67

Rural-urban migration, since 1936, 37–38

Russia, in Guayana boundary dispute, 29

Salinas de Araya, 12–14, 32

San Antonio, on map, 22

San Carlos, on map, 9, 19, 22, 25, 41

San Carlos de Rio Negro, on map, 28, 41, 111

San Cristóbal: 20; on map, 9, 11, 19, 25, 41

San Felipe, on map, 19, 41

San Fernando de Apure, on map, 9, 25, 41, 111

San Fernando de Atabapo, on map, 28, 41

San Francisco, Franciscan Convent of, 86

San Juan de los Morros, on map, 22, 25, 41

San Luis, on map, 19

San Mateo, on map, 41

San Sebastián Valley, 21

San Sebastián, on map, 22, 25

San Tomé, on map, 111

Sangre patricia, 259

Santa Catalina, on map, 13

Santa Cruz de Caracas, Franciscan Province of, 86–87

Santa Lucía, on map, 22

Santa María de Ipire, on map, 13

Santa Teresa, on map, 41

Santo Domingo, as market for Indian slaves, 64

Sarmiento, Domingo F., 259

Second Republic, 141–42

Segovia Highlands Region: 8, 10; description, 17–18; on map, 11, 19

Seminary of Caracas becomes university, 106

Serpent's Mouth, on map, 41

Settlement: and conquest compared to Mexico and Peru, 68–69; of Llanos, by Capuchins, 89–90

Sierra de Pacaraima, on map, 9, 41

Sierra de Perijá, on map, 9, 41

Sierra Parima, on map, 9, 41

Silvas americanas, 257–58

Silver, 30

Slave trade: eliminated, 40, 125; African, 44–45; and the Caracas Company, 95–103

Slavery, abolition of, 186

Slaves, black: occupations, 45; basis of identification as, 48; revolts, 57; runaway communities, 57; trade, 76–77; during Páez regime, 176. See also Blacks, Race

Smallpox, 71

Social: structure, challenges to colonial, 49–50 goals of development after 1935, 217; expectations as a result of petroleum, 248

Society, as described by foreigners, 254

Soublette, Carlos: in 1816 expedition from Haiti, 149; in Páez regime, 168; serves out Vargas' term, 170; presidency, 181

Spain: Civil War immigrants, 50;

eighteenth-century decline, 112–15; resistance to French rule of Napoleon, 119–20; events in 1820 and independence, 151
Steamship contracts, 35
Steel industry, 37
Sucre State, on map, 41
Sugar, as a colonial crop, 34

Tacarigua, Lake, 67
Táchira Depression, on map, 19
Táchira State, on map, 41
Tar-Sand Belt, 40
Táriba, on map, 41
Taxes, Spanish colonial, 78
Telegraph: during Guzmán Blanco regime, 194; in Castro regime, 202–4
Terrorism, against Betancourt regime, 234
Tinaco, on map, 25
Tinaquillo, on map, 41
Tiznados River, on map, 25
Tobago, on map, 41
Tocuyo River, on map, 9, 19, 41
Tocuyo de la Costa, on map, 41
Toro, Fermín, 258
Tourism in Guayana, 27
Tovar y Tovar, Martín, 253
Tovar, Count, 125
Town council. See *Cabildo*
Towns founded by missionaries, 88, 89, 90
Trade: Spanish regulations and contraband, 75; colonial, 75–76, 77–78; Spanish regulations and contraband, 75; and the Caracas Company, 95–103; free and the independence, 112, 118; changes for republican period, 160; exports during Páez regime, 175–76
Transportation, 35–36
Trinidad: Franciscans in, 86; on map, 41

Trujillo State, on map, 41
Trujillo: founded, 68; on map, 9, 19, 25, 41, 111
Tucacas, on map, 13, 41
Tucoyo River, on map, 13
Tucupita, on map, 13, 41
Turmero, on map, 41
Tuy River, on map, 13, 22, 41

Unare Basin: 20, 24; description, 14; as impediment to expansion from Caracas, 63–64; difficulties in conquest of, 70; and Franciscan mission of Piritu, 87–88; Subregion, on map, 13
Unare Depression, 23
Unare River, on map, 9, 13, 22, 25, 41
Unión Patriótica Militar, coup d'etat in 1945, 223
Unión Republicana Democrática: policy, 224; under Pérez Jiménez, 226–27; profile after 1958, 238–39
United States: 50, in Guayana boundary dispute, 29; independence compared to South America, 115–16; as major supplier of Venezuelan imports, 249
Universidad de Caracas, Real y Pontífica, 106
Upata, on map, 28, 41
Urama River, on map, 19
Urban: system as focus of Venezuelan history, 5; increasing concentration, 36, 211; network growth by eighteenth century, 83–85; network function in Venezuelan politics, 199; public works after 1935, 215; concentration since 1958 and land reform, 236; expansion as a result of petroleum boom, 246; framework as main theme of Venezuelan history, 266–68

Urica, battle of, 148
Uslar Pietri, Arturo, 262

Valencia: founded, 67; on map, 9,
    11, 22, 25, 41, 111
Valencia Basin Subregion: 21; on
    map, 22
Valera, on map, 41
Valle de la Pascua, on map, 41
Vallenilla Lanz, Laureano, 260
Vargas, José María, 168–69
Venezuela: *gobernacion,* and *cabildo*
    of Caracas, 81; eighteenth-century
    provinces, map, 111; as ideal case
    study of independence, 117; on
    map, 41
Ventuari River: 26; on map, 9, 28, 41
Villa de Cura, on map, 22, 41
Villalba, Jóvito, 224, 238–39
Villegas, Juan, 67

War to the Death, decree of, 139–40
Welser, German period of explora-
    tion, 65–66
Wheat, as a major colonial crop, 34
Whites: 48; as major population
    group, 46–48; elite groups within,
    47–48. *See also* Race
Willemstad, on map, 41
Women, in literature, 261
World War II, impact on Venezuelan
    politics, 223

Yaracuy River: entryway into plains,
    15; on map, 13, 19, 22, 41
Yaracuy Valley, 20

Zamora, Ezequiel, 189–90
Zaraza, on map, 13
Zuata, on map, 25
Zulia State, on map, 41